Culture and Liberty
in the Age of the
American Revolution

Jeffersonian America

Jan Ellen Lewis, Peter S. Onuf,
and Andrew O'Shaughnessy, Editors

Michal Jan Rozbicki

Culture and Liberty

IN THE AGE OF THE

American Revolution

UNIVERSITY OF VIRGINIA PRESS
Charlottesville and London

University of Virginia Press
© 2011 by the Rector and Visitors of the University of Virginia
All rights reserved
Printed in the United States of America on acid-free paper

First published 2011
First paperback edition published 2013
ISBN 978-08139-3413-6 (paper)

1 3 5 7 9 8 6 4 2

The Library of Congress has cataloged the hardcover edition as follows:

LIBRARY OF CONGRESS CATALOGING-IN-PUBLICATION DATA
Rozbicki, Michal.
Culture and liberty in the age of the American Revolution / Michal Jan Rozbicki.
p.   cm. — (Jeffersonian America)
Includes bibliographical references and index.
ISBN 978-0-8139-3064-0 (cloth : alk. paper)
1. United States—History—Revolution, 1775–1783—Social aspects. 2. Liberty—Social
aspects—United States—History—18th century. 3. Liberty—Political aspects—United
States—History—18th century. 4. Social status—United States—History—18th
century. 5. Social classes—United States—History—18th century. 6. Elites
(Social sciences)—United States—History—18th century.
7. Founding Fathers of the United States. I. Title.
E209.R89 2011
973.3'1—dc22
2010020855

For Jody

My life, liberty, and happiness

Contents

Acknowledgments

T HE ORIGINS OF THIS BOOK go back to a remark once made by Jack P. Greene calling for attention to the "deep and abiding commitment" of the American Founders to inequality. I have always felt that the nature of this commitment needed to be examined more fully, and what follows is an attempt to do so. My debt to Jack P. Greene's inspiring scholarship in American cultural history and to his generous spirit is deep and enduring.

Very special thanks go to Dick Holway, my editor at the University of Virginia Press. His good faith as well as his curiosity and willingness to look beyond established historiographical trends have been an unfailing source of encouragement. My gratitude is also due to my project editor, Ruth Steinberg, whose kind assistance brought technical harmony to the manuscript, and to Susan Murray, who copyedited it and whose patience and sharp eye helped smoothen my relationship with grammar.

I am indebted to many colleagues, friends, and students who have over the years offered generous advice on my project. For their insightful comments and suggestions I wish to thank Alan Tully, Peter S. Onuf, Jack R. Pole, Jack N. Rakove, Walter Nugent, Nelson D. Lankford, Natalie Zacek, Daniel Hulsebosch, Julie Winch, Jeffory A. Clymer, Tom Sosnowski, Sara van den Berg, Tony Hastert, Peter and Basia Sokolowski, Angie Dietz, Ted Listerman, and Scott McDermott. It is a special pleasure to thank the staff of the History Department at Saint Louis University, Kathy Bonsack and Chris Pudlowski, for their ever cheerful and efficient assistance.

For their help when I was working on this project, I would also like to thank the librarians at the Huntington Library in San Marino, the Newberry Library in Chicago, the Pius XII Memorial Library at Saint Louis University, the Olin Library at Washington University in St. Louis, and the Special

Collections and Rare Books of the Ellis Library at the University of Missouri, Columbia.

I am obliged for the financial assistance I received during my research and writing of this study in the form of Mellon Foundation Research Grants through Saint Louis University, and a research fellowship from the Virginia Historical Society.

A fragment of my book was presented as a paper at the 2001 Seventh Annual Conference of the Omohundro Institute of Early American History and Culture in Glasgow, Scotland, and subsequently published as "Between Private and Public Spheres: Liberty as Cultural Property in Eighteenth-Century British America," in Robert Olwell and Alan Tully, eds., *Cultures and Identities in Colonial British America,* pp. 293–318, 367–71 (© 2005 The Johns Hopkins University Press. Reprinted with permission of the Johns Hopkins University Press). The quote from Camillo Querno in chapter 4 is from Gale, *Eighteenth Century Collections Online* (© Gale, a part of Cengage Learning, Inc. Reproduced by permission. www.cengage.com/permissions). Parts of chapter 2 were published as "To Save Them from Themselves: Proposals to Enslave the British Poor, 1698–1755," in *Slavery and Abolition* 22, no. 2 (2001): 29–50 (reprinted by permission of the publisher, Taylor and Francis Ltd., http://www.tandf.co.uk/journals).

Culture and Liberty
in the Age of the
American Revolution

Introduction

Perhaps the sentiments contained in the following pages, are not yet sufficiently fashionable to procure them general favor; a long habit of not thinking a thing wrong, gives it a superficial appearance of being right, and raises
at first a formidable outcry in defence of custom.

—Thomas Paine, *Common Sense,* 1776

THIS BOOK IS NOT A HISTORY of liberty in the age of the American
Revolution. It is a book *about* the history of liberty in the age of the
American Revolution. It is less concerned with constitutional issues, juris-
prudence, and philosophical theories (which already have a very large literature), and more with extending our knowledge about the various modes of
liberty's existence in the minds and experiences of eighteenth-century actors.
It looks not only at what we know, but at how we know what we know. The
intention is to recover the contemporary meaning of liberty—the core concept of the era—and in the process suggest revising some of the ways we
currently understand the founding of the nation. The reflections that follow
are exploratory, and are offered in the spirit of inquiry. They do not seek to
dismiss, endorse, or replace the existing scholarship, but to advance a different
way to interpret its subject, one that bridges the current gap between the
political and cultural history of the Revolution and that encourages these two
fields to "speak" to each other more often and more creatively.

   The constructions of eighteenth-century culture by present-day academ-
ics were not on the minds of the people who populated late colonial British
America and were immersed in the realities of their own experiences. "Liberty" and its role in the American Founding has been wrapped in so many
veils of modern analyses, politics, social conflicts, morality, and hindsight that

the only way for us to more fully recover its actual nature is to historicize our subject as deeply as possible. To this end, attention will be called to two dimensions of "liberty" that have hitherto not been widely considered, and even less often applied together. The first is the exercise of power through culture, and, more specifically, through the ownership of liberty and the ability to define its public meaning. The second dimension, crucial to any such exercise, is the peculiar existence of liberty in this era as an intricate synthesis of political practices and symbolic forms.

The point of departure is that, contrary to our ingrained illusion, the meaning of "liberty," as outlined by the Founders and understood by their contemporaries, was one of "privilege"—that is, of advantage, or of power, over those who did not possess it—and therefore an ingredient of a world view that inherently assumed social inequality. This is why trying to capture its nature—as is so frequently done—by asking to what extent it was, or was not, modern and egalitarian is an attempt to fit a square peg into a round hole. The revolutionaries of 1776 could not suddenly discard a concept of society made up of ranks (with a corresponding hierarchy of liberties) while holding on to all the other norms and views of the world contained in the ethos of British culture. It would be like expecting the inhabitants of Salem in 1692 to selectively discard their belief in the existence of witches while retaining the rest of their theologically based world views. Early modern liberty was a social relation between unequals, and as such could not have existed in and of itself as an abstract right, nor should it be examined as such. Mindful that it took two more centuries for its proclaimed, symbolic equality to evolve into literal practice, we should be looking more closely at the origins of this transformation to understand its nature.

For decades, the historiography of the Revolution has been divided between those who stressed the centrality of the Founders and those who offered alternative accounts highlighting the contributions of women, poor whites, African Americans, and Indians, long left out of the traditional narrative. The latter approach revealed conflicts and differences of interest rather than consensus, and demonstrated that the stage was populated by many different actors—the "unknown revolutionaries" of Gary Nash, the "forced founders" of Woody Holton, and the "common people" of Alfred F. Young.[1] The former stance still reigns in popular history. Both schools have been moving along their separate ways, and have yet to produce an integrated story. This is unfortunate. To attempt to create an acceptable account of the era that does not include both the elites and the non-elites, both the disadvantaged and those who had a stake in that disadvantage, is to follow a blind alley. Any account of Revolutionary liberty in particular should be deeply rooted in the relationship between these two groups—that is, between those who enjoyed the full privileges of freedom and those who held only a few, or none. Privilege cannot be construed without the existence of the unprivileged, in the same way that a single person living on a desert island cannot be said to possess liberty.

Examining this relationship requires much more than looking at class inequalities. It is something of a wonder how many authors succumb to the popular fantasy that liberty is essentially self-evident, instead of examining its historical development as peculiar to a time and place. Ever the children of Enlightenment, we are tempted to assume that liberty simply exists, and that, historically, it has been either disregarded or acknowledged by human reason—as if there was such a thing as collective "human reason," located somewhere beyond human history and experience. We are perhaps inadvertently borrowing from the main thinkers of the American Revolution, who, like so many minds of the era, did believe that Reason could free the people from the predicaments of History. But to do so is to play God. The development of equal liberties and rights in eighteenth-century America was, like all human developments, the outcome of specific historical experiences, and not a discovery of transcendent and timeless truths. With all due reverence to Jefferson, who, for political ends, converted English philosophical and constitutional traditions (in themselves products of Britain's unique experiences) into abstract, "self-evident" truths, we simply cannot do justice to history by studying them as such, outside of the framework of these experiences. Something self-evident for all humanity would have to exist outside of history. Jefferson himself provides ample evidence for this—for instance, he did not view political rights for Indians as self-evident.

The second assertion of this study is that liberty exists in society at the factual and the symbolic levels simultaneously, and that the two are neither separate nor mutually exclusive. To examine them as mutually exclusive often leads us into a dead end, where we end up comparing what people say about freedom with the political reality, in order to see whether the two correspond. The reality, alas, is rarely a mirror reflection of the abstract statements made

3

about it. If we can agree that the early modern concept of liberty was a relation of unequal power and privilege between certain classes of people, then these ideas also existed—had to exist—at the symbolic level, where such a relationship could be communicated and where a shared experience of such an order of things could be articulated. In other words, "liberty" operated not just at the level of institutions but also at the level of norms, values, and ideals. This second level was not some Baconian corner populated by illusory "idols of the theater," outside of empirical experience. Both the politics and the symbolism of "liberty" constituted reality for the people. Liberty was neither entirely factual nor entirely fictional, neither institutionalized as executable law nor a timeless ideal, but rather a dynamic combination of both, peculiar to a place and time. Just as we speak of the politics of knowledge, we should speak of the politics of representations, concepts, and vocabularies. It mattered a great deal who could effectively portray what; whose values and interests were embedded in these characterizations; and by what means and to what political effect they were disseminated and absorbed by the culture. To a great extent, we may say that "liberty" was defined by its most successful portrayal.

The challenge, therefore, is to look more closely at these two bodies of Lady Liberty, not so much to uncover the differences between them, but to understand the nature of their bond. The symbolic body cannot usefully be separated from the factual one, as was once the case with the trimly abstract Marxian twosome of "base" and "superstructure." The theatrics of power—whether in words, stories, ceremonies, flags, or liberty poles—is not just a reflection of power, it is its very lifeblood. These representations make power visible, legitimate, justifiable, and real—both to the rulers and the ruled.[2] And it takes two—the rulers and the ruled—to play this game. Both must attend the same playhouse and share the same representations of reality, if these representations are to represent reality at all. Both must employ the dominant legitimacies, even if they argue for divergent goals and interests. In post-Revolutionary America, the rebel leader Daniel Shays invoked the same symbols as the rulers in Boston to demand that the latter revise their understanding of rights and liberties and acquiesce to the view held by the farmers he represented. All actors on the stage of history thus find themselves following two scripts: that of the formal, legal system, which codifies and enforces relations of power, and that of the larger symbolic order, which provides the tools through which the world—including relations of power—is articulated.

This dual system works well—and remains stable—only when the center of power finds successful expression in a symbolic order of shared representations. When revolutions happen, this correspondence is usually undermined, and the role of the cultural sphere in mediating the relations of freedom and power suddenly becomes much more visible. Claude Lefort noted adroitly, "Until such time as a fracture appears in society, it is tempting to study the structure of power, class structure, the workings of institutions, and social actors' modes of behavior as though they were meaningful in themselves, and overlook the imaginary and the symbolic foundations of their 'reality.' "[3] This is because cultural presuppositions are so deeply implanted in social practice that they are often invisible. It is like the act of seeing: when we look at things, we do not ordinarily reflect on the fact of our having eyes to see with; we only do so when there is a physical problem and our vision becomes distorted. Revolutionary events bring the political significance of cultural representations to the surface. Patriotic pride in England's long traditions of certain rights and freedoms was taken for granted among the American colonials, but after 1764 these rights and freedoms unexpectedly emerged as a vehicle for protests *against* London. The appeal of this new provincial self-representation thus reached over and beyond its original meaning and became an integral part of the Revolutionary action. To fully understand these events, we need to go beyond power struggles per se and to reflect on how the new situation was interpreted through the cultural assumptions and narratives employed to make sense of them. We will find that any recipe we devise for making sense of events will require both imaginary and factual ingredients. The American Revolution and its immediate impact on liberty can be fully understood only if we grasp how it generated a depiction of itself, and how this imaginary representation contributed to the way people experienced and understood the political and social world.

In seeking to uncover how a major historical episode such as the American Revolution was construed in the minds of the people who experienced it, we need to attend to at least three different dynamics, none of which is independent of the others: the events themselves; the beliefs used to make sense of them at the time; and the intentional manipulations of those assumptions by those with power and a public voice. It would seem natural that all three should be a part of any interpretation of the Revolution, but that has not been the case. Although immense intellectual energy has been directed at the study of liberty in this period (mostly focused on its political and constitutional dimensions), there have been few attempts to combine culture and politics. Neither the newly sophisticated theories of culture nor the linguistic and postmodern turns in historiography have generated many such endeavors. Historical writing remains rather untheoretical, and the reasons for this are understandable. Historians are naturally wary of postmodern exercises in abstraction. They do not want to be colonized by cultural studies. They dislike textual criticism that rather than listen to the text itself, reads into it the interpreter's agenda. They know the past is much more unruly than our theories about it. They feel uneasy about intimations of far-reaching relativism, about reducing complex processes to mere power struggles, and, not least, about leaving the comfort zone of their own discipline.[4] And yet, ignoring the advances of semiotics and hermeneutics is not an option if we are serious about historicizing liberty in this era and understanding more fully what it meant for those who lived it. Subjectivity needs to be better attended to, but there is no reason to capitulate before its altar for fear of being accused of naive realism. A non-naive realism is quite achievable; the meanings of a text can be numerous, but they are not infinite, and they are to a great degree knowable. "History is not the province of the ladies" may, for example, mean a number of different things; but it certainly does not mean "The winter of 1694 in Salem was cold."

If we are to make a much-needed reassessment of the ideological origins of the Revolution, we must attempt to integrate culture and politics into that history. Most would agree that islands of liberty were the rare exceptions in the ocean of early modern unfreedom and inequality. It is therefore important to uncover the peculiar circumstances that made them possible, as well as the conditions that then allowed for liberty to expand beyond the narrow circle of those who originally enjoyed its privileges and into new segments of society. To reconstruct how people created and experienced freedom, we must reach beyond traditional disciplinary frameworks.[5] We historians need new insights, in order to become better aware of the unexamined premises, rooted in modern culture, that we bring to our writing. The old, Parkmanesque style, with its all-knowing author and a unified narrative, is long gone, replaced by a multitude of approaches, angles, and perspectives. But this new medley is not necessarily coherently organized and conceptually linked, something that the cautious use of theory could help overcome. Such an attempt, if successful, could bring substantial rewards, by freeing us to be realistic about Revolutionary liberty without being cynical; to be thrilled by the power of the language of rights without being naive and misty-eyed about its historical realities; and by allowing us to acknowledge the lasting value of the Founders' vision without asking them to be more modern than they knew.

One reason why liberty is infrequently examined through the lens of culture is that the very focus on culture implies daunting ambiguities. It conjures up a Babel of voices, identities, ambitions, and interests that appear vexingly jumbled and resist neat categorizations. But that very difficulty is precisely the reason why the story of liberty needs to be told in the language of culture as much as in the language of law and politics. Culture tries to make a sensible and coherent order out of the myriad of differing and often contradictory ingredients that make up people's experience. We cannot expect human experience to be internally consistent in a purely logical sense, just as it is futile to analyze it in terms of certitudes (which ultimately may only be justified on metaphysical grounds).[6] Even the briefest reflection makes evident that people of all social classes, positions, and education say one thing and do another. Their actions are rarely consistent with their declared aims and values, because they are driven by a legion of conflicting forces which they often are not aware of, or which they do not comprehend. But culture need not be consistent to be real for people, to motivate their actions, and to create sense and order in their world (a fact that exasperated Enlightenment-rooted thinkers like Karl Marx or Antonio Gramsci, who saw in it the source of an unscientific outlook on the world, imposed by the rulers).[7] Law, political theory, and the history of ideas—all of which by nature stress continuity and internal coherence—are not able to fully capture this reality, because they cannot easily accommodate in their stories the various fictions, rationalizations, imaginings, and other ways by which culture creates meaning for people.[8] By integrating cultural and political perspectives, we can help to overcome some of these dilemmas. Such an approach may also help to stem complaints that cultural history overstresses impersonal forces at the expense of politics and events, while political history overemphasizes personal (mostly elite) power struggles at the expense of the larger forces that affect societies. Finally, this approach also better addresses the issue of different time frames for the different spheres of people's experience. Political events may have happened fairly rapidly during the American Revolution, but the expansion of the social space of liberty simply could not have transpired at the same rate. We should heed here the lessons of Fernand Braudel, who in his study of the Mediterranean showed three different rates of change over time: one for geographic space, one for the social order, and one for political developments; and of Jacques Le Goff, who pointed out similar differences in the pace of time with respect to the Medieval Church and the merchants of that era.[9]

That is why this book will look especially closely at the intersection of political idiom and cultural identity. It will ask what exactly was being communicated about order and authority by the Revolutionary rhetoric of universal liberty; what the historical actors believed this rhetoric meant; how it helped them to comprehend contemporary social and political reality; and how the meanings of this rhetoric changed when, to use Michel de Certeau's concept, it was creatively adapted by ordinary people.[10] Such adaptations were possible because ordinary people actively participated in the dominant cultural economy, while not being altogether dominated by it. Rather than study this participation traditionally, as a case of an imposed world view which precluded an "objective" one reflecting the people's interests, I will examine why and how they utilized and manipulated it for their own ends. This will help explain the striking difference between the meaning of liberty in 1764 and in 1800, between the still restricted social space it occupied at the beginning of this period and the significantly expanded space it occupied at end of it. This disparity was not the result of a "delay" caused by the "resistance" of the ruling class to the supposedly inevitable progress of modern liberty. Instead, this period represents a time of rapid acceleration of a universalized and inclusive perception of freedom that was prompted by a radicalized—to the extent of being almost open-ended—Revolutionary narrative. It was the injection of this ideological vocabulary into the mainstream of language, thus making it part of the common cultural capital, that for the first time gave both political presence and legitimacy to ordinary people as an entity that, by definition, possessed rights and liberties. The loci of these dramatic changes were not so much to be found in the enactments of 1776 or 1787, still tied to the older, inherited view of society held by the Founders, but in the politicization of society and in the intense public conversation about freedom which took place during the two or three decades following these events. It was then that the new representations of liberty were harnessed by various protesters, insurgents, and radicals who wished to justify their cause against the new rulers. It was also a time when the established political class—rapidly coming apart along factional lines and trying to attract broader support across social ranks—increasingly invoked a universalist, egalitarian, and accessible language of liberty to fashion new party ideologies, and in the process delivered even more fuel to the symbolic torch of freedom.

An argument will be made here that the symbolic manifestations of freedom as a rule *preceded* the factual ones—until the culture changed sufficiently to make turning them into practice and law imaginable. In some cases, such as those of women's rights and civil rights, such manifestations preceded legally sanctioned liberties by as much as a century and a half. This is why an attempt to bring together the symbolic and the factual in our examination of freedom is so important. Without such an endeavor, students of liberty risk ending up like Marc Bloch's oceanographers, who neglected looking at the stars—seemingly so distant from the ocean they were studying—and thereby rendered themselves incapable of explaining what causes the tides.[11]

The structure of the book reflects this goal. Chapter 1 addresses the intellectual origins of the pervasively axiomatic treatments of liberty in the historiography, and demonstrates that such assumptions preclude the critically important question of why and how it emerged in history. Chapter 2 surveys the origins of early modern British liberty and spells out the reasons why privilege remained a core ingredient of its meaning up to the end of the eighteenth century. Chapter 3 shows how and why this restricted meaning of liberty was successfully transmitted to colonial America, despite considerable structural differences between the provincial and metropolitan societies. The liberty-centered narrative of the American Revolution is examined in chapter 4, which discusses its intended and unintended outcomes—for the rulers and the ruled. Chapter 5 focuses on the power of symbolic depictions of liberty as embodied in the country's faith in progress, in the concept of representation, and in political conduct. Chapter 6 looks at the various attempts to harness the symbolic lexicon of Revolutionary liberty by both anti-government rebels and rival factions within the ruling class during the last two decades of the century. It also shows how the growing involvement of the unprivileged in the debate over liberty triggered a backlash from the political class. The conclusion reflects on the need to move beyond the two prevailing models of interpreting Revolutionary liberty: the one that assumes the Founders invested it with a modern meaning which has in essence continued in a linear manner to the present day; and the other that also takes such a modern meaning for granted but focuses on its "betrayal" by the new rulers' intransigent commitment to inequality. I propose replacing both of these perspectives with one that integrates the story of the Founders who fashioned the new rhetoric of freedom, with that of the ordinary people who took up this new rhetoric to insist that its symbolic inclusiveness include them in fact.

A FEW WORDS NOW ABOUT HOW "liberty" and "culture" are understood here. In order to grasp how liberty existed in people's experience, it is not very practical to rely on traditional definitions, which tend to focus on intellectual formulations and legal concepts, at the expense of the broader historical context. A more usable definition must begin with two premises. First, liberty can exist only as a component of the network of ties that bind society. People as a rule wish to be free to act, but they also wish to live in a society, and all societies institute constraints on how much freedom one is permitted. Since people's desires are often contradictory, to realize what we want usually means that others need to give up some of their wants. To speak of liberty is to speak of the area within which society allows us to make free choices. In other words, we are not talking here about liberty as an instinctive will among humans to be free from constraints, but about man-made, historically specific, restricted freedoms. These do not derive from the nature of our existence, but from our membership in society, with its culture and laws that permit certain things and proscribe others. Second, because liberties often conflict with one another, and because their very functioning is dependent upon the constraints imposed on them, to understand their particular nature, as well as the social value placed on them, we must look at the entire system that makes them possible.[12] Only then can we see how the culture of the time and place balanced them against one another in its attempts to create order. There is no way to assess the meaning of a particular liberty other than by viewing it within the larger culture in which it functions.

A more subtle appreciation of the meaning of eighteenth-century liberty in its full cultural and social context—not just in terms of power relations and political theories—will open the doors to a better understanding of its nature, and especially of what may be called the inverse proportionality principle that lies at its core. This effect came to the surface every time certain rights were granted to new groups who had not held them before. Although we may like to think that granting such rights was an inevitable and natural development, a simple recognition of universally existing entitlements, it was historically a highly atypical concession—usually fiercely resisted—because it not only inherently involved a cutback of privileges for those who had secured them earlier, but also undermined the identity they had built around these privileges. Without a fuller examination of these tensions, and of the conditions which made such concessions possible, a comprehensive explanation of why modern American liberty emerged when it did would remain elusive.

This is why "liberty" will be used in this text much as it was used in the eighteenth-century British world: as a metaphor for a cluster of specific immunities and entitlements existing along a continuum, with different portions of this spectrum available to different social ranks, and with their fullest enjoyment exclusive to members of the uppermost elites. For American provincials such freedoms would include the right of habeas corpus, ("The habeas corpus act . . . that second Magna Charta and stable bulwark of the subjects liberties . . ."); trial by jury ("The parliament has attempted to take from us the darling privilege of Tryal by Juries of the Vicinage"); representative government ("It is essential to Liberty that the Subject be bound by no Laws to which he does not assent by himself or his representative; a Privilege which forms the distinction between Freemen and Slaves"); the levying of taxes through representation ("Let the Americans enjoy . . . the privilege of to give and grant by their own representatives . . ."); and the franchise ("The Constitution of No. Carolina permits not the Privilege of Citizens to any who have not resided therein 12 months, and paid taxes").[13] The intention here is not to look at specific liberties in their legal and constitutional embodiments, but at the changing cultural context that made them possible and allowed their expansion to embrace new segments of society (this is why the traditional verbal distinction between liberty as constituting specific entitlements and freedom as a more universal concept is not useful here—contemporaries widely used both terms interchangeably). Eighteenth-century liberty was primarily a *relation of difference* between people, one that divided and separated them. To be free meant there had to be others who were less free; to become more free meant that others, already more free, had to relinquish some of the freedom they held.[14]

To think of this relation primarily in terms of hegemony, as has often been the case, is not very useful, especially in trying to explain the dynamic of change involving liberty. One has only to consider those groups who at any given time broke away to some degree from the current system and succeeded in obtaining new liberties they had not held before. When such a change occurred, the entire social configuration, which made the existing asymmetrical distribution of liberty possible, had to accommodate those who had successfully wrestled new privileges. A new balance of social inequalities was created as the newly empowered began to participate in supremacy over those who possessed fewer liberties. For instance, the Glorious Revolution of 1688 in England expanded the space for action available to the gentry, but it did so by limiting the previously existing privileges of the monarch, the court, and the aristocracy. The same mechanism would have operated if, hypothetically, the Virginia planters and smallholders (who were the main addressees of Jefferson's rhetoric in 1776) had agreed to actually grant equal freedom to all. They would then have had to give up substantial benefits stemming from their own privileges (with some perhaps having to return to England), a scenario contradicting their basic interests. Eighteenth-century liberty was not a nonpartisan bowl of soup from which all could eat. Consuming it gave distinct—and ardently defended—advantage to some over others.

It will be argued that this advantage, rather than being exclusively an obstacle, also provided—however obliquely—a major incentive for the progress of American liberty in the late eighteenth century. If we can agree that liberty was invented as a means to provide a privileged position for its inventors, we have to accept that it could not have been invented as an egalitarian right. Acknowledging this means that we need to develop a whole new way of looking at the Revolutionary era. The founding elite cannot be said to have founded modern freedom, or to have prevented it. They had a huge stake in selective liberty because it gave them a privileged role as enlightened rulers, but it was precisely this stake that also made them promote, cultivate, and legitimize liberty as natural and universal, setting off a process which made wider equality of rights thinkable.

"Culture"—the context that produces specific meanings of liberty—will here be viewed from an anthropological angle, not in the sense of "high culture" (literature, art, drama, etc.), a field already ably examined by Kenneth Silverman. The term is used here to mean a framework of socially established and transmitted practices, ideas, and institutions shared by members of a particular society. Terry Eagleton has usefully called culture the complex of values, customs, beliefs, and practices which constitute the way of life of a specific group.[15] In other words, it is an assemblage of subjective meanings people hold about themselves and their world. But for a historian, culture is also an objective, external phenomenon, and it needs to be considered together with social and economic structures as well as institutions which articulate its constituent values and beliefs and thus help "translate" them into specific behaviors. Culture's main role is to generate order and coherence in a chaotic world by providing people with norms and prescriptions for living. It is by no means a fixed structure to which people must acquiesce; on the contrary, it is constantly active in trying to create order and to make sense of a changing world. The coherence it produces bears only a fuzzy correspondence to the coherence required to build a bridge. Culture is a very artful entity; it does not generate order by forcing uniformity upon societies, but by supplying people with categories and boundaries to help them assign everything its proper, "natural" place, and define how everything ought to be arranged. Because it is a system of conceptions which convey knowledge about life, it can be said that culture supplies people with meaning that makes sense of their existence in the world. As Zygmunt Bauman once noted, an omelet is an omelet on a breakfast table plate, but when on a pillow—in the wrong place, out of its order—it becomes a stain. In other words, dirt has no objective existence; it exists as such only because our culture has provided us with such a belief.[16] A liberty pole is just a piece of wood, and a dollar bill a piece of paper, unless society assigns *meanings* to them.

Another kind of "magic" wielded by culture is its ability to create metaphors and narratives, which come to be conceived by people as frameworks of the "natural" world. Over time, an early modern metaphor for Englishmen as a "free-born people" merged with what it was a metaphor for, and could no longer be separated from the way Britons thought of themselves. This is why liberty is not a thing in itself, but is defined by the specific, historical mind and the experiences which shaped it. The manner in which it is represented in people's minds determines the way they use it to make society's networks of rank and power sensible and coherent.

Because culture is socially and historically transmitted, we must bear in mind that a great deal of the knowledge it provides is of the taken-for-granted type. It would therefore be erroneous to look at culture as some sort of external entity that tells people what to do. Instead, it is for them the deepest reality, something they live for and that defines who they are. It is critical for historians to understand this, because people's actions are rarely an outcome of purely rational, conscious analysis of their situation; in large part, they are motivated pre-reflexively, by the cultural givens of their time and place. These givens constitute the historical reality of their being. Political theory and philosophical ideas—as elaborated, for instance, in the classical works of authors like Bernard Bailyn and J. G. A. Pocock—are only some of the many bodies of knowledge that constitute such reality, and only partially illuminate what historical events meant to historical actors.[17]

An important point to note is that culture insists that all social groups collaborate in it (though not necessarily intentionally or consciously). This partnership is sometimes obscured by the omnipresence of class analysis—an otherwise eminently useful method of anyalsis—in historiography, an approach that tends to examine elites separately from non-elites. The result is that the interactions between elites and non-elites still remains a rather gray area. Granted that dominant elites have a disproportionate influence on shaping the norms and values for all, we should not look narrowly upon the beliefs and practices diffused by them across society as having been merely imposed upon the passive masses by an act of domination. This inclines us to study such beliefs as an anomaly of sorts. We should pay more attention to the fact that, once internalized, these beliefs—and not historians' abstract interpretive categories—become the reality for people, a reality through which they perceive and interpret the world, and which motivates their actions. To interpret this reality against an abstraction or a yardstick from another era is to try to understand what things meant to them through criteria outside of their culture. A farmer's son in early eighteenth-century Virginia had to know that a periwig worn by a man he saw riding on the road nearby was a "distinguishing badge of gentlefolk." Without the boy's participation in the culture through this knowledge, the periwig would not have communicated the message that deference was expected and that he "ought to" take off his hat. Conversely, the youngster's coarse breeches and Osnabruck shirt signaled to the rider that he had encountered a commoner, and should "expect" a gesture of respect.[18] For these meanings to be conveyed, both had to collaborate in observing the culture's conventions. Both had to be conditioned to perceive these conventions as a "natural," taken-for-granted reality.

Finally, a note on language, one of the symbolic systems of signs used to communicate meanings in cultures, and a major part of what we know as reality. Language works much like "periwigs" and "breeches"—which is to say, particular words can only reflect the particular social experiences of a particular time.[19] A given word still appears the same today, but its meanings, like the portrait of Dorian Gray, have changed with time. To recover the older meanings, we must make sure that they are congruent with the cultural setting and specific social relations within which they were created. Jefferson's words in the Declaration "ring true and strong more than two centuries after he wrote them," marvels one historian. They do, indeed, but the ringing is in our ears, not Jefferson's. Timeless content can only be bought at the expense of historicism. Not only is liberty not universal, but it is not even predictable over longer periods of time. No one could have foretold in 1776 what would happen to the then current meanings of "liberty" by 1830. Contrary to otherwise gratifying popular perceptions, there was no directional path or concealed "purpose" residing in early modern American history to offer equal liberty to all. Events did not "flow" toward freedom any more than the late Middle Ages "flowed" toward Enlightenment.[20] Similarly, there was no unified meaning of "free" within any one culture, nor across cultures.

We should also be mindful that the concept of "meaning," especially when associated with politically loaded words such as "liberty" or "equality," is far from simple. At this point, let us only note that "meaning" implies two different, though closely overlapping types of signification—a distinction that will be brought into play throughout this book. The first is denotation— that is, the consensus, or "dictionary," meaning that most people in a given culture and time would recognize. The second is connotation—which refers to the varying associations that the word might have for members of various groups of people with different class, gender, and race experiences.[21] In the Virginia encounter mentioned above, the term "gentlefolk" would have been immediately recognizable to both the farmer's son and the gentleman, but it would have had very different connotations for each of them.

A Critique of
Self-Evident Liberty

For the liberal humanist's mistake is not to insist that human beings from very different contexts may share values in common, but to imagine that these values are invariably what is most important in a cultural artefact. It is also to assume that they are always, in however cunningly disguised form, the values of his own civilization.

—Terry Eagleton, *The Idea of Culture*

I F LIBERTY WAS THE conceptual axis of the ideology of the American Founding, it was also its dominant metaphor. The overlapping of the two has diverted our attention from the fact that both were political and cultural instruments rather than objective descriptions of the essence of the Revolution. Patriot speeches, constitutional debates, and sermons on liberty were more often depictions of ideal models than measured representations of the Revolutionary process, but modern commentators often make no clear distinction between the two.

A necessary point of departure in reconstructing the eighteenth-century American sense of liberty must be a realization that freedom ultimately derives from the intricate webs of culture and society in which we are all entangled; people are "free" or "equal" only as members of society, not as people as such.[1] Eighteenth-century formulations of freedom could carry only the meanings allowed by the contemporary social and cultural market. This means that when we hold up such articulations for analysis, they first ought to be placed in the practical context of social and cultural relations of power. In other words, intellectual conceptualizations of liberty are not liberty. In 1776, as a few gentlemen were declaring in Philadelphia that all people are by nature created equal and endowed with unalienable rights, slaves, Indians, women, and the propertyless remained, and were long to remain, untouched by the universalism of these formulations. A few years later, heads rolled off the Paris guillotine on orders justified by the defense of liberty, fraternity, and equality. It is not the rhetorical or legal elegance of a given formulation of liberty but the uses to which it is put that tangibly affect lives, and define its real meaning. The issue before us, therefore, should be less whether liberty was verbally defined in this or that way, or whether it derived from this or that philosopher, but what exactly was being communicated by the language of liberty in the Revolutionary era about actual relations within American society.

Such an approach will help avoid a recurrent interpretative problem in studies of freedom in the eighteenth-century Anglo-American world: a uniform, self-evident, and unproblematic concept of equal freedom that has quietly, almost imperceptibly, been adopted as an abstract norm against which all actors and actions are gauged and sweeping classifications of events and individuals are made. Indeed, it is not too much to say that it has made much of American scholarship in this area a history of *constraints* on liberty, rather than a history *of* liberty. It is time to reposition the debate and modify this reductionist model, which effectively obscures the fundamentally nonegalitarian nature of early modern liberty. This model endows it with an abstract, teleological universalism and produces a propensity to uncover limitations and contradictions, instead of striving to understand what is truly important: how and why certain liberties surfaced at a particular time and place, who was able to claim them and why, and how those who did not hold them before acquired them when they did. As such, it has had a profound effect on the overall assessment of the role of the Revolution in American history. Alan Taylor's impressive survey of early America, a volume intended to cover United States history, may illustrate this effect; it has only two out of 480 pages devoted to the American Revolution. As the author explains in the introduction, the Revolution and the Founders' ideology do not warrant much attention, because they promoted a liberty that was restricted to well-off Euro-Americans, they encouraged the dispossession of Indians, they did not abolish slavery, and they inspired colonization.[2] In other words, because Revolutionary-era liberty still existed in a restricted form and was not universally applied, it does not merit our consideration. It is a view that is not only idealistic, it is startlingly perfectionistic, suggesting that historians should not drink from a glass that is half full. What it tells us is that we need to make a better effort to look beyond the seductive, but often illusory intellectual cocktail of American idealism, ingrained faith in ideas as movers of history, wishful thinking, current politics, and intuitive presentism that our own culture has mixed for us.

And yet, practically all current historiographical models explaining Revolutionary change are to some degree premised on the meaning of liberty as an essentialized notion implying universal rights for all classes of people. Broadly speaking, one may discern three major subcategories among these models. One school posits that, with the Revolution, the colonial elite transcended their well-entrenched identity as a dominant class by wrenching their understanding of liberty from its long-standing symbiotic attachment to rank and privilege, to espouse a fundamentally new, universal meaning of freedom. "The language of equality in the Declaration was sincere," writes one author, stressing that the Founders "set up a government that did what no democracy had done before: It combined majority rule with effective protection for minority rights." Others note that "what in the end remains remarkable is the degree to which they accepted the equality of all people," and that the Revolution radically changed "the pattern of beliefs and customs that mediates between men who govern and the people they rule," with the result that "the year 1776 saw the collapse of virtually all old political relations."[3]

A second view, sometimes partially overlapping with the previous one, postulates that Revolutionary society rapidly moved on toward greater egalitarianism, while the republican elite, which initially promoted radical ideas of equality, *did not live up to them* in political and social practice. America in this period was a country "where social differences were considered incidental rather than essential to community order." The polity created by the Founders was therefore essentially a "response to the pressures of democratic politics," and was "peculiarly the product of a democratic society." The Patriot elite were "unsettled and fearful not because the American Revolution failed but because it had succeeded, and succeeded only too well. What happened in America in the decades following the Declaration of Independence was after all only an extension of all that revolutionary leaders advocated."[4] Such a reading of the Revolution assumes that the whole episode was built on an essentially new and wide-reaching meaning of liberty, antagonistic to the old. It typically ends up with the historian rather puzzled by the gap between this supposedly modern meaning promoted by the Founders and the resistance to such modernity by the very same individuals.

A third orientation, today not as prominent but still commanding a sizeable following, derives from Marxist traditions and builds its narrative around class struggle. It emphasizes the use of equal liberty by the Founders as essentially instrumental and therefore hypocritical: "The reality behind the words of the Declaration of Independence (issued in the same year as Adam Smith's capitalist manifesto, *The Wealth of Nations*) was that a rising class of important people needed to enlist on their side enough Americans to defeat England, without disturbing too much the relations of wealth and power that have developed over 150 years of colonial history."[5]

Both the "reactionary" and the "radical" perspectives on the Founders' liberty have long roots in American historiography. The Progressives, who saw the economic realm as the main battleground where the struggle for freedom took place, promoted a framework which stressed the disparity of interests between the propertied ruling class and the common people, and suggested that the rulers successfully marketed a rhetoric of liberty in order to preserve their economic domination. From the 1950s, the "consensus" school pushed the pendulum to the right and deemphasized social conflict, putting stress on an ideology of liberty widely shared across social classes.[6] By the 1970s, this perspective had waned, replaced by a wide variety of studies of colonial British America viewed through the prism of society and culture, especially race, class, and gender. Meanwhile, scholarship devoted specifically to the Revolution has remained mostly focused on the political. All these approaches uphold the centrality of liberty, but their methods and outcomes diverge. Political historians tend to highlight continuity, and stress the causal role of ideas, laws, constitutional design, and political philosophy. By contrast, many social historians tend to use the antagonistic class model, contrasting the powerful and the powerless: slave owners and slaves, urban laborers and the merchants, sailors and captains.[7] It is certainly a germane method, because privilege and exclusion were omnipresent in human history, but the model tends to exert too much power over the interpretation by becoming a self-fulfilling prophecy, readily supported with abundant evidence showing tension between the possessors of freedom, clinging to their possession and resisting change, and the excluded, resisting exclusion and subjection. In the process, we often lose sight of the substantial collaboration between elites seeking popular support and ordinary people taking advantage of this opportunity to push for their own interests.

What is most striking is that so many authors on both the left and right ends of the methodological spectrum share assumptions of liberty that are nothing short of axiomatic. The results are sometimes akin to replacing George Washington's wig with a baseball cap. Consensus and conservative historians tend to view the Revolution as a struggle for modern liberty, a view that would have surprised a Virginia or South Carolina gentleman acutely proud of his privileged freedoms. Their persuasion is that the Founders "agreed that all men are created equal,' only disagreeing on "the application of that principle." Their principle was universal; they just differed on how to enforce it, because some worried that the poor and uneducated would not make responsible decisions.[8] By contrast, for many liberal historians, the story of early American liberty has often been a morality play staged as a war of social classes. It therefore required uncovering all the ways in which the Age of the Founding did not ensure equal freedom. One may say that consensus historians essentialize the idea of liberty, and class struggle historians essentialize the social subject. The former want a pure beginning of the nation; the latter assume that it should have been pure. Both, however, reveal a pietistic strain in their devotion to abstract liberty.[9]

All these interpretations reflect a perennial American predicament: what to do with an apparent contradiction implied by the coexistence of freedom and inequality at the birth of the nation. Despite a mountainous historiography, this dilemma is far from resolved. It remains the source of a lively academic debate as the pendulum swings back and forth between views of the Founders as either progressives or reactionaries, and the Revolution as either a struggle for power or a struggle for liberty. This predicament is not likely to be unequivocally resolved, but the dynamic of this controversy and the intellectual ferment it has generated is of great interest to a historian.

Different authors have dealt with this dilemma in different ways, but the axiomatic and perfectionist assumptions continue to dominate the historiographical marketplace. Over the last several decades—at least since the demise of the consensus school of history—the most common interpretive response to the Founders' language of freedom has been to point to their presumed inconsistency. After all, they not only showed more interest in protecting the received, limited meaning of liberty than in any major expansion of its social space, but also appeared oblivious to the ongoing transformation of liberty from an exclusive privilege, attached to the elite, to a more abstract and universal right of citizenry. Surely, nothing short of invoking contradiction can make sense of the gap between their progressive language of equal freedom and what Jack P. Greene has rightly called the "deep and abiding commitment of the revolutionary generation to inequality."[10] It is not unusual to find a serious and important volume devoted to the origins of liberty in the new American republic start by denouncing its "narrow and selfishly motivated beginnings," and going on to portray its post-Revolutionary unfolding as "constrained by old traditions and institutions hard to move."[11]

Two premises behind statements of this type deserve attention. First, liberty appears as a timeless *Geist* of sorts, outside of a specific culture and social order, ready to shower its blessings equally on all if only it were not impeded by the self-serving "American reactionaries," defending their rank and property.[12] The second, quietly stashed behind the logic of the first, is that the Founders should have voluntarily given up their advantaged positions in society—expressed in their possession of fuller liberties than the rest of the people—in the name of a more modern and egalitarian understanding of liberty. This would have gained them a more honorable and "unselfish" place in history. It has become fairly commonplace even among the most renowned colonial historians to explain the "paradox" of liberty and inequality —without questioning its doubtful logic—by the inconsistency rooted in the "flawed" characters of the Founders, who in their lives were unable to reconcile the contradictions they presumably ought to have reconciled. Their proclamations on equal rights have been called a case of "amaurosis," a "truly wondrous" argument, and an "obvious suggestion of hypocrisy." Francis Jennings has pointed to the same by asking, "Where is there any thought of the majority of South Carolinians enslaved by the passionate defenders of liberty?" Along the same lines, Thomas Jefferson has been labeled a "self-righteous hypocrite." Elsewhere, the author of the Declaration of Independence has been treated to a complex logical analysis showing that his views of liberty revealed "a deep incoherence of his theoretical structure." His culpability lay in sacrificing his "moral sense" by rationalizing slavery with the concept of "tranquility," which he considered of greater value to society. Others have pointed to the "logical incompatibility" between slavery and republican ideology, resulting in inherent "inconsistencies" within the latter; have decried the "moral absurdity of a society of slaveholders proclaiming the concepts of natural rights, equality, and liberty"; or have tagged the Founders as insincere, because they "spoke of the liberty and equality of citizens," while "the reality was different" because "promises were not fulfilled."[13] Although references to the Founders as "flawed" often seem to be mere liturgical devices to ensure that a recognition of their impressive contribution is not confused with an approval of the various unfreedoms they approved, the implication is clearly that their rhetoric of equal liberty contained modern, egalitarian meanings (one might note that being "flawed" could not have been a distinctive feature of the Founders, because it is a feature of all people—unless the measure is taken against an ahistorical model of perfection). These charges of hypocrisy begin to look a bit eerie when we realize that we are applying our ideal fictions to reproach the Founders for getting carried away by their ideal fictions.

Another group of commentators have emphasized the neglect and even rejection by republican elites of their own rhetoric of virtue for egoistic reasons: to preserve themselves as a ruling class, and to hold on to wealth and social ranks established over the preceding century. "If American independence depended on public virtue," they ask, "how could one resolve the conflict between the demanding ideals and the sharp practice that betrayed them?" A frequent answer is that this "betrayal" took the form of a "repudiation of equality" in the pursuit of ambitions that were "unembarrassedly aristocratic." The toleration of bondage was a "glaring contradiction in the Republicans' popular creed." This behavior reflected "partisan and aristocratic purposes that belied the . . . democratic language." Jefferson's words on liberty were merely "glittering generalities" that defied "reality." The architects of the Constitution made no less than "a colossal error of judgment" in not immediately expanding the rights of American citizens.[14] What is striking in these citations is that reality seems to reside in the new and revolutionary *statements* of universal liberty, while age-old *practices* not conforming to them are made to seem aberrant. In other words, the ideals being "repudiated" are presumed real, and the historically entrenched social order a departure from the normative. It is this kind of a priori assumption that has led one author to conclude that Thomas Jefferson's words about the political strife in the United States were a case of "treason against the hopes of the world," and should apply to Jefferson himself for not living up to his language of equality and unalienable rights. His words are "those of a liberty-loving man of Enlightenment," but his deeds are "those of a self-indulgent and negrophobic Virginia planter."[15] In all these quotations, Lady Liberty's cloak has an anachronistic shine to it. The criterion of consistency seems to have been tailored to suit our own taste.

The fact that the above examples represent the thoughts of a group of distinguished scholars without whom there would be no modern history of the American Revolution only serves to illustrate the depth of the epistemological dilemma being raised here. It is not just that they all tend to treat equal liberty as a given; a bigger issue is that this premise has effectively prevented us from appreciating the core of *privilege* at the heart of early modern liberty. It simply takes freedom out of its complex sociohistorical context, much like Louis Hartz did when he suggested that a cohesive, liberal "fragment" was somehow extracted from the European matrix (a single thread from a spider web of culture, as it were) and transferred to America, where, deprived of burdensome "feudal" elements, it "had been established from the outset in colonial life."[16] Such an essentialist approach confuses symbolic elements of the Founders' vision with intentions to reengineer society by levelling its ranks. It makes their belief in inequality an anomaly, a live dinosaur of sorts, surprisingly discovered beyond the 1776 boundary line that was supposed to mark its extinction. But liberty did not have an autonomous existence, nor would it have been "normal" for everyone in late eighteenth-century America to be equally endowed with it. This is why one cannot tell "the story of liberty," much as one cannot tell "the story of beauty." It was not a natural phenomenon, an entity waiting to be claimed or denied and surfacing in this or that incarnation at different points in history. If only it were so, it would be a historian's dream come true: once the permanent quintessence of such a liberty were discovered, we would not only know why and when it came to light in history, but could perhaps even predict when it would emerge again.[17]

Another unwelcome consequence of the self-evident treatment of equal liberty is that it facilitates the assumption that liberty had one, core meaning, widely shared among various social ranks in eighteenth-century America (and in some cases, even across the whole world). This conjecture implies that behind the Revolution there operated some grand force of ideas that imparted unity and consistency to the whole historical event, even if this unity was not always respected or even acknowledged. This is a case of supplying more coherence to a historical scene than it contained. Historians simply cannot speak of liberties inherent to human society. They should know better than anyone else that humans no more have an inherent concept of habeas corpus than they have an inherent concept of an internal combustion engine. Both had to be "invented" at some point and place in the course of history. This applies to each specific liberty, which is why it cannot be lineally tracked through the ages. To do so, we would have to assume that there existed across history core concepts of certain liberties, much like the genus of the juniper exists through its various cultivars. The result would be ahistorical, even mythical; one would need to "find" some inner conceptual essence of freedom shared between communal-oriented, medieval peasant uprisings and the twentieth-century American civil rights movement which focused on individual liberties. Similarly, without a focus on historical peculiarities, we would not be able to see that in early British colonial America the concept of free speech referred most of the time to the right of the elites to freely speak in assemblies, but not to the right of all individuals to do so in public.[18] What should be of primary interest to us is the peculiar confluence of circumstances that made this specific liberty viable at the time.

We are inheritors of a powerful, Enlightenment-inspired tradition of speaking about liberty in the Age of the Revolutions as a common value, shared not only by various classes of American society, but also by other peoples. Such a notion includes those who exercised all the freedoms then available, as well as those who yearned to obtain them but were met with denial. Some authors have even suggested that "egalitarian, multiethnic conceptions of humanity had not evolved in isolation, but rather through solidarity and connection," and that those who struggled for liberty were part of a "planetary" movement. Others have similarly concluded that Indians, slaves, merchants, and the gentry in Revolutionary America had two "traits in common": "a dream of freedom," and an awareness that they should act as groups toward that end.[19] While it is true that most humans wish to ease the various constraints on their lives, it does not follow that people from different social backgrounds, histories, and cultures share the same concept of liberty (which, incidentally, in most such studies, happens to be a modern, Western-type concept). A close scrutiny of the emergence—not the future history—of specific liberties suggests that there is little explanatory value in the assumptions of unified liberty, however attractive and inspiring they may appear. If freedom exists only as a relation between people in a given society, with its network of interdependencies, then its meanings are primarily local and defined by this network of relationships (other societies in other times have different networks of relations).[20] These meanings (as today's tensions, triggered by globalism, amply testify) have as a rule encountered resistance when crossing borders. For instance, the eighteenth-century idea of "Britishness" held very different degrees of attractiveness to different peoples, such as the Scots or the Irish, who found themselves a part of the British world.[21]

Our faith in shared, grand ideas driving historical change has probably much to do with the fact that for a long time the Revolution has been viewed primarily as an event in the history of ideas, and the public discourse which drove it was seen as primarily a civic one, where ideologies were central. Debates among the Founders on the nature of power and the role of government took center stage, and the search for the long genealogy of concepts that were influential among them, such as virtue and corruption, sometimes took historians as far back as fifteenth-century Florence. The problem with the history of abstracts and ideas, as Michel Foucault once sagely noted, is that it "usually credits the discourse it analyzes with [a] coherence" that in the actual life of societies did not usually exist. Only fairly recently has a more holistic and inclusive treatment of the subject emerged, as society, economy, and culture have been brought into the picture, revealing more fully the subjectivity of ideologies. Important, pioneering work in this area—most of it covering the post-Revolutionary period, and dealing with civil society rather than language and meaning—has been done by a group of historians, some of them inspired by the "public sphere" theory of Jürgen Habermas, who examined how the cultural space for liberty and political participation grew as a result of changes in public discourse. John Brooke, focusing on public institutions, analyzed political culture in Massachusetts in terms of republican and Harringtonian versus liberal and Lockean "visions" of polity. By examining voluntary associations, Albrecht Koschnik has shown how, through them, ordinary citizens were able to enter public space and participate in political life by giving expression to a variety of partisan interests. In an improvement on Habermas, he reveals how specific institutional structures helped politicize and give voice to ordinary people. Johann N. Neem carried this line of inquiry further by demonstrating that a pluralistic "civil society," opposed by both Federalist and Anti-Federalist elites, was not a direct outcome of the American Revolution, but emerged only by the 1830s with the decline of the republican political model and the growth of popular politics, so feared by Jefferson. Peter Onuf, writing about the early nineteenth century, has argued effectively for a similar approach: not to idolize or indict, but to historicize, and then to look at how new political space opened up through changing frameworks of thinking, and not through presentist criteria. This enabled him to successfully show how the Revolutionary language of rights provided both Republicans and Federalists with arguments to pursue their divergent political goals.[22]

Because idea-centered studies naturally focused on abstracts, they paid less attention to the changing meanings of ideas, and to their different meanings for different social groups. For instance, a Belgian lace blouse worn by a wealthy selectman's wife in colonial Salem served to confirm her membership within the local upper class, while the same blouse purchased with much financial sacrifice by a modest shoemaker for his wife signified an aspiration to greater respectability and social equality, a meaning often objectionable to the upper class. In other words, once particular beliefs and values were diffused across society, various groups of people exploited them for their own, distinct purposes—an ongoing process by which their meanings were constantly altered. We are now much better aware that ideas are not simply hegemonically imposed upon society; many successful recent studies of popular opinion have turned their attention from ideas per se to how certain political beliefs and values spread across the social space.[23] How people experience life cannot be discovered by historical analysis from ideas, as people's actions do not primarily "reflect" ideas, nor can we derive people's ideology from behavior. A philosopher's observation that "the fact that the snail's behavior observes biological laws does not mean that the snail is aware of them" holds true for the history of liberty, too.[24]

In colonial American historiography, the now widespread "from-the-bottom-up" approach has moved scholarship well beyond the former deification of the Founders (accompanied by the omission of the common soldier, artisan, woman, and slave), toward the inclusion of all as participants in the Revolution. This may be one reason why we have inadvertently neglected to pay attention to the differences in the meaning and value of liberty for different classes who had different stakes in the unfolding events.[25] Because in late colonial America the working classes, the poor, and the enslaved were the ones who knew better than anyone else what unfreedom and oppression meant in real life, and who had the most to gain by an expansion of liberties, it has not infrequently been suggested that these groups in particular shared a fairly well-defined concept of freedom. The contrary, however, is much more likely to be true. As a relatively small ruling class with a well-defined identity and a vested interest in maintaining power, the gentry elite across British America tended to share the same understanding of liberty to a much greater degree than the non-elite. Ordinary people, urban laborers, slaves, the backcountry poor, and others like them were much less swayed by the abstractions related to privilege and honor that constituted elite liberty; they were instead immersed in deeply localized experiences of life, experiences which were the source of their values. They rebelled, protested, and resisted their unfreedoms in a myriad of ways, but this did not mean they shared a unified concept of liberty as a single and universal norm. To say so would simply be too Hegelian. Paul Gilje has perceptively pointed out in a recent study that the liberty of the sailor, "as he came reeling along the docks with money bulging in his pocket," expressed primarily a freedom from order and hierarchy in the world of *his* experience. His joining in a Revolutionary riot might have been motivated by a lofty concept of liberty, or by a simple joy of fighting—even if it did indirectly express a denial of the usual social constraints.[26]

The elites, by virtue of possessing property and political privileges, could afford to focus on the security (and stylish articulations) of their individual freedoms, while the non-elites' primary interest lay in the removal of various taxing and burdensome restrictions under which they labored. The former wanted to ensure that their positive liberties—that is, their existing, privileged freedom to act—were safeguarded. They were defending a prized possession to the extent that they developed a cult around it—with sacralized values guarded by honor. In other words, those who were more free had more power to dominate and control those who were not, and so it was far from paradoxical that they were the ones who placed the highest value on freedom. The non-elites, on the other hand, primarily yearned for freedom *from* the constraints that bound them, and so were focused mainly on reducing oppression rather than gaining the freedom to run for office or being able to export one's products to a market of one's choice.[27] Furthermore, the different value put on liberty by the two groups was also acutely affected by the fact that they existed within a specific, unequal order of society, institutionalized and legitimized by culture and collective memory. A Jefferson or a Washington would not be able to continue to achieve their ambitions without maintaining the privileged liberties they already held as gentry, and so they attached a great value to them. A poor ferryman, interacting with the Maryland physician Dr. Alexander Hamilton, existed within the same unequal order, and was not simply free to reject its inequalities and demand the right to, say, run for the position of delegate to the colonial assembly, or even to address such an assembly. Indeed, he was strongly reprimanded by Hamilton for the mere possession of a teapot, reserved as a sign of social position for those above his rank. The ferryman, though clearly not without aspirations to respectability and the bettering of his status, would not place as much value on liberty as it was understood by the upper class, simply because any *realistic* attainment of his goals would not be much affected by it.[28] In other words, he did not share the same worth of liberty with Hamilton. This is why a single, generic meaning of freedom as a sort of classless ideal common to all sectors of society—despite vastly differing experiences of reality—is not a very usable interpretive device. It prevents us from exploring a major route through which an expansion of liberty took place: the one which began with conceptualizing and articulating specific freedoms—such as taxation through representation or the right of habeas corpus—by those who originally and exclusively owned them, and ended with these concepts being taken up and claimed by those who did not yet possess them.

A recent study of merchant seamen may illuminate this historiographic "blind spot." It focuses on the oppression of seamen by captains who, with the support of British Crown officials and merchants, held "near dictatorial powers" over them, all in the service of "a capitalist system rapidly covering the globe." The sailors are in a constant struggle over conditions of work, pay, and control by the captains. The focus throughout is on resistance: even piracy is presented as a case of class warfare against the merchant establishment. The sailors are the sole fighters "for democracy and freedom," and all others play only one role on this historical stage—that of being an obstacle to progress.[29] Consequently, in this story, those who were most free, and so defined the various existing freedoms, do not play any significant role in construing freedom. Such a binary model is very efficient in showing social tensions and political struggles, but it is not sufficient to explain how liberty increased its social sphere when it did. It does not—cannot—allow that the ruling class could simultaneously produce reactionary and progressive contributions to this process. It does not reflect the important fact that in the eighteenth century the normativeness of the dominant culture, including its values and social order, exerted a much stronger pull on people—all people—than is the case for the postmodern, individualistic American society of today. The rebellious and the radical were usually marginal, while most people functioned within the bounds of the cultural system, more often appropriating and modifying its existing elements to advance their own aspirations, than rejecting them.

Instead of assuming a unity of shared meanings, we should acknowledge that there have always existed a great many varieties and degrees of liberty. If we look only at the eighteenth-century British colonial forms of labor along a broad spectrum from the free to the unfree, including varieties of convict labor and indentured servitude, we find an assortment of configurations characterized by different degrees of coercion and relative freedom.[30] While liberty may have been a homogenizing metaphor, widely used for this reason in the Age of the Founding, its signification for different social classes would have differed greatly. For some it denoted legally protected, real freedom to act, while for others it was more of a rhetorical form, perhaps providing uplift for their identity and dignity, but with much less corresponding legal or political empowerment. Prominent early modern writers who gave their approval to equality, and therefore at least implied that liberty should be more equitably distributed, operated within the realm of theory and accepted much of the existing order, almost never proposing material social reform (Thomas Paine's truly democratizing postulates were an exception, and were met with much hostility, only confirming this rule). Social equality was not their goal, and, in any case, they mostly referred—as Locke did—to relations between monarchs and peoples, rather than between classes and individuals. Ultimately, the deepest rationale for why no shared idea of eighteenth-century liberty was possible lay in its very social ontology: positive freedom—that is, the power to act in certain ways—was a license granted selectively, and as such could not be conceived of as an equally distributed possession. Should someone have suggested to the Founders that all liberties were socially neutral and were to be equally parceled out to adult residents of the new republic, they would no doubt have replied that such liberty would cease to be liberty. Liberty to them was less an individual right and more a state of being permitted by laws and a collection of rules to allow them to do certain things. It therefore, by definition, presumed that there existed things not permitted for others. The then commonly used argument about the anarchistic state of nature, where everything was permitted, was a popular fiction employed to stress this point.[31] The Founders may have devised a theoretically modern, liberal polity for the new American republic, but the "self-evident" concepts of order, such as the assignation of different degrees of freedom according to one's rank, were much too deeply ingrained in the culture to be wiped out by the events of 1776 or 1787.

There was, however, one thing that metropolitan and colonial Britons did share in their understanding of freedom: a common core of privilege, a belief that liberty essentially existed as an unequal social relation. It was part of a larger world view, buttressed by cosmology; the innate order of society was the same as that of Nature, comprising inequalities and dependencies. An invidual's situation was tied to some kind of dependence or social attachment, the most common being the master-servant relation. Christopher Hill has shown that early modern "masterless men" were marginalized and ostracized as outcasts because they were not attached to anyone in a socially subordinate relationship.[32] The very term "masterless" is revealing: it categorizes a class of people as being out of social order based on a master-servant correlation. The masters were seen as independent, by virtue of their ownership of property (and therefore, rightfully, the most free), just as the servants, who did not own any, were dependent on others (and therefore, by definition, did not qualify for the same degree of freedom). This inequality may have been economic at its roots, but it operated in society as a cultural norm that effectively defined who had what amount of freedom.

Finally, a number of reasons for the historiographic persistence of idealized liberty may be directly linked to certain peculiarities of modern American culture. One of these is of an unsurprising nature: we investigate what is important to us; equal freedom is important, so we look for where it existed and where it was "absent." In this, we often resemble a modern-day Herodotus for whom "our" world is the taken-for-granted norm. Because we have been conditioned to believe in equal rights as essential—that is, as the equivalent of objective truth—other norms in other societies seem either inessential or anomalous. We thus bring our idea of order into their world.[33] A set of premises shared by us and the actors in 1776 is tacitly assumed; surely, we too would have acted like they did, if we had been there. As one eminent author explained, the Founders had a coherent cultural and political vision, "based on the concept of equality, which had provided the justification for revolution and served as the norm for the reordering of society." It was only due to confusion and lack of "clear self-understanding" that they "found meaning in difference which involved excluding and separating groups of people one from the other," a course that was "fundamentally contradictory" to their original vision.[34] What this demonstrates is how genuinely difficult it is to place ourselves in the early modern mind-set, with its inherently hierarchical world view and its understanding of liberty, not as a widely shared right but as a specific empowerment over others. To succeed, we need to look more closely at our own categories, metaphors, and values. We have objectified them—which is to say, we are often no longer aware that they are merely products of our culture—and we gladly use them to organize our knowledge of the past. In this we are not unlike our eighteenth-century counterparts, who used categories like "savagery" and "civilization," or the "mob" and the "better sort," to organize their knowledge of the American scene. It would be a good idea to try and de-objectify some of our investigative tools.

Another source of distortion is the dramatic pull extended over historians by the current political culture of equal rights. We are professionally obliged to depict early modern inequalities as normative, for that is what they were, but the expectations of our current culture—and indeed the larger American civil religion of liberty—oblige us to represent such inequalities as aberrant. For instance, in his richly insightful book, Philip Morgan rightly points out that slavery was "no curious abnormality, no aberration, no marginal feature of early America," but rather "a fundamental, acceptable, thoroughly American institution," which he immediately defines as "the core contradiction of slavery."[35] He is, of course, perfectly correct on both points, but the two points come from different normative systems, with the result that early modern cultural norms may inadvertently be rendered as historically idiosyncratic.

A uniquely American predisposition affecting perceptions of liberty is the assumption that historical actors were primarily driven by free will rather than by the imperatives of cultural norms, social psychology, and group interests.[36] In other words, not only is freedom seen as self-evident, but also as originating primarily from one's individual desire and not from external circumstances. This seems to be a legacy of the modern historical experience of freedom *and* prosperity, however relative their distribution, for large segments of society. Prosperity has been vital as a resource for exercising freedom (as we can see even today among those who are free, in the Bill of Rights sense, but too poor to pursue their aims freely). This is why for so many Americans individual action seems primarily voluntary, and freedom appears to be an *absence* of prohibitions. Restrictions on freedom are seen as mainly external barriers, mere constraints on our commonly shared will to liberty. George Washington would have found it rather difficult to identify with such a view.

Lastly, because American culture has always been pluralistic, and, as such, in need of a stable, shared core of identity, we have developed a deep and popular faith in the permanence of the founding documents, and in the constancy of their intent. Few people in France today agonize over Napoleon Bonaparte's original intent in this or that provision of the Civil Code. In America, the ritualization of the Declaration of Independence and the Constitution, combined with a continued reverence for the legal and the constitutional, has given the language of these documents an imaginary aura of timelessness that disguises the historical shifts in their meanings over the centuries. The endless debates over the Second Amendment may serve as an example: no matter how divergent the opposing views, historicism is often ignored as all parties attempt to mine the "original" meaning of the document for legitimacy. It is not that we are all Rip van Winkles and have missed the change over time. It is that this fiction works well for us—but only if we assume that the original meaning is changeless (it usually just happens to be the one favored by the arguing party). It is this perceived immutability that nourishes the belief in the oneness of liberty today and in the Founding era.

British Legacies

I. Privilege at the Heart of Freedom

> One privilege is taken away after another, and where we shall be landed God knows, and I trust will protect and provide for us even should we be driven and persecuted into a more western wilderness on the score of liberty, civil and religious, as many of our ancestors were to these once unhospitable shores of America.
> —James Otis, *Rights of the British Colonies Asserted and Proved,* 1764

THE HISTORICAL GENESIS of early modern British liberty was insepa- rably tied to privilege, and American liberty as formulated and under- stood by the Founders was part of this blueprint. Acknowledging this more fully would bring about profound historiographical consequences. First of all, it would make clear that the widespread acceptance of various forms of unfreedom (including even slavery) by eighteenth-century advocates of liberty in the British world was neither an aberration nor an exception.[1] What these advocates were saying was not antithetical to all inequality and exclusion. In fact, claiming allegiance to the liberty of the people effectively enabled the claimers to assert authority and advantage in society. This em- powerment was concealed in the contention that they spoke for all people. The political attraction of this stance, and not any abstract idea of uni- versal rights, became the main catalyst for putting liberty on a pedestal. Only if we recognize this pattern can we attempt to explain why and how originally elite-bound freedom successfully expanded within a few decades of 1776 into non-elite social space.

Although this may not be immediately obvious, if we look closely at the centuries preceding the American Revolution, we will observe that for all liberties (as a rule granted exclusively to select groups) to make sense as privileges, they had to be denied to others. Only then could they effectively construct social order and mark clear lines of class distinction. One person's liberty was another's constraint. Particular liberties carried cultural substance only if within their very essence privilege was bound up with exclusion, and different *amounts* of freedom were dispensed across society in proportion to social rank. For instance, the medieval spectrum of this distribution extended from the freedom of an ordinary freeman, through the more expansive freedom of a nobleman, to the imperial liberty of the king. In medieval as well as early modern England, the meaning of a particular liberty to its owner existed as his or her relation to other people. When a sixteenth-century English merchant obtained the privilege of a royal monopoly to import lumber from the Grand Duchy of Lithuania, its meaning to him depended on his relation to those who did not hold such a privilege, and were excluded from the trade. If a seventeenth-century propertied freeman was free from arbitrary arrest (by virtue of the privilege of habeas corpus), the worth of this freedom to him lay in his relation to those—the poor, the masterless, the unemployed—who could be arrested and sold as indentured servants to the colonies against their will. One can track this manner of identifying freedom with unfreedom all the way back to ancient Rome, where unfreedom was defined by both law and culture more fully than freedom: in the broadest sense, a free person was someone who was not a slave. It was especially visible in the attitude to those who had been freed from slavery; they sometimes continued to be called freedmen—that is, "no longer slaves"—for more than a generation.[2]

If we can agree that the origin of liberty was located in privilege, then we must also acknowledge that there have always been arbiters who defined who could be granted such privileges and who were backed by sufficient power to enforce their definitions. They were the ones who defined the contemporary paradigm of liberty: what it meant and how it should properly be interpreted, what liberties were "natural," and who should possess them. The scope of their influence was usually limited by the current balance of power. Particular freedoms were almost never freely given; any analysis of their genealogy must begin with the relationship between the controlling arbiters and those who at a given point had sufficient bargaining muscle to extract concessions.

Perhaps the reason we do not always pay sufficient attention to this pattern has something to do with our frequent focus on legal and constitutional history when studying the expansion of freedom. Law may at times create an illusion of being timeless and absolute. While it provides a crucial framework for thinking about the functioning of liberty, it does not have an intrinsic dynamic, outside of a given sociopolitical environment, much as the authors of laws are not able to authorize their particular uses in different contexts. This seems to have been already understood by one of England's greatest legal minds, Sir Edward Coke, who observed in 1628 that not only should English rights based on the Common Law not be considered universal, but they did not even apply to Britons living in the American colonies. During a debate on whether it was lawful for the king to use martial law against civilians, when a reference was made to such use in Virginia, Coke declared that the common law "meddles with nothing done beyond the seas," suggesting that he saw the meaning of liberty as definable only by the jurisdiction of English, but not British or imperial courts.[3]

For a good illustration of the essence of early liberty one may point to the English Magna Charta of 1215 and its history since then. It exemplifies especially well the triple nature of most privileges of freedom: that of a compromise agreement; an exemption from some constraint by the rulers; and a precedent into which, at a later point, people would read new meanings. Like most liberties in history, those contained in the Magna Charta were a give-and-take exchange involving *concessions* wrested under pressure. When King John returned, defeated, from his Poitou expedition, the barons, dissatisfied with heavy scutages, made their demands and—supported by the Church and much of the country—brought the confrontation to the brink of war, forcing the king to reluctantly sign the charter that clarified, and thus delimited, the financial demands that a monarch could make on barons, townsmen, tenants, and merchants. It was a classic medieval grant of privileges, a contract between the estates and the monarch, born of a conflict of interests between them, and made possible by mutual trade-offs. Close similarities may be found in the agreements made in 1356 between Duchess Joan of Brabant and the estates (with the latter obtaining the right of approval of the marriages of her daughters), and between Margrave Albrecht Hohenzollern with the Brandenburg estates in 1472, where the gentry and the cities agreed to help pay war debts in return for the right to approve taxation.[4] Typically, such agreements represented an exemption—for a select group—

from some area of governmental control over them. In each case, the way the power equation was altered resembled a zero-sum pattern: the addition of liberties granted to the new party was balanced by a reduction in the former authority of the rulers, a decrease roughly equal to the number of new privileges given to the grantees. We should note that in the process, the social space of liberty increased to accommodate the newly empowered.

Over time, any such change takes on a historical dynamic of its own, because it also begins to function as a precedent and as a potential symbol of liberty for others. Culture is exceedingly artful in turning facts of the past into usable symbols, and then employing them as tools to fight current struggles. Those who had an interest in preserving their privileges often glorified and mythologized such facts into a cult of sorts, with roots in the immemorial depths of history. This was how Magna Charta reemerged in mid-seventeenth-century England from relative obscurity. The Parliamentary faction usefully "discovered" in it a centuries-old commitment by the monarch to respect certain rights of the British people. Its medieval nature was conveniently forgotten and replaced by a mythical one with a contemporary interpretation: limited, constitutional monarchy was as "ancient" as the Magna Charta. This enabled the anti-Stuart faction to claim that the Parliament was merely preserving archetypal political principles, while the monarch was violating them. Such culturally tailored "precedents" were a common pattern in history. In 1687, William Penn, fighting against the fines and forfeitures imposed upon Dissenters, invoked the "native rights" of Englishmen to their liberty and property, as well as the "Great Charter, what we all of us call, our birthright." The Victorian author William Stubbs embellished the thirteenth-century product with modernity when he wrote in his study celebrating the English constitutional system that the Magna Charta was one of the first "collective" acts of the "people" who served as the "other high contracting party," and that it secured "by one bond the interests and rights of each other severally and of all together." John Adams, in his comments on the canon and feudal law, promoted the Mayflower Compact in a similar way—as a founding codification of a modern American system of liberty. The Magna Charta itself surfaced repeatedly during the American Revolution. A Patriot author posed this challenge in 1776: "I would be much obliged to any one who will shew me *the Brittano-American Magna Charta* wherein the terms of our limited dependence are precisely stated."[5] The question would soon be answered by the Declaration of Independence, another document destined to be viewed as a collective act of the "people."

In seventeenth-century England, liberty was widely understood as a privilege whose main value lay in the fact that it protected those who held it from the state. A government respecting liberty, declared John Pym, the leader of the Long Parliament, is one whose goal is to "limit and restrain the excessive power and violence of *great* men." By the time of the Glorious Revolution, "British liberty" had become a well-established metaphor for a body of privileges enjoyed by free persons, designed to protect their personal freedom and property from the Crown (rather than to enable them to speak, publish, etc.). "Now, by enjoying Liberty," wrote an English colonial gentleman, "I understand, the Liberty of their persons being free from Arbitrary, illegal imprisonments."[6] The defining relation here was that between the privileged groups and the state.

New claimants to liberty aspired above all to join the ranks of those who held such privileges, rather than demanding equal freedoms for everyone. Because we are today deeply conditioned to see liberty as an antithesis of elite privilege, we at times miss the fact that it was the ambition of upward social advancement that frequently provided the impetus for such claims. Even when opposition to privilege was ostensibly voiced, its opponents did not necessarily aim to negate the privileges of the privileged, but to wrestle concessions which would grant them rights already held by others. Historically, the progression of rights and liberties in English culture has almost always involved building on preexisting privileges. This holds true even if intellectual arguments for such changes were couched in terms of abstract, "universal" principles. The grievances of colonial Britons in America after the French and Indian War are a case in point. At the outset, both colonial leaders and ordinary people believed they were defending already existing rights. They looked back to English political culture and precedent much more than they cast forward to any systemic novelties, a position that Jack Rakove has called so traditionalist as to be almost anachronistic. There is no reason to assume that the meanings they attached to specific liberties were any less traditional. For instance, their references to the English Declaration of Rights of 1689 were most likely understood in terms of checks on the arbitrary power of monarchy (standing army, excessive fines, cruel punishment), rather than in a more modern sense, as an enumeration of primarily individual rights.[7] They also clearly understood the various rights traditionally—as privileges, that is, as the power to do things. In 1788, the Massachusetts Anti-Federalist John de Witt characterized the people's enumerated rights as "titles of power." At the Virginia ratifying convention, Edmund Randolph referred to the "liberty of the press" and the "right of conscience" as "powers."[8]

The English Whig authors of *Cato's Letters* (1773), widely admired by the Revolutionary generation in America, clearly saw liberty both as a social relation and as a power. In fact, they referred to arbitrary power as a form of excessively concentrated liberty. They envisioned freedom as a wide spectrum. At one extreme was "tyranny," defined as "unlimited restraint put upon natural liberty, by the will of one or a few." At the opposite extreme was "natural and absolute Liberty." Man entered into political society and gave up some of this freedom to preserve as much of that original liberty as possible. Oppressive government happened when too much of this natural freedom was concentrated into a few hands: "Tyranny is a brutish struggle for unlimited liberty to one or a few, who would rob all others of their liberty; and act by no rule but lawless lust." In other words, they saw it as a zero-sum relationship of sorts: the people lost liberty when government accumulated too much of it, and government gained power by occupying the space in which liberty had been previously held by the people. They especially stressed that the enjoyment of liberty was personal, strictly tied to one's property and not to an idea of equal rights: "True and impartial Liberty is therefore the Right of every Man to pursue the natural, reasonable, and religious Dictates of his own Mind; to think what he will, and act as he thinks, provided he acts not to the Prejudice of another; to spend his own money himself, and lay out the Produce of his Labour his own Way; and to Labour his own Way; and to labour for his own Pleasure and Profit, and not for others who are idle, and would live and riot by pillaging and oppressing him and those who are like him."[9]

When we take a long-term perspective on liberty understood as a power, it becomes clear that it was much more than simply an increased freedom to act. To possess it was to hold some sort of membership in the ruling class. It was the centrality of privilege, rather than titles, that ultimately defined membership in this class; after all, a commoner, too, could receive privileges and enter the club.[10] Liberties as legal entitlements have received most of the historians' attention, but they also produced cultural effects which were at least as important as formal powers. They supplied those who possessed them with prestige and identity. They created a shared social consciousness based on the distinction of owning privileges—in contrast to those who did not. This was facilitated by two facts. First, many privileged liberties in history were hereditary and so over long periods became entrenched as ingredients of prestige and authority for their possessors. Sanctioned by time and ultimately viewed as parts of a "naturally" existing order, they became vital parts of their owners' selfhood. Second, monarchs not infrequently granted them, especially from the thirteenth century onward, to whole groups of people—such as knights or cities—rather than to individuals. Antoni Mączak has usefully identified five broad categories of such privileges: exemptions from taxation, or agreements to seek approval for new taxation; various judicial privileges such as more lenient forms of punishment, additional weight given to the grantee's court testimony, or the right to a specific sphere of private jurisdiction; economic advantages, usually monopolies or, in the case of towns, trading privileges; exclusive prestige attributes, such as the right to wear certain clothes symbolically expressive of social position; and, finally, certain political privileges such as access to offices and, in the early modern period, the right to vote. The result of all this was that groups possessing these liberties became internally integrated not only by legal status, but also by their collective self-perception. For instance, Roman elites invoked Ciceronian virtues such as independence, integrity, civic spirit, control of passions, and magnanimity to protect their exclusive liberties. Plebeians who were able to quickly advance to the patriciate were notably more prosaic, and valued liberty primarily for its empowerment to influence politics and government. Once established, they attempted to redefine virtue to reflect their social origins, and stressed achievement rather than lineage.[11] But what they all had in common was the belief that it was the possession of distinctive virtues that gave them the title to own *libertas*.

We may distinguish two major paths along which such group privileges-cum-identities developed in England. One involved the landed classes of gentry and aristocracy; the other originally involved cities, which were granted certain privileges, usually related to taxation, as corporations. By the eighteenth century, however, wealthy urban elites were able to vie for social respectability and acceptance with the much longer-established landed nobility. The "new gentry" sought to revise pedigree-centered values, which defined an elite, by basing value on merit, a quality that, unlike noble birth, was achievable by the middle class. That this competition was transmitted to eighteenth-century America can be seen in the fact that Revolutionary elites condemned (unobtainable) pedigrees, and instead endorsed (obtainable) merit as the primary virtue legitimizing them as an upper class. Although they were otherwise emulating many of the old values of landed nobility, the historically new American elite was in fact in a situation closest to that of the contemporary English commercial class in their struggle for respectability. Like the metropolitan merchants, they attained their wealth not through a long line of inheritances but through their own economic activities. As Zygmunt Bauman has compellingly argued, the newness of the elevated position of such self-made men made it easier for them to claim rights and liberties they did not previously possess because their very lives showed that change was possible. This, combined with the growing Enlightenment faith in human perfectibility, encouraged those who insisted that what thus far had been an ancient and impregnable social order could be modified to accept them.[12] It was a path tailor-made for Americans. In England, the link between birth and rights continued unbroken until the early nineteenth century. What matters for our argument is that whatever the divergences existed between them in the eighteenth century, both the metropolis and the colonies witnessed a firm nexus between privilege, in the form of exclusively held liberties, and the cultural identity of those who held them.

II. *The Marriage of Rights and Inequality*

They are silly People who imagine, that the Good of the Whole is consistent with the Good of every Individual; and at best they are insincere.
—Bernard Mandeville, *A Letter to Dion,* 1732

ONE OF THE MOST intellectually thorny discoveries for students of Enlightenment in England and America is that natural rights not only coexisted, but coexisted quite effortlessly with inequalities and unfreedoms. Upon deeper examination, an even more inconvenient truth emerges—they did not just coexist, they were closely tied in a bond of matrimony. Liberty, as pointed out earlier, denoted a spectrum of enforceable rights, with their fullest enjoyment exclusive to members of the elite. It was a selective entitlement to which one was admitted under certain conditions. At its core lay what one Massachusetts author called the freeholders' "privilege of becoming party to the laws." Notably, those few liberties that were granted to the non-elites tended to be viewed as passive rights, implying the lack of full control over them by those who nominally held them. Henry Parker, the great theorist of the English Revolution, offered a particularly clear explanation of the reasoning behind the distribution of liberty in proportion to social rank: "Liberty is the due birth-right, of every Englishman: but Liberty has its bounds, and rules. . . . By the laws of Liberty every man is to injoy, that which is his own: but since one man has far greater, and better things to injoy, than another, the liberties of one may extend further, than the Liberties of another."[13]

In America one encounters this understanding throughout the eighteenth century. As the Massachusetts Congregationalist Abraham Williams observed in a sermon on the eve of the Stamp Act, "All Men being naturally equal, [they are] embued with like Faculties and propensities, having originally equal Rights and Properties . . . yet Men not being equally industrious and frugal, their Properties and Enjoyments would be unequal." These differences led to a natural hierarchy: "A Society without different Orders and Offices, like a Body without Eyes, Hands, and other Members, would be uncapable of acting, either to secure an internal Order and well-being or defend itself from external injuries." "I think it must be manifest," wrote Timothy Ford more than thirty years later, "that men cannot be considered equal in their natural endowments, nor in their personal acquisitions; nor in their civil rights, as regards those acquisitions: that is to say, that though a man worth but 10l. has as clear a right to what he holds, as the one worth 10 000l. yet the latter surely has more extensive civil rights guaranteed by society, than the former." "A fly, or a worm," noted John Allen, "by the law of nature, has as great a right to Liberty, and Freedom, (according to their little sphere in life,) as the most potent monarch on earth."[14]

What, then, are we to think about all those Enlightenment authors who produced a substantial body of writings arguing that people equally possess natural rights, and that laws should be equally applied to all? We have long since come to believe that by the middle of the eighteenth century a caesura had been reached: the concept of equal liberty was intellectually sufficiently well established that it not only could provide a solid basis for the abolitionist movement but also would make thinking about bondage in Britain no longer possible.[15] Part of the confusion on these issues is probably linked to the erroneous assumption that the Enlightenment represented a relatively unified system of progressive thought, but the main problem seems to be that too much attention has been paid to the abstract intellectual content of the texts in question, and too little to their contemporary meanings and their relationship to the existing social order. To illuminate the latter point, it will be useful to take a brief look at three proposals, published between 1698 and 1755, to legally enslave the poor in Britain. The question asked of their authors, all prominent Enlightenment figures, will be, What do these propositions tell us about the contemporary meanings of freedom and unfreedom among the British political and intellectual class? Of special interest is the fact that all three emphatically rejected the incompatibility between natural rights and the ultimate form of unfreedom—slavery. How could these sophisticated theoreticians of freedom accommodate such polarities within their world views in a non-contradictory way?

Andrew Fletcher of Saltoun, an eminent political thinker and fiery defender of liberty against autocratic government, proposed in his 1689 petition to Parliament a legal enslavement of the Scottish poor as a means of eliminating vagabondage and beggary. His reasoning is illuminating for our argument. "There are at this day in Scotland . . . two hundred thousand people begging from door to door," he estimated. "These are not only no way advantageous, but a very grievous burden to so poor a country." These vagabonds live "without any regard or subjection either to the laws of the land, or even those of God and nature." They are "perpetually drunk, cursing, blaspheming, and fighting together." The problem, Fletcher concluded, was not in overpopulation ("numbers of people being great riches"), but in that these people were not productive, and since in a country as poor as Scotland neither manufactures nor public workhouses could ensure their employment, he proposed to introduce, as a remedy, a form of bond labor already well known in colonial British America—slavery. He would assign such slaves to landowners, much as the poor laws in the past had assigned the parish unemployed to serve. A landowner would be obliged by the new law to "take a proportionable number of these vagabonds, and either employ them in hedging and ditching his grounds, or any other sort of work in town and country; or if they happen to be children and young that he should educate them in the knowledge of some mechanical art, so that every man of estate might have a little manufacture at home which might maintain those servants, and bring great profit to the master, as they did to the ancients." This would immediately ensure basic food and clothing for them, but would also "go a great way towards the present relief of other poor people who have been oppressed by them" by having to pay welfare taxes. Fletcher's argument here reflects a traditional distinction made by the ruling classes between the deserving poor ("people born with natural endowments, perhaps not inferior to our own, and fellow citizens") and the undeserving poor ("idle vagabonds, as no laws could ever restrain"). The latter category implied not only unproductiveness but also moral degradation and a threat to social stability, which was why it was seen as requiring policing as much as relief.[16] Fletcher was deeply convinced that enslavement was a tool that would successfully combine both objectives.

It is revealing that Fletcher saw the genesis of contemporary poverty in what he believed was an unwarranted expansion of the meaning of liberty and its dangerously growing divorce from property. He criticized past churchmen, who "confound things spiritual with temporal." They had persuaded slave owners to free their slaves upon baptism, thus disrupting the good order of society and creating a multitude of people who had "no other estate but their liberty." This had produced a need for charity, but "provisions by hospitals, alms-houses, and the contributions of churches and parishes have by experience been found to increase the numbers that live by them." Furthermore, freedom—in Fletcher's view—was organically inseparable from responsibility, and when applied to vagrants, it could only become its own parody, a "liberty every idle and lazy person has of burdening the society in which he lives, with his maintenance." He saw that the only means of reversing this process lay in reinstating control over the labor of the underclass to masters who would by nature have an economic interest in the laborer, for "when such an economy comes under the inspection of every master of a family, and that he himself is to reap the profit of the right management; the thing not only turns to a far better account, but by reason of his power to sell those workmen to others who may have use for them . . . the profit is permanent to the society." In an argument also used by colonial defenders of slavery, Fletcher pointed to its supposed built-in protections against any abuse and mistreatment of the slave: "As long as the servant is not unfit for work, all these things are against the interest of the master: that the most brutal man will not use his beast ill only out of a humour."[17]

Anticipating potential criticism on the grounds of natural rights and religion, Fletcher responded to the hypothetical question, "Shall men of immortal souls and by nature equal to any, be sold as beasts?" with, "I regard not names but things," firmly asserting the primacy of social reality over mere ideas. His version of slavery would be limited, and the allowable degree of subjection strictly justified by the higher needs of "a well-regulated common-wealth." The masters would have no power over the life of their slaves ("The life of the master should go for the life of the servant"), nor freedom to mistreat them (in case it did happen, the slave should "not only have his freedom . . . but a sufficient yearly pension so long as he should live from his said master"). Clothing, food, and lodging were to be ensured for the slave's family; the slaves should be taught reading and religion; they should not work on Sundays; public "hospitals" should be provided for those who no longer could work, and "in everything, except their duty as servants, they should not be under the will of their masters, but the protection of the law." Fletcher insisted that under this kind of rule the slave still retained his basic liberty, because "in the most essential things he is only subject to the law and not to the will of his master." Fletcher thus made a clear distinction between true slavery and his own concept of a legally regulated form of slavery, which he believed should more accurately be seen as a harsh subcategory of servitude for those who should not be "abandoned to their own conduct." In his definition, a slave is "one who is absolutely subjected to the will of another man without any remedy: and not one who is only subjected under certain limitations, and upon certain accounts necessary for the good of the com-monwealth, though such a one may go under that name." True slavery might be witnessed, for example, in Turkey, where "they are all slaves to the Grand Signior, and have no remedy against his will." Even with the introduction of his reforms, such a degree of dependence would be impossible in Britain: "We are all subjected to the laws: and the easier or harder conditions imposed by them upon the several ranks of men in any society, make not the distinction that is between a freeman and a slave." Clearly, for Fletcher liberty meant the rule of law within which a gamut of rights was applied in different degrees to different social ranks. This socially selective treatment by the law, to which all were "equally" subject, was practiced throughout the eighteenth century, in England as well as in its New World colonies. One can even find references to such ancient exemptions for the elite as the "Benefit of Clergy" in legal decisions made by American Revolutionary authorities.[18]

More than three decades later, George Berkeley, by then the Bishop of Cloyne and a widely celebrated philosopher, came up with a strikingly similar scenario to cure severe poverty in Ireland. He publicized it in *The Querist* (1735–37), a tract written entirely in the form of rhetorical questions intended to trigger a wider discussion on the economic predicament of the island. He pointed out that the existing system of poor relief based on the "poor-tax" had not only been a failure but had increased the number of people on the poor rolls, and he argued, therefore, that the time was ripe for the state to use all means possible in the battle against "idleness and all idle folk." While his ideas of economic reform were intended to help all the poor, he singled out "the most indolent" and "those who cannot or who will not find employment for themselves" for more dramatic treatment. Asking the public "whether temporary servitude would not be the best cure for idleness and beggary," he proposed legislation that would require all beggars to be "seized and made slaves to the public for a certain term of years."[19]

Like Fletcher, he viewed this kind of slavery as an act of charity, and suggested that its benevolent outcome would be that the idle would end up "well worked, fed and clothed," a state much preferable to their current existence. It would be rightful for the nation to legislate such a system, because it would bring about public good, the supreme yardstick of policy. The society would also be repaid with various public works for the damages and losses caused by the unproductive. Berkeley rhetorically asked "whether other nations have not found great benefit from the use of slaves in repairing high roads, making rivers navigable, draining bogs, erecting public buildings, bridges and manufactures." Both Fletcher and Berkeley typically shared a degree of contempt for the poor as a class of lesser people. Both held it as a given that the sorry state of this underclass was in good part a result of their own moral decline. Wrote Berkeley: "In this fertile and plentiful island, none can perish for want but the idle and improvident. None who have industry, frugality, and foresight but may get into tolerable, if not wealthy, circum-

stances." The "lusty vagabonds" begged all over Ireland but showed no interest when offered employment. The threat of severe treatment would have the
additional advantages of both striking terror into hardened criminals and
providing motivation for industry among the other poor; slaves chained in
pairs, Berkeley suggested, would be "very edifying to the multitude." Fletcher,
we may note, envisioned similar psychological measures when he suggested
that, "for example and terror three or four hundred of the most notorious of
these villains which we call jockys, might be presented by the government to
the state of Venice, to serve in their galleys."[20]

Most importantly, Berkeley believed that his limited form of bondage
would not violate individual rights or liberties, because the conduct of criminals and able-bodied beggars was already punishable. He made two main
points on this issue. First, he asked the rhetorical question: "Whether he who
is chained in a jail or dungeon hath not, for the time, lost his liberty? And if
so, whether temporary slavery be not already admitted among us?" And then:
"Whether criminals in the freest country may not forefeit their liberty, and
repair the damage they have done to the public by hard labour?" Furthermore, he then argued, the society at large had a "right to employ" those who
would not work. As to the principle of religious equality, he did not see it as
contradictory to slavery, and, like colonial American slave owners, he argued
that God's equal love for all was in perfect harmony with the need for social
hierarchy and the existence of a servile class. This could be seen as consistent with his broader philosophical views, especially his belief that although reason could lead men to moral existence, truth was accessible only to
a small elite.[21]

Berkeley's brief sojourn in colonial America in the years preceding the
publication of *The Querist* indicates that his enslavement plans were not
merely an exotic sideline, and that servitude and slavery coexisted in his
world view with liberty and Christianity in a non-contradictory way. He
sailed to the colonies in 1729 to pursue his semi-utopian plan of founding a
college in Bermuda to educate "the Youth of our English Plantations," alongside "a number of young American savages," as a means of strengthening the
British rule in the colonies. After a brief spell in Virginia, he ended up in
Newport, Rhode Island, where, awaiting funds to be raised for Bermuda, he
settled on a ninety-six-acre farm. There he purchased three slaves, whom
he baptized as "Philip, Anthony and Agnes Berkeley." At the same time, he

spoke out publicly—despite protests from West Indian slave owners—against racism (which he called "an irrational Contempt for the Blacks, as Creatures of another Species") and for a better treatment of slaves. He argued that baptism was not contradictory to slave status, and protested that "small care hath been taken to convert the Negroes of our Plantations, who, to the Infamy of England, and Scandal of the World, continue Heathen under Christian Masters and in Christian Countries." On the issue of the baptizing of slaves by their masters, he noted, it "would be of Advantage to their Affairs, to have Slaves who should obey in all Things their Masters according to the Flesh, not with Eye-service as Man-pleasers, but, in Singleness of Heart as fearing God." Although slaves remained free before God, he argued, "Gospel-Liberty consists with temporal Servitude," and "Slaves would only become better Slaves by being Christians."[22] Apparently, Berkeley's later vision of slaves as the bottom rung of a stable and orderly society back in Ireland was quite consistent with these views, and almost certainly was to some extent animated by his experience in the colonies.

The third major voice advocating the enslavement of certain categories of the homeless and unemployed in Britain was that of Francis Hutcheson, professor at the University of Glasgow, teacher of Adam Smith, and a leading philosopher of the Scottish Enlightenment. His thought is widely considered to have given a strong impetus to the antislavery movement. He is widely regarded as a philosophical influence on such American Founders as Thomas Jefferson and Gouverneur Morris. His proposal was contained in the treatise *A System of Moral Philosophy* (1755), in which Hutcheson propounded the theory that people possess an inner sense of benevolence toward humanity, and that this—and not the Hobbesian principle of egoism—is the primary human impulse, one that links individual interest and the good of society. But, like Fletcher and Berkeley, he too viewed natural rights in the context of their benefits to society. Hence, proper conduct should be "such as is necessary for the general good," and individual rights to liberty by natural law should be subordinate to collective interest. It was this premise that informed the justifications for Hutcheson's call to enslave all "idle" poor in Britain.[23]

The very existence of unproductive people was antithetical to a well-ordered society, which Hutcheson, like most of his contemporaries, saw as founded on an interdependence between two groups fundamental to the constitution of such a society: masters and servants. He derived this concept from the fact that population was constantly growing, while land remained finite. Hence, there would always be those without property or the employment needed to support themselves, just as those who did own property would always need laborers and would be willing to offer them some sort of compensation for their service. This "relation of master and servant" was universal in history, and the question whether servitude itself was for a term only or for life was "not of much consequence." Both sides of this relationship had fundamental duties: "The servant is bound to fidelity, and willing service, as in the sight of God, by whose providence this lot is appointed to him; and the master to mercy and lenity, as toward a fellow-creature in less fortunate circumstances, who yet has the like affections, and is capable of the like virtues, and happiness or misery with himself." A limited form of slavery could and should be applied to the idle poor—a category that violated this organic relationship—primarily because it would restore and enforce mutual master-servant obligations. It would also have a punitive function. Hutcheson was emphatic about this: "No law could be more effectual to promote a general industry, and refrain sloth and idleness in the lower conditions, than making perpetual slavery of this sort the ordinary punishment of such idle vagrants as, after proper admonitions and tryals of temporary servitude, cannot be engaged to support themselves and their families by any useful labours." Hutcheson defined the category of enslavables rather broadly by also including some of those on public welfare, especially those, "such as by intemperance or other vices ruined themselves and their families, and made them a publick burden."[24]

Hutcheson too saw slavery as a subcategory of servitude, only more severe. It was fully justified legally and morally, providing it was "in consequence of damages injuriously done, or of debts incurred, which they have by their gross vices made themselves incapable of discharging." As he argued: "The person whom they have thus injured has a perfect right to compensation by their labours during their lives, if they cannot sooner discharge the claim. A criminal too, by way of punishment, may justly be adjudged to perpetual labours of the severest sort." The labor of such people could therefore be lawfully bought and sold without their consent.[25]

Of particular interest for our understanding of the ontology of freedom in the early modern British world is Hutcheson's emphasis that establishing bondage for certain categories of people in no way detracted from their sacrosanct British rights and liberties. The newly enslaved should be offered an opportunity to earn their freedom, if they reformed themselves: "There might be a trial first made, according to the Jewish custom of servitude for seven years; and then they might be allowed their liberty, in case they acquired an habit of diligence; but if not, they should be adjudged to slavery for life." Hutcheson recognized that such slaves "are still our fellow-creatures," and stressed that even in "this worst condition of servitude, neither the criminal, after he has endured any publick punishment which the common safety may require, nor much less the debtor, have lost any of the natural rights of mankind beside that one to their own labours." These included the right to "defend themselves by violence against any savage useless tortures, any attempts of maiming them or prostituting them to the lusts of their masters, or forcing them in any worship against their consciences." Slaves should also be able to "acquire rights by contract or by any legal deed," so they could pay off debts or "compensate part or whole of the value of their labour." Hutcheson explicitly contrasted his own, enlightened notion of slavery with that of the Ancients, who derived bondage from captivity in war. The latter principle was, in his view, an unjust and cruel custom depriving men of all rights; slavery should be considered punishment, and innocent individuals should not be punished for decisions by rulers to make war. "No damage done or crime committed," Hutcheson also claimed, "can change a rational creature into a piece of goods void of all right." At the same time, he argued, much like Berkeley, that it was a fallacy to apply natural law in an absolute manner, without regard to the larger principle of public utility. To do so might erroneously lead to the rejection of all slavery. In fact, Hutcheson believed, "some nations favour liberty immoderately by never admitting the perpetual servitude of any citizen." By contrast, a carefully marked-out slavery "has a just foundation."[26] Hutcheson's treatise contains several arguments —such as his reasoning against absolute bondage and his universal principle of human happiness—that have received most of the historians' attention as foreshadowing future progressive developments, especially abolitionism. But this should not prevent us from noting how deeply his abstract philosophical notions were rooted in assumptions about social order—assumptions that eighteenth-century English culture still took for granted. David Brion Davis has observed that Hutcheson "preached the universality of benevolence, and held that our sympathy for the most remote members of our species was proof of our disinterested virtue."[27] We should, however, bear in mind that disinterested virtue was an old and essentially aristocratic concept, and was assumed to be an attribute only of an elite that could afford—through property and education—to possess it.

Finally, a closer look at Hutcheson's supposedly universal instinct of benevolence shows that he is not speaking of all men, but of the genteel elites. "Men of virtue, distinction, wit, and kindness," he wrote, "often get together without expecting profit or glory, and without attempting to boast of themselves or to ridicule or revile others." Elsewhere, Hutcheson noted that where there is "no social enjoyment or affection, no finer perceptions, or exercise of the intellectual powers; the state is below many brutes." Like Shaftesbury, he believed that the lower orders of men were often driven by sensuality, which, when dominant, was "shameful and despicable." In contrast, "the superior orders in this world probably experience all the sensations of the lower orders, and can judge of them." But "the inferior do not experience the enjoyments of the superior. . . . God has assigned to each order . . . their peculiar powers and tastes." A similar selectivity can be observed in Hutcheson's application of natural rights. While he did strongly criticize inheritable, "perpetual slavery," on the grounds that "each man is the original proprietor of his liberty" and that the proof of anyone's losing this liberty "must be incumbent on those who deprive him of it by force," he accepted slavery as legitimate if the enslaved had in some way "forfeited" their liberty. This argument could easily be used to justify the enslavement of Africans in the colonies, since he allowed that if a merchant bought and transported captives (and thus saved their lives), then "these captives are his debtors" and must repay with interest by an appropriate period of service, after which they should be set free.[28] The very point that idleness justified forced labor, but only in application to the class of the unemployed and the masterless, should make us sensible to the fact that, at the deepest level, the meaning of liberty used in the whole argument was still inherently exclusionary and elitist rather than universal.

We need to bear in mind that all three authors were staunch champions of individual liberties and natural rights; Hutcheson even went so far as to suggest that the American colonies were entitled to resist oppressive rule from London. In this context, their arguments for the compatibility of slavery with natural rights tell us much about the meaning of liberty among the British political classes in the period leading up to the American Revolution.

They are also a good example of the perennially puzzling "contradictions" among political and intellectual figures of the British Enlightenment, including the American Founders. David Brion Davis in his monumental *Problem of Slavery in Western Culture* pointed to "the curious capacity of slavery for generating or accommodating itself to dualisms of thought." Locke was a case in point; he put slavery entirely outside of the social contract, a premise that allowed him to defend the former and still extol the rights of man.[29]

But the arguments of Fletcher, Berkeley, and Hutcheson suggest that these men did not represent such an "inconsistent" dualism. Rather, all three wrestled with the burning issues of their societies by applying currently legitimate ideas to specific, real-life problems. Their answers show that it was not equality and rights that were somehow primary and universal, while slavery and unequal treatment of the underclass had to be reconciled with them, but rather, the reverse: a deeply hierarchical understanding of society based on the master/laborer dichotomy was primary, and liberty—even if it was rhetorically defined as an abstract and universal concept—continued to be largely understood as a privilege applicable in full only to a group entitled to it by property, reason, and virtue. These men did not see it as a unified concept, but as a broad range of particular freedoms distributed in rank-specific shares.[30]

Another belief that clearly emerges from these writings is that the stability of social order was an inseparable condition of preserving liberty itself. The idea of enslaving vagrants may appear somewhat less radical when it is realized that servitude had long been perceived as a form of ensuring order by subordinating unruly elements to a master's authority. Since the Statute of Labourers (1350–51) and, later, the Statute of Artificers (1562–63), all able-bodied unemployed under sixty were forced to serve; and after 1572, even the children of beggars were bound out as a form of welfare. One of the central premises of poor laws after the decline of feudalism and serfdom was to protect eroding relations of authority that had been disrupted by mobile, "masterless" men, fluid wages, and increasingly frequent changes of employers. A beggar was, after all, one of those who "observe no law, obey no governor, use no religion." The three proposals discussed here fit right into this traditional line of reasoning about the underclass. Elite-authored relief projects were as a rule designed to clothe and feed the destitute, but not to open the way for them to relinquish their status in the lower order.

Like Berkeley's slaves, the poor were to be made better poor. When in 1700 Fletcher's contemporary, James Donaldson, published his own plan of economic reforms, he warned that they were not intended "to make all Men rich, for that were not only contrarie to the order GOD has established, and Foretold, that there shall alwise be some Poor in the World, but also is in its own Nature impossible, for as one increases in Riches, some others must Decrease as natively as one Scale of a Ballance goes up when other is pressed down." In this context, it made perfect and non-ironic sense for one colonial promoter in 1735 to solemnly call on the West Indian slaves to "contentedly possess the happy, humble Lot assigned to you by Heaven"—assuredly a stirring appeal to its addressees, especially when published in the *Gentleman's Magazine*.[31]

The primacy of order over equal liberty should not surprise. First, a characteristic feature of English Enlightenment—unlike the more theoretically inclined European variant—was that it intermixed theory and practice, and was much less sharp than its French counterpart in its attacks against the institutions of state and society. Second, the Enlightenment notion of liberty was a cultural artifact created by the elites. This was why a pauper and a property owner would be disciplined differently for the same "licentious" conduct and the liberties of neither would be seen as violated by such inequality. For Fletcher, equality existed in the equal subjection to the law, but he had no misgivings about the law imposing "different conditions" on people according to the distinctions between the "several ranks of men." In this he was by no means exceptional among intellectuals. A long line of theorists, from Luis de Molina, through Hugo Grotius and John Selden, to Thomas Hobbes, not only accepted slavery, but also separated *ius* from *dominium*, where inferiors had a *ius* but not *dominium* against superiors—that is, a passive, not an active, right. It appears that for Fletcher, Berkeley, and Hutcheson, servants and slaves retained such passive rights, but they had no sovereignty over their rights, nor were these rights separate from their duties as a lower, laboring order. The liberty invoked here was subjective liberty, an intellectual construct. It was referred to as absolute only to make a theoretical point about its essence, but in real life it had to be restricted by law and by God-ordered obligations differentially assigned to social ranks.[32]

It is crucial to understand that these broad, symbolic liberties could quite readily coexist with limited but enforceable ones in various English and American bills of rights. We should most certainly pause before throwing the liberty referred to in the Declaration of Independence into the dustbin, as some authors do, solely because it did not include slaves in the language of "all men are created equal," or before viewing the Northwest Ordinance, which did not include Native Americans as legal persons, as nothing more than a case of "British imperialism." Neither English theorists nor the political classes of the time had yet included the English poor in their concepts of full rights, because rights were not yet viewed as existing autonomously and were still inherently tied to ranks, and therefore, inequalities. This view thrived in America throughout the eighteenth century. Supreme Court Justice Samuel Chase observed in 1803 that, contrary to popular usage, people did not posses rights in a state of nature: "I really consider a state of nature as a creature of the imagination. . . . Personal liberty and rights can only be acquired by becoming a member of the community."[33] Behind his statement stood centuries-long British beliefs that those without property had no attachment to the community, and that liberty was a man-made device to protect property.

It is this correlation between rank, property, and liberty that explains why bondage and other forms of unfreedom could be viewed as forms of charity. Forced deportation of vagrants and other criminals and their sale into servitude in colonial America had been practiced since the first British settlements there. The Court Books of Bridewell have several entries mentioning vagrants, "kept for Virginia" and Barbados, as early as 1619 and 1622. John Donne, preaching to the Virginia Company in 1622, evoked a vision of America as a huge house of corrections, noting, "If the whole Countrey were but such a Bridewell, to force idle persons to work, it had a good vse." Hugh Jones, a colonial promoter who was Berkeley's contemporary, called for more forced immigration of bond servants to Virginia, noting, "There can be no Injury in such moderate legal Compulsion as forces People to be honest and industrious, though it be contrary to their false Notions, which ought to be subject to publick Good." The respected economic thinker John Oldmixon observed in 1741 that the unemployed have "no Value to a Nation." In his argument promoting British colonies, he explained the merits of forced emigration to America: "Tis said, People are the Wealth of a Nation, and to take away their people is to impoverish them; those that say it, mean only laborious and industrious People, and not such as have no Employ, or, which is worse, are employed only in disturbing and robbing such as have any." Most early theorists of natural rights found bondage permissible in certain circumstances, such as when a person could be assumed to have traded away his natural liberty.[34]

To sum up, extreme forms of unfreedom within the eighteenth-century British world were not as "socially and legally anomalous" as we have been told. To explain the enslavement proposals examined above in terms of inconsistencies would clearly be an error of retrospective history. It would blur what J. R. Pole once called the distinction between "rhetorical and literal commitment to equality," a separation that seems to have its origins in the dual nature of liberty as both an intellectual construction and a social relation.[35] Apparently, natural rights resided in the former sphere, and selective unfreedom in the latter. For British intellectuals, the former was not incongruent with the latter; rather, their mutual correspondence was indispensable in harmonizing the various contending class interests. It was also a prime justification of the elite's own cult of independence, a cult that required both the real-life unfreedom of some and the symbolic apparatus of equal liberty. It was this meaning of liberty that the late colonial American political class inherited from British culture.

The Transmission of Restricted Liberty to Colonial America

I. Reproducing the Old World Order in the Provinces

Nobility in Men is worth as much as it is in Horses Asses or Rams: but the meanest blooded Puppy, in the World, if he gets a little money, is as good a man as the best of them.

—John Adams, 1813

IT HAS LONG BEEN a commonplace that late colonial American society was less structured than the mother country. This undisputed fact is often flanked by a belief that an order of ranks had never meant much to the provincials, and that "Americans, conscious that they lacked the extremes of wealth characteristic of older European countries, generally accepted equality as a characteristic of their society and of the governments they were founding."[1] There is much evidence, however, that points in the opposite direction, revealing a persistent quest to reproduce at least some of the major distinctions present in the mother country. In fact, the more undifferentiated colonial society appeared to be, the more the provincial elite, and those aspiring to enter its ranks, struggled to re-create at least a semblance of hierarchy. Their principal means of achieving this goal was to emulate the characteristics of the English gentry, an unsurprising fact since throughout the colonial period the political, economic, and cultural identity of British America—an imperial outpost—was deeply dependent on the metropolis. The sheer intensity of these mimetic efforts, and the strength of the provincials' ambition—ever futile—to be considered equals with their English counterparts were quite remarkable. They tell us much about how the concept of restricted, rank-specific liberty was transmitted to the colonies, and of how it held sway throughout the Revolutionary era—even if the various declarations of independence from London, with their sweeping use of egalitarian rhetoric, suggested otherwise.

Without going into the details of an otherwise well-covered subject, it is today a little disputed fact that by the third decade of the eighteenth century, British America—despite its relative social homogeneity—had witnessed the emergence of a genuine, creole upper class confidently claiming to be free and independent. Any fresh discussion of the nature and species of contemporary liberty must take a new, sober look at this elite, not as bearers of a "reactionary" or "progressive" liberty, but as a socioeconomic class that dominated the public scene in late colonial America, monopolized the educational and political capital of the colony, and by 1764 had a grand stake in preserving their social station. In New England, the elite was made up of a combination of the clergy, powerful lawyers, and men of wealth, and comprised a ruling class that Abraham Bishop of Connecticut saw in 1800 as a form of continuing "aristocracy." In the South, the elite comprised a slaveholding, landed class, which in some colonies developed into a virtual oligarchy. In 1774, John Day, who had lived in British America for decades, identified a colonial upper class consisting of "the landed or moneyed interest," "the "commercial men," "practitioners of the law," and the "clergy," a classificatory scheme that does not much depart from the social composition of the few dozen men who devised the Constitution. The elite / non-elite distinction remained a basic cultural norm. As late as 1791, William Brewster, an ambitious Connecticut shoemaker (and so a member of the class of "mechanics") who published political articles on taxation in the *Norwich Packet,* complained that the public ignored or ridiculed him for having taken up an activity beyond his station.[2] The term "elite" used here is not merely an economic one; it refers to a class that, in relation to the rest of society, was the most free, one whose autonomy depended on their control of property and cultural resources, and who had the power to influence collective beliefs and behavior—especially by imposing a conceptual vocabulary which legitimized such an order and made it appear natural.

While the existence of elites is not in dispute, historians have differed over the degree of their authority. Progressives divided the elites into conservatives and radicals. Charles Beard defined their elitism by their "economic interests," mostly ignoring their identity as a class. Consensus historians shoved them under the carpet by emphasizing shared, egalitarian values. More recently, they have been presented as a dominant class that transformed itself with the Revolution and created a democratic ideological framework. The newest studies by historians with a culturalist bent are uncovering a more complex colonial world in which even a relatively broad popular participation in political life only served to uphold the domination of the gentry—through webs of dependence within a still traditional and stratified society.[3]

Why should we pay special attention to privileged elites when examining the late eighteenth-century progress of American liberty? First, because they controlled the production of political reality and its symbolic representations. Second, because elites and non-elites were integral parts of a closely interconnected network of culture encompassing all of society. Third, because there is no reason whatsoever to assume that positive, modern liberties did not, in good part, derive from privilege. In much of the historiography of the past four decades, however, the elitist and non-egalitarian sources of liberty have been downplayed. Such a pedigree simply grinds in the teeth of Americans, who tend to take for granted that one is simply free, unless one's freedom is somehow constrained. But modern, democratic practices did not have to originate from sources unblemished by inequality or injustice. As we shall see, they could, and did, also derive from class-bound inequalities, fabricated traditions, and a political idiom generated by power struggles.

When the Revolution broke out, the provincial gentry as a group were mature in their distinctiveness. Despite marked regional differences, its members could instantly recognize one another as such, whether it was a Bostonian visiting Charleston, or vice versa. This was made easier by the fact that, unlike in Europe, where early modern elites had a long history behind them and were usually differentiated into groups based on property (merchants, bankers), prestige (the gentry, the aristocracy), or political power (governmental officials), the British colonial elite often combined all these criteria, minus the noble pedigree.[4] But aspirants to high office who possessed wealth but no ancestry did not pose much of a problem in the colonies, and there were no rivalries between estates, as in France before the Revolution. The

Patriot gentry assembled in the Continental Congress were a fairly homogeneous upper class, and most evidence points to the fact that their consciousness of being members of this class still trumped political divisions, which they disdainfully called factions. What is more, this social and cultural identity endured throughout the contests between Federalists and Anti-Federalists in the last two decades of the century.

It was neither an accident nor an anomaly that ambitious, newly wealthy provincial Americans eagerly championed metropolitan genteel values. They did so because such values contained desirable prescriptive assumptions about who qualified for authority, and who did not. These prescriptions functioned as legitimizers of rank, power, and prestige. They included material requirements (property) and cultural requisites (education, virtue, taste), all subtly interwoven within the fabric of culture. Property was an indispensable guarantor of the full enjoyment of liberty, and liberty from arbitrary power protected property and personal security. Property also provided independence, which, in turn, was a prerequisite of disinterestedness. Disinterestedness was deemed the foundation of public virtue, and thus a condition of occupying offices of influence. For these representations to function as part of a "natural" arrangement of the world, they had to be absorbed and domesticated by both the elites and ordinary people. A habitual usage of such assumptions "naturalizes real differences, converting differences into nature."[5] Only then could the elite come to be popularly perceived as intrinsic proprietors of certain attributes—such as, for instance, public virtue—and, by extension, claim title to be carriers of fullest liberty. This was why in the culture of the Revolutionary era a successful claim to be a member of the gentry still carried considerable social plausibility, and was far from being outmoded.

These elements of elite identity—essentially, emulations of metropolitan society—were especially alluring to the rising colonial upper class because they hierarchized society. The essence of this identity lay in difference. It helped define its owners *against* others, inside and outside of their circle, and to circumscribe their place in the larger order of society. This was why they so often emphasized contrasts with other groups. This was why they construed condescension by stereotyping the uncivil mob, the materialistic petty bourgeois, and those deficient in taste. They marked out approved behavior and censured those who violated it. When someone clearly outside of their class assumed any of the reserved attributes or styles, he could usually count on being viewed as a usurper, and when someone from within their group exhibited styles appropriate to ordinary people, he could expect ostracism for unbecoming behavior. In other words, for one to be approved for membership in the class meant that another had to be excluded. Any wider openness for membership would instantly democratize such an order, and nullify the very raison d'être of an elite. Possessing exclusive liberties worked in much the same way as possessing exclusive personal qualities, or even styles of dress. The whole social order was conceived, instituted, and made stable by maintaining an equilibrium between those with the fullest degree of freedom and those with restricted freedom. The only way the privileged free could exercise their privilege was for the freedom of others to be restricted. The unfree were the alter ego of the free.[6]

Of all the distinctive features of American gentry, identity, virtue, and independence were the most jealously defended. This only makes sense when we view them in the context of an organic concept of a free and unequal society, a British legacy asserted in America throughout the eighteenth century. *Private* attributes were assumed to make them immune to licentiousness and interest, the main threats to *public* liberty. "There is seldom an Instance of a man guilty of betraying his Country," noted Samuel Adams, "who had not before lost the feeling of moral Obligation in his private Connection." Their self-definition by virtue thus validated their authority and their claim to be guardians of the public good. They saw themselves as the true "political nation," entitled to both civil liberty, which protected their persons and their property, and political liberty, which gave them the power to vote and to hold offices. The rights of yeomen to vote were widely recognized, but this did not imply their being equal to the elite as bearers of all liberties, or having an equal public voice. Reflecting on the latter point in their letters to George Washington, John Kirkpatrick warned about relying on the promises of "the Vulgar," and James Wood noted that the "common herd" was not to be depended upon for political responsibility. Whenever the terms "free men" or "independent men" were used as euphemisms for the propertied class, and whenever comments were made on government and laws as a goal of "free people," the references were usually not to all people, but to "the virtuous and sensible part of the community." Only within such a concept of society could the gentry's privileged position be seen as consistent with the popular idea of a free nation.

This view of a unified, "free," and "ordered" society, resting on the premise that the elites would "naturally" be elected to power by the non-elites, retained validity among the American elite throughout the eighteenth century. John Adams was far from being exceptional when he found Thomas Paine's radical redefinition of the powers of the people, presented in *Common Sense,* "so democratical . . . that it must produce confusion and every evil work."[7]

To better understand why *new* elites in both England and America attached so much value to defending their honor and claims to certain privileges of liberty, we should note the similarities between them. They both found themselves on the receiving end of condescension from the old ruling class. In one prominent English case, Daniel Defoe, the son of a butcher and a very successful writer, devised a coat of arms for himself and bought land in order to obtain respect as a gentleman, yet was still ridiculed by London high society for his low birth. But there would have been no Defoe if the rigid concepts of hierarchy had not already been dented by the anti-absolutist edge of the Cromwellian rebellion and the Glorious Revolution of 1688. The collapse of the Stuart dynasty diminished the influence of the court and the aristocracy. A parallel growth of commerce and manufacturing generated ambitions among the newly rising moneyed class to gain cultural and political acceptance, a goal possible only if the traditional social order, dominated by an elite of property and birth, were altered. Although the established class resisted such change by fighting a cultural war of sorts with the nouveaux riches, by the mid-eighteenth century property instead of birth was increasingly becoming the criterion of political and social authority. It was this new bourgeoisie that came up with the idea—long before the American revolutionaries did—of an elite based solely on merit replacing the old heraldic one, a cultural change that would give greater respectability to merchants and businessmen, as well as a greater share of political liberty. It was this tension between the old defenders of privilege and the various types of new aspirants to elite status, aided by the various disaffected voices of the unpropertied classes, that created a public conversation in which both sides increasingly introduced a more socially inclusive and consensual political language. What is most important to realize is that Defoe—who contemptuously referred to the lower classes as "the despicable throng of the Plaebeii"—and those like him, by no means advocated social levelling; they wanted to rise, to be accepted and included among the dominant class as equals. Their campaign was never intended to expand the liberty of non-elites, but only to include newly propertied men in its privileged circle. As the new men succeeded in their aspirations—and as Parliament increasingly came to reflect their interests—they themselves became the jealous guardians of their new privileges and opposed expanding the sphere of liberty to others.[8] New American elites developed along similar trajectory, especially since, as the only high society in the colonies, they had fewer local competitors in their drive for authority.

Although, for the purposes of argument, the term "gentry" is used here to collectively denote the colonial upper classes, it must be emphasized that there existed a variety of distinct, regional elites across British America. Although they may have shared key assumptions about gentility, there were also significant differences between them. Prominent among these differences was their attitude toward the commercial class. The British landed class had traditionally defined their values in opposition to the "interested" and materialist world view of urban moneyed men. In the plantation colonies of America, where the landed lifestyle was closest to this metropolitan prototype, such an attitude was much more common than in the North. The views of Jefferson in this matter are perhaps the best known, but already in the 1730s one can find a number of distinctly hostile comments about commercial men. From the ranks of the great Virginian planters, William Byrd II spoke contemptuously of the aspirations to wealth of "people who [stand] behind the counters," and Landon Carter believed that a trader "generally has too much of the theif [sic] in him." The fear of the commercial classes intruding on the gentry's reserved sphere of liberties continued throughout the Revolution, and well after. Richard Henry Lee was appalled by the "rapacious Trader," and James Duane contrasted the "disinterested Patriot," who placed his "happiness in Reputation," with "clamorous Creditors and insidious Speculators."[9]

But contempt for the mercantile world view was not limited to the South, which suggests that transmitted metropolitan values were often stronger than the specific regional life experiences of their bearers. When John Adams recommended Robert Morris to General Horatio Gates, he wrote that Morris "has vast designs in the mercantile Way. And no doubt pursues mercantile Ends, which are always gain; but he is an excellent Member of our Body [Congress]." Elsewhere, Adams noted that "the Spirit of Commerce . . . is incompatible with that purity of Heart, and Greatness of soul which is necessary for an happy Republic." Even Thomas Paine, with all his radicalism, viewed mercantile society and the business ethos with suspicion, because they were based on self-interest. It would appear that after the Revolution many of the dire warnings by Anti-Federalists of a new "aristocracy" (a common code word for oppressive government), which they feared might emerge from the Constitution, implied a potential "consolidation" of central power by the newly wealthy, and thus unvirtuous, elites. One author generously allowed that "many commercial and moneyed men . . . ought to be respected," but his deeper point was that most of them sought only material gain instead of the public good, and therefore "are to be despised." Clearly, even by the late 1780s, a good part of the gentry's identity, and not only in the South, was still tied by the umbilical cord of culture to the Old World landed ethos. It was an ethos that endowed landowners with the independence and virtue required to fully bear the responsibilities of liberty, and that branded the rapidly rising merchant class as nouveaux riches whose involvement with commerce would never allow them to exercise power disinterestedly. For the Americans, a bitter irony in all of this was that London cheerfully branded the colonial elites with the very same label. Recurring themes in descriptions of the colonists included their "eager desire speedily to raise a Fortune," and the lack of genteel virtue among them, "for the fathers of those men were Tinkers and Peddlers."[10]

Another regional difference between the colonial elites can be seen in the fairly common perception of the New England upper class that their Southern counterparts were too Old World and aristocratic. Jonathan Blanchard, a delegate to Continental Congress from New Hampshire, was of the opinion that "the Southern Gentry prefer extravagance to Oeconomy . . . and were it not for New-England Delegates, the Lord only knows to what lengths the Congress would run." John Adams, referring to Southern planters, observed: "These Gentlemen are accustomed, habituated to higher Notions of themselves, and the distinction between them and the common People, than We are." The huge differences in wealth among the Southerners, he thought, gave "an aristocratical turn to all their proceedings," and even an "aversion to Common Sense." "The Southern Nabob's," noted Ephraim Paine, "behave as thoug they viewed themselves a superior Order of animals when Compared with those of the other end of the Confederacy." He added, "This Sir you know Dos not agree with the great Spiritt of the Northern Gentry." Charles Thomson was appalled by the corrupting effects of slavery on the Southern elite, and worried that it might impede the creation of a federal state, because, "such is the fiery pride of South Carolina, such a dissipation in her morals & her insolence occasioned by the multitude of slaves that she will not cordially join in any Union." It is important to note, however, that all of these authors were merely pointing to differences that existed among members of *same class,* one to which they felt they all unshakably belonged. Their shared status as members of the elite was stronger than their regional or political alliances. This was not the case between elites in the metropole and those in the colonies: during the War of Independence, a British gentleman officer did not hesitate to characterize the Loyalist groups who fought for *his* royal cause in the Southern backcountry of America as "mere rabble."[11]

II. Fear of Levelling and Licentiousness

> Since every Commonwealth consists of Two Orders of Men, the People properly so called, and the Populace, or Inferior Multitude; we may accordingly reckon two orders only of Citizens, the Noble and the Plebeian.
> —Wawrzyniec Goślicki, *The Accomplished Senator,* 1773

ONE OF THE REASONS for the colonials' urge to reproduce familiar and recognizable social structures was their fear of chaos—the antithesis of a well-ordered society, traditionally understood as one based on a harmonious balance between its unequal ranks. The provincial intelligentsia was genuinely worried that the excessive social homogeneity posed a threat to the stability of the colonies, and they persistently called for the reinstatement of some semblance of hierarchy. A recurring theme in New England sermons was the fear of social "levelling," which was seen as the route to anarchy. The same concern was behind the early eighteenth-century voices who opposed the creation of a land bank, arguing that it would cause "levelling and licentiousness" among the poorer sort. The lack of readily identifiable social classes in early Maryland appeared to Lord Baltimore to be such a serious threat to the survival of that colony that he urged Governor Charles Calvert to come up with a device "for the making of some visible distinction" between people. The Proprietor's suggestion that "the Best of the People" wear some sort of "habbits, Medals, or otherwise" may seem a bit grotesque, but it was motivated by a sincere concern that without at least a symbolic distinction between classes, an orderly society would not be possible. Baltimore's proposal helps us understand why American colonials attached such importance to imitating metropolitan styles. In Europe the elements of one's clothing and lifestyle immediately signaled rank and authority, but few such symbolic indicators were available to the colonists. Thus, emulating the dress, lifestyle, and residential architecture of the metropolis became crucial—not so much for their aesthetics, but for their practical ability to signal the stratifications within a society where few other means to do so existed. This phenomenon was also present throughout the nineteenth century, when imitating genteel styles continued to be enormously popular among Americans busily engaged in upward mobility. More democratization and prosperity produced more, not less, emulation of the upper classes as the newly rich sought higher social status and respectability.[12]

The fact that the eighteenth-century American ruling class faced contempt and the rejection of their legitimacy as true gentry by the English upper classes in no way slowed their pursuit of such ambitions or weakened their faith in natural inequality of social classes. The opposite seemed to be the case: because of their relatively fragile nature as a new elite, they stressed social distance, set themselves off from ordinary folk wherever possible, and embraced a traditional, restricted sense of freedom. In this, they willingly pursued a pattern that was fairly common in early modern history: once an exclusive set of liberties was successfully obtained, their newly empowered owners—usually a group rather than individuals—became staunchly motivated to close ranks in order to make their privilege secure and permanent. This was achieved not only by political maneuvering and legal enactments but also through developing certain institutional structures, as well as distinctive identities. As long as these were exclusively held, attributes such as honor, virtue, lifestyle, and taste all contributed to this inner unity of the privileged.[13] Eligible British Americans employed all these methods to create and maintain the stratification of society, and to preserve the patron-client relationships central to it.

There is little doubt that, on the eve of the Revolution, the colonial political class overwhelmingly adhered to this traditional vision of a well-ordered society. When after the Seven Years War the fateful dispute with the London government broke out, it was this established meaning that the provincial leaders primarily had in mind. When they invoked liberty, it was in defense of "all the franchises, privileges, and immunities of the free people," against "a lately adopted system of plantation government." They explicitly wished to "preserve in its greatest purity the excellent Constitution of England as settled at the Revolution." Liberty did not signify a self-evident abstraction. It was for them a social reality, one rooted in their selective exemption from the constrictions of state power with respect to jurisdiction, taxation, or other obligations, rather than in a right to do things (such an exemption is still traceable in the "Congress shall make no laws" language). Only some, but not others, were granted freedom from a particular constraint, or allowed some participation in government. Liberty was not something one was entitled to, but something one was invested with, if proper conditions were met. This sense was deeply rooted in English traditions: during the English Revolution, the Levellers, with their radical program of democratizing the political system, clearly saw liberty as a privilege, and explicitly excluded servants, the poor, and women from the franchise, because these groups were dependent on the will of other men; even their use of the term "people" excluded more than half of the population. In the colonies, New Hampshire had defined enfranchised freemen as those who had over "£20. rateable estate," and tellingly referred to them as "admitted to ye liberty of being freemen in this Province." Thomas Jefferson, discussing property qualifications for the franchise with Edmund Pendleton, referred to those eligible as people "whom you would admit to a vote." The American Articles of Confederation of 1777 contained similar limitations: Article IV defined "the people" as the "free inhabitants of each of these states, paupers, vagabonds and fugitives from justice excepted," who "shall be entitled to all privileges and immunities of free citizens in the several states."[14]

This concept of liberty was enmeshed in an organic and hierarchical vision of society. In 1772 a New England Whig explained how the widely held principle of equality of all freemen carried meaning only within a larger world view involving different social ranks: "Resignation and *obedience to the laws,* and *orders,* of society to which we belong are *political* duties necessary for its very being and security, without which it must soon degenerate into a state of license and anarchy. The welfare, nay, the nature of civil society requires, that there should be a subordination of order, or diversity of ranks and conditions in it; that certain men or orders of men be appointed to superintend and manage such affairs as concern the public safety and happiness." Similarly, the concept of equality referred not to the private "interests and feelings" of individuals, but to an equality that would be ensured by chosen representatives of freemen—that is, by "such a number as shall most fully comprehend, and most equally represent, their *common feelings* and *common interests*." Throughout the era of the American Revolution, liberty continued to be understood as a *social relation of difference,* with its survival dependent on "admitting" some and excluding others. In 1776, John Adams vehemently opposed any tinkering with the system of property qualifications for voting in Massachusetts. It would be dangerous to "open so fruitful a Source of Controversy and altercation," he wrote. "There would be no end of it. New Claims will arise. Women will demand a Vote. Lads from 12 to 21 will think their Rights not attended to, and every Man, who has not a Farthing, will demand an equal Voice with any other in all acts of State. It tends to confound and destroy all Distinctions, and prostrate all Ranks, to one common Levell." When in 1780 Jefferson was advocating adding the Indian lands on the Ohio to his Empire of Liberty, he tacitly understood that the freedom of the Euro-Americans carried more worth than the freedom of the Native Americans, and as such, was unavoidably linked to the unequal relationships between various groups of people. The liberty of the European would be legitimately enhanced by constraining that of the Indian. It was this belief that made possible the declaration, with regard to the Ohio Indians, that "the end proposed should be their extermination, or their removal beyond the lakes or Illinois river."[15]

We need to be very cautious about inadvertently translating the cultural vernacular of early modern social order into our own idiom of equal rights. Capitalism and the exploitation of other groups were not the only sources of class structure in pre-Revolutionary America.[16] Passing over culture and its deeply embedded world views as insufferably "subjective" does not take us very far in reconstructing contemporary meanings of inequality and explaining how people's understanding of that concept corresponded to their broader outlook upon the world. Most evidence suggests that in colonial

British America and in the early republic the sense of social hierarchy was deeply ingrained. In fact, the relatively feeble popular opposition to bondage, from the introduction of the first slaves down through the entire eighteenth century, stands as perhaps the greatest single indicator that "natural" inequality remained self-evident in the culture of white inhabitants.

Because early modern America is often thought of as a society where a sense of class did not play a major role (with slavery as a glaring exception), those who did stress hierarchy are consequently portrayed as being out of the ordinary and marginal. One example commonly cited to support this inaccurate view is the existence of a militia in colonial and early republican society. Since the signers of the Constitution and the Bill of Rights called for a "well regulated militia" consisting of ordinary people as an institutionalized, military arm of the new republic, the supposed implication was that they held an egalitarian view of society and trusted its individual citizens. There is little evidence for such a conclusion. In England at that time the Tories were great supporters of a militia, and saw it as a conservative force composed mostly of local, rural men loyal to the landed aristocracy. In colonial Virginia, the militia was closely regulated, beginning in 1757, to protect the system of social rank and to sustain the local patron-client relationships between major planters and freeholders, as well as tenants. Officers of the militia had to live in the county where they were commissioned. Those who were free but of the "servile" class (identified as "free mulattoes, negroes, and Indians") were allowed to participate, but only in certain roles, such as drummers and trumpeters. The act also had a clause about militia patrols, clearly assigning policing duties—such as preventing unlawful assemblies of servants and slaves—only to the officers. Musters were used as an opportunity to publicly display and confirm this hierarchy of rank.[17]

This is not to say that the social structure of the colonies, more flat and less rigid than that of Europe, did not have an effect on the shaping of Revolutionary perceptions of liberty. Because egalitarianism was far from a guiding principle in provincial culture, the simplified social makeup at first caused fears of levelling and of chaos, but as the conflict with Britain developed, this very makeup became part of the political reality that the revolutionaries had to take into account. Unlike the leaders of the French Revolution, they had no royal court, no aristocracy, and no church hierarchy to deal with, and so there were no elaborate structures and configurations of power, held together by the monarchy, that would collapse at the point of separation from the Crown. This lack of other local groups that could serve as potential allies was an incentive to seek a symbolic partnership with "the people" against London, even if it carried a risk of greater politicization of the masses. In a sense, such a partnership was a practical strategy similar to that of the French bourgeoisie who sought political support among the plebeians against the nobles. But the American strategy tended to stress freedom, while the French put the accent on levelling and on citizens' duties to the state.[18] It therefore made perfect sense for the leaders of the rebellious colonies to invoke liberties and rights protecting private property, while London called for respecting civic obligations to the state.

III. Property and the Cult of Liberty

Power always follows Property.
—John Adams, 1776

An effective social hierarchy did emerge in British America by the early eighteenth century, but it developed along different lines than in England, in that it was almost exclusively centered around property. In contrast to the metropolis and its celebration of lineage, the rise in the 1730s of a stable colonial upper class was primarily based on economics. The resulting convergence between commercial activities and a genteel lifestyle was more effortless than in Britain. The American elite were a hybrid breed, in some ways resembling the bourgeoisie that was to crystallize in Europe in the nineteenth century. Even Southern slave-owning planters who styled themselves as landed gentry were in essence agrarian capitalists and entrepreneurs. Ambitious provincials were fortunate that at home they did not need to overcome the barriers of birth faced by "new men" in England. Sometimes, they were rudely reminded of the continuing importance of such criteria: when the wealthy Virginia planter William Byrd II visited the mother country and tried to marry into the English upper classes, he was shocked at the contempt and rejection he encountered.[19] The title to elite privilege in America was almost entirely based on property, something that, unlike heredity, could be achieved. Successfully amassed wealth bestowed status within a relatively short time, even on a former indentured servant. Unlike in England, rank based on property alone carried little cultural stigma. For all practical purposes, there were no old gentry. Only a few of the "better sort" had been in this category for more than a generation or two, and their efforts to achieve gentility were mostly a case of self-fashioning, not a battle with condescending, pedigree-waving neighbors. Rivalry with the old nobility was not an issue; separation from the non-elite was.

Although the American gentry were atypical in their rise through property alone, property in eighteenth-century British culture did remain the bridge that conjoined political privilege and the cultural identity of the privileged. In people's minds, property affirmed unequal liberty by demarcating divisions across society, and by assigning degrees of freedom. Property qualifications were also liberty qualifications. Those with the greatest amount of property claimed the fullest amount of liberty. They, in fact, claimed property in liberty as the only ones who could rightfully own it. The unpropertied ranks could not do so, just as peasants in England were seen as incapable of properly owning a library or portraits of ancestors, because they had no use for them. In short, the value placed on property and its legal security was not simply a means of preserving one's possessions, it was equivalent to a defense of liberty. This link between property and freedom was common in early modern Western cultures. One need only recall the almost material value placed on exclusive liberties in contemporary France, where privilege was defined not only as a "useful and honorable distinction which certain members of society enjoy," but also as property of sorts, with value measurable in coin. The value in this case was created by the power of the state, which sold monopolies and was then able to able to enforce their protection. Offices and rents were literally listed as "immeubles"—that is, property attached to houses or land—and were passed on to the next generation. Such property in privilege was often more secure than money, and so could be traded on the market.[20] It is not difficult to see why privileges of liberty impressed themselves so powerfully on the identities of their owners.

The property-based meaning of liberty remained prominent in American culture throughout the eighteenth century. In his 1754 election sermon, Jonathan Mayhew defined the purpose of all good government as one of achieving "a good land, flowing with milk and honey; that they might there possess property, enjoy the blessings of equal laws, and be happy." That he listed property first was predictable, for his point rested on two common premises: first, that only the propertied were free, while the poor lacked sufficiently independent will and principle; and second, that without protections for property, no freedom was possible. These beliefs were not cut short by the Revolution. An essay in the *Columbian Magazine* censured European authors for lavishing encomiums on the natural liberty of "our savage neighbors," the Indians, and explained that such views could only "arise from an ignorance of the influence of property on the human mind." The piece concluded: "Property, and a regard for law, are born together in all societies." At the dedication of the Tree of Liberty in Providence, Rhode Island, in 1768, Silas Downer, in his fiery oration about the rights of Americans, included the statement, "It hath been fully proved, and is a point not to be controverted, that in our constitution the having of property, especially a landed estate, entitles the subject to a share in government and framing of laws." In his 1774 address to the British people, Richard Henry Lee stressed that it should not even be necessary for Americans to demonstrate they shared the British principle that the safety of property is the security of liberty, as "every page of history proves their generous, brave attachment to these principles." John Adams observed: "Harrington has Shewn that Power always follows Property. This I believe to be as infallible a maxim, in Politicks, as, that Action and reaction are equal, is in Mechanicks." James Madison strongly believed that "in all civilized Societies, distinctions are various and unavoidable," and argued that a "distinction of property results from that very protection which a free Government gives to unequal faculties of acquiring it."[21] It is no wonder that almost until the end of the eighteenth century the majority of states not only still had property requirements for office holding but required senators to have more wealth than representatives.

But property itself, independent of people's collective consciousness, did not create class. Class happened only when the people, equipped with culturally created, subjective representations of class, perceived it as such. Although the economic criteria of class have long received the most attention, in actual society class was constantly produced and reproduced symbolically through various means of communication between people. This was why aspiring American provincials eagerly sought out material objects that communicated rank—wigs, carriages, teapots, portraits of horses, fashionable residences, and gardens. In a sense, this self-stylization made creating class distinctions for upwardly mobile colonials relatively more straightforward than in the Old World. A working man staying at a Pennsylvania inn in 1744 who was "desireous to pass for a gentleman" had no reticence about boasting over dinner to other guests that he possessed a linen, rather than a worsted, nightcap, a silver buckle, and "two Holland shirts"—all emblematic of polite society—to signal that he deserved the label. But for those provincials who had already ascended to higher rank, non-material possessions, such as certain exclusively held liberties (entitlement to hold elected office, exemption from corporal punishment, etc.) were even more important as signs of class.[22]

While material objects symbolized status directly, non-material attributes had to be communicated to the wider society to be effective. Once the culture recognized a person as occupying this or that position in social space, it signaled that the person possessed certain distinctive attributes that qualified him for that position. For instance, in colonial America the attribute of respectability was linked to those groups of individuals who were qualified by birth (prominent foreigners, like Rochambeau, Lafayette, and Chastellux), by the ownership of slaves, by the ownership of land, by profession (doctors), by political office (the members of colonial assemblies), or by several such positions combined. Demonstrating certain symbols of that attribute was crucial to maintaining one's membership in that particular class of people. When Silas Deane advised a young man to take a position with General Horatio Gates as a secretary, he explained that it was desirable, as "it will place you in the best Company for improving in knowledge and good breeding and be in a genteel Station." But to hold on to that distinction required that the young man read "the best Treatises on Warr & histories of sieges" and acquaint himself with "every Military operation of any Consequence," because demonstrating such knowledge was one of the expected attributes of someone claiming such a station.[23]

Although most colonial elites lacked pedigrees, one huge attraction for them of assuming the identity gentry in the metropolitan style was its implication of a much greater freedom to act than that of ordinary people. This identity was usefully essentialist—it did not depend on one's profession or activities to confer privilege. Once successfully self-fashioned in this manner, the provincial elite could derive their prestige from who they were—that is, from the representations of themselves which they instilled into the culture. Because membership in this rank became an effective metaphor for certain qualities, the very claims to such qualities could serve as rhetorical weapons against those who trespassed into the territory of the virtuous. When in 1778 Gouverneur Morris rebuked Thomas Paine for questioning certain powers of the Congress, he pointed to Paine's low social origins, contemptuously calling him a "mere adventurer from England, without fortune, without family connections, ignorant even of grammar."[24]

Once these genteel traits came to be "naturally" associated with the upper class, their selfhood and prestige then became dependent on their continued connection with such qualities. Members of the colonial elite defended their status zealously, and were often forced to live up to at least some of these standards. For instance, if the early modern gentry believed themselves to be distinctive as a group in their ability to control their passions by means of reason, then such control became a prized personal quality. Thus, they now ostracized public displays of anger as vulgar, and any heated clash with an ordinary person could be used to justify their position that commoners were driven by emotions and therefore lacked the public virtue needed to exercise full liberty. Put another way, class was created by means of the values placed by the culture on certain representations, and by the ability of certain individuals to control these symbolic meanings. Those who best succeeded in doing so usually attained the most power, because they were able to assign to their own class certain qualifying characteristics (such as virtue) and to label others as posessing inferior, servile traits (such as passion). This cultural power hierarchized early American society more effectively and directly than the mere possession of economic resources.

This is why George Washington's insistent quest for an English coat of arms and his meticulous stylizing of Mount Vernon to resemble a manor house were not quixotic acts in an otherwise egalitarian society. The elite took the utmost care to reproduce, defend, and cultivate the attributes of their distinctiveness, and the new elite had to do so with even more attention. To appreciate the immense power of such culturally approved identity, one can envision a young eighteenth-century English aristocrat driving a carriage by himself: he would be condemned for behavior improper to his social rank, but he would still be recognized as a nobleman, perhaps temporarily out of his mien and just wanting to amuse himself. However, a polite and elegantly dressed commoner would not be so easily excused for committing the same impropriety; his misstep would most likely be seen as exposing him as a newly rich upstart. In other words, his socially recognized identity as a *gentleman* gave the young carriage driver more freedom to act outside of his social rank. The aspiring *parvenu,* by contrast, had to be careful to avoid being caught out as a transgressor. Deeply sensitive to propriety and the opinion of her social equals, the wife of Joseph Galloway, a prominent leader in the Pennsylvania Assembly, strongly believed that her husband was *obliged* to publicly apologize for their choice of a minister to marry them when the clergyman's doubtful reputation raised eyebrows among the "people of fashion." "I doubt not," she wrote, "he will condemn it rather than disoblige the society."[25]

In the eyes of the English upper classes, however, provincial American elites exhibited illegitimate pretensions to genteel virtues and privileges. This lack of respect was a constant irritant for leading colonists. It became especially painful after the Seven Years War, in the context of sharp exchanges with Britain in which concerns about the dignity and ambitions of the provincials suffused their legal and constitutional arguments. This angst was made worse by the fact that the colonials had developed a solid sense of British patriotism, rooted in a proud exceptionalism centered around liberty. As George Mason put it, "Few men had stronger prejudices in favor of that form of government [British] under which I was born and bred, or a greater aversion to changing it . . . without an absolute necessity." Meanwhile, British newspapers printed cartoons of semi-savage American leaders, which they contrasted with refined and elegant British statesmen. The hurt pride of one provincial was unmistakable in a letter Benjamin Franklin wrote to Earl Howe, in which he took note of the metropolitan opinion of the colonists' "Ignorance, Baseness, and Insensibility."[26]

This is where issue of identity and its representations intersected with the ideological prominence of liberty during the American Revolution. Even though up to the early 1770s the colonial propertied class saw itself as part of the British culture and the British political nation, its members were in practice quite distant from the central state in England. Their lives were lived mainly within a local orbit. It was within this framework that they developed a fierce veneration for personal independence. Such a cult of freedom was, of course, a luxury of the already anointed; exalting it as something greater than themselves was a form of defending their most precious personal possession.

William Byrd II exuded confidence when he observed in 1735 that the Virginia landed class was financially and politically self-determining, and lived "in health and plenty." Local government was firmly in their control, he noted: "Our governor must first out wit us, before he can oppress us. And if ever he squeeze mony out of us he must first take care to deserve it."[27] By mid-century, the provincial gentry had created what amounted to a cult around their own, distinct identity as a provincial upper class defined by their possession of the greatest degree of freedom. This selfhood was soon to become a prism that reflected the shifting mix of old English traditions and new American circumstances. The approaching Revolutionary conflict would add much fuel to this belief, by bringing into sharp relief the provincial elite's strong sense of ownership of most of the privileges of liberty, and by giving rise to newly sophisticated arguments for their continued local leadership and autonomy. The restrictions placed on colonial self-rule by London became such an outrage not just for economic reasons, but because they were imposed in the wake of such a long and bitter history of the metropolitan political class looking down on the provincials.

Without the development by the American provincial elite of a class-bound cult of personal independence and genteel virtue, the issue of liberty would not have surfaced after 1764 in the same way that it did. When the confrontation with the old authority came, it was this identity that provided the best readily available resource for justifying resistance. It is striking that of all the distinctive values claimed by the American provincial elite, and insistently invoked during the conflict, public virtue was given the most weight. The claim to public virtue was not merely a "venerable abstraction" or a "schematic notion," as has sometimes been suggested, but a preeminent instrument of power, for only those who had been legitimized by culture as possessing it were to be trusted as the bearers and protectors of full liberty. Worrying about the outcome of the Revolutionary struggle, Arthur Lee, a future delegate to the Continental Congress, wrote in 1770 that he was overwhelmed with anxiety that "there was not enough virtue in the country to sustain her liberties." There is little doubt that he understood liberty as an attribute only of those who were capable of being fully free. "Liberty," he noted, quoting Rousseau, "does not consist in any form of government, it exists in the heart of a free man; he bears it everywhere with him; a base man bears everywhere servitude." Being free was understood primarily as being autonomous enough to resist dependence. According to Carter Braxton, a signer of the Declaration of Independence, "Public virtue . . . means a disinterested attachment to the public good, exclusive and independent of all private and selfish interest, and which, though sometimes possessed by a few individuals, never characterized the mass of the people in any state." Such altruism was seen as a guarantee of political equality, "on which the security of the government depends," because it was supposed to preclude "preferment." One author writing in the *South Carolina Gazette* argued that only men with "great public virtue"—that is, men without material or private interests—could be protectors of "liberty and the right in the people," and that therefore, "it must be on the virtues of such men only that freedom, justice, and security can ever rest."[28]

The self-identification of the American political class as gentry was cultivated well into the early nineteenth century. Its members continued to see themselves as exclusively holding the cultural imprimatur of the ultimate bearers and guardians of liberty. This view was perhaps best summed up by the Anti-Federalist "Farmer" who in 1788 observed in the *Maryland Gazette*: "The order of the gentry . . . is essential to perfect government, founded on representation. Every other model of introducing wealth into power, has proved vicious and abominable." Acknowledging that members of the American elite were meritocratic, and not "fixed and permanent" through heredity as in England, the writer suggested the necessity for "an executive for life," as a countermeasure necessary for the survival of liberty in the new republic. When he described "the people" as being free to govern themselves locally, he clearly was referring only to those who qualified, namely "landholders and consequently the most independent of mankind, mild by nature, moderate by manners, and persevering in every honest pursuit." In case this was not unambiguous enough, he clarified: "I mean not the lowest populace—I mean that class of citizens to whom the country belongs." Characteristically, referring to the political class as "gentry" was common usage in the halls of the Continental Congress. When William Hooper worried about raising an army in 1776, he noted that the Eastern gentry were "not yet satisfied" as to the costs, but that "these gentry will soon I hope be brought to reason, and we shall have a formidable force on reasonable Terms." Edward Hand referred to the New England delegates to Congress simply as "the Eastern Gentry."[29] Just as in the minds of the American elites of the founding era the concept of the ruling class was interchangeable with that of the gentry, the "ownership" of the country by this political class was still inseparable from their "ownership" of the most complete range of existing liberties.

The liberty argument exploded with great force at the start of the American Revolution, and almost immediately became the symbol of the entire contest with Britain. Four developments that preceded the Revolution made this outcome possible: the transmission of restricted liberty to the colonies; the rise by mid-century of a genuine provincial elite; the cultivation by that class of an identity based on personal independence; and a humiliating struggle with the metropolitan ruling class over legitimacy. It was the combination of these cultural catalysts that gave liberty much of its power as the principal metaphor defining the struggle for independence, as well as the character of the new republic.

4

The Revolution

I. A Radical Script for a Preservationist Struggle

Liberty is an inestimable treasure: the delight and passion of mankind. It is the source of almost all human felicity: the parent of virtue, pleasure, plenty and security: And the love of it is an appetite so strongly implanted in the nature and constitution of all living creatures, that even the principle of self-preservation, which is allowed to be the strongest, seems to be contained in it.

—Hugh Allison, *Spiritual Liberty*, 1769

THE CLASSICAL ARGUMENT in American historiography has long been that the old signification of liberty was renounced during the Revolution and replaced by a much more universal and socially progressive understanding, reflected in the language of the Declaration of Independence. The inference is that such a modern meaning should be used as a criterion of interpretation. Hence, a Thomas Paine would appear not so much as an individual ahead of his time but as someone who simply complied with the essence of the Founders' new sense of liberty, while a John Adams with his Federalist views of social hierarchy would appear to be somewhat anomalous, a holdover from an earlier chapter of history. In his study of Revolutionary radicalism, Gordon Wood, one of the great historians of the Founding era, acknowledges the existence of an upper class as a distinct group, but contends that "any resemblance between colonial society and that of the mother country remained superficial and partial"; that the "hierarchies and patronage connections of American society were brittle"; and that "little in the society had much chance to solidify." Consequently, even though some parts of

America "seemed to be becoming more like England," the reason that Revolutionary change was more radical than anywhere else at the time was because "society in the New World was already more republican, more shallow, and more fragile." From this premise comes a conclusion that the Founders intended to reengineer the English social order as they knew it: "The revolutionaries aimed at nothing less than a reconstitution of American society," and "to destroy the bonds holding together the older monarchical society."[1]

This perspective, in its deepest sense, has also long been at the core of the popular narrative of the Founding, upheld by a long and venerable tradition of inserting a disconnecting caesura between colonial and Revolutionary history. And yet, on closer examination, its implications are intellectually startling. Wood suggests the late colonial American ruling elite, who had thus far tirelessly modeled themselves on the English gentry, convinced themselves within a very short span of time that the value of their distinct identity as a class, as well as the exclusive liberties that were inseparably attached to this identity, should now be discarded, their usefulness outweighed by the urgent need for a new, egalitarian order in which their class would no longer occupy a privileged position. Moreover, following Wood, such a decision would also require them to sever freedom from rank, until that time an inseparable conceptual entity. But ruling classes are not historically known to vote themselves out of power, and the American elite were not fighting London to do so, but rather to hold on to their prominent position in society. It was to achieve this end that they turned to their own cult of liberty and deployed its full rhetorical potential. Their constitutional argument was directed against England, but their popular rhetoric was aimed at the American public, without whose support the entire project would have had no chance of success. Their colonial worship of *exclusive* liberty was turned into a Revolutionary ideology that worshiped *inclusive* liberty. It was a fighting ideology, not an objective description of social reality. To grasp the full depth of this change, we must read the language of the Declaration of Independence, intended for public and political consumption, together with contemporary letters and diaries revealing closely held, personal worldviews.

The apparent incongruity between the two has been the source of much of the historiographical debate about liberty during the Revolution and the early national period. A recurring and endlessly baffling question of this discussion is why those who produced the language of the Declaration of

Independence, and the Constitution with its Bill of Rights, said one thing and did another. How could their pronouncements read like a litany of modern rights and freedoms, while they simultaneously tolerated inequality of access to such freedoms, and did not even put an end to slavery? How could Samuel Adams solemnly condemn those "who are afraid of a free Government, lest it should be perverted and made use of as a Cloke for Licentiousness," and think it ridiculous that "the Fear of the Peoples abusing their Liberty is made an Argument against their having the Enjoyment of it," but demand the most severe punishment for the Shaysite farmers who were trying to use their rights to demand relief from oppressive taxation?[2]

To find an answer, we need to turn to the circumstances that gave meaning to the new rhetoric. In most major historical conflicts it is usually the articulate elite of the winning side who shapes the standard account of events and disseminates it among the people at large. The Bayeux Tapestry depicts William the Conqueror's invasion of England and his success at the Battle of Hastings. Predictably, the tapestry shows the Norman version of events, and for a millennium it has exerted influence on how the story was told. The culture absorbs such accounts in condensed forms, as stories, images, formulas, slogans, and clichés (in America—the City upon a Hill, Manifest Destiny, the Land of the Free, etc.), because that is how people code knowledge in their collective memories. Formulaic statements are necessary, whether in oral or writing cultures, because they make it possible for societies to "preserve their knowledge and recall it when needed."[3]

One of the greatest contributions of the Founders to America's future was their creation of a persuasive narrative of the Revolution, built from top to bottom around the notion of liberty. The universalist inclusiveness of Enlightenment philosophy could not, in itself, initiate a major change in the way a whole society thought about liberty. For such a turn to take place, history had to supply a moment of opportunity. That moment was provided by the conflict with Britain, which drove the provincial ruling class to overhaul the public portrait of freedom in ways they might otherwise not have done. They skillfully transformed the conflict over taxes into a struggle for the universal rights of "freeborn" Britons, presented as a universal battle between liberty and tyranny. To sustain this interpretive blueprint they delegitimized monarchy and aristocracy, anchored American liberty in divine will, fabricated new patriotic traditions, invented "the people," and redefined representation.

It was a remarkable conceptual package, cast into the public marketplace to be consumed by a society still largely attached to the world of British culture.[4] This narrative has proved enduring beyond all expectations, and its energy and sway has extended far beyond documents and the law, beyond the era of its making, and beyond the original intent of its authors. It is a script that is still playing in the theater of national memory, powerfully affecting the way we construe American history. What has long disappeared from our line of vision, however, is that it was originally framed as a radical script for an essentially preservationist struggle. As we shall see, acknowledging this not only does not negate its historic importance, but, to the contrary, it allows us to shine new light on the persistently baffling linkage between its traditionalist origins and its progressive impact.

The making of this narrative was a response to three demands of the historical moment: the development of a credible set of arguments against the new imperial policy of London; the making of a case for the legitimacy of the new, republican polity and its political class; and the promotion of a new kind of patriotism to unite Americans across the thirteen former colonies. Before analyzing these three impulses, we should take note of one crucial fact: most revolutionaries in modern times were entangled in the extreme political tensions that come with destroying and building, and have had to urgently justify their newly found power, as well as their conduct in the struggle to obtain it. They therefore have tended to muster ideologically seductive political language—more seductive than they would have done in quieter times —to depict their cause. To give reason for their endeavor to the world and to themselves, they had had to reach for the strongest arguments that the arsenal of their culture had at hand. Usually, the most effective of these arguments have relied on mythical themes. The mythical and the practical in political language, then as now, are not only closely related but they each contain elements of the other. When the goal is justification, broadly mythical themes, like "society's deepest interests," "birthrights," or "sacred traditions," are much more powerful than references to specific legal or executive precedents, which do not immediately relate to the general good of the people. For this reason, politically contingent, revolutionary language is usually a hybrid blending of the fictional and the real. The real is expressed in semi-fictional terms, as if the rulers were practicing a Midas touch of sorts: everything they hope to bring about turns into widespread public good. This should be viewed not so much as a case of "saying one thing and doing another" (as in conscious manipulation, where two rational entities are deliberately separated), but as a case of expressing reality in terms of a culturally approved symbolic language.

Oliver Cromwell presided over the English Revolution by waving, to much applause, the banner of widespread liberty, but he was unyielding in preserving the privileges of his own, landed class, and in eradicating the "levelling" radicals who called for extending privileged liberties to the non-elites. Perhaps the most blatant example of a dissonance between the language of equal liberty and the actual political regime is provided by the leaders of the French Revolution, who fervently proclaimed the principle of absolute equality while employing it to legitimize a state at times more centralized than the monarchy they overthrew, and who used such talk to justify their own astonishingly elitist prerogatives—all done, of course, in the name of ordinary people. In Revolutionary America, the fighting language of equality was subject to a similar dualism, and only by ignoring this fact can one treat the texts of the leaders as representations of an immediately implementable social reality. One need only recall how the Loyalists were treated by the colonists. As we know, the Patriots' rhetoric of equal rights was widely used to justify jailing, fining, lynching, forced oath-taking, and other repressions not only of Loyalists, but also of faith-based pacifists, such as the Moravians and the Quakers. Not even Thomas Paine equated liberty with economic equality. "Let the rich man enjoy his riches, and the poor man comfort himself in his poverty," he wrote, "but the floor of freedom is as level as water." Nor should free speech be absolute; Paine insisted that "none other be heard among us" than followers of the Revolutionary cause.[5] The more the Patriots tried to reverse what had thus far constituted a prevailing norm—loyalty to Britain—and force law-abiding people to change their long-held assumptions, the more they deprived them of their long-held political rights, all the while justifying such actions with the radical rhetoric of equal liberty.

The new egalitarian rhetoric was much like an elegant façade added on to the massive and still sturdy mansion of culture that had been built in the preceding era. The stylish frontage was designed to demonstrate the architects' progressive disposition. The mansion where they still lived, however, was built of historically accumulated knowledge about how the world was "naturally" ordered. The façade was not erected to disguise the mansion; it revealed how the inhabitants saw themselves. The house was built of taken-for-granted and unquestioned material, while the façade was a conscious effort to reflect the enlightened character of the residents. Even a brief glance at a letter written in 1775 to George Washington by Richard Henry Lee, Patrick Henry, and Thomas Jefferson demonstrates that old, unspoken assumptions still carried much power. The authors asked for Washington's "patronage and favor" in securing a prominent position for another member of the Virginia planter elite, Edmund Randolph. They specifically commended Randolph for his "gentlemans abilities," for his social origins (he represented "our young gentry"), for his "extensive connections," and for "his desire to serve his Country." Unaffected by the universalistic rhetoric flying around, gentry rank and genteel virtue remained—for these authors—exclusive cultural qualifiers for public office. Similarly, Benjamin Franklin's son William, who became governor of New Jersey in 1762, may have read his father's admonition to rise in society by one's own hard work, but it did not stop him from seeking patronage through the elder Franklin's connections in order to obtain a government position. William's two letters written in 1762 to Lord Bute reveal a very traditional approach: "Mr. Wood informs me there is a Governor to be appointed for New Jersey in America" (an overt hint at the desired position); and "I am well known to many of the principal gentlemen of the Country and have some influence with them" (a reference to William's connections within the power circles of the colonies). William also mentions the governmental services of his father; exhibits a highly deferential attitude toward his addressee, whom he addresses in paternal terms; and ends with an assurance that he, William, would assume the office "with Ease and Honour."[6]

It would be wrong to assume that we are simply dealing here with a case of cultural inertia that somehow stands in the way of rejecting old notions of order in favor of professed Revolutionary equality. The Revolution itself was originally a conserving, not a disruptive, undertaking. The preservation of the existing privileges of the American provincial elite was not some aberration, but at the heart of their initial purpose. Extensive literature exists on the political and economic interests of the late colonial elite, and there is no need to recount its various arguments here. It is generally accepted today that their mobilization against Britain was motivated by the fact that they, as a group, had the most to lose as a result of London's new imperial policy, in terms not only of authority and honor, but also wealth, already threatened by the specter of insolvency. Colonial elites were used to being in command of the public scene, and sometime during the Stamp Act Congress they came to believe that the prospect that they would no longer be in charge was very real, and that they must attempt to reassert control as a last-chance option. At stake was their vantage ground in society, as well as their ownership of the fullest liberty in British America. These goals were manifested in their abiding interest in political practice rather than theory, in how to secure rights rather than define their permanent meaning. After all, the Federalist Papers were more an explication of brilliant political propaganda than a purely theoretical treatise. It was no accident that many of the arguments for separation were simultaneously arguments for the upholding of those norms and practices of colonial American society that anchored the gentry's preeminent role in that society and their prized independence (their accusations against the Crown included the dissolving of the Assemblies, making territorial expansion difficult, erecting royal offices to control provincials, and preventing trade with the rest of the world).[7] It was primarily for the purpose of *legitimating* this struggle by means of liberal, enlightened positions that they produced an open-ended narrative built around such highly abstract notions as "life, liberty, and the pursuit of happiness" and "natural rights."

Modern and postmodern models of historiography so often stress political power as the force driving all ruling classes that we do not always appreciate that the Revolutionary leaders sought to preserve not only their political supremacy but something of equal, if not greater, worth to them: their station in the social and cultural space of America. It was a space filled by a complex network of asymmetrical relationships involving not only economic class and political control, but also identity, religion, education, and prestige, all of which made sense of people's experiences but also divided them into ranks.[8] The provincial elites, who had gained their elevated positions fairly recently, had an immense stake in holding on to them, and none in overturning this order of things. Even if we hypothesize, purely for the sake of argument, that they did have such radical intentions, we would also have to assume that they were somehow able—in 1764, 1776, or 1787—to transcend a deeply rooted belief in self-evident inequality. It would have been a near-miraculous case of culture change that in real historical time would have taken at least several decades, if not a century to complete. To appreciate the immense power and durability of such established beliefs, one need only recall the case of the nineteenth-century white abolitionists who fiercely invoked scriptural and constitutional vocabularies of equality to reject slavery, but who could not yet bring themselves to accept the novelty of full social equality with African Americans, which would require a long and laborious transformation of collective world views that would continue well into the late twentieth century.

Those who had the capability to define—for the people—the meanings of events, from the Stamp Act to the Bill of Rights, were also the ones best able to preserve their privileged standing in society. For instance, by naming a minor riot in Boston a "massacre," the namers could assign to it a specific meaning, loaded with emotional and political implications. Once popularized, this meaning became impressed on the public consciousness as an objective perception of the event, and thus became an immensely effective instrument for furthering the agenda of the assigners. To fully appreciate the communicative power of the speaking elite, one need only reflect on how relatively quickly they were able to reverse the meanings of the terms "patriotism" and "treason" in America after the War of Independence broke out. As they endeavored to make sense of events by placing them within a purposeful order, they were also able to reap major dividends by reserving the central role in the story for themselves.

We should also note that much of the language of liberty they used against Britain was not novel. In this sense, the revolutionaries were preserving, not dethroning, the existing vocabulary of freedom. Unlike Jean-Jacques Rousseau's theory of equality, which inspired much of the rhetoric of the French Revolution, theirs was not a dramatically new ideology. Most of the rights they invoked—trial by jury, habeas corpus, representation, and government by consent—had not been devised by them to counter British imperial policies, but had already been there, supplied by history. Indeed, it is only because these rights already existed within the reputable lexicon of British freedom that the revolutionary leaders were able to take them up so effectively after 1764.[9] The long historical pedigree gave their arguments coveted cultural legitimacy, much as Greek and Roman architectural designs were usefully adopted as a distinctively American style during the Federal era because they, too, embodied so much legitimacy.

Perhaps the most important, and, at the same time, least understood aspect of the Founders' efforts to protect the social status quo was the impact of their rhetoric on the future of liberty in American history. Contrary to what we have often been told, the preservationist traits of the Revolution, when channeled through the culture's intertwined webs of myth and fact, produced more than mere obstacles to progress. In fact, it is far more likely that it was the Founders' relative *conservatism* and their faith that after Independence the social order *would not* be seriously undermined, that made it easier for them to invoke a radical narrative for the Revolution. It enabled them, at least initially, to put aside their fears that ordinary people would become too politicized and threaten the stability of society. Furthermore, because they did not propose a radical restructuring of society, they could plausibly claim that they were only defending the rights already sanctioned by the collective ethos of English culture, a stance that became a major asset for them in a time of crisis. People have an instinctive need for continuity. To be able to perceive dramatic historical change as an act of choice, and to feel that one is participating in a justifiable struggle rather than one driven by unfamiliar or random forces, can soften the turmoil of war with a sense of comforting continuity.[10] At the end of the day, it was this sense of sitting confidently at the top of the social matrix that allowed the Patriot intelligentsia to transcend the limitations imposed by tradition, and to design a new state that was responsible before the voters and that offered broad guarantees of individual rights. In constructing such a liberal polity, they were able to be as boldly pioneering as seemed possible, without voting themselves out of authority.

In all of this, their English-modeled identity turned out to be far from a "cultural burden" preventing them from expanding freedom, as some historians have suggested.[11] Instead, it helped to consolidate the provincial political class on the eve of the Revolution. Had they been socially and culturally fragmented and insecure, the likelihood of them promoting a daringly egalitarian language of liberty would have been much smaller. It was the homogeneity of their identity that produced the requisite *cultural capital* to be spent on such boldness. It was this capital, consisting of shared elite values of public virtue, honor, and responsibility for enlightened leadership, that made solidarity and reciprocity within their class possible, and, more importantly, enabled unified collective action during the turmoil of war.

86

II. The Universalization of the Language of Freedom

Columbia, Columbia, to glory arise, the queen of the world and the child of the skies!

— Timothy Dwight, *Columbia, Gem of the Ocean,* 1777

PERHAPS THE FOREMOST REASON why we today perceive such a discrepancy between the Revolutionary narrative and contemporary political practice is that its authors had a penchant for speaking about liberty in absolute and all-embracing, rather than specific, terms. It was a mannerism de rigueur among late-Enlightenment writers, although it was also practiced, to a lesser extent, in the seventeenth century. Not only did monarchs traditionally speak for all the people, but, after the English Revolution, so did officials and theorists, using broadly inclusive language and drawing on its power to validate their political arguments. The great theorist of natural law, John Selden, best explained the persuasiveness of such idiom when he observed that calling liberty absolute was "just as a line is often extended indefinitely to demonstrate something in geometry." James Madison was clearly aware of this when he wrote that the equality of the consent principle was a hypothesis of sorts, rather than a literal goal to be pursued. A society that would achieve it would no doubt be "happy," but "this is a Theory, which like most Theories, confessedly requires limitations and modifications" when applied. "Experience alone," he noted, "can decide how far the practice in this case would correspond with Theory."[12] Awareness of their rhetorical value notwithstanding, such "theories" were nevertheless at the heart of Revolutionary thinking. Both Jefferson and Franklin believed that there existed a basic universality of human experience, and that its understanding could be achieved through reason and then applied to improve the human condition.

A second source of the broad inclusiveness of contemporary American language of liberty was the pressing necessity to defend the Revolution and Independence. It was a most urgent incentive. Not only had an entire people who had heretofore been part of one nation, all subjects of the Crown, been abruptly separated from the mother country, but the new republican state, facing a world map of monarchies, cried out for intellectual justification.

87

American leaders needed to assure themselves and the unprepared public that the disruption of a system sanctioned by long history and deeply entrenched in social psychology was based on principles sufficiently valid to override loyalty to Britain. At the level of political philosophy, Locke had already provided highly abstract and transnational arguments for equality and natural rights—an enormously useful arsenal for colonial leaders, because it enabled them to double-dip, bringing up principles ostensibly higher than traditions limited to British history even as they proclaimed themselves to be the true defenders of these very traditions. But at the grassroots level, amid the disorder and uncertainty of war, their greatest challenge was to transform the political language used to describe liberty in order to make it both more sweeping and more accessible to ordinary people. It was this challenge, rather than the weight of philosophical theories, that prompted the American political class to formulate in a short period of time a rhetoric of freedom so dramatically inclusive that almost as soon as it was introduced, its authors began to express fears that the social stability and order might be upset if ordinary folk took it too literally.

There already existed a well-established tradition among British elites of using a universal and inclusive language of rights and liberties, especially in struggles for political influence. In 1754 the English landowner Thomas Beckford became engaged in a blatant manipulation of elections through the corrupt system of "rotten boroughs," in an attempt to have all four of his brothers elected to Parliament. But in his plea to the Duke of Bedford, who controlled the boroughs, he not only asserted that "the liberty of the country" was at stake, but he also insisted that there were "not four men in the kingdom more zealously attached to . . . the liberties of the people." To properly understand the meaning of such claims is to realize that they did not derive from a world view based on the political primacy of the people, but from one that presumed that only the elites could represent the entire population. The colonial American speaking class widely employed the same meta-language to express their own, provincial interests. Prominent Virginians like Edmund Pendleton, George Mason, and William Preston were dismayed by London's Proclamation of 1763 because it conflicted with their plans for acquiring property in Kentucky, but none of them, of course, raised the issue of profitable land speculation involved in these projects. Instead, the proclamation was referred to as a grand conspiracy to deprive all colonists of liberty, "by restraining Settlements to the Westward, to facilitate that Subjugation of

America which they had planned." Such use of the symbolic power of language not only buttressed its effectiveness, it also reinforced the elite's self-portrayal as spokesmen for the public good. The young Marquis de Lafayette, who had not indicated much interest in the appalling condition of his French peasants, waxed universal on his way to join the American Revolution: "The welfare of America is intimately linked with the welfare of all humanity. She is going to become the respected and secure refuge of virtue, good character, tolerance, equality, and a peaceful liberty."[13] An enlightened figure of authority would not be complete without uttering such broad and exalted abstractions.

The revolutionaries took up the same style to express their cause. John Hancock spoke of the British army as "enemies of Liberty & the Rights of Mankind," and George Washington called them violators of "the most essential & valuable rights of mankind." When Virginia delegates to the Continental Congress condemned the war waged by England "against their countrymen," they praised the American goal as "the common cause of freedom and mankind." The South Carolina planter Thomas Lynch believed that America was "looked up to as the last resource of liberty, and the common cause of mankind," and he concluded, "Brave and generous, we fight for mankind." Reflecting on the Declaration of Independence, Joseph Reed noted, "It is a Principle of universal Extent." This common cause of mankind was usually framed as liberty deriving from Nature or from God. The two absolutes provided a transcendent, immutable point of reference for a variety of political arguments. Employing absolute concepts (God, Nature, the People's Will, the Laws of History) to sanction new regimes and to anchor them in universals and inalienables, is a strategy common to many revolutions in history. Leaders of the French Revolution famously used the concept of "general will," derived from Jean-Jacques Rousseau's notion of popular sovereignty. Since they assumed the mantle of representing such "general will"— a highly abstract concept transcending specific political differences—all opposition could be (and usually was) portrayed as acting irrationally, against the inevitable tide of history. The leaders were thus not only affirmed, but also obtained a compelling rationale to suppress opponents. A similar logic was widely employed in America from the Revolution to the advent of the Alien and Sedition Acts, although suppression never came close to the French level, and after the war was conducted mostly by legal means. An attack on the republican system was routinely portrayed as an attack on "the people." "Under such a government as this," noted one writer, "every insurrection against constitutional authorities, or opposition to them, is a revolt of a part against the general will, by which those authorities exist, and is highly criminal." This new rhetoric highlighted the transcendent sources of republican liberties; whether presented as secular or divine in origin, they were cast as preexisting absolutes. "There can be no prescription old enough," wrote James Otis, "to supersede the law of nature and the grant of God almighty; who has given to all men a natural right to be free." One of the most important goals for the Continental Congress with regard to freedoms, wrote Silas Deane of Connecticut, was "fixing them rightly, with precision, yet sufficiently explicit, & on certain, and durable basis, such as Reason & Nature of things, the Natural Rights of Mankind." William Pierce, commenting on the English political heritage of the Americans, emphasized that "the absolute rights of Englishmen are founded in nature and reason, and are co-eval with the English Constitution itself. . . . The same spirit was breathed into the Americans, and they still retain it." The new rulers thus did not have to claim to be the source of such principles; a transcendent point of reference allowed them to publicly assume the modest role of disinterested intermediaries who merely articulated the timeless laws on behalf of the people. "Our Cause . . . will be supported," remarked Samuel Adams. "It is the Cause of God & Men, and virtuous Men by the Smiles of Heaven will bring it to a happy Issue."[14]

After 1764 colonial leaders found themselves under pressure to elucidate more exactly what rights Americans had. It was not an area with much existing theory or precision, and this gave them some freedom to formulate their points in ways best suited for justifying the grievances against London. Their efforts typically were a combination of their struggle to deal with these specific issues and their creative use of serviceable concepts available in the culture's repository. The latter included items from British history, such as the Magna Charta, the Habeas Corpus Act of 1679, and the Bill of Rights of 1689 (all carrying a certain mystical sanctity of "ancient" precedents), as well as appeals to philosophically justified "natural rights." The earliest debates in the Continental Congress revealed divisions between those delegates, like Richard Henry Lee, who emphasized natural rights, and those, like Edward Rutledge and Joseph Galloway, who stressed precedents in the constitution of England. Both points of view were adapted and incorporated into the political rationales offered for the Revolution.[15] But as the conflict expanded, the argument of eternal, natural rights visibly gained more prominence.

If London could be shown to have stood against timeless norms that defined people's rights, the colonists' claims that it represented tyranny would acquire a near cosmic sanction. James Otis effectively used the metaphorical force of such concepts when he argued that he was basing his exposition of the rights of the colonists on the authority of "natural laws, which are immutably true." John Adams spoke in the name of the common man, but summoned divine design when he wrote: "The great . . . have accordingly laboured, in all ages, to wrest from the populace, as they are contemptuously called, the knowledge of their rights and wrongs, and the power to assert the former or redress the latter. I say RIGHTS, for such they have, undoubtedly, antecedent to all earthly government—*Rights* that cannot be repealed or restrained by human laws—*Rights* derived from the great legislator of the universe." During the Stamp Act crisis, Silas Downer expressed a formula that would be endlessly used in contemporary discourse—that Americans are as entitled as the English to that "liberty which the GOD of nature hath given us." He also stressed equality as a general principle, but it was equality with English freemen, not equality for all, as is clear from his emphasis on the point that only "the having of property, especially a landed estate, entitles the subject to a share in government." Natural law construed from abstractions and imbued with reasonableness was placed above positive law, a product of particular historical circumstances, and as such became a compelling instrument of political change. We should not forget, however, that despite its apparent universalism, natural law was ultimately an elite-made instrument. As early as 1607, Sir Edward Coke politely reminded King James I—when the latter expressed interest in deciding cases in the Court of King's Bench—that legal and constitutional matters were to be interpreted and decided not by "naturall reason" but "by artificiall reason and judgment of the Law," open only to those equipped to do so by "long study and experience."[16] What the American leaders could not quite foresee was that the very same attraction of timelessness and universality that gave "natural," "inalienable," or "God-given" freedoms their persuasive political power, would also hold a strong and novel appeal for ordinary people—because it offered them, as never before, a compelling, if still symbolic justification for participating in the world of rights and liberties.

Some of the most persuasive encouragement for such participation came from arguments rooted in religious experience. If the grand plan for Revolutionary liberty was divinely justified, it carried promise for all humanity:

Liberty! Thou darling of mankind,
Celest'al born, thou source of all delight,
Caress'd by ev'ry rank with fond desire,
From Princely thrones down to the humble cot.

With the society already permeated by religious frameworks of reference and a pietistic lexicon, this kind of political language readily resonated with the culture. American Enlightenment was Franklinian, not Voltairean, and treated knowledge and reason not as antithetical to, but compatible with, religion. In this unique matrix, transcendent absolutes of equal liberty fitted in easily, echoing the spiritual equality of believers before God. This religious bent helped make freedom an article of faith in American culture quite apart from its specific existence in law and actual societal relations. Jefferson himself seems to have believed that anchoring American freedoms in a divine source was needed to firmly implant them in the collective conscience, when he asked, "Can the liberties of a nation be thought secure when we have removed their only firm basis, a conviction in the minds of people that these liberties are of the gift of God?" Churches became a major channel for the popularization, through sermons, of republican concepts of freedom, a process all the more intense because the various competing denominations sought the republican vision to legitimate their own authority. Revolutionary sermons frequently merged political issues with religious themes so closely that they produced a form of divinely justified propaganda. "The devil and his infernal ministers, under whose administration they were by nature," preached Hugh Allison, "are continually *imposing taxes* and exacting a *revenue* from the children of God, and exerting every malicious scheme to bring them into their former state of servitude and subjection." "Upon the whole, nothing appears to me more manifest than that the separation of this country from Britain, has been of God," preached John Witherspoon.[17] In this way, some of the penumbra of divinity associated with the old monarchy was transferred to the new republican state. When the nature of cultural continuity is considered, a leap from the divine source of royal sovereignty to the divine source of rights and liberties of the new sovereign, the people, was not as great as it might seem. Freedom was the quintessence of the emerging American national identity, and its enshrinement as such owed much to the transcendent shroud that popular religion spread over the new political system.

The above examples show the degree to which trendy rhetoric of enlightened inclusion and unconditional rights became the archetypical mode of articulating even the most diverse of political goals. The most important point to note is that such rhetoric coexisted unreservedly with a broad variety of inequalities. Even arguments for openly exclusionary policies were framed—in order to be intellectually respectable—in terms of the very same poetics of inclusion. When in 1768 pioneer settlers on the western frontier of South Carolina (dissatisfied with the Tidewater planter elite in the Charleston Assembly for their reluctance to provide protection against lawless elements, their refusal to create new counties for the administration of justice, and the refusal to allow a more equitable representation in the colony's government) organized into armed Regulator groups, they met with a rejection of their remonstrance, accusations of treason, and, ultimately, military suppression. But when, a year later, the same Assembly sent (without the approval of the royal representative, Lieutenant Governor William Bull II) support money to John Wilkes, the famed crusader for the expansion of political rights and a critic of the London government, and consequently became involved in a protracted conflict with the Privy Council, great planters like Henry Laurens and Arthur Lee consistently described their own position vis-à-vis London as representing the "right of the People," "rights and Privileges of British subjects," and the "inalienable Birthright of English subjects." There was no inkling of irony; whether the assemblymen were denying rights demanded by the frontiersmen, or whether they were being denied rights by the British government, the authoritative rhetoric of response was one of universalized rights and liberties. At the level of political decisions, however, the meaning and application of those rights was still defined by the received cultural axiom of a naturally unequal social order. Notably, the same pattern would later reappear in the much more radically egalitarian French Revolution. Abbé Sieyès, who sincerely despised inequality, not only asserted that absolutely no one should hold any power unless it flowed directly from the will of the people, but was anguished that the wealthy had carriages while the poor had to walk. Yet, the same Sieyès also demanded forced deportations of all unemployed to the colonies, taking for granted that the poor did not possess the same extent of natural rights as others.[18]

Broadly egalitarian rhetoric used to publicly express political arguments became the norm in post-Revolutionary America. When Patrick Henry, speaking to the Virginia Ratification Convention of 1788, criticized the federal Constitution for taking away power from the state government—of which he was a part—he assumed the persona of the people, inclusive of all classes. The dangers of the new system, he said, "are out of sight of the common people: They cannot foresee latent consequences; I dread the operation of it on the middling and lower class of people: It is for them I fear the adoption of this system." But when Edmund Pendleton, a conservative and a supporter of the Constitution, criticized Henry's radicalism, he too spoke in the name of the common man. He accused Henry of being "an advocate for the middling and lower classes of men" only, while Pendleton professed to be "a friend to the equal liberty of all men, from the palace to the cottage, without any other distinction than that between good and bad men." He spoke against social distinctions and for "giving to the poor man free liberty in his person and property." And yet, they both assumed the necessity of a government by the elite if liberty were to be protected from the passions of ordinary people. Pendleton could claim that the people were "the fountain of all power," but he also took it for granted that "they cannot act personally, and must delegate powers."[19] This symbolic use of language merged with its practical and political functions to such an extent that separating them was difficult, if not impossible.

What caused this dramatic democratization of political language? The two most frequent answers are that it was either Enlightenment thought (the idealistic position) or political contingency (the cynical position). In truth, they were far from mutually exclusive. The Enlightenment defined intellectually progressive ways of representing political goals. As we have seen, an all-embracing vocabulary of rights was used well before the Revolution. The contingency of war did not create it; it only intensified its use, shifted its political goals, and altered its style. The last change was especially significant. Not only did the vocabulary of freedom become more inclusive, but the rhetorical style was rapidly metamorphosing from hermetic and elitist to one more attractive to ordinary people. The Revolutionary political class was not fashioning a utopia; they were interested in a practical ideology for a workable government. They were in their majority experienced, highly pragmatic politicians and seasoned public speakers, used to intricate, often contentious, debates in colonial assemblies and courtrooms. Despite the fact that they had so far operated primarily within their own circles, where insider language and symbols were instantly recognizable because they were shared within the culture of their class, they could now hardly afford a "Let them eat cake," European-style aristocratic detachment. They had to win broader support for their designs from a society unsure about the meaning of unfolding events. A refashioning of rhetoric soon became noticeable. It was bolstered by the rapidly growing role of the printed word, as well as by the spread of public oratory—both of which helped expand the receiving audiences. This process was already noticeable in the prosecutions of such causes as the writs of assistance, the well-known speech of James Otis on this topic being a case in point. Lawyers now introduced more color and flamboyance into their legal speeches to enhance their public reception. The new linguistic bridges between social ranks came to mirror the Revolutionary political coalitions across ranks. Thomas Hutchinson marveled at the novelty of such alliances, noting that the public rallies following the Boston Tea Party "consisted principally of Lower ranks of the People & even Journeymen Tradesmen were brought in to increase the number & the Rabble ... yet there were divers Gentlemen of Good Fortunes among them."[20]

One striking indication that the need to appeal to a wider public was recognized was the elite's reluctant but tangible abandonment of one of the most hallowed norms of gentility in the eighteenth-century British world: keeping emotions under control and out of public speech. Earlier in the century, as the Great Awakening preachers had successfully employed emotionally charged language in their public addresses, the gentry had considered such displays vulgar and unbecoming, but now they began to overcome their contempt and disgust. It was no longer reasonable to entirely suppress the passions, argued the Massachusetts minister and patriot, Henry Cumings, in 1781, who pointed out that it was "both rational, and a duty, to stir them up into exercise, when suitable objects are presented to view." James Otis and Patrick Henry were among the first members of the ruling classes to have altered their speaking style to accommodate feelings, but even the traditionalist, John Adams, who, like George Washington, had always looked down on those who were guided by emotion, was willing to make exceptions to enlighten the minds of ordinary people and better instill Revolutionary ideology. Emotional oratory was simply more effective: "Sound, is I apprehend a more powerful Instrument of moving Passions than sense." While still cautious about "passions," Adams allowed that they might be used "to rouse in the Breasts of the Audience a gallant Spirit of Liberty."[21] It was a communicative transformation of great importance. Ideas presented in new ways were much more understandable to the wider public than the purely rational and intellectual arguments formerly used in internal exchanges among the political class.

This adjustment was not painless. A political necessity for the rulers, it was still considered a case of crowd-pleasing. John Adams, commenting on the mounting "theatrical exhibition of politics" (involving, for instance, such popular symbolic actions as mock funerals) remarked, with barely veiled resentment, that George Washington had "understood this art very well, and we may say of him, if he was not the greatest President, he was the best actor of presidency we have ever had. His address to the states when he left the army, his solemn leave taken of Congress when he resigned his commission, his Farewell Address to the people when he resigned his presidency: these were all in a strain of Shakespearean and Garrickal excellence in dramatical exhibitions." Robert Munford's play *The Patriots,* written in the midst of the Revolution, ridiculed those who would sacrifice good style to please the mob. The character of an old Virginia gentleman is contemptuous of Mr. Tuckabout, who, though privately conservative, pretends to be a Whig and panders to the crowd. "If your baseness was not perfectly plebeian, Mr. Tuckabout," he comments, "the exteriors of a gentleman might perhaps keep you concealed." But critics missed the point; what they perhaps should have feared much more than the loss of good taste was that such pleasing of the vulgar actually did please the vulgar. Ordinary people found abstract canons of liberty conveyed and explained to them in evocative language more accessible and appealing. What they heard was an enticing vision of all social ranks assimilated within a free society:

> Men of every size and station,
> Ev'ry age and occupation,
> Foes to party—friends to reason,
> Taste the fruit that's now in season,
> Taste the fruit—revere the tree
> Which nature plants, call'd Liberty.[22]

Such texts, widely diffused by new and old means of mass communication, may have invited some who were out of the mainstream of political life to see themselves as actors and participants (it surely undermined the stigma placed on social "levelling" as being against Nature). They would, however, still face a wall of cultural assumptions, shared by all classes, about an inherently unequal order of ranks in society. The possibility of the Founding elite instantly freeing themselves of this inherited world view was near zero; it would take America two more centuries to remove inequality from liberty. This was why the words and concepts of Revolutionary authors who otherwise gave us some of the most compelling language of equal rights for all people had specific, distinctly limited meanings. In his defense of the right of the American colonies to consent to taxation, Richard Bland wrote emphatically that "this natural Right remains with every Man and he cannot justly be deprived of it by any civil Authority"—but his universalistic "every Man" still rather unambiguously meant *freemen* and not slaves, Indians, or women. Thomas Jefferson's Declaration of Independence, in its reference to a collective and undifferentiated body of "Indian Savages," tacitly assumed that liberty was an attribute applicable primarily to Europeans. Benjamin Franklin was outraged that Samuel Johnson would suggest "hiring the Indian Savages to assassinate our Planters in the Back Settlements." As he noted, "They are the poorest and most innocent of all People; and the Indian manner is to murder and scalp Men Women & Children." James Duane noted that the country's "northern and Eastern frontiers are at the mercy of the Canadians and the savages long in their alliance," and that the Indians were "entirely without Faith and Humanity." The Northwest Ordinances of 1784–87 did not even bring up the question of the Indian inhabitants' rights to the territories covered by the legislation—it was a non-issue, a part of silent history. Women, as a class, were excluded not just from political positions or voting, but even from taking up certain subjects. Mercy Otis Warren, perhaps the most prominent woman intellectual in eighteenth-century America, had to issue caveats in her political publications, stressing that she only wished to "cultivate the sentiments of public and private virtue," and that the role of a mother remained "peculiarly" hers—because it was not appropriate for women to write about politics.[23] Our aim should not be to once again confirm that various groups were not included in the club of equal rights during the Revolutionary era, but to better understand why this was not an anomaly.

Finally, aside from its Enlightenment credentials and its pro-Revolutionary political rewards, the all-inclusive language of liberty carried another important attribute. It supplied coherence in an incoherent world, and tempered the wildly differing and contradictory experiences of people caught in the turmoil of war by offering them a sensible and composed vision of reality. The impact of such language was enhanced by the speaking elite's rhetorical credibility, which often allowed them to define the meaning of reality for the people. We instinctively tend to focus on the contradictions between language and reality (in this case, between the rhetoric of equality and the practice of inequality), but language may carry meaning even without referring to anything objectively existing—if enough people acknowledge it as a true representation of some thing. Fictionality need not reduce the power of language to shape social space.[24] For instance, there was a widespread belief in early modern England that all social ranks were virtually represented in Parliament, and that all possessed liberty, even though in real life liberty was distributed unequally among unequal ranks. Similarly, Americans of various classes could share a belief that equality and liberty reigned in the new republic. Linguistic fictions made the world more consistent for them by *symbolically* reconciling freedom and unfreedom. The imagined nature of such claims did not diminish this conciliatory power. On the contrary, they were so appealing because objectively existing contradictions could not be reconciled. It was this attraction that contributed significantly to the rapid absorption of such rhetoric into American culture, and to making equal liberty one of its givens.

III. Delegitimizing Pedigreed Advantage

> It has been my hobby-horse to see rising in America an empire of liberty, and a prospect of two or three millions of freemen, without one noble or one king among them.
>
> —John Adams, *The True Interests of America,* 1776

IN ORDER TO DELEGITIMIZE the main enemy—the metropolitan ruling class—American Revolutionary authors created a dark image of hereditary nobility in England. They characterized its members as a parasitic, immoral group, wallowing in luxury and debauchery, who betrayed the nation's ancient ideals of liberty and defended an "aristocratical tyranny." The popularity among all social classes of this vision, of a "corrupt aristocracy which at present rules the British councils," exceeded its creators' expectations. For ordinary working people it was a validation of their worth vis-à-vis the powerful and the well-born. For the American political class, the enthusiasm to diminish metropolitan nobility offered the joy of payback for having been looked down upon as second-rate Englishmen. This indignity had a long history. Patriot elites were used to having power, and, in this sense, defended the status quo, but what they never attained was recognition as a valid upper class—even when they acquired genteel polish and taste—because, by metropolitan criteria, they were mostly of humble social origins. During his stay in London, the Virginian Carter Braxton irately noted in his diary: "The people of England generally behold, or rather affect to behold, the American with contempt. . . . In my mind, a man of virtue and propriety of conduct, has as fair a claim to attention, and much fairer too, than he on whom fortune has showered titles or riches." After 1764 the tone of English comments on developments in America became even more contemptuous, and laden with epithets suggesting low birth. References such as "Mr. John Hancock (now PRESIDENT of the Congress, but formerly a most notorious Smuggler)" were commonplace. Satirists called upon the British to stand up to "Hancock with his rabble . . . the wrath of Congress, or its lords the mob," and to the "the new-born statesmen" who, like rats, emerged from "garrets" and "cellars." The Revolution provided a tremendous opportunity for the Americans to end this humiliating treatment by portraying themselves as genuinely virtuous and by branding English aristocrats as artificial. The otherwise inaccessible criterion of noble ancestry was now cast off—publicly and with jubilation. The people of America would have a true elite of quality, "in whose Wisdom and Virtue They could confide."[25]

A typical interpretation of this assault on British aristocracy has been that the Patriots rejected the old hierarchic order in order to create a more modern and egalitarian one. Since there was no nobility of birth in America to speak of, the argument goes, rebellious colonists had neither use for nor appreciation of the privileged classes, especially when such a class system was intrinsically linked to monarchy. The barrage of rhetoric directed at hereditary nobility has been seen as testimony of such a principled rejection of inequality. But if that were so, how are we to account for the fact that late colonial and Revolutionary elites strived intensely to be recognized as gentry;

FIGURE 1. Lord North and other aristocrats rejoice at the news of General Howe's victories in America. A commoner woman symbolizing America sits weeping on the ground holding a tattered liberty cap. Etching from the *London Magazine,* November 1776. (Courtesy Library of Congress, Washington, D.C.)

enthusiastically joined exclusive societies, juntos, clubs, and Masonic lodges; keenly sought out symbols of politeness; bought coats of arms; built fashionable residences modeled on English country manors; studied genteel subjects; and revered aristocrats like the Marquis de Lafayette, Baron von Steuben, the Chevalier de Chastellux, or the Comte de Rochambeau? It is often difficult for us today to understand the immense symbolic power of pedigree in the world of eighteenth-century British culture. We tend to—mistakenly— dismiss the ambitions of someone like George Washington (by then already President of the United States), eagerly requesting a coat of arms from the College of Heralds in London, and engraving one on his silver service, as insignificant and idiosyncratic.[26] They were neither. They testified instead to the durability and power of established cultural symbols to confer respectability and identity—long after the political context had changed.

Nor should late colonial and Revolutionary denunciations of hereditary privileges be confused with qualms about the social order of ranks, or about the genteel ethos, with its distinctive features of public virtue, taste, politeness, and honor—all taken straight from the old aristocratic textbook. As the conflict progressed, the need to invalidate the prestige of hereditary nobility as the imperial ruling elite, and to blame them for the mistreatment of the colonies, became a political imperative. But this particular campaign was carefully limited to pedigreed privilege, and was not an attack on all hierarchic distinctions as such. Only in this way could the former provincial rulers claim to be an honorable elite, as opposed to an undeserving, hereditary one. What was new was the separation of birth from merit, otherwise simply an acknowledgment of colonial reality. Jefferson had no doubts as to his own membership in the gentry class, but he found French hereditary offices, titles, and "perpetual monopolies in commerce, the arts and sciences" as outrageous as entail in British America.[27]

Colonial elites detested hereditary entitlements not only because they reminded them of the metropolitan rejection of their gentility, but also because such rejection cast doubt on their title to full liberty. Samuel Johnson explicitly questioned this title in 1775 by tying it to birth. Referring to the Revolutionary leaders, he pointed out with his trademark sarcasm that these "heroes of Boston" who blustered about liberty were originally of low social descent and neither possessed "all the privileges of Englishmen" nor were they entitled to "a vote in making laws." In a similar reaction to colonial claims, James Macpherson ridiculed the Americans' "warm encomiums on the ancestors," noting that these forebears were poor and "could scarcely obtain credit." From this perspective, the colonists' arguments about their right of consent to taxation were really an "endeavor to establish into an inherent right what was actually an indulgence." Public sentiment in England supported such views. In the words of one pro-American observer in London, "There was not a Cobbler in the Kingdom but considered the Americans as Indentured servants and Convicts."[28]

The attacks on aristocracy and the claims of colonial leaders' virtue were plainly designed as an argument for the equality of the colonials with their metropolitan counterparts, and not for equalizing American society. In 1776, Edward Rutledge, a South Carolinian signer of the Declaration of Independence, reflecting on the future of an independent America, noted that he above all dreaded those "levelling Principles which Men without Character and without Fortune in general Possess, which are so captivating to the lower Class of Mankind." The New Yorker Alexander McDougall, worried about the dangerous "habits of thinking" and "levelling principles" of the Northern "yeomanry," placed his hope in their military officers, who, being more conservative, would "temper" the commoners. John Adams was concerned that the Massachusetts assembly debating the state constitution might introduce "dangerous Innovations," because "the Spirit of Levelling . . . is afloat." Jonathan Dickinson Sergeant shared the same fears about New Jersey, writing about "the mad Fellows who now compose that Body," and noting hopefully that "the great & mighty ones in the Colony are preparing to make their last stand against the Principle of levelling which prevails in it."[29]

Long-term culture change is seldom predictable for the contemporary participants in that change. In the decade following the end of the Revolution, when English-style hereditary privilege had been successfully discredited and anti-aristocratism had established itself as part of the emerging national distinctiveness, the public conversation about class and authority set off by this debate began to take a new turn, surprising to many of its initiators. The case of the Society of the Cincinnati may serve as a telling illustration. The founders of the order, George Washington among them, were members of the very elite that had originally assailed English nobility, yet they felt that coming up with a proposal for an exclusive association was perfectly appropriate for American Patriot gentlemen who had distinguished themselves in the War of Independence. Their project, however, triggered an immediate and unexpected backlash. John Adams, upon hearing about a society where membership was to be hereditary, found himself distraught. "Is that order of chivalry, that inroad upon our first principle, equality, to be connived at?" he asked. "Is it not an effectual subversion of our equality? Inequalities of riches cannot be avoided as long as nature gives inequality of understanding and activity. And these inequalities are not unuseful. But artificial inequalities of decorations, birth and title not accompanying public truth, are those very inequalities which have exterminated virtue and liberty, and substituted ambition and slavery in all ages and countries." Elbridge

Gerry, too, was concerned that a new hereditary elite could potentially concentrate power in the elected bodies of the Confederation. He and other Massachusetts congressional delegates warned that many of those calling for "more power in Congress" were really seeking "lucrative Employments, civil and military. . . . Such a government is an Aristocracy." Mercy Otis Warren was no less exasperated. Her comments on the new organization dripped with irony; she referred to it, using old, aristocratic vocabulary, as a "hereditary claim to the peerage of the Order of Cincinnati, and the privileges annexed thereto," and as an "honor of hereditary knighthood, entailed in their posterity." Even Washington's membership could not "sanction the design in the eye of the sober republican, and other men of moderate views in the common grades of life." The same view was voiced by Aedanus Burke, chief justice of South Carolina, who thought that it was nothing less than "a deep laid plan, to beget and perpetuate family grandeur in an aristocratic nobility." A national aristocracy of birth could become a rival to the republican elite, only recently defined as one based on personal quality. Burke thundered that "the order of Cincinnati usurp a nobility without gift or grant, in defiance of Congress and the States," and that "in less than a century . . . the country will be composed only of two ranks of men the patricians or nobles and the rabble." This new aristocracy would be "in a republican government extremely hazardous and highly censurable." Attending a Fourth of July celebration in 1786, the Massachusetts delegate to Congress, Rufus King, was shocked by members of the Order, who put up "splendor exceeding any thing within the practice of government." Jefferson, in a letter to Washington, respectfully but firmly objected to the principle—contained in the Order—of "preeminence by birth," noting that it was "against the spirit" of all the state constitutions, and that "experience has shewn that the hereditary branches of modern governments are the patrons of privilege and prerogative, and not of the natural rights of the people."[30]

It is striking that most of these criticisms came from people who considered themselves to be members of an American upper class and bearers of the higher virtues, such as "equality, liberty, simplicity, and interest of the nation at large." Their negative reaction—even if the arguments were, as a rule, framed in defense of egalitarianism—was really against the strict exclusiveness of Cincinnati-type clubs, not against a society of ranks. Aedanus Burke considered the Society "an establishment, which ere long must strip the posterity of the middling and lower classes of every influence and authority, and leave them nothing but insignificance, contempt, and the wretched privilege of murmuring when it is too late." The Federalist preacher, David Osgood, cautioned the members of such societies that "every club, formed for political purposes, is an aristocracy established over their brethren. It has all the properties of an aristocracy, and all the effects of tyranny. It is a literal truth, that democratic clubs in the United States, while running mad with the abhorrence of aristocratic influence, are attempting to establish precisely the same influence under a different name." Such righteous populism was quite typical of contemporary intellectual elites (and is far from absent among them today). French Enlightenment figures like Voltaire or Abbé Raynal, who came to epitomize the principles of equal liberty, saw themselves firmly as members of "le monde," society's cream of the crop, representing progress, taste, and reason—perched not only above the commoners but also above the money-oriented bourgeoisie.[31]

Revolutionary anti-aristocratism, originally directed against England, thus led to an unanticipated outcome: it also discredited claims of privilege made by the existing elites—such as those asserted by the Society of the Cincinnati—by cutting into conceptions of social order in Anglo-American traditions to a much greater degree than the Patriot leaders would have wished. What started as an ideological device to discredit the English aristocracy's unelected rule, ultimately ended up putting a ceiling on the authority of the republican gentry. It helped not only to gradually destroy among Americans whatever remained of traditional deference to monarchy and nobility, but also contributed to a gradual breakdown of deference to privileged elites as such. This was, historically, the inner logic of Revolutionary rhetoric; a preservationist device became a democratizing instrument. For such deep changes to happen, new schemata of articulating the world had to be introduced and accepted by the people. Only when the networks of values, norms, and beliefs that had organized the earlier system of power changed could a shift reducing the extent to which privilege was acceptable take place. What this episode demonstrates is that the first steps toward an equality of rights and liberties took place in the sphere of the symbolic. True revolutionary changes, to recall an observation by Claude Lefort, "occur at the moment when the transcendence of power vanishes, and when its symbolic efficacy is destroyed."[32] Anti-aristocratism, a countercultural device used to undercut the authority of the British ruling class, retained its power after its original target had lost its significance, and, like Banquo's ghost, returned to haunt its authors.

IV. Inventing Patriotic Traditions

To one however who adores liberty, and the noble virtues of which it is the parent, there is some consolation seeing, while we lament the fall of British liberty, the rise of that of America. Yes, my friend, like a young phoenix she will rise full plumed and glorious from her mother's ashes.

—Arthur Lee to Samuel Adams, 1772

ON AUGUST 22, 1768, the *Boston Evening Post* carried an announcement of an "extraordinary festivity" in town to commemorate the original demonstration by the Sons of Liberty on August 14, 1765, when the effigies of Stamp Act supporters had been hanged. At dawn, "the British flag was displayed on the Tree of liberty, and a discharge of fourteen cannon, ranged under the venerable elm, saluted the joyous day." At 11 o'clock, "a very large company of the principal gentlemen and respectable inhabitants of the town, met at the hall under the tree, while the streets were crowded with a concourse of people of all ranks." This was followed by music, "performed on various instruments," and the singing of the "universally admired American Song of Liberty," providing "sublime entertainment to a numerous audience, fraught with a noble ardour in the cause of freedom." Then followed more firings of cannon, fourteen toasts, more music and cannon, an elegant dinner for the gentry at the Greyhound Tavern at Roxbury, and, finally, a "slow & orderly procession thro' the principal streets, and round the state-house."[33]

Rapid political change in the early modern Western world was usually accompanied by a struggle to control the collective memory, as such change was much more easily accepted when dressed up in a costume tailored from the cloth of familiar history. Because this memory is an important glue that bonds and stabilizes society, it has also usually been (and remains) an area of intense political competition. Until collective remembrance is successfully restructured—a job that by and large fell to the speaking class—no major upheaval could be considered complete. American Revolutionary leaders understood early and well that the core values and grand principles of their struggle needed to be expressed and kept alive by encouraging and cultivating new traditions. Soon after the implementation of the Stamp Act, a set of existing customs were converted into patriotic ceremonies, with the explicit aim of uniting the people. Such practices—as acts of collective communication—proved especially valuable as strategies of political inclusion. They are of particular interest to us because they provided incentives for the expansion of the sphere of liberty.

When we speak of traditions, we are usually referring to recurring values, customs, and expectations, expressed both in ideologies and in social rituals. Traditions tell us about the normative order that dominates a given society and that allows its various groups and circles to thrive. They also tell us much about a society's ethos, that is, the disposition or orientation of the whole culture, its "style" expressed in systems of values and ideals.[34] Examining traditions allows us to peek into the hierarchy of these values. A specific ritual, for instance, can be indicative of the values which at the time were considered essential enough to be honored by public celebrations. Since a number of popular rituals during the Revolution and the early national period symbolized liberty, the question to ask is what they meant to their organizers and to their participants.

The newly invented traditions of the Revolutionary era, such as popular celebrations of Washington's birthday and of the Fourth of July, revolved around a number of stock concepts: republican virtue, sovereign people, public spirit, natural rights, and equality before the law. Within a short span of years, the now abandoned components of the traditional British ethos, such as the loyalty of subjects to the Crown and deference to nobility, had been replaced by veneration for an idealized American liberty. By the 1790s, with the emergence of parties and the rivalries between them, celebrations and street rituals had taken on a more partisan character, but the propaganda of all factions continued to make use of abstract, sweeping visions of liberty, aimed at engaging a wide circle of supporters. Such festivities not only nourished the emerging national selfhood but—more importantly for our subject —helped disseminate a lexicon of modern freedom. Despite the fact that these early patriotic celebrations usually focused on broad universals rather than on particular rights, the message of a shared "legacy of freedom" reverberated among ordinary people, who found in it an affirmation of their dignity and a symbolic political empowerment.

The elite organizers of such events, on the other hand, were motivated by different goals. They stressed a shared legacy, hoping to call attention to the unity of all Americans and to promote solidarity between classes. During the war, the main stress had been on creating a united front against the enemy, with "all ranks of people united in sentiment to repel every principle that seemed derogating from freedom, suspicious of infringing their darling rights." In the postwar years, the theme of social cohesion gained in importance; the expectation was that "the generality of citizens" would draw pride and satisfaction from the symbolic fusion of nation and liberty, while confirming the authority of the local elite. As early as July 3, 1776, John Adams had called for organized symbolic rituals aimed at uniting all ranks of the people. Now that the question of independence had been decided, he wrote to General James Warren, "the second day of July, 1776, will be the most memorable Epocha in the History of America." As he proposed: "It ought to be commemorated as the day of deliverance, by solemn acts of devotion to Almighty God. It ought to be solemnized with Pomp, Shews, Games, Sports, Guns, Bells, Bonfires and Illuminations from one end of this Continent to the other from this time forever more." His detailed designs for such ceremonies offered, to use Joseph Ellis's apt term, "a romantic rendering" of the anniversary. Adams understood well that to control the language and the ritual was to constitute a new reality in the collective American mind. He also knew something that it may be somewhat difficult for today's readers to appreciate, given our postmodern mentality—namely, that the eighteenth-century mind still held great faith in the power of words as symbolic gestures. A good example may be found in the requirement of an oath of loyalty, widespread by 1778. Although the actual oath was probably worthless, because it was taken under a threat of property confiscation or exile (many colonists re-swore their loyalty back to England as soon as the British army entered an area), a steadfast reliance on the magic of this ritual persisted among the Revolutionary leaders throughout the war.[35]

Adams was quite far-sighted in his proposal. One of the first widely mythologized national themes to emerge was that of a new nation created on the foundation of liberty. In the early decades of the republic, the bulk of patriotic festivities celebrated the Beginning, idealizing it as an august caesura in history, a sublime point of reference for all current affairs of the country. To emphasize a long and respectable *American* pedigree, this centrality of liberty was extended backward, into the colonial beginnings. David Ramsay, in his history of the Revolution, pared down all conflict among the first Puritan settlers, and presented an early society united around the principles of equality and republican freedom. Puritan communities were depicted as committed to "a conviction that tyranny, whether in church or state, was contrary to nature, reason and revelation," and it was noted that their opinions "were favourable to liberty and hostile to all undue exercise of authority." Colonial society "favored a spirit of liberty and independence," because the inhabitants "were all of one rank."[36] The Founding was thus fashioned as a shared sign that combined the beginning of European settlement in America with the cause of equal freedom.

Similarly, once the revered milestone of 1776 became an all-purpose symbol of American liberty, it could be, and was, used to validate a wide variety of partisan political goals, which were now presented as consistent with the mythical "essence" of the Founding (not unlike many of today's political arguments, which are eagerly clothed in the legitimacy of the Founders' "intentions"). By the late 1790s, both Federalists and Anti-Federalists invoked in their celebratory toasts what had become a canonical lexicon of freedom: "republican spirit," "virtue," "the rights of man," "the people," and "the sovereignty of the people." Simon Newman has shown how, during the July 4th festivities of 1796 in Philadelphia, Democratic Republican opponents of the Federalist government used their loyalty to the "Patriots of '76" to symbolically exclude Federalist members of the Order of the Cincinnati by not saluting after their toasts. The local newspaper hinted that Washington, as a member of the Society, had betrayed the republican principles enshrined in the Constitution. During similar celebrations in 1798, the Declaration of Independence was read aloud, allowing the assembled Republicans to frame their anti-government opposition in terms of the supposed "original intent" of the Founders. In their toasts they routinely identified themselves with the early, "genuine principles" of republicanism. Invented traditions thus gave birth to usable cultural givens. They could now be employed by groups other than just party partisans to plead for rights. During Federalist Independence Day celebrations in York, Pennsylvania, several local ladies cheerily raised a toast to the "rights of women," something that would not have been very likely a few decades earlier.[37]

The burgeoning public rituals displayed a dazzlingly creative assortment of symbols. In 1793 prominent sympathizers of the French Revolution in Boston organized a celebration, with a procession through the streets; a barbecue; the renaming of Oliver's Dock to "Liberty Square"; and a banquet at Faneuil Hall with the mottoes of Liberty and Equality, fireworks, and children parading a cake with the words "Liberty and Equality" through the streets, "to impress the tender minds of rising generations." Five years later, the Federalists began wearing black cockades as a symbol of opposition to the tricolor ones of the pro-Revolution Anti-Federalists. The latter promptly responded with their own parody, for instance, by sporting four-inch-long "dried cow-dung" cockades. Songs were used in similar manner: Abigail Adams related that, during a visit to the theater, there had been "something like disorder," with one group singing "Yankee Doodle" while " 'Ca Ira' was vociferated from the other."[38] The use of such signs, easily and efficiently conveyed, condensed messages of social order and political identity. In the long run, however, their use also promulgated a nonpartisan, generalized belief in universal, equal, and natural liberty, and thus helped ensure that this concept became dominant in the cultural liturgy of the young nation.

To fully understand the remarkable success of these forms of liberty talk in early modern America, we need to realize just how profoundly they were rooted in earlier English custom. The revolutionaries and the early national historiography of the event understandably emphasized the newness and the peculiarly American characteristics of patriotic traditions related to freedom. But a closer look at them shows that continuity had as much to do with their success as originality. New traditions that could be effortlessly related to those already familiar made it easier for the public to absorb the Revolutionary changes that had upset many of the mechanisms for making sense of the world. Part intentionally, part instinctively, Patriot leaders tapped into an already existing deep veneration of liberty in British society, widely shared as one component of the country's national pride. They harnessed this tradition by persuading people that America was now the true bearer and protector of its key principles. This was why post-Revolutionary celebrations of patriotic holidays so often involved toasts to "ancient British liberties." In other words, only a part of the old narrative had to be altered; the rest came wholesale from well-established metropolitan usages.[39] There was no problem with the old British wine filling the new American vessel, because much of it was already there. Since traditions, as a rule, express the reigning model of a world order (and so involve a strong reluctance among the people to abandon them), it was much easier for the rulers to make use of old traditions for new political purposes than to introduce new ones not rooted in familiar notions of order.

Consider the example of one of the central tenets of the worship of freedom in Britain: exceptionalism. From early seventeenth-century poetry to late eighteenth-century newspapers, a recurring theme was that of pride in England's uniqueness as a free nation. It was common fare in editorials and letters from readers to observe that while the greater part of mankind are "held in the most abject state of slavery," and "an established tyranny holds them in perpetual bondage," in Britain the "constitution has . . . delivered us from the ravages of despotism, and the fangs of unrestrained tyrants." The people had at their disposal "a glorious constitution committed to their care, by gallant forefathers." This patriotic identification with freedom was usually portrayed as going back as far as the Celtic struggle with Roman rule, when "in the earliest hour of Britain's morn, A Briton's hate of tyranny was born." The nation's "sturdy ancestors," driven by "their country's love," had been vehement in defending their freedom:

> Fierce for hereditary claims they fight,
> And ev'n till death maintain a Briton's right.
> Hence rose *our* liberties, a common cause
> To these succeed, their best support, the laws.

England could justifiably be proud; it stood in awe "of no pow'r upon earth, but Justice and Law; No wrongs to redress, and no rights to restore." Of all the world's countries, it was the best home to Lady Liberty:

> Fair Liberty! if on a throne
> Thy own unfetter'd wishes own,
> Where Discord, War, and Murder cease
> I seek thee—lo—thy form is seen
> On Albion's plains, her worshipped Queen.

Throughout the eighteenth century, both high and popular culture associated freedom with Britain and with that nation's singular place in the world. This sentiment received an additional boost from the French Revolution:

While France is struggling with oppressive woe,
To gain such favors, few but Britons know,
And other nations are in slav'ry bound,
We live securely on thy happy ground.[40]

The colonists were part and parcel of this tradition, so when the need arose, it was a relatively effortless undertaking to weave a separatist theme out of the old yarn and make America the new home of historic British liberty. As Samuel Adams wrote: "Men of Virtue throughout Europe heartily wish well to our Cause. They look upon it, as indeed it is, as the Cause of Mankind. Liberty seems to be driven from every other Part of the Globe. The prospect of affording its Friends Asylum in this New World, gives them universal Joy." "Civil Liberty, in my opinion," noted Edward Carrington, "never before took up her residence in a country so likely to afford her a long and grateful protection as the United States." And as John Francis Mercer wrote in his address to the public: "Liberty! Thou emanation from the all-beauteous and celestial mind, to Americans thou hast committed the guardianship of the darling rights of mankind, leaving the eastern world where indolence has bowed the neck to the yoke of tyranny; in this Western hemisphere hast thou fixed thy sacred empire." In the decades that followed, endless sermons delivered on Independence Day commemorated "the principles of men, who sought not to subvert the government, under which they lived, but to save it from degeneracy; not to create new rights, but to preserve inviolate such, as they had ever possessed."[41]

The former provincials saw themselves as having owned these rights all along by virtue of participating in a proud tradition. Charles Thomson, commenting on the Boston Tea Party, noted that it was common cause in America at the time that the controversy with London be settled in a way that would "leave the people of Boston upon their ancient footing of constitutional liberty." The denial of their preexisting freedom by tax men was expressed by the colonists in the streets by the "funerals of Liberty," where stamp distributors were symbolically killed and buried. A popular 1776 patriotic song ridiculed the once great but now disgraced and corrupt England: "The Lustre of your former Deeds, whole Ages of Renown, Lost in a moment, or transferr'd to US and WASHINGTON." The new "birthrights" were thus solidly founded on a heritage of old legitimacy (something modern

American exceptionalist historians had little sense of). There was nothing unusual about such continuity; as Eric Hobsbawm has shown, invented traditions, precisely because they are invented, seek a connection with an established historic past.[42] Such use of British history was, of course, selective; rather than mine for strict precedents, it aimed to validate revolutionary change, making it appear normative rather than subversive.

Devised traditions also tell us much about the close collaboration of elites and non-elites. The American Patriots' effective attack on certain British values had the potential to undermine the established order in society, hitherto expressed and maintained through such values. Removing the old center of allegiance did not in itself make it easy for the new one to immediately command loyalty, because new values, in order to successfully integrate society, first had to become sufficiently shared and respected. This was why their intense public promotion was so important: the speaking elites hoped that the new ethos, once widely diffused, would help maintain an order in which the elite and non-elite classes (with their competing interests) would coexist in relative harmony. Their belief was that the new country, designed around the principle of liberty, should by definition ensure a peaceful coexistence of the rulers and the ruled. As Washington put it, "The very idea of the right and the power of the people to establish government presupposes the duty of every individual to obey the established government."[43] This was the grand stake that the Patriot elite had in the effectiveness of invented traditions. But a concerted effort to popularize the new folklore of freedom not only helped to politically consolidate society; it also produced an unanticipated effect of encouraging the politicization of ordinary people. It was a case study of the non-linear and non-teleological expansion of freedom.

The relative social homogeneity of Revolutionary America, the need to gain wider social support for the war, and the urgency of legitimizing the new polity contributed to the fact that new traditions in America played a more equalizing role than did similar traditions introduced in Europe. When the Dutch Republic of United Provinces underwent a crisis under the reign of William V, the anti-William, "Patriot" faction invoked a mythical Batavia, a country of liberty, unspoiled virtue, and a pure church, from which all free citizens of the Republic supposedly originated. The 1768 rebellion of Polish nobility and gentry against the reformist king Stanislaus Augustus was ideologically justified with a spectrum of values supposedly deriving from ancient, mythical ancestors of the gentry, the Sarmatians, who represented the now

An East View of GRAY'S FERRY, near Philadelphia, with the TRIUMPHAL ARCHES, &c. erected for the Reception of General Washington, April 20ᵗʰ 1789.

FIGURE 2. Triumphal arches, decorated with laurel, cedar, and banners, erected for the reception of General Washington in Gray's Ferry near Philadelphia. Flagpole from which a flag with the rattlesnake symbol is flying also holds a liberty cap on top. Etching by James Trenchard after Charles Wilson Peale. From the *Columbian Magazine,* Philadelphia, May 1789. (Courtesy Library of Congress, Washington, D.C.)

lost ideals of pure virtue and republican liberty.[44] In both countries, the rebels' language was full of phrases referring to their disinterested sacrifice for the cause of freedom. In reality, both cases essentially involved a struggle of one elite against another, each defending its privileges. By contrast, the American elite was not battling another elite, but seeking support and acceptance from a broad social base, and so its invented traditions played a more democratizing role.

It has sometimes been pointed out that these new traditions and celebrations in the early post-Revolutionary period contained a deep irony, because they made citizenship "too imaginary" and "symbolic," instead of opening it up for broader political participation.[45] Invented traditions were indeed symbolic, but the inference that they were essentially ironic goes a bit too far, because it assumes that the Revolution should have much more radically opened up the legal sphere of civic involvement to more literally "correspond" to its rhetoric of freedom. We run the risk of what has fittingly been called logocentrism—when words are assigned too much substance as representations of reality, and attributed with significations they do not contemporarily contain.

The argument should be reversed; it was precisely the imaginary, cere-monial inclusion that became a prime instrument of agency for those not yet admitted to full ownership of freedom. It undermined (symbolically, to be sure, but all communication is symbolic) the defining paradigm of order and helped open the door to future admittance of the excluded. It delivered this message regardless of the fact that one of the intentions behind patriotic rituals was to affirm the political dominance of the gentry, and that many were explicitly designed as didactic measures to that effect. Social and politi-cal distinctions were indeed conspicuously present in them; for instance, invited participants included only those who were expected to share the elite-made interpretation of events being commemorated, while the Loyalists and the unsure were explicitly barred. But the rituals were also indisputably at-tractive for ordinary people, for whom participation implied agency and social worth. It gave them political standing by signaling that they belonged to a circle of insiders identified with a progressive cause. Contrary to the view of history as being grounded in incompatible class antagonisms, patriotic rituals affirmed both the authority of the ruling elites and allowed for a growing inclusion and engagement of the non-elites.[46] Their participation ensured that certain liberty-related concepts would spread widely across the social space and be absorbed into the cultural fabric. One such concept was that Americans as a nation were collectively free; another, that, in contrast to European monarchies, everyone had a stake in the new republic.

V. Constituting the People

> That all power is vested in, and consequently derived from, the people; that magistrates are their trustees and servants, and at all times amenable to them.
>
> —George Mason, *Virginia Bill of Rights,* 1776

THROUGHOUT THE REVOLUTION, a struggle to attach names to events was an integral component of the political conflict. For instance, if London's policy of taxation could successfully be labeled as a case of "slavery," the contest for the meaning of reality would tilt toward the Americans.

Revolutionaries had to fight with England for a free government, insisted Samuel Adams in 1775, because there was nothing "so much to be dreaded by Mankind as Slavery."[47] If the "revolution" were instead to be referred to as "rebellion," a London-made label, its persuasive edge would tilt toward England. Representations could attack, mediate, or defuse tensions. One such cultural device produced by the era was the invention of a sovereign "people." It was an extraordinary instrument through which Enlightenment idealism was fused with political practice. Combined with the accompanying substitution of the voice of those in power for the voice of the people, it both helped prolong a traditionally ranked society, and undermine it. Its echoes reverberated through the American, the French, and the Bolshevik Revolutions, and it is widely used to this day on the American political scene.

Who exactly were "the people" for the Revolutionary leaders? The answer is far from simple, and must begin with the realization that the Revolution's leaders viewed the representations and the reality of "the people" as two different, but parallel entities. The rhetorical "people" were a unified, homogeneous body, possessors of collective wisdom, and carriers of natural rights (symbolic oneness and homogeneity were crucial if the elite were to be able to speak "in their name"). The empirical "people" were stratified into unequal classes, with the majority viewed as unqualified for certain liberties and for self-governing, and at times possessing the characteristics of a "mob" rather than those of responsible citizens. We intuitively tend to see this as a paradox, but doing so prevents us from fully understanding the logic of this cultural-cum-political mechanism. The idealized people, created as the essential anchor of the whole Revolutionary creed of liberty, could play this role successfully only if a clear distinction was made between them and the common populace. The rulers could not speak for the "common herd," but they could speak for "the people." The abstract people held the ultimate power, while the empirical populace had to be constantly constrained—needless to say, in the name of the people's liberty. What may appear today as contradictory, in fact made the whole design functional. Absent a hereditary monarchy as a legitimizer of government, it was only through this symbolic representation of a judicious people, unified in their equal rights and fully conscious of their political responsibilities, that the entire Revolutionary ideology of liberty could be constructed and validated. And only by assuming to be the *voice* of such a people could the Jeffersons and Madisons of the age claim their authority. As Francois Furet once brilliantly observed, in early modern revolutionary situations, the old locus of power, in the person of the king, migrated to the language—where the people's power would now reside.[48] By speaking on behalf of the people and not of themselves, the signers of the Declaration of Independence moved the locus of power from George III to their Philadelphia summit. At the same time, they could effectively assume this power only if their language did not reveal that they had. In other words, what appears contradictory was a perfectly rational arrangement; had the symbolic "people" been defined with any empirical specificity, the whole notion would have become politically unattractive to the leaders.

Quite apart from the contemporary political uses of "the people," there was another, even more important, long-term effect of this novelty. By widely publicizing such an entity as the ultimate and infallible foundation of republican polity, the revolutionaries may be said to have constituted "the people" as a category of thinking about American society and its rights. The concept of a free people had existed in the British world earlier, but Americans turned it into a foundational icon and a cultural commonplace. By making everyone believe that it existed and was real, *they created it*. By the late 1770s, representations of America as a country "abounding with free men all of one rank, where property is equally diffused, where estates are held in fee simple," had become customary. "The people" came to function both as a mandatory element of political and legal language, and as a romanticized figure of speech to serve celebratory ends. Fourth of July orations routinely exulted the new nation, which, the contemporary historian and physician David Ramsay noted, had "hit the happy medium between despotism and anarchy." Ramsay went on: "Every citizen is perfectly free of the will of every other citizen, while all are equally subject to the laws. . . . Our rulers, taken from the people, and at stated periods returning to them, have the strongest incitement to make the public will their guide, and the public good their end." In America, "the views and wishes of the legislature, are for the most part the views and wishes of the people; but in England, the reverse is often the case."[49] Without this symbolic presence of the people as a subject, acquiring new liberties by any subset of the population in the future would have been more difficult. Unlike the elites, who were always visible, various non-elite groups would remain in the shadows, much as women were invisible on the public stage before the feminist and suffrage movements impressed their presence—as a group with distinctive interests—on the society's consciousness. One might compare this phenomenon to today's issue of the spotted owl. The spotted owl had been around for a long time, but only when environmental groups became effective spokespersons for its preservation did it become widely identifiable on the public stage as a distinctive (and endangered) species. In other words, the objective existence of spotted owls did not automatically translate into their conspicuous presence in the public mind as a collective entity. This presence had to become a prerequisite if their current plight was to be reflected upon and action taken.

At this point, an inevitable question that arises is how the invention of a sovereign people could play a progressive role, considering that it was being used by the few to rule the many. It is an important problem, calling for serious epistemological reflection. Two decades ago, in his study of popular sovereignty in England and America, Edmund Morgan suggested that the "success of government requires the acceptance of fictions, requires the willing suspension of disbelief," and concluded that the governments of Britain and United States "rest on fictions as much as the governments of Russia and China."[50] Morgan was entirely correct that the governing of the many by the few would hardly be possible without imaginary narratives (putting aside the fact that in their real-world applications the governmental fictions of democracies and dictatorships are similar, but only in the way that an easy chair is similar to an electric chair). However, to dismiss these narratives as mere fictions—that is, as something presumably less than scientific—is to obstruct our access to large territories within the world of culture. Culture stands on fictions. Dressing political issues in somewhat mythical clothing reflecting current norms and expectations is not simply manipulation. It is essential to communicating. When guests visit our home, we do not expect them to comment in the doorway, "Oh, what ugly, tasteless décor" (even if it is true), but to utter something like, "Nice home you have here," and thus remain within the parameters of convention. Anyone who doubts the binding power of such culturally approved conventions should try ignoring them, and then observe the results.

The traditional juxtaposition of "real" events and "fictitious" representations is also deceptive in another way. At the level of culture, supposedly objective "events" were often prefabricated and assigned meanings by certain political actors. Naked "facts," like the Stamp Act or the Boston Massacre, drove the Revolution much less than the ways in which these facts were defined, presented, and dressed. It was this manufactured reality that became actual reality in people's minds. The "naked" events, in themselves, did not contain portrayals of colonial leaders as representatives of the people's ancient rights, or of Britain as the betrayer of these traditions—but their representations supplied to the people did. In order to grasp the historical ontology of Revolutionary liberty, we need to pay much more attention to the role of such narratives. Whether the discussion was of "rights," "liberties," or "the people," the meanings of such terms were invariably formed by a language that was part fiction (that is, having few or no objective referents) and part concrete fact (such as events, executable contracts, laws). To situate cultural beliefs—in this case, those labeled as "fictions"—as being opposed to "observable facts," is to bind ourselves to a dated, positivist dichotomy. This can lead to the pointless pursuit of supposed certitudes; but many beliefs that make up a culture exist only as representations, and appear to participants as no less real than cathedrals or battles. Deference to the king on account of his divine right to rule was real, irrespective of the fact that such a godly designation would be rather difficult to prove empirically. The natural rights of man, on which so much of the eighteenth-century edifice of liberty was built, would be equally hard to locate in the world of Nature. Early modern English nationalism was to a large extent based on a popular belief that, as William Blackstone put it, the Parliament and the laws of England, unlike those of all other countries, were "particularly adapted to the preservation of this inestimable blessing [of civil liberty] even in the meanest subject."[51] We moderns today are much more inclined than our eighteenth-century ancestors to separate the imaginary and the real.

The meanings of any symbolic structure, whether a ritual, an institution, or a written text, are a blend of objective historical reality and the reality of their interpretation (the way they are understood). For a student of cultural history, this duality should be an important focus of inquiry. Many shared social beliefs that function effectively are not premised on empirical fact. A "suspension of disbelief" would be required only if our interpretative yardstick assumed (wrongly) a strict correspondence between words and objective truth—that is, the existence of a literal reality that the words must reflect. Words did not materially produce "the people" (or, for that matter, "the gentry" or "the poor"), but designating such a group in public conversation as a distinctive body instituted its existence in the collective mind, so that the people could now perceive it as an expression of the reality of their existence. When the shoemaker George Robert Twelves Hewes reminisced on the moments following the Boston Massacre, to which he had been a witness, he recalled that "the people then immediately chose a committee to report to the governor the result of Captain Preston's conduct, and to demand of him satisfaction." In Hewes's mind, there was little doubt that the primary actors in the events were "the people." It was a representation through which he had learned to describe reality, and, more importantly, his own place in society as a citizen. It mattered little that the committee was actually a self-formed group of gentlemen.[52]

Another point that often escapes us is that "the people" was an elite-made concept. It was employed by the political class mainly to denote a certain type of government, and it served as a symbolic core of American polity (a polar opposite of the metropolitan one, rooted in monarchy), as in "All power is vested in, and consequently derived from, the people," or "The people have a right to uniform government." It was still a long way from signifying individual and equal ownership of liberties. Let us consider, for example, the stance taken by Jefferson and Washington toward Shays's Rebellion. Although the two differed in their reactions—which reflected opposing party affiliations and agendas—there was clearly a common paternalistic thread in their comments, a thread which originated from the traditions they both shared. To Washington, who worried that the original republican hopes were based on "too good an opinion of human nature," the unrest in Massachusetts only demonstrated that to uphold the new system, "founded on the basis of equal liberty," there must be an institutionalized "coercive power," so that "the better kind of people" and "respectable characters" would not abandon the American experiment. Jefferson, in turn, pointed out that the position taken by the farmers was essentially "founded on ignorance," and that the best remedy was to "set them right as to facts, pardon, and pacify them." It had to be ignorance; were it otherwise, it would be a violation of good sense, a case of "popular absurdity," since proper liberty for all was already ensured by the existence of a Congress which represented all the people—including the disaffected Massachusetts farmers. Although Jefferson fully expected such representatives to be chosen from among the upper class, he was confident that if only they would "mingle frequently with the mass of citizens," the delegates would become sufficiently aware of the needs of ordinary folk. John

Adams advocated that "the Representatives may often mix with their Constituents," and Thomas Paine hoped that the elected would often "return and mix again with the general body of the electors."[53] The prescription for "mixing" showed a new consideration for the common people, but it left old assumptions of rank mostly intact.

To be who they were, the Jeffersons and Washingtons acutely needed "the people." The creation of such a symbolic, collective body was a prerequisite to any claims of representing them politically. Within a few years from the outbreak of the Revolution, the authority of the new rulers came to be entirely founded on representing "the people" as the archetypal owners of all rights and liberties. In this sense, the people constituted the republican elite as much as the elite constituted the people. I am not talking here about political representation as a formal delegation of power (such as that constitutionally given to congressmen to represent their constituents), but about the fact that the political elite, as well as ordinary people, existed through one another, representatives through the represented, and vice versa. Quite apart from the underlying economic criteria that divided them, both these classes were in large part constructed culturally, in people's minds, through symbolic depictions which gave them a presence in the public domain.[54] In the Revolutionary battle of words about who truly represented the people's interests, the king was able to draw on historical legitimacy, but the Patriot elite found itself compelled to rely on rhetorical arguments, naming themselves into existence as an exclusive group of defenders of everyone's liberty. The novelty was that they presented themselves not as an elite per se, but as a subset of the people for whom they substituted their voice; the first words written by a small group of gentlemen who assembled in 1787 behind closed doors in Philadelphia to design a constitution were, "We the People."

Various monarchs and aristocracies had, of course, for ages spoken "in the name of all people." Virtual representation, so reviled in Revolutionary America, had functioned there without much opposition until 1764. The notion of "the people" propagated by the Founders to counter London's policies was initially not very different from the notion of "the people" that had been invented in the seventeenth century by the English Parliament to counter the authority of the Stuart monarchs. Neither group intended to undermine the existing social systems that privileged them. Even in 1776, a printed circular in South Carolina praised the newly independent government of the former colony for deriving from the people, *as well as* for its gentry makeup: "Every good citizen must be happy in the consideration of the choice of these officers, appointed in the administration of our present Government, as well in the impartial mode of an appointment arising from the people themselves ... as in their personal characters as men, justly beloved and revered by their country, and whose merits and virtues entitle them to every preeminence."[55] The difference was that old, hereditary elites were not as dependent on the people for their legitimacy as were the American ones.

As the Revolution progressed, signs of this dependence became manifest; members of the American ruling class began to downplay their identity as rulers and to shift their public image from that of "the better sort" to one of "disinterested servants of the populace." It suddenly became good taste to style themselves as simple, ordinary citizens, by assuming the persona of an "Honest Farmer," a "John Homely," or, simply, "Citizen." Benjamin Franklin famously fashioned himself as "Poor Richard," John Adams as "Humphrey Ploughjogger," and Thomas Paine as "Vox Populi." Humility was in vogue. "Modest Merit," observed Samuel Adams, "declines pushing it self into pub-lick View." Federalist Elias Boudinot of New Jersey served prominently in the Continental Congress, but claimed that his real desire was to be "the humble Peasant of Baskenridge, in the enjoyment of domestic Happiness with a beloved family . . . as unenvied as undisturbed." His colleague, Benjamin Rush, was determined to fulfill his public duties, but longed for "a cottage, a single cow, and horse—a faithful diary [dairy] maid—a black Jack—a book—with my dear Julia to pick—to talk & to smile by my side." Perhaps the greatest early propagator of this popular fiction was the Connecticut minister and poet Timothy Dwight. In his 1794 "Greenfield Hill," the namesake town had no mansions or pretensions, no upper class, no high and courtly tradi-tions. Instead, it was populated by humble and gentle people—honest, inde-pendent, and equal:

> Here every class (if classes those we call,
> Where one extended class embraces all,
> All mingling, as the rainbow's beauty blends,
> Unknown where every hue begins or ends)

The fact that very little of this pastoral fantasy was a reflection of real society was immaterial to its appeal. In fact, it only strengthened it: the gentry wanted to believe it because it made them part of the people they claimed to represent, and ordinary people wanted to believe it because it made them feel on a par with the gentry.[56]

Once the notion of a sovereign people possessing rights became an integral part of the cultural and political scene, its usage and meaning began to slowly but surely shift toward a more democratic and unrestricted understanding. At the outset of the conflict with Britain, references to the people were mostly made in the sense (inherited from the Old World) of a polity, an abstract, collective body connoting a system of government, rather than of citizens with individually held rights. "In general I believe," wrote Jefferson, "the decisions of the people, in a body, will be more honest and more disinterested than those of wealthy men." With time, the meaning of the term began to imply a more individual ownership of liberties. This was facilitated by electoral practices already socially broader and less rooted in hierarchical traditions than in England, a fact that made it easier to begin detaching freedom from rank. By the time of the Constitution, some codified rights, such as the right to bear arms, contained in the Second Amendment, still referred to "people" in the collective sense, while other rights, such as the freedom of religion in the Virginia Bill of Rights ("All men are equally entitled to the free exercise of religion") were already unambiguously attached to individuals. Conceptualizations of liberty were evolving along similar lines. Alexander Hamilton was still convinced in 1775 that limits on the power of the rulers over the ruled were essentially determined by a compact between them, a compact which also served as a guarantee of the rights of both the rulers and the ruled. But by 1787 his formulations had changed to a broader justification for the liberty of the ruled. While conceding that rights were "in their origin, stipulations between kings and their subjects, abridgements of prerogative in favor of privilege, reservations of rights not surrendered to the prince," he now emphatically noted that this had "no application to constitutions professedly founded upon the power of the people."[57]

Looking back at the entire Revolutionary era, it is clear that the first serious instance in which abstract founding ideals met political reality was in the process of framing the state constitutions. In the intense debates over the meanings of the various liberty-related concepts bandied about by the Revolutionary leaders, competing interests and values visibly surfaced, and popular sovereignty became the main bone of contention. In May 1776, as the New York provincial congress began deliberations on a new constitution, it suddenly faced opposition from the mechanics of the city and county of New York, who questioned the congress's right to pass into law a constitution without a vote of "the inhabitants at large." In the same month, Pittsfield town sent a petition to the Massachusetts General Assembly firmly reminding them that "the people are the fountain of power," and that it was therefore unacceptable that "the Representatives of the people may form Just what fundamental Constitution they please & impose it upon the people." To be valid, they argued, such a document had to be approved by all the freeholders of the state. Some of these tensions were resolved by pragmatic compromise. But their larger and irreversible effect was a marked increase in the political polarization of the public. The struggle with London had tended to unify the Americans, but the debates over the state constitutions were rooted in local power relations and hierarchies of deference, and so tended to separate conservatives from radicals, as well as cause friction between state power and that of the central government. In the latter case, the "sovereign people" became a crucial fiction used by the states to assert local rights against federal authority. Peter Onuf has superbly shown how this tension became a vehicle for many political struggles that ultimately contributed to the democratization of the country. In the two decades after the Revolution—in an unprecedented mobilization of people who had to that time not been politically active or who did not identify with any well-defined ideological orientation—these conflicts helped crystallize the political parties, highlight divisions within the parties and within the social hierarchy, and solidify popular loyalties and popular ideas of what liberty was.[58]

In sum, there were two types of effects once "the people" had been established as one of the key conceptual building blocks of American political discourse. The first, a result of intentional design, was to preserve an order in which the political elite would continue as a ruling class. This was achieved by successfully rallying the population around a name, "the people," and by elites positioning themselves as the preeminent spokesmen for the rights of all. The second effect was the result of a convergence of historical forces, over which the authors of this terminology had little control. The rulers supplied a term through which the social and political world could be perceived and interpreted by ordinary folk, a symbol the folk could identify as their own once it entered the cultural bloodstream as a shared belief. (To appreciate how naming can impose mental structures, one need only recall one change in

FIGURE 3. Allegorical scene of America's unity. Concord stands next to Clio, who is about to write down a historical message, "We are one," delivered by Cupid holding the Constitution. Behind is a temple with thirteen columns and an inscription, "Sacred to Liberty Justice and Peace." Etching by James Trenchard. From the *Columbian Magazine,* Philadelphia, 1788. (Courtesy Library of Congress, Washington, D.C.)

American terminology that occurred over the past few decades: the term "hobo," or "bum," has now shifted to "homeless," which changes its connotation from one of blaming a category of people for their situation to portraying them as victims of ill fate.) To present all political struggles in terms of the interest of the people at large was to create an obligatory conceptual link between them and the rulers, a link that ensured the people's (symbolic) presence in all such public conversation. This presentment of "the people" as the supreme authority was not yet fully modern (in the sense of referring to an egalitarian social order). Yet, to say that it was nothing but a device to mask the exclusion of the many from a full repertoire of liberties would be misleading. It is not infrequently said that "one of the supreme ironies of the Revolution was that the assumption of authority by the 'body of the people' . . . served to oppress as well as to liberate."[59] It would only have been a historically genuine irony had a standard of social equality already been a valid norm at the outset of the Revolution; it was not, and so the case for its "ironic" violation is not a strong one. On the other hand, had the upper class had no stake of its own in putting the authority of the people on a pedestal, the "liberating" changes would have taken place much later.

To say that it was the speaking elite who had created "the people" in American political culture is to take nothing away from the agency of ordinary citizens, who successively utilized this new conceptual tool to their own advantage. Because of the evident ambivalence of this elite contribution, it has been either unnecessarily overemphasized as fully intentional and modern, or neglected as immaterial for progressive change. What is lost in both views is that non-elites enjoyed, at that point, few means of public expression, and had a relatively much weaker awareness of their collective identity than the gentry. It was difficult, if not impossible, for them to impose from below any significant changes in the shared symbolic sphere. The wealthy and educated elites, by contrast, held a near monopoly of communication through the pulpit, print media, or public oratory. It was through a considerable *collaboration* between the two that a good portion of the conceptual universe created by the speaking class also became, by cultural osmosis, the property of ordinary people.

Ultimately, however, the effectiveness of "people rhetoric" emanated not so much from the texts of the leaders as from specific relations of power. Unlike their European counterparts, late colonial American political elites historically emerged without being closely attached to a centralized state. They also developed in the relative simplicity and newness of a provincial social structure, where as a class they practically had no other discrete social group, such as a unified church, an aristocracy, or a grand bourgeoisie, with which to seek collaboration. The only partner they could effectively ally themselves with against England was an abstraction—"the people." In an early modern, still largely traditional, society, this was mostly a marriage of convenience rather than love, one of rhetoric rather than consummation, but its contribution to the fashioning of a new cultural and intellectual habitat for liberty cannot be overstated.

VI. Equality as the Future of America

Without learning, men are incapable of knowing their rights, and where learning is confined to a few people, liberty can be neither equal nor universal.

—Benjamin Rush, 1786

To return to the query posed earlier about the apparent discrepancy between the words and actions of the Revolutionary leaders regarding equal liberty, a careful examination of their writings reveals that they were well aware that equal rights, so central to their rhetoric, were more figurative and symbolic than factual. This, however, was not inconsistent with their larger world view. They made a distinction between the universal principle of including all people in the sphere of liberty, and the deficient realities of contemporary life, which had not yet made its full application feasible. Whenever any specifics about literal inclusion came up, they invariably pointed to some undefined moment in the future when ordinary people would acquire the attributes qualifying them to own all liberties. What is especially telling when one looks at the list of attributes that the common people needed to someday attain to qualify for full liberty is that it was a carbon copy of the qualities traditionally claimed by those who already did possess the full range of liberties. When John Adams contemplated the future effects of the new system of government on the population, he anticipated that a "Constitution like this . . . naturally introduces generally Knowledge into the community and inspires the People with a conscious Dignity. . . . Pride which is introduced by such a Government among the People, makes them brave and enterprising. That ambition which is introduced into every Rank makes them sober, industrious and frugal." David Ramsay went even further in his enthusiasm for the changes to be effected by the new republic, noting with scientific certainty: "I flatter myself that in a few centuries the negroes will lose their black color. I think they are less black in Jersey than in Carolina, their [lips] less thick, their noses flat. The state of society has an influence no less than climate."[60] In his mind, there was a certain cultural rationale for such beliefs; liberty was a privilege, and acceptance of new members to the club of the free was conditional on them becoming *like* those who thought of themselves as normative members.

Faith in progress was not infrequently intertwined with overt acknowledgments of the symbolic nature of liberty. In a 1787 essay in *Worcester Magazine,* the author, reacting to the threats spread by "the lawless hand of faction," calls for more education: "If America would flourish as a republic, she need only attend to the education of its youth. Learning is the *palladium* of her rights—as this flourishes her greatness will encrease." In a republican government, the author continued, where "every citizen has an equal right of election to the chief offices of the state," learning should be "universally diffused." But the caveat that follows is revealing of the nominal nature of this statement, as the authors notes that "those who are busied in the humbler walks of life need not the aid of literature to become proficients in their occupation," and that he "would not insinuate that every man ought to aspire at the chief magistracy [since] this would throw a community into great confusion."[61]

It was quite consistent with such perceptions that the Founding era placed so much emphasis on the education of the masses. Soon after Independence, the future enlightenment of ordinary people became a prominent component of the public conversation on freedom. "Ignorance, darkness and superstition, have ever had their source in oppression and injustice; while truth and science have been constant attendants upon liberty," observed David Griffith, in a sermon he preached at Williamsburg in 1775. The Anti-Federalist "Farmer," who otherwise unequivocally excluded the lowest populace from the current political scene, nevertheless declared solemnly that someday they, too, would become educated in "the principles of free government," and that "light would penetrate, where mental darkness now reigns." David Ramsay saw a "zeal for promoting learning" across America, with various emerging institutions of learning "which must light up such a blaze of knowledge, as cannot fail to burn, and catch, and spread, until it has finally illuminated, with the rays of science, the most distant retreats of ignorance and barbarity." The Massachusetts lawyer, Theophilus Parsons, noted that any future "free permanent constitution" must harmoniously unite the opinion of the "bulk of the people," who do not have "the means of furnishing themselves with proper information," with that of the "men of education and fortune," who possessed virtues that "a liberal education aided by wealth can furnish," and who were capable of determining "what is the true interest of any state." From those who were not "gentlemen of leisure," the latter abilities "are not to be generally expected." "Freemen should always acquire knowledge," wrote Israel Evans. "This is a privilege . . . unknown to slaves; this creates a conscious dignity of his importance as a rational creature, and a free agent. . . . Where there is wisdom, virtue, and liberty, there mankind are men." "If America would flourish as a republick, she need only attend to the education of her youth," noted another author, and so "in a republican government, learning ought to be universally diffused." John Adams, in his *Thoughts on Government,* expressed the belief of many that clear, commonsensical laws might have the same prescriptive effect: through them people would ultimately acquire "good humor, sociability, good manners, and good morals." The reigning assumption was that "if the Youth are carefully educated—if the Principles of Morality are strongly inculcated on the Minds of the People—the End and Design of Government clearly understood, and the Love of our Country the ruling Passion, uncorrupted Men will be chosen for the Representatives of the People."[62] All these authors represented the elite view that in the future the spread of learning would allow for more people from the general "bulk" to become enlightened enough to deserve full political participation. The culture, as was so often the case, was quite content to play the unifier by reconciling discrepancies; it confirmed the current, "natural" political monopoly of the ruling class, and at the same time eagerly promoted a truly open-ended and inclusive vision of an educated society of the future.

To be sure, it was an image that the gentry evidently devised by looking in the mirror. To expect they could have done otherwise would be unrealistic. It was a deeply entrenched eighteenth-century tradition that a gentleman's education prepared him for a public, political role, rather than for a mere professional career. When the young Theodorick Bland, son of a prominent colonial family and a future officer in Washington's army, was sent to Edinburgh in 1761 to study, he saw his sojourn there as, above all, a preparation for

FIGURE 4. Instruction of American Youth. Engraving by John Norman, 1783. A girl representing young Americans meets four muses. The goddess of Peace implores her to pay attention to "Religion, Liberty, and Commerce." Other children are studying the "useful sciences" of Grammar, Astronomy, and Husbandry. Frontispiece, *Boston Magazine,* December 1783. (Courtesy Library of Congress, Washington, D.C.)

some sort of political office, appropriate for his rank, in Virginia. In a letter to his father, he wrote, "At four years, the farthest, by a diligent application, I shall be perfectly qualified to enter on that scene of action which I have been so long preparing for, and which . . . I hope will yield the proposed advantages, honour and happiness to myself, my parents, and country."[63] If educational capital thus privileged those who acquired it, then the envisioned goal of ordinary people equally possessing it in a remote future carried no immediate costs to the position of the elite. This is crucial if we are to understand how they could so eagerly promote it as part of their vision of progress, even if the end of this process, if successful, would spell the demise of their own class.

But in the genteel tradition, education itself, if separated from property, was not a sufficient qualifier for enjoying full liberty. This was why another recurring theme in their vision of the future was the link made between landowning and public virtue. Thus, a future citizenry of educated land-owners was at the heart of Jefferson's dream of a new American society and state, securely based on "the will of the majority" and capable of correcting any errors that might be made in governing. "I think," he wrote in 1787, "our governments will remain virtuous for many centuries; as long as they are chiefly agricultural" and if "the education of the common people will be attended to." Since "very few Men, who have no property, have any Judgment of their own," noted John Adams, "the only possible way of preserving the Ballance of Power on the side of equal Liberty and Public Virtue, is to make the Acquisition of Land easy to every Member of Society . . . so that the Multitude may be possessed of landed Estates." Charles Pinckney believed that of all classes in the United States neither the "commercial men" nor the "professional men," but the "landed interest, the owners and cultivators of the soil . . . are and ought ever to be the governing spring in the system." This agrarian tilt was characteristic for America. While Thomas Paine feared that Americans would become a mercantile society, driven by self-interest instead of republican virtue, in Britain, Adam Smith and David Hume promoted similar ideas, but with distinctly more capitalist overtones. They envisioned future society acquiring political maturity through participation in the mar-ket. Hume believed that "industry, knowledge, and humanity are not advan-tageous in private life alone: They diffuse their beneficial influence on the public, and render the government as great and flourishing as they make individuals happy and prosperous." This would generate sufficient civility and public virtue among common people to make liberty secure for all.[64] The shared core of all these views was that only when, someday, wealth made common folk resemble the gentry, could the former be trusted with more authority.

To grasp why the dual elitist and democratic thrusts within Revolution-ary political discourse did not nullify each other, but moved along parallel trajectories leading to very different outcomes, is to appreciate that the vision emanating from the political class could play not only a conservative but also a dramatically progressive role in shaping the American ethos. At the heart of this vision lay the intensely promoted belief that all classes were now included in one homogeneous concept of "the people." The most consequential novelty was that the gentry, while continuing to assume they were the only legitimate spokesmen for the country's interests, came to identify this role inseparably with "the people," a social entity whose existence they had to assert as undeniable in order to claim the authority of representing it. It was also novel in that the new egalitarian and universalist language, originally devised to symbolically recompense for the unequal distribution of rights and liberties, elevated the general principle of inclusion to unprecedented heights. This was not a mere paternalistic fiction. An imaginary society of equal rights, expressed in liberty poles and Fourth of July festivities, did not have to immediately correspond to an objective reality of constitutionally guaranteed equal rights to be a vital part of advancing the public discourse of liberty toward such rights. Its success lay elsewhere, in opening the doors to a wide assortment of claims—from those of the abolitionists to the feminists—by giving them a lexicon to effectively articulate their interests and ambitions which heretofore had had no readily available, legitimate names.

5

The Sway of Symbolic Power

I. Captains of the Ship of Progress

To see it in our power to make the world happy—to teach mankind the art
of being so—to exhibit, on the theatre of the universe a character hitherto
unknown—and to have, as it were, a new creation entrusted to our hands,
are honors that command reflection, and can neither be too highly estimated, nor too gratefully received.

—Thomas Paine, *America in Crisis,* 1783

BEFORE ASKING WHY THE Founders did not implement the system of
universalist liberty they so enthusiastically embraced in their rhetoric, we
should inquire into what caused their enthusiasm in the first place. What did
the challenge of devising a new, republican state as an empire of liberty mean
to them? When viewed from a cultural rather than political or constitutional
angle, what comes through most clearly is that they found the whole project
exciting not because of its egalitarian implications, but because it bestowed
new authority on them, an authority beyond anything they had experienced
earlier. They had always expected to remain in power, but now their power
was attached to a vision of catholic magnitude. First, they were not just the
leaders of the new nation; they were the leaders of America as the avant-garde
of progress for the entire world. Second, they were unlike members of governing bodies in the past; they were an emanation of a sovereign people, with a
title to rule that seemed greater than any known earlier. Elite privileges
hitherto presented as self-evident in a "naturally" unequal society were now
replaced by privileges derived from being spokesmen for a society of equals,
and from being shepherds of that society toward a historic advancement of its
condition. It was intellectually and politically a glamorous combination.

One of the central attractions of this grand vision of improvement was that it required a qualified elite to implement it. To ensure that people's rights and happiness were founded on solid ground made it imperative that affairs of state be directed by "the Virtuous and impartial part of Mankind." "It is a great Satisfaction to me to be informed," wrote Samuel Adams, "that some of the best Men in the Commonwealth are elected into the principal Departments of Government. Men . . . who by the Wisdom of their Councils and their exemplary Manners, will establish the public Liberty on the Foundation of a Rock." Framing a new polity needed the best knowledge available: "The settlement of American government being as we hope for ages, or even to the end of time, we may well take time for it, use all proper means, and get all possible light." It also required selfless dedication. The power of the British government was based on "the mysterious doctrine of undefinable privileges," and therefore it was "a government where all authority is founded on usurpation," while in America leaders emanating from the people would be less inclined to "stretch their authority."[1]

The rulers would now present themselves modestly, as impartial leaders available to correct the course of the political ship, if the people erred. For instance, when problems arose in the state assemblies, Madison expressed hope that if only "a few enlightened & disinterested members would step forward in each Legislature as advocates for the necessary plans" and counter ill-advised "popular prepossessions," an outcome conducive to larger public good could be achieved. Throughout his life, Samuel Adams put faith in the curative role of his class; he fervently believed that because the principles of republicanism had been established in America "by continued efforts of men of science and virtue, they will extend more and more till the turbulent and destructive spirit of war shall cease" and all people "shall eventually enjoy perfect peace and safety until time shall be no more."[2]

Compared to earlier rationales for elite preeminence, the new design was indeed cosmic. While it partially drew on British traditions of providential destiny and exceptionalism, its grand concepts of progress through Reason were supplied by Enlightenment thought, which gave huge preferentiality to intellectual capital. "It has been the Will of Heaven," observed John Adams, "that We should be thrown into Existence at a Period, when the greatest Philosophers and Lawgivers of Antiquity would have wished to have lived: a Period, when the Coincidence of Circumstances, without Example, has afforded to thirteen Colonies at once an opportunity, of beginning Government anew from the Foundation and building as they choose. How few of the human Race, have ever had an opportunity of choosing a System of Government for themselves and their Children?" His tone was almost millennial when he noted that there was "nothing on this side of the new Jerusalem, of equal importance to Mankind," and that "when a revolution seems to be in the designs of providence," it is "as important as any that ever happened in the affairs of mankind." No wonder Benjamin Rush could say in his speech to Congress: "I am not pleading the Cause of Pennsylvania. . . . No Sir—I am pleading the cause of the Continent—of mankind—of posterity." The conservative New Jersey Whig Elias Boudinot spoke for many of the Patriot leaders when he wrote: "The Contemplation of this Epocha, almost overcomes me at times. It opens a new Scene to Mankind, and I believe is big with inconceivable Effects in the political & I hope in the moral world." Washington, commenting on the end of the War of Independence, observed that the "citizens of America" had now become "actors on a most conspicuous theatre, which seems to be peculiarly designated by Providence for the display of human greatness and felicity." "The foundation of our empire," he noted, "was not laid in the gloomy age of Ignorance and Superstition, but at an Epocha when the rights of mankind were better understood and more clearly defined, than at any former period; the researches of the human mind, after social happiness, have been carried to a great extent, the Treasures of knowledge, acquired through a long succession of years, by the labours of Philosophers, Sages, and Legislatures, are laid open for our use." Seventeen years later, Madison declared that "with the life of Washington is connected a new era in the history of man. He seems to have been called forth by Heaven, as the instrument of establishing principles fundamental in social happiness, and which must and will pervade the civilized world." Jefferson saw America as an empire of liberty stretching into the future, "for our descendents to the thousandth and thousandth generation."[3]

Until the American Revolution, the sphere of liberty within the British world was circumscribed by contests between various power elites: country vs. court, King vs. Parliament, or royal government vs. colonial assemblies. In these rivalries, liberties, mostly understood as the rights of "not being tyrannized," were extracted from those in control by those who had sufficient clout to obtain them. In the new, American vision of progress, political power was justified as a means of improving the condition of people, and of ensuring their rights. This view carried a vital implication that liberty could more usefully be defined as a right to pursue happiness rather than as freedom from constraints by the powers that be. Once this new sense was established, the whole way of thinking about what it meant to be free would be substantially redirected toward the individual. Power struggles would, of course, continue as they always did, but the *language* of such contests would now markedly shift from obtaining privileges to achieving self-fulfillment. By the mid-1780s, when a delegate to the Continental Congress wanted to express his suspicion of strong federal power, he was more likely to attack those who stood for such power for being "not confined to a Government that will best promote Happiness of the people," than simply for craving excessive authority. Roy Porter has aptly identified this broad recognition of all people's aspirations as a language of "nominal inclusion"—that is, as an attempt to symbolically embrace as many people as possible in order to mollify social tensions and to guarantee the stability needed for the gentry to continue its rule.[4] This approach was not merely a political strategy; it was also a part of the changing self-perception of the political class. Just as it was bad taste for a public figure—both in America and Europe—to wear an unpowdered wig, from the 1780s on it was no longer fashionable when speaking in public to exclude ordinary people from the goals of an improved and enlightened society.

The open-ended definition of liberty, and the new role of the political elites as spokesmen for the People and for Progress offered immense new power to the rulers. They would no longer speak for their own class, but for all people. Tench Coxe, reflecting on the unanimous election of George Washington to the presidency in 1789, observed that "Genl. W. will have the united voice of a free people—a transcendent honor infinitely beyond the proudest triumphs of ancient times." They would increasingly self-fashion as agents of historical purpose. As a group exclusive by virtue of education, wealth, and personal independence, they would turn themselves into engineers of human happiness. They metamorphosed from guardians of a traditional right of the upper class to rule into instruments of ushering in the age of liberty, equality, and the advancement of the human condition. "May Heaven inspire the present Rulers with Wisdom & sound Understanding," anticipated Samuel Adams. "In all Probability they will stamp the Character of the People."[5] One might even say that in some ways the authority stemming from this new ideology exceeded the power of hereditary privilege; frequent justifications of the rulers' power based on cosmic forces of history sometimes brought it close to the divine rights of monarchs. It was one of the most consequential cultural shifts brought about by modernity and Enlightenment, albeit with a double edge to be revealed by future history; there would have been neither twentieth-century democracies nor collectivist dictatorships without it (one suspects that as long as governments legitimate their actions this way, the temptation of illiberal policies "in the name of the people" will lurk in the halls of power).

For a Jefferson, a Madison, or an Adams, the new vision could not but be a thrilling project. Classically educated, they readily saw in it a powerful sanction for their own centrality in society, an affirmation of their forward-looking role in history, and a fascinating personal sense of mission. Socially and politically, it allowed them to have the cake and eat it too: while it continued to set them apart from non-elites, it symbolically included them among the idealized entity of "the people." "I suppose," wrote John Adams, "that in this enlightened Age, there will be no dispute, in Speculation, that the Happiness of the People, the great end of Man, is the End of Government, and therefore, that Form of government, which will produce the greatest Quantity of Happiness, is the best."[6]

The will of the people became an authoritative instrument of all political debate. When a dispute in Congress divided delegates, one could always make a statement like "The nefarious Act of State Governments have proceeded not from the will of the people" to obtain instant legitimacy for one's position. This was possible because the culture had already absorbed this criterion as an accepted justification for governing. Anything else would be "complete Tyranny," because "In democracies there should be no single will above the will of the people at large." This in no way meant that the political elite no longer recognized social hierarchy. When a substantial group of members of the North Carolina Assembly opposed the ratification of the Constitution, Madison invoked "the people" to criticize the faction, but he still acknowledged their patrician social station, writing that "the body of the people are better disposed than some of the superior order."[7]

The immediate result of all this was that, at least in political rhetoric, the old line of separation between the elite and non-elite had begun to weaken. But another, long-term effect was also in the offing, and it would have startled the rulers had they been able to foresee it. If the gentry's legitimacy were now to stand entirely on their being spokesmen for the people, the definition of the people had to be modified to include new worth and qualities. The ruling class could not rule by deriving its authority from the mentally "dark" masses, or worse, the "mob." This was why, as the Revolution progressed, references to the collective wisdom of the people and the infallibility of their judgment became increasingly frequent. It was not uncommon to hear references to Americans as a "people more generally enlightened than any other under the Sun." After all, only such a people could be entrusted with liberty, for those "in the habits of owning, instead of being mere tenants in, the Soil, must be proportionably alive to her sacred rights, and quallified to guard them." What was new and peculiar to this process of lionizing the people was that elite writers were crediting them with ennobling attributes so far associated exclusively with the gentry. The possession of virtue was now being extended to the whole population. "What difficulties are unsurmountable," asked Samuel Holten, "when a virtuous and enlightened people are striving for all that is dear & and all that is worth living in this world to enjoy & not ownly for them selves but for posterity." Massachusetts school teacher and politician George Partridge felt "happy in retiring to private life" in 1785, because he was "confident that a Country so enlightened as ours, will not fail to build on this foundation a National Character . . . where Justice, Wisdom and every Principle of Virtue may operate unrestrained." In the words of Philip Freneau:

> So shall our nation, form'd on Virtue's plan,
> Remain the guardian of the Rights of Man,
> A vast republic, famed through every clime,
> Without a king, to see the end of time.[8]

These may have been manifestly idealized representations, serving specific and limited political ends, but they permanently changed the poetics of political language. It moved from an already increased inclusiveness to promoting even more democratizing propositions: that the ultimate locus of authority lay outside the political elite, and that the people have not only an intrinsic worth but also collective wisdom. That this promotion was effective was evidenced by the fact that most arguments raised by various rebels and opponents of the government in the 1780s and 1790s invoked the premise that the rulers' sole title to rule derived from the people, and that they therefore should better exercise their obligation to serve the people.

Until the end of the century, however, the people principle served the rulers far better than it served their critics. If the people could never be wrong, the rulers who stood for them could not be wrong either. Even a pedigreed aristocrat in old England could not summon such a broad-based rationale. This claim became typical of most modern revolutions. Its extreme (at least by eighteenth-century standards) but also exceptionally lucid example was found in Maximilien de Robespierre's 1794 justification of *autocratic* power as essential to preserving the *democratic* achievements of the French Revolution. "A king, a proud senate, a Caesar, a Cromwell," he observed, "oppress and deceive the people in order to attain the end of their perfidious ambition." He and other leaders, in stark contrast, were not there to exercise power, but merely to protect liberty for all. In their service, they were entirely disinterested and answered only to transcendent ideals such as truth, "which is eternal," "eternal justice," and "the destiny of man." They would merely help create a society free of "egotism" and "vice," where people will be "magnanimous, powerful, happy." They were only speaking for the people, and since the people could not be wrong, any opposition would be simply irrational. The new rulers were implementing a cosmic ideal of liberty and happiness, and "all that tends to corrupt it is counter-revolutionary." In this vision, enemies were not merely political opponents; they were enemies of good, and as such, needed to be eliminated by means of "terror, without which virtue is impotent." The only way to eradicate old despotism, as well as "ancient habits" and "imperfections" still regrettably present among some people, was with "the despotism of liberty against tyranny." However harsh, it was a *good* despotism: "the severity of tyrants has barbarity for its principle; that of a republican government is founded on beneficence."[9] This pattern of justification by the people also functioned in Revolutionary America, but because the issue there, unlike in France, was preserving an existing elite instead of elevating a new one, its application was much less militant, and far more concerned with order and practical governance than with imposing virtue and happiness by force. Robespierre's text is explicitly belligerent, and even bears a ghastly resemblance to the language of twentieth-century dictatorships, while Thomas Jefferson's Declaration of Independence and Thomas

Paine's *Common Sense* are relatively unthreatening and emphasize confidence and optimism in American society's ability to carry out the authors' revolutionary vision. This was no small contribution to future American democracy, because forced happiness, just like forced unity, has been the province of all modern despotisms.

Another feature of contemporary culture that should be taken into account when considering how a dramatically egalitarian language, with a sovereign and free people at its center, could initially boost, instead of reducing, the privileges of the rulers, is the monopoly of public communication held by the speaking elite. The ability to assign meaning to these new concepts, and to apply them to people's experiences—in forums such as churches and political gatherings as well as in print—gave them a distinct advantage (much as today an editor or television anchor, speaking to millions, can name an event in one way and not another, and thus exercise immense power by attaching a particular meaning to that event). In contrast, the ability of ordinary people to effectively offer competing interpretations of liberty on the larger public stage was still severely constrained, and in the very few major cases when they did attempt to do so, as in Shays's and the Whiskey Rebellions, the authors were promptly branded as usurpers—that is, as illegitimate interpreters of ideas.

One of the ways restrictive meanings were created was through certain styles of public speech, accessible only to educated elites, which advantaged their explanations of reality. Elevated, non-colloquial forms of speech had long functioned as symbols of authority. The speaking elites of the Revolutionary era took full advantage of this fact, even as they tried to make political language more accessible. For instance, the following words by John Quincy Adams could not be confused by the public with a text produced by a shoemaker or a blacksmith. Speaking of the origins of American Independence, Adams observed: "The field is extensive: it is fruitful: but the copious treasures of its fragrance have already been gathered by the hands of genius: and there now remains for the gleaning of mental indigence; nought but the thinly scattered sweets which have escaped the vigilance of their industry." When on the Fourth of July, 1783, Dr. Joseph Warren, brother of General James Warren, spoke of liberty at a Massachusetts gathering, his style unmistakably signaled authority: "Transported from a distant clime less friendly to its nature, you have planted here the stately tree of Liberty, and lived to see it flourish. . . . Go, search the vaults where lay enshrined the relics of your martyred fellow-citizens, and from their dust receive a lesson, on the value of your freedom!" The Reverend Jacob Duché, chaplain to the Continental Congress, in his opening prayer to Congress in 1774, spoke of the rebellious American colonies when he called out: "Take them therefore, Heavenly father, under thy nurturing care: give them wisdom in council, valour in the field. Defeat the malicious designs of our cruel adversaries. Convince them of the unrighteousness of their cause. And if they persist in their sanguinary purposes, O! let the voice of thy unerring justice sounding in their hearts constrain them to drop the weapons of war from their ennerved hands in the day of battle." John Francis Mercer assured the public in 1783 that although there were divisions in America, "there is still a light, although it glimmers at a distance.... The cause ... can never be deserted or betrayed, not the lustre of our rising Empire tarnished, nor its glory pass away like the blazing meteor that streams for a moment through the sky, and quickly vanishes in endless night. No! it shall be fixed as a constellation, to give light to revolving ages."[10]

Few would have associated these long-winded texts with exchanges among ordinary "mechanics." Lofty style—quite apart from any political substance it contained—communicated the speaker's prominence. Those who "owned" this style held an instrument of considerable power, for such a manner was unavailable to ordinary people. Just as the elite culture censured a farm worker for purchasing home furnishings above his rank, it would ridicule a warehouse laborer who used an exalted oratorical style that would have been deemed appropriate on the floor of the state assembly. One might say that, in such cases, form itself, aside from the content, carried meaning: it announced that the speaker was already entitled to dominance, and that his interpretation was privileged. When in 1786 Massachusetts governor James Bowdoin called upon the people of the state to oppose farmers demanding tax relief, his text was soaring in its historical, even cosmic inferences; he expressed hope in the citizens' "faith, which in the sight of GOD and the work they pledged to one another and to the people of the United States, when they adopted the present Constitution of Government—as they would not disappoint the hopes, and thereby become contemptible in the eyes of other nations, in the view of whom they have risen to glory and empire."[11] The style, as much as the arguments, communicated his authority.

All this allows us to better understand why the Founders' dazzling vision of progress did not have to be—as is sometimes assumed—a fundamental concession to some preexisting principle of equal access to liberty. This vision would preserve, not compromise, their prominent rank within the social order. The new rhetoric carried certain risks to that order, but the power of new authority that it gave them neutralized most worries, and enhanced the leaders' enormous confidence in the wisdom of their cause:

> Thus we shall see, and triumph in the Sight,
> While Malice frets and fumes, and gnaws her Chains,
> AMERICA shall blast her fiercest Foes,
> Shall brave the dismal Shocks of Bloody War
> And in unrivall'd Pomp resplendent rise,
> And shine sole Empress of the WESTERN WORLD.[12]

Without this confidence, the social inclusiveness of the Revolutionary narrative would have been much more modest. It took a self-interested elite, animated by its new authority and its new mission in history, to promote on such a grand scale an egalitarian parlance of freedom that transcended class boundaries. Without tangible dividends they would not have had the motivation to democratize public political conversation to the extent they did. It would have been impossible for non-elites alone to do so. It was not just that they lacked sufficient public voice; more importantly, their world views were rooted in the same culture that still took many inequalities for granted. The elite very much expected this, and until the mid-1780s did not worry too much about rising political consciousness among ordinary people. There was little in their buoyant pronouncements to suggest the disillusionment that came at the end of the century, when increasing political activity involving the non-elites began to dent the position of the privileged.

II. *The Meaning of Representation*

The people of a free state have a right to expect from those whom they have honoured with the direction of their public concerns, a faithful and unremitting attention to these concerns. He who accepts a public trust, pledges himself, his sacred honour, and by his official oath appeals to his God, that with all good fidelity, and to the utmost of his capacity he will discharge this trust.

—Samuel Cooper, *A Sermon,* 1780

THE FACT THAT PROMINENT political texts of the era contained copious references to genuine, as opposed to virtual, representation of the American colonists (not to be confused with the term "representation" used elsewhere in this book to denote a symbolic portrayal) has sometimes led us to believe that the authors understood it in a way more modern than was the case.

When Americans raised the issue of their lack of delegates in Westminster, Prime Minister George Grenville responded with genuine surprise, emphasizing that the authority on which the Stamp Act was founded was soundly based on virtual representation. He observed that fewer than 5 percent of the people in England had ever been directly represented (i.e., were electors), and that the colonies had thus far approved of this system.[13] He was right; for the colonists, the issue was mostly tactical, and after independence the political elite almost immediately assumed a role closely resembling that of virtual representatives of "the people." It was not likely that the colonial authors of demands for direct representation actually wished to travel across the Atlantic for each session of the English Parliament. And yet, unlike Grenville, who looked back into history for the sources and validity of this idea, the American political class had placed it in a new context by stressing equality, and by defining "representatives" as deriving authority from a sovereign people.

Does this mean that once Americans won independence these progressive concepts turned out to be merely instrumental, and were abandoned in favor of "returning" to traditional rule by elites? Was Revolutionary ideology betrayed when only a few years after the Constitution many of the framers openly expressed their conviction that a representative recruited from their class would—on account of superior virtue and education—better articulate the will of the people than the people themselves? Some historians have viewed this as an outright reversal, where the "concept of representation ceased to be a revolutionary engine with a single thrust" and was "returned" to its old, elitist meaning. The result was that "American representative government . . . would exclude the represented from governance."[14] When we look more closely at the contemporary understanding of political representation, however, it does not seem likely that such a "return" to elitist meaning could have occurred—because the ship had never left the harbor. Nor was it technically possible to "exclude" some of the represented; they had not been included before, and most were not going to be for a very long time.

For the American political class, whether one was a Federalist or an Anti-Federalist, the original importance of representation in assemblies derived not so much from elections and responsibility before constituents, but from the right of privilege. A belief that they possessed a great degree of autonomy as representatives cannot realistically be labeled reactionary just because it continued beyond the Revolution. For instance, it was thoroughly consistent with such assumptions to devise the new constitutional system entirely without the people. As Edward Carrington noted: "The debates and proceedings of the Convention are kept in profound secrecy. Opinions of the probable result of their deliberations can only be formed from the prevailing impressions of men of reflection and understanding." "Everything was covered with the veil of secrecy," marveled William Pierce. Those who tend to stress the modernity of the writers of the Constitution and claim that they reached to the "people themselves" in order to "assure the legacy of freedom" for all, sometimes gloss over the significance of the fact that constitutional proceedings took the form of essentially private meetings, not open to the public. These were usually limited to about forty gentlemen, and conducted much like the colonial assemblies, the members of which rarely sought public opinion, kept debates closed, did not publish them in newspapers, and did not, as a rule, feel themselves to be primarily in the role of democratically mandated agents of voters. On the contrary, once elected—as William Blackstone explained—delegates to parliaments held "uncontrolable authority," and such an assembly was "the place where that absolute despotic power which must reside in all governments somewhere, is intrusted by the constitution."[15]

Yet, the sovereignty of the delegates to which he referred was not viewed as in any way tyrannical. Quite the opposite; it was intended to be a guarantee against the potential despotism of the monarch, a trade-off to ensure liberty for the people, much as William Ball argued on the eve of the trial of Charles I in London, that "the Law is more powerful than the King" and "the whole body of the people are more powerful than the law" but in practice the Parliament that represented them was sovereign. This understanding was echoed in Noah Webster's arguments against a bill of rights in 1787, when he asserted that it was unnecessary, because in America "the supreme power *is the people in their Representatives*" and "in our governments, there is no power of legislation, independent of the people; no power that has an interest detached from that of the public." From this premise he drew a conclusion that "the collective body of Representatives is the collective sense and authority of the people, and that "it can be proved that the reservation of any power in the hands of the people, may at times interfere with the power of the Legislature to consult the public interest." Clearly, the concept of the rulers and the ruled was still an organic one: "The liberty of the people does not rest on any reservation of power in their hands aside their Legislature; it rests singly on the principle, a union of interests between the governors and the governed."[16]

Madison made it plain that the considerations of representatives chosen from among the educated elite would be "more consonant with the public good than if pronounced by the people themselves," because the delegates' "wisdom may best discern the true interest of their country." Other leaders literally worried about the harmful "dependence which the representatives feel upon their immediate constituents," because it might confuse the representatives' judgment of what is best for the public. The rise of Anti-Federalist voices generated rhetoric more egalitarian than ever before, but even they saw proper representation possible only if the system ensured that the representatives were not "common people." One might say that once the political class framed themselves as a substitute for the people, they felt even more entitled than before to substitute their view of the world for that of the people. There was nothing exceptional in this outlook. It was common among early modern European and British upper classes to think of the political nation as extending from the elite—who represented it, for all practical purposes. Enlightenment references to the "public," a concept less abstract than the "people," typically implied that membership in this group was circumscribed by knowledge, reason, appreciation of letters, taste, the sublime, and the ability to see the universal over the parochial. "Patriotism is a virtue which a few men possess," noted Meriwether Smith in a letter to the *Pennsylvania Packet*, "and a real patriot, of distinguished abilities to serve his country, is a jewel of inestimable value."[17]

Jefferson, who saw the goal of any new electoral system as getting "wise men chosen," was firm in his conviction that at least the delegates to the Senate should be "perfectly independent of their electors," and preferably chosen for nine years or for a lifetime, or else they might be "currying favor with the electors, and consequently dependent on them." This belief only grew among the political class as the century approached its end. Noah Webster noted that the people as a sovereign were mainly a theoretical construct; by electing their "agents and substitutes," they "delegate away their own power to them" and therefore can no longer exercise it. For the same reason, he saw the universal right of suffrage as "absurd," because it would only multiply "the number of corruptible electors" who lacked quality, easily succumbed to demagogues, and thus endangered liberty. In a manner typical for his age, he used a gendered comparison to make his point. "The people," he noted, "like artless females, are liable to be seduced, not by the men they hate or suspect, but by those they love." Theodore Sedgwick, reflecting on his retirement from public life, emphasized that what ultimately mattered to him was only the esteem of other gentlemen delegates in the Continental Congress: "Vulgar applause was never to me a cause for exultation, and I think that I am not degraded in the opinion of the respectable, & virtuous." This meaning of representation had a long tradition, perhaps most famously articulated by Thomas Hobbes, who wrote that the only way to create a government that could effectively provide people with security was for them to "confer all their Power and Strength upon one Man, or upon one Assembly of Men, that may reduce all their Wills, by plurality of Voices, into one Will . . . and therein to submit their Wills, every one to his Will, and their Judgments to his Judgment."[18]

Such historically ingrained elitism was only minimally disturbed by the Revolution. And yet, the very debate epitomized by Webster and others provides a glimpse of a critical cultural change brewing in the relations between the elites and ordinary people. As we have seen, in the post-Revolutionary reality both elite and non-elite increasingly needed each other in order to construct and affirm their existence as subjects in the public arena. David Ramsay captured this well when he observed that "it is the great happiness of America, that her independent constitutions were agreed upon by common consent, at the time when her leading men needed the utmost support of the multitude, and therefore could have no other object in view, but the formation of such constitutions as would best suit the people at large." Although the "common consent" was plainly far from common, "taking the sense of the people by representatives" in one way or another was fast becoming mandatory. The elites were now credibly anointed as the symbolic embodiment of all society. As delegated guardians of freedom, they gained power and autonomy that was much larger than that of the people who voted them in. These developments tied the political fate of the elites to the non-elites as never before. For the former, their new public identity now required that they pay keener attention to ordinary Americans, not only through lip service, but also through more consideration given to their expectations and interests. In order to even nominally include the people's sentiments, they had to learn more about ordinary folk, and to understand better their priorities and their world views. The new and enlightened way of maintaining authority was to make an effort to at least symbolically involve common people in political life. As John Adams advised Princeton lawyer Jonathan Dickinson Sergeant: "Gentlemen cannot expect the Confidence of the common People if they treat them ill, or refuse haughtily to comply with some of their favorite Notions which may often be most obligingly done, without the least deviation from Honour and Virtue." Appealing to constituents was, of course, not entirely new. Late-colonial elites had grown quite expert in presenting themselves as representatives of the people. Even though "electioneering" was ostensibly below their dignity, most made certain they were known to the local freemen (to which end some candidates appeared at the local church or sent out letters announcing their willingness to serve), and they made sure they were personally present at election time. In Virginia, the candidates traditionally financed liquor and other picnic treats, at times even music, for the voters on election day. This hospitality was expected to be generous because liberality indicated personal independence, a prerequisite of political virtue that qualified candidates to properly represent their electorate. Whatever the methods used, acceptability to the voters was not just a theoretical requirement. In British America, a wholly detached, aristocratic stance toward ordinary people was not a good option for those aspiring to elected office.[19]

One of the indications of accelerated attempts to more effectively appeal to the electorate was the peculiar shift in political language after 1776 to a more down-to-earth phrasing, routine substitution of the speaking subject by a highly idealized people, the presentation of elite-oriented goals as fundamentally desirable for all citizens, an increasing avoidance of outright statements that such goals were devised by the "better sort," and efforts to disconnect these goals from the elite by references to the Public Interest, Reason, or the Creator. After the Declaration of Independence was signed, delegates referred to it not as *their* decision, but as "the universal demand of the people, justly exasperated by the obstinate perseverance of the Crown in its tyrannical and destructive measures, and [that] the Congress were very unanimous in complying with that demand." When the Georgia delegates to Congress sent a letter of praise to General Nathaniel Greene for his military achievements, they wrote "in the name of the people of that State," and offered "grateful and sincere thanks," assuring him that "it is the constant theme of all orders and ranks of men this way." Similarly, Rhode Island representative Henry Marchant informed Governor William Greene that he "communicated to Congress the spirited Measures which continue to be exerted by the Legislature, and by all ranks and Degrees of the good People of the State I have the Honor to represent."[20] These now obligatory references to "the people" by their delegates in government did more than just legitimize the delegates. They also served to ensure a conspicuous *presence* of the people as a political entity on the public stage. Such presence could not have been gained unless there existed representatives who were perceived to be the people's public voice.[21] The representatives of the people, in order to be whom they claimed they were, had to convince the public mind that both the people and the rights being represented existed.

It was a vital step in moving away from a still-dominant holistic understanding of society, a step that was a prerequisite for liberty to be extended to new sectors of the population. The effects of this change did not begin to more fully materialize until the end of the eighteenth century. As Richard Primus has compellingly shown, the whole Revolutionary argument against England was still expressed in terms of collective, rather than individual, rights. Governments, colonies, and various social groups, but not individuals, were viewed as collective bearers of liberty. The "people" thus consisted of those who were only virtually represented, those who actually voted, and those who did the representing. It was essential for a free government to have "a full and equal representation of the people in the legislature," wrote the Federal Farmer in 1787, but this representation "should be so regulated that every order of men in the community, according to the common course of elections, can have a share in it—in order to allow professional men, merchants, traders, farmers, mechanics, etc. to bring a just proportion of their best informed men respectively into the legislature." All these communities were seen as having a right to self-government, but this did not mean that every member of such a community had the same right to participate in governing. Possessing liberty by the people was not understood as possessing actual power. Noah Webster, commenting on the sovereign power of the people, bemoaned that the English language, unlike Latin, did not "distinguish the *populus* from the *plebs;* the free citizens who have not the privilege of suffrage," and insisted that it would have been more precise to say that power was only "*derived from* the people."[22]

It was not just an American dilemma. Montesquieu worried that "the power of the people" could be confused with "the liberty of the people." People's liberty consisted only of the right to do what the laws permitted; if all people had broad power to do things, including what the law prohibited, none would possess liberty. This distinction provides a crucial glimpse into the inherent inequality programmed into the meaning of eighteenth-century liberty. The individual was expected to be subservient to the larger public good, presented as the collective will of the people. But since the people could not collectively speak, their will was expressed by those who were qualified to do so. Samuel Johnson was fairly typical in his belief that this was the only system that made liberty possible at all: it was a natural state of things that "the business of the publick must be done by delegation. The choice of delegates is made by a select number, and those who are not electors stand idle and helpless spectators of the commonweal."[23] It was this duality of Enlightenment liberty that made it possible for the elites to symbolically substitute themselves for the people, while retaining their own, exclusive liberties. Those today who see the coexistence of these two forces as a paradox need to recognize that for such coexistence to have been questioned then, the Johnsonian duality would have to have been rejected first, something that did not happen until the waning years of the century. A bit of epistemological humility would be helpful in appreciating this; after all, our own references to "universal human rights" today are often made with little awareness that we are bringing up a product of Western history and culture, which in many ways (equal rights for women, full religious tolerance) is incongruent with "universal" values held by other cultures with other histories standing behind them.

The larger point is that, at the time, there was no inherent contradiction in this duality. As Emmanuel Le Roy Ladurie has shown, hierarchic societies divided and separated people, but they invariably did so in the name of interdependence and unity of the whole. In 1787, a Boston author observed: "Every state . . . contains three classes of men. Those who have small estates in land, and little money; those who have large estates in one, or both of these; and those who depend for their support, upon salaries, or wages, given for personal service." The object of good government, he argued, was to allow for an appropriate "influence" of both the independent and the dependent classes of people, but not reduce the distance between classes. In the words of another writer, the idea was that "common people should have a part and share of influence," a set of liberties appropriate to their rank but not encroaching on the fuller liberties of the privileged. For instance, to "hold open to them the offices of senators, judges, and offices to fill which expensive education is required, cannot answer any valuable purposes for them; they are not in a situation to be brought forward and to fill these offices." On the eve of Independence, Edmund Pendleton, the president of Virginia's Committee on Safety, was unyielding in the belief that a "democracy, considered as *referring determinations,* either legislative or executive, TO THE PEOPLE AT LARGE, is the worst form (of government) imaginable." He went on: "Of all others, I own, I prefer the true English constitution, which consists of a proper combination of the principles of honor, virtue, and fear." A New York author similarly asserted that "men of good education and deep reflection, only, are judges of the form of government," and he expressed apprehension that, in order to obtain the political support of non-elites, overly ambitious gentlemen would appeal to "the passions and prejudices of the less discerning classes of citizens and yeomanry," thus deceiving the "unthinking" into believing that their "liberty is invaded," and inviting "anarchy and wild uproar." These views of society were so organic that it should not surprise that they naturally lent themselves to invocations of religious sanction. Jonathan Edwards Jr. told potential voters that, "Of all forms of government a republic most essentially requires virtue," and therefore, "By the same reasons by which you are obligated to choose the Lord for your God, you are obligated to seek out and by your suffrages to promote to legislative authority, such as are of the same character"—that is, "to promote the wisest and the best."[24]

The ideal was a "system of Government, that sending its equitable Energy thro all Ranks & Classes of Men, defends the poor from the rich, the weak from the powerful, the industrious from the rapacious, the peaceable from the violent, Tenants from the Lords, and all from their Superiors." If such a balance were not achieved, and "if the representation be so formed as to give one or more of the natural classes of men in society an undue ascendancy over the others," worried an Anti-Federalist author, "the former will gradually become masters and the latter slaves." He added, "It is the first of all among the political balances to preserve in its proper station each of these classes."[25]

Although the concept of natural law is usually viewed in historiography as progressive in its implied egalitarianism, it could serve traditional as much as modern ends. It was usually linked to the divine source of nature, with its moralism consistently justifying an "appropriate" social hierarchy of ranks as well as an unequal scope of freedoms befitting each rank. We tend to focus on rights as such, but contemporaries emphasized duties as inseparable from rights, with the premise that the two had to be balanced. It was this stress on obligations that made rights an aspect of one's ties to society and its collective good and not just an individual entitlement. It was a belief rooted in Christian morality; the Princeton lectures of John Witherspoon, for instance, used the concept of duty to discourage believers from confusing God's purpose with their own, individual one.[26]

Although the Founders lived on the brink of modernity, they still largely viewed the nature of the people in collectivist rather than individualistic terms, and the role of the government as an articulator of the will of the people through its superior knowledge and not through direct delegation. This dovetailed well with the dual character of liberty as a symbolic construction and a concrete social relation; representatives, once elected in the name of *nominally* sovereign people, would *practically* exercise sovereign power. For us to downplay this inherent elitism is to risk misreading some of the Revolutionary texts. For instance, even if we were to take Richard Bland's call for rights that would apply, "without respect to the dignity of the persons concerned," as a broader social statement and not just as a call for equality between colonial and metropolitan leaders, we would still need to recognize that such broad equality at the time implied, as Jack P. Greene has insightfully observed, the "equivalence only of those who were entitled to similar rights."[27] Only in the last decade of the eighteenth century did this understanding begin to include more stress on the rulers' role in shielding individuals from encroachments on their liberties, a perspective that gradually led to the de-collectivization of the notion of "the people."

The notions of representation and legislative sovereignty offered the Patriot leaders a coherent framework for confirming their role as a new type of ruler and for preserving liberty as they defined it. Within a short time, however, they saw their plan undermined by the emergence of party factions. Their deep disappointment at this development suggests that their idea of representation was not yet a modern one. It was instead tied to an earlier notion of the gentry functioning as spokesmen for all of their countrymen, a concept rooted in the English and the Glorious Revolutions, with their accompanying contests between the Crown and the Parliament over the King's arbitrary powers. The English Parliament came to portray itself as a bulwark—by virtue of being a representative body—to the violations of rights by the monarch. This tradition was particularly dear to the American elites steeped in their longtime rivalry between colonial assemblies and royal power.[28]

This rather conventional position on representation was not only not at odds with their Revolutionary ideology, but it meshed exceptionally well with their sweeping vision of themselves as the vanguard of enlightenment. It is therefore important that we not consider this view as simply a cloak, consciously worn to cover naked domination. Like their English predecessors of the preceding century, post-Independence delegates believed they were autonomous, and did not feel closely bound by the specific agendas of those they represented. There is no reason to believe that within a few years the late-colonial elite would have eradicated this deeply ingrained belief from their world view. To think they could do so would be not only to assume that they had much more control over culture than was likely, but also that they were willing to relinquish their new role as leaders of humanity's progress.

III. Claims of Liberty Claim Their Authors

Ye men of SENSE and VIRTUE—Ye ADVOCATES for American Liberty, rouse up and espouse the cause of Humanity and general Liberty. Bear a testimony against the vice which degrades human nature, and dissolves that universal tie of benevolence which should connect all the children of men together in one great Family.—The plant of liberty is of so tender a Nature, that it cannot thrive long in the neighborhood of slavery.

—Benjamin Rush, *An Address to the Inhabitants of the British Settlements in America upon Slave-Keeping,* 1773

WE ARE OFTEN TEMPTED to view the lofty statements about virtue and freedom made by Revolutionary leaders with the knowledge of hindsight—as cases of self-fashioning or political propaganda that should be separated from social realities. We would be wrong to make such a separation. Although their liberty talk was certainly not a mirror reflection of the factual state of things, there did exist one peculiar sphere where facts and behavior came to reflect the talk. It was in the area of cultural feedback, where certain symbolic claims made by the speaking class appropriated the speakers, compelling them to act in ways that reflected these claims. For instance, they may have invented "the people" as an abstract entity, but once this notion successfully impressed itself upon the collective mind, they found themselves under no small pressure to demonstrate that the virtues which they claimed entitled them to rule in the name of the people were indeed authentic. They had identified with these virtues as a class long before the Revolution, but now this identity became part of the new political ideology. Attributes such as honor, disinterestedness, and public virtue were no longer just indicators of refinement mostly confined to gentry circles, but became traits that the much larger stage of public opinion expected them to demonstrate. We are all familiar with Washington's uncommon care not to say or do anything that might blemish his virtuous image among the people. Claims to such upright qualities thus bound the claimers, often obliging them to live up to their self-ascribed qualities in practice, both before the audience of their peers and before a broader public. The familiar question of why their actions were at odds with their words has been ubiquitous, but it is also worth asking to what extent these principles claimed the leaders themselves, affecting their behavior and decisions.

This influence of cultural identity on politics has not always been well understood. For some scholars, the Revolutionaries' claims of "virtue" were not only historically meaningless but even "too disgusting for detailed discussion," because they came from the mouths of slaveholders, speculators, and power-seekers. Authors influenced by the political economy of class have tended to see such claims as mere rationalizations, secondary to the real interests of power and therefore without possible significance as a force toward any progressive end. There are two problems with this approach. The first is that America was not a Panglossian paradise and as we examine early modern liberty we can and should study only the real (often not pretty) world, not the one wished for. The second is that power-seekers rarely sought pure power as such; rather, they desired that which power bestowed—a unique identity and a privileged position in society. Virtue made sense for those who claimed it because it made sense of who they were. What should interest us is the fact that once they became identifiable on the public stage through such attributes, they also became *dependent* on a continued attachment to these characteristics, and on cultivating and defending them as their distinctive features. The cult of disinterestedness may serve as an example. Once developed as a peculiar quality of the new, republican political class, it became much more than a rhetorical device. In many instances it compellingly *obliged* them to play the part, or risk ostracism and disgrace for not living up to the consecrated norms. Attributes appropriated their owners. For instance, Thomas Paine, who otherwise questioned many premises of the old social order, thought it immensely important that all his political activities were seen as impartial, and he took pains to let the world know that he was not merely serving his personal agenda. "If, in the course of more than seven years," he wrote in 1783, "I have rendered her [America] any service, I have likewise added something to the reputation of literature, by freely and disinterestedly employing it in the great cause of mankind, and showing that there may be genius without prostitution."[29]

Revolutionary stress on the superiority of a meritorious ruling class brought the virtue of selflessness to the forefront. Merit combined with selflessness was to be the guarantee that the people and their interests would be included in all political conversation. This emphasis on the people was novel, but there already existed certain traditions of such inclusion in the paternalistic culture of the British gentry, which the provincial elite drew upon. An early modern English gentleman would not duel with a peasant (because the latter was not his equal), but he was expected to respect the rule of good manners which required that in dealings with common people he demonstrate nominal equality ("Always talk to your carriage driver politely") and "condescend" to treat them civilly as equals. Only the despised social upstart would feel the urge to overtly demonstrate his superiority over the "lesser sort," something that would only reveal his parvenu origins. For instance, one author recounted with approbation that when Virginia governor Sir William Gooch was criticized for the inappropriateness of his returning the salutation of a bondsman, he responded, "I should be very sorry that a slave should be more polite than myself." Count Rochambeau was admired by the American gentry because of his "polite unaffected easy manner of address, the kindness and abundance of good nature, with which he treats all ranks and orders of men." This did not imply social equality, but was expected as "honorable" behavior, indicative of the generosity and benevolence of the upper ranks. This context of the "condescension" and "obligations" of the elites helps us understand better the practice of nominal inclusion in late eighteenth-century America. As Solomon Stoddard, the famed minister of the church at Northampton, Massachusetts, explained, some must be more free to act than others in order for freedom to even exist in a society: "God hath appointed divers Orders of men . . . that in the Common-wealth, some should be Rulers, and others Ruled. It is agreeable to the light of nature that it be so: if there were an equality all things would run into confusion: if there were none to Govern, there would be many to Tyrannize. If there were no Order among them, there would quickly be intolerable disorder." Common people should reject "disobedience" and submit to "the sentences of rulers." But by the same token, the better sort had grave obligations to the common people: "Good carriages in men of publick place, do stir up others to imitation; their good carriages make others fear to carry badly." They must be "honourable," for only then is it "an honour to a people to have choice men for Magistrates and for Ministers."[30]

Once the virtue of disinterestedness was elevated to a standard in republican political culture, the need to publicly demonstrate it began to affect the behavior and decisions of prominent figures more than before. In 1775, when the eyes of the colonies were focused on Massachusetts, Samuel Adams wrote to Elbridge Gerry: "It behooves our friends, therefore, to be very circumspect, and in all their public conduct to convince the world, that they are influenced not by partial or private motives, but altogether with a view of promoting public welfare." For many Americans, the ultimate embodiment of this particular virtue was George Washington. As John Adams observed: "There is something charming to me in the conduct of Washington, a gentleman of one of the first fortunes upon the continent, leaving his delicious retirement, his family and friends, sacrificing his ease, and hazarding all in the cause of his country! His views are noble and disinterested." To betray in a major political debate a conspicuously narrow, petty interest would have been embarrassing. The republican elite viewed Shays's Rebellion with much hostility, but once it was over, they pardoned the accused and reinstated their citizenship fairly quickly. This leniency elicited much self-applause as the triumph of selflessness over factionalism. The point to note is that they acted upon their claimed qualities. Henry Laurens solemnly explained to the Marquis de Lafayette that he would gladly see "speculators" and other "mischievous Knaves" punished, but he would deal gently with "those whose errors are of the head, whose general tone speaks the public good. And at all hazards & expences I will to the utmost of my abilities Support & defend the disinterested patriot—at the same time most sedulously avoid every whisper which may tend to fan the flame of party." A 1776 pamphlet contained the following "American Patriots Prayer" that well pinpoints this moral requirement of political conduct:

> Let me not Faction's partial hate
> Pursue to *this Land's* woe;
> Nor grasp the thunder of the state,
> To wound a private foe.

Such claims were not a mere Potemkin village masking the elite's power, but in many ways became genuine articles of their selfhood. To be who they were they had to firmly believe in their professed virtues, and to respect the constraints that came with them, lest they undermined the foundations of their identity. To be a member of the ruling class was to believe one should serve as model citizen, "in duty bound to contribute to the safety and good of the whole, and when subject is of such importance as the liberty and happiness of a country, every inferior consideration, as well as the inconvenience of a few individuals, must give place to it." Without such rules of honor, the exclusiveness of their identity could not be properly secured. For those involved on the political stage, it was not enough to proclaim these values; the pressure of peer expectations often demanded that they act upon them. Elbridge Gerry found himself in such a situation. He opposed the Constitution, and so when he reluctantly agreed to be elected to Congress, he explained that his private views had to take second place to national interest: "I am and always was a Federalist, but not in their sense of the term. I feel bound by honour to support a system that has been ratified by a majority of my fellow citizens; to oppose it would sow the seeds of civil war, and to lay a foundation of military tyranny." Similarly, he put the public good over his own objections to the constitutional plan proposed for Massachusetts when he declared that he personally disagreed with it, "but the convention being of a different opinion, I acquiesced in it, being fully convinced, that to preserve the union, an efficient government was indispensably necessary."[31]

When disinterestedness combined with the veneration for liberty, it could even motivate some to defy the existing social order (which privileged those who were speaking out) and confront otherwise widely accepted injustices. Voices against slavery were perhaps the best examples; their most notable feature was that they called for enlarging the meaning of Revolutionary liberty. "Extend the privileges we enjoy," wrote Benjamin Rush, "to every human creature born amongst us, and let not the Journals of our Assemblies be disgraced with the records of laws, which allow exclusive privileges to men of one color in preference to another." Stephen Hopkins, a statesman from Rhode Island and a signer of the Declaration of Independence, invoked its principles to condemn slavery and to point out that "the Africans, and the blacks in servitude among us, were really as much included in these assertions as ourselves; and their right, *unalienable right* to liberty, and to procure and possess property, is as much asserted as ours. . . . And if we have not allowed them to enjoy these unalienable rights . . . we are guilty of a ridiculous wicked contradiction and inconsistence." David Rice, a delegate to the Kentucky constitutional convention, similarly urged his colleagues to do away with what he saw as an intolerable "inconsistency" in American government, in which a slave "is declared by the united voice of America, to be by nature free, and entitled to the privilege of acquiring and enjoying property; and yet by laws past and enforced in these states, retained in slavery, and dispossessed of all property and capacity of acquiring any." "By the immutable laws of nature *all men* are entitled to life and liberty," wrote New Jersey's David Cooper, recalling the Declaration of Independence, and pointing out that "We need not now turn over the libraries of Europe for authorities to prove that blacks are born equally free with whites; it is declared and recorded as the sense of America." St. George Tucker, a prominent member of the Virginia aristocracy, saw bitter irony in that, "whilst we were offering up vows at the shrine of Liberty, and sacrificing hecatombs upon her altars; whilst we swore irreconcilable hostility to her enemies . . . we were imposing upon our fellowmen, who differ in complexion from us, a *slavery* ten thousand times more cruel than the utmost extremity of those grievances and oppressions, of which we complained." Such calls encouraged others to raise new demands for rights and liberties. The black mathematician and astronomer Benjamin Banneker wrote to Secretary of State Thomas Jefferson: "Sir, suffer me to recall to your mind that time, in which the arms and tyranny of the British crown were exerted, with every powerful effort, in order to reduce you to a state of servitude. . . . This, Sir, was a time when you clearly saw into the injustice of slavery, and in which you had just apprehensions of the horrors of its condition." There were also calls demanding voting rights for women. Virginia's Richard Henry Lee believed that the principle of representation ought to be extended to embrace widows with property, and a New Jersey author, writing in the *New-York Journal* in 1776, concluded that taxpaying widows were subsumed under the Revolutionary concepts of suffrage.[32] What linked these voices was that they took the Revolutionary vocabulary of freedom and pushed it beyond its dominant meanings.

We should also take notice of cases in which claims of disinterestedness were applied to parliamentary custom, because they anticipated later, modern practices that would take place in a much more pluralistic context. For instance, the need to show generosity and consideration for opposing views —as a display of higher value placed on public than on private good—was a frequent theme. Pierce Butler, a wealthy planter and South Carolina delegate to the Constitutional Convention, strongly opposed Elbridge Gerry's plan for a federal government, but his words of response leave little doubt that the sense of shared identity as a member of the gentry remained for him a value superior to political differences. He wrote that he only wished he were "in unison with a person for whom I have so great an esteem as for Mr. Gerry, but I shall not less admire his independent spirit, his disinterested conduct and his private worth because we differ on measures of great public concern." When, on June 8, 1789, Madison responded to Anti-Federalist demands that a bill of rights be added to the Constitution, he recommended in his speech to the House that such amendments be composed in the spirit of "deference and concession" to those electors who desired such a bill. When Thomas Jefferson became vice president to John Adams—and suspicions swirled that because the two came from opposing parties there might emerge a paralyzing political hostility between them—Jefferson insisted that among impartial gentlemen such differences could at most be a source of private uneasiness, but that "neither of us are capable of letting it have effect on our public duties."[33]

To realize how intense was the pressure to live up to such professed qualities, one only need look at the enormous regulatory power of honor. Preserving reputation was no small matter. Michael Keane, of a prominent St. Vincent family, harshly admonished his friend Samuel Lynch for not paying his debts: "I was very much mortified and grieved at . . . [the] very unaccountable and unhandsome manner in which you quitted nevis an island in which you were much respected. My Dear Sam! I shall not even hazard to think that having been driven by necessity to have once taken a wrong step, should make you for ever after indifferent & regardless of your Honor and good name." Robert Munford, writing from a camp near Fort Cumberland during a 1758 expedition against Indians, complained about the self-centered and ungentlemanly attitudes of some of his colleagues, that in his view cast a shadow on the honor of all officers, which was "in a manner ruin'd by persons whose souls scorn a thought that tends not immediately to their own advantage." He went on, "I am sorry to live upon my country when I have so small a prospect of repaying her by any service." One may argue to what degree these were cases of self-fashioning, but they clearly were also real and binding commitments, obliging the claimers to behavior reflecting the proclaimed values. Some had shown genuine courage in defending personal honor, an indication of the weight it carried in their lives. When in 1765 Henry Laurens's house in Charleston was invaded by an angry crowd seeking "Stamp'd Paper" and asking about his connections with Governor James

Grant of East Florida, he told the attackers: "You are very strong & may if you please Barbicue me. I can but die, but you shall not by any force or means whatsoever compel me to renounce my friendships or to speak ill of Men that I think well of." He was left alone.[34]

The Revolution changed little in the existing repertoire of elite values considered honorable. These values remained so powerful in their ability to identify rank that they even operated across enemy lines in war. Patrick Henry thought it would violate the virtue of "that hospitality which our country gentlemen show to strangers" not to allow proper civilities between General William Phillips (held captive in Virginia since the Battle of Saratoga) and his social equals. Even a brief survey of the pronouncements of Revolutionary leaders shows that the duty to serve public good over private interests ascended to the top of the honor list. Henry Laurens, commenting on the alleged illegal trading of George McIntosh with the British in Florida, had this warning to Patriot leaders: "A transgression against our Associations against our laws is a greater Crime than Housebreaking, & by a Man vested with public confidence is aggravated in proportion to its pernicious influence and effects. Let us . . . know no Man as a friend or a Brother who in the strictest sense of the term, falls short of the duty of a friend and a Brother." Writing of those in public office, he noted that it was "their duty through good Report & through evil Report to strive against the powerful Stream of popular error without uniting in party Spirit on either side." Samuel Adams echoed the same stern expectation that no "illiberal party spirit" should govern the actions of public figures, whose "political existence" should not depend on being "the Governors friends" but on "the Honor and Safety of the Commonwealth." "We ought to have the Interest of our Country and the Good of Mankind to Act as the main Spring in all our Public Conduct," wrote Pennsylvania revolutionary Robert Morris, noting that it was the duty of those in office to "weigh well the Consequences of every determination we come to and in short to lay aside all prejudices, resentments and sanguine Notions of our own Strength in order that reason may influence and Wisdom guide our Councils." Edward Langworthy, a Revolutionary leader and delegate to the Continental Congress from Georgia, distressed that his friend, Colonel William Palfrey, intended to retire from politics into private life, expressed his objection in no uncertain terms: "Tho' I'm conscious you could do more for your family in a Private Station & that your Abilities and

Knowledge of mercantile affairs could not fail of procuring you great success; but my Dear Sir, it may be dangerous to the great & glorious Cause to suffer private motives to influence you at this time."[35]

A good way to understand such cultural feedback is to look at identity, political authority, and elite / non-elite interactions as parts of the communication process. Claimers of virtue craved a wider, public recognition of their qualities. Their new role as selfless spokesmen for the country provided them with additional authority, but only if the non-elites collaborated in this communication process by accepting the message. But if and when such recognition materialized, it came with increased public expectations of virtuous behavior. The more effective the self-propagation, the greater the obligations imposed on the propagators. The ultimate outcome of this collaboration was a democratizing one: the ruling class had to pay more attention to non-elites and their views than was the case before the Revolution, sometimes even at the risk of potentially diminishing their own influence. Even conservative Federalists were aware of this; Fisher Ames argued for a quick suppression of the 1786 Massachusetts rebellion, but he nevertheless warned the rulers to take note of public opinion: "At present, it is necessary that the public counsels should have the public approbation. This is peculiarly necessary at a time when the Constitution of the people's own choice is in danger."[36] Although it was clearly not his intention, such alertness to public opinion was an important step toward a future expansion of the sphere of liberty.

It was characteristic that in regions where the ruling class was well established and secure they were more willing to translate some of their claimed virtues into practice, by allowing more toleration and egalitarianism, than in areas where they were weak or threatened. Pennsylvania under the Constitution of 1776 has usually been considered the most radically democratic of the newly created states. But the freedom of speech it guaranteed was limited to those who did not speak against "the American cause": voting for the convention was allowed only if one was not listed as "an enemy to the liberties of America" by the Committees on Safety; and sweeping test laws against sedition threatened dissenters with imprisonment. In fact, the Council of Safety, which governed the state immediately after the Declaration of Independence, assumed remarkably broad powers ranging from detention to execution of those whose "conduct or conversation" were deemed suspect—powers to which they would have strenuously objected had they been exercised over them by the British government. By contrast, Virginia, where the slaveholding elite was more independent and solidly entrenched, allowed for comparatively more religious tolerance and political liberty in its Declaration of Rights, leading a New England writer to observe grudgingly that "wherever slavery is encouraged, there are among the free inhabitants very high ideas of liberty; though not so much from a sense of common rights of man, as from their own feelings of superiority." Similarly, in 1810 South Carolina became one of the first coastal states in the South to allow universal white male suffrage, and as Robert Weir pointed out, it was not so much from popular political pressure as from the self-assurance of the ruling circles.[37] This was not a paradox. When elite identities were secure, it was easier for members to live up to their proclaimed distinctive values, and to be more generous in permitting changes in the existing order. There was a reason why Southerners were so prominent in producing much of the radical language of liberty during the Revolution.

The value of the public good as a measure of political action, respect for opposing opinions, and disinterested service beyond personal and material gain were clearly used by the gentry to legitimize their power and privilege. That fact notwithstanding, these virtues also mattered in the history of liberty because they happened to be the very same values that make possible a modern, tolerant, and egalitarian democracy. Such values survived much longer than the ruling class of the Revolutionary era, but their survival had much to do with the fact that these rulers made them part of the national conversation. This imprinted the worth attached to these qualities on American political culture. Societies that have developed elite "fictions" of disinterested public service and the sovereignty of the people have historically been better disposed toward democracy than those that have not. If we take a position that the Revolutionary elite simply "held their world together with violence disguised as gentility," this important dynamic vanishes from our line of sight. In this view, we also have trouble appreciating another important role of the gentry's values for the history of liberty: the mark they left on legal and constitutional acts of long-term significance. It is not too much to say that the specific shape of such dramatically progressive articulations of liberty as the Declaration of Independence, the Constitution, and the Bill of Rights were affected not only by the appeal of certain philosophical theories but also by the *cultural obligations* compelling the authors to demonstrate their enlightened principles and virtuous probity.[38] Few would disagree that they wrote the documents in an admirably clear, uncluttered style, and—despite the various limitations which future amendments would have to remedy—with an open-minded, forward-looking respect for a wide array of people's liberties. Without considering these obligations together with their self-perception as the avant-garde of enlightened progress, it would be difficult to explain why the American Founders were more generous in sanctioning a catalog of citizens' individual rights than the culture of the English world allowed at the time (freedom of religion being perhaps the most obvious example). After all, many of these rights implied future constraints on the power of the rulers. Only when we realize that the ideological and cultural claims which they summoned during the Revolution also took possession of them, are we able to grasp why they at times followed up on them further than might have been expected.

6

Usurpers and Dupes

The Backlash

I. Revolutionary Vocabulary against Revolutionary Government

> Bodies of men, under any denomination whatsoever, who convene them-
> selves for the purpose of deliberating upon and adopting measures which
> are cognizable by legislatures only will, if continued, bring legislatures to
> contempt and dissolution.
>
> —Samuel Adams, 1784

THE TWO DECADES FOLLOWING Independence were a laboratory where the Revolutionary conceptual package was tested. The environment had changed; justifying the war and the Patriot cause gave way to the practice of governing. At the same time, various groups began to voice their grievances in terms of the new language of rights popularized by the Revolution. This caused a good deal of friction with the new leaders, who were beginning to have second thoughts about the growing involvement of ordinary people. The tensions soon turned into a struggle over the meaning of new, republican liberty. The upper ranks increasingly worried that "the everlasting flattery of the people as sovereigns" would result in commoners redefining and "democratizing" liberty. They warned that "no counterfeit sense of the people expressed in mob meetings, and dictated by the loudest bawls of the man who happens to rise upon a hogshead, ought to control or prevent the measures of the nation and its government." This tension inspired first a disillusionment and then a backlash among the political class. Their response was aimed at regaining control over the meaning of liberty, holding back the spread of an egalitarian mentality, and, in cases of insurgency, countering the "spirit of rebellion" contained in the voices of the "usurpers," who not only had "the insolence to wear badges of their character," but whose "boldness [wa]s countenanced in many places by popular elections of them to local offices." This backlash was far from being a case of moral declension or, as we are sometimes told, a betrayal of previously proclaimed values. Instead, it confirmed that there was nothing to betray; the rulers were only defending the logic of freedom tied to a social order they had always accepted as proper.

The truly novel story of this period was that of the masses of common people seeking respect and independence by eagerly invoking the principles which the Revolutionary leaders designed for *another* vision of society—one inspired by classical republics ruled by virtuous elites. George Minot correctly identified this eagerness as "that thirst for freedom which the people have discovered in the late revolution," even as he expressed fear that it might develop into "an unqualified opposition to authority."[1] The earliest and most prominent dispute about the meaning of the Revolutionary narrative was occasioned by the 1786 Shays's Rebellion in Massachusetts.

Most literature on this episode has focused either on the economic conflict involved or on the influence of the event on the shape of the Constitution. At one level, it was certainly a confrontation over economic policy. The state legislature, overwhelmed by public debt, refused to reduce taxes, forcing many farmers into insolvency. Unable to pay debts with hard money, backcountry towns sent moderately phrased petitions to the legislature, which refused to act upon them. Only in response to this inaction did a convention of selectmen from several towns adopt a more dramatic agenda of political demands, including abolishing the upper house and establishing annual elections. They also assembled militiamen, led by former commanders of Revolutionary units like Joel Billings, Joseph Hines, and John Thompson, to block a number of county courts where debt cases were tried.[2] In all of this, the protesters did not have the destruction of the newly established political system as their aim; their interest was in easing the debt burden by putting pressure on the courts. It is striking that both the rebels and the governing bodies widely invoked the Revolutionary vocabulary of rights and liberties to justify their positions. This offered an early demonstration of the extraordinary versatility of this vocabulary as a political tool, a usefulness that would continue over the next two centuries. Both sides carefully framed the events as a threat to American liberty. The farmers saw the relief of their debt burden as the duty of a government elected to represent the people's will, and to pursue broader public good. Creditors and the well-to-do across America viewed it as an issue of protecting their sacred right to property, enshrined as a sine qua non of a free society.

An examination of this debate leaves little doubt that for the new rulers the social meaning of liberty continued to be defined by pre-Revolutionary assumptions of hierarchical order, now clothed in a mantle of the new state. To them, the rhetoric of liberty made sense only within such an order. For instance, the proud Revolutionary war record of Daniel Shays, one of the leaders of the uprising, ultimately carried less weight to the rulers than his rank in society. He was a yeoman farmer, not a member of the gentry, and he had obtained his captain's rank on his own, without patronage, through his service in the war. His credentials as an American patriot and soldier were impeccable: he was a minuteman in Lexington in 1775, and he had fought at Bunker Hill, Ticonderoga, and Saratoga. Yet, when he became actively involved in leading the movement against foreclosures, and thus encountered the wrath of an array of government figures from John Hancock to Samuel Adams, the lesser position he occupied in social space mattered more than his Revolutionary pedigree. The nominally shared concepts of political ideology turned out to have dramatically different meanings.

The insurgents rolled out a whole catalog of liberty-related terms popularized by the Revolution, including the enslavement of the people by a tyrannical government, violations of the natural rights of man, and a denial of appropriate representation. It was especially notable that this cache also contained two concepts commonly used by the Patriot elite to justify their authority: disinterested service and public virtue—evidence that the proclaimed identity of the rulers produced certain expectations to which they were held accountable, even by people outside of their class. According to the Shaysites, the current state government had abandoned these qualities and the rebels were merely demanding that they live by their word. During the War of Independence, identical accusations were, of course, frequently made against the metropolitan ruling class, portrayed as having betrayed ancient British liberty—driven by a devotion to excessive luxury and the pursuit of private interests. Only six years earlier, Samuel Adams was cautioning America that similarly corrupted individuals might "steal into Places of highest

Trust" in the country, as some of its leaders were "distracted with the Pursuit of Pleasure & exorbitant Riches."[3]

These very same anti-aristocratic arguments were now applied to question the legitimacy of the Massachusetts elite, who had for years justified their political domination by claiming to practice true public virtue in serving the people. Shays's petition of January 30, 1778, to General Lincoln clearly stressed that it was the insurgents who were guided by genuine republican values. This cast doubt not only on the rulers' policies but also on the main tenets of their identity, something that—coming from the mouths of ordinary people—could not fail to irritate men like Samuel Adams or Fisher Ames. The rebels wrote that it was they, not the governor, who were defending the "credit and honour of the Commonwealth" and promoting the "principles of our Constitution," as well as "piety and virtue." Petitions and letters from western towns to newspapers spoke of "the virtuous yeomanry of Massachusetts," in contrast to "the aristocratical principle . . . prevalent among the wealthy men." Sylvanus Billings called the powers that be in Boston "tirants who are fighting for the promotion and to advance their Intrest wich will Destroy the good people of this Land," while others spoke of the government as resembling "British tyranny" and leading the backcountry farmers "into slavery." One letter to the *Boston Independent Chronicle* asserted that the republican rulers reigned like an aristocracy, and another called them "Tories and Enemies to America." Joseph French insisted that the farmers only wanted to reform, not to destroy, the republican government, "to do ourselves justice which the laws of God and man dictate to us." A group of farmers pleading for paper money to pay debts pointed to the corruption among the Boston elite, who "riot in grandeur and luxury." Inhabitants of Dracut believed the elite "have greater love to their own interests than they have to that of their neighbors."[4] Exclusive cultural attributes of the gentry tied to their ownership of fullest liberty were thus used to question their authority. A small shift in the social meaning of words was all it took to turn them into potent anti-establishment weapons.

The vocabulary of liberty inculcated in the popular mind by the Revolution had been used to question the new government before. It was prominently present in public complaints in 1778 over the proposed Massachusetts constitution, especially against limiting suffrage to those owning more than 60 pounds' worth of property. For instance, objecting to property qualifications, the town of Colerain wrote, "Taxation without Representation we Consider unreasonable," and New Salem complained that it was "unfair and unjust to Tax Men without their Consent."[5] This shows that the meanings of words did not reside in the words themselves, but in the circumstances in which they were used. The complaints of 1780 were not viewed as a major breach of order by the authorities in Boston because they were not accompanied by organized actions of protest. By contrast, it was the militant actions of the Shaysites in 1786 that gave the very same vocabulary of liberty a new social and political context, and consequently triggered a fiery struggle over its sense. The Massachusetts elite may have assumed new, post-Revolutionary selfhood as meritorious rulers and guardians of republican freedom, but culturally they remained deeply set in their earlier identity as gentry. This was why they saw the organized protests of farmers not as an expression of real grievances, but as an open challenge to their authority, political as much as social and cultural.

To counter this challenge, the elite applied the very same lexicon, forged in the late struggle for independence. "What, gracious God, is man! That there should be such inconsistency and perfidiousness in his conduct?" lamented Washington. "It is but the other day," he wrote, "that we were shedding our blood to obtain the Constitutions under which we now live; Constitutions of our choice and making; and now we are unsheathing the sword to overturn them." Former Revolutionary radical Samuel Adams was aghast at what he viewed as the people assailing the new political order that was supposed to embody their very liberties. He called for a harsh suppression of the protests and demanded the execution of their leaders. Tellingly, he shared this view with the much more conservative Fisher Ames, who wrote about the rebels that "It ought to be provided, that the punishment of death or a total or partial confiscation of their estates . . . shall be inflicted." While in a monarchy rebellion was justifiable, proclaimed Samuel Adams on the pages of the *Columbian Centinel,* once the new American polity had been established, "the man who dares rebel against the laws of a republic ought to suffer death."[6] Their arguments, eerily resembling future Robespierrean reasoning, can serve as a reminder of the ever-looming threat to free societies—that of using liberty and democracy to justify even the most undemocratic measures against political opponents.

Because the rulers substituted themselves for the people as their voice, they had a huge stake in defending this reasoning. Two years before Shays's Rebellion, Samuel Adams wrote, "Those men, who under any Pretence or by any Means whatever, would lessen the Weight of Government lawfully exercised must be Enemies of our happy Revolution and the Common Liberty." This view was not an attempt to reduce the political role of the people and violate "American Revolutionary thought," as some scholars have suggested. The war brought changes in the rhetoric, but changes in the perceptions of social order were much slower, with the gentry fully expecting to continue as rulers. This was why the 1786 protests against the new regime were viewed as a rebellion against freedom itself, threatening to reverse the achievements of the Revolution. Some sounded the alarm that the rebels yearned for dictatorship and even monarchy. Samuel Adams even accused the insolvent farmer rebels of living in "luxury," a widely used code word during the Revolutionary years for metropolitan corruption. They were also called "internal despots," in resemblance of "foreign tyrants." Only the elite truly stood for all people, and therefore they had to act decisively when "the Constitution of the people's own choice is in danger." It stood to wit: since a "Constitution is the free act of the people," there should be no doubt that "treason against such a constitution implies a high degree of moral depravity." George Minot noted that "the object of the insurgents evidently was, to annihilate the perfect happy constitution," and that their success, "as it would be the result of force, indirected by moral principle, . . . must finally terminate in despotism, in the worst of its forms."[7] The protesters were thus reduced to an anarchistic, reactionary mob by those who only a few years earlier were described in identical terms by the English ruling class and by American Loyalists.

The term "people" appeared prominently in the debate as both sides struggled to delineate its connotation. It was a measure of the huge weight that this concept had gained since 1764 that both the Shaysites and the government framed so many of their claims around it, and that each accused the other side of usurping it for their narrow interests. A January 31, 1787, petition by Shays began: "As officers of the people, now convened in defence of their rights and privileges . . . we justly expect that hostilities may cease." The Shaysites' "people talk" was grounded in subsistence economy, frontier individualism, and suspicion of external authority. The leaders repeatedly asserted that they stood for "the body of the people," and that they merely fought to protect the "lives and liberties of the people" against the new tyranny of government. They saw their militia as an entity delegated by the people at large, and their demands as nothing more than calls for change "favorable to the people." Before 1781, leaders of the Revolution frequently invoked the Whig theories of Locke and Harrington to justify their resistance to London; the Shaysites did not bring up the names of philosophers, but nonetheless justified their right to protest in much the same, if more popularly phrased, terms. They defined themselves as free and responsible citizens, backed by ownership of property, and their actions—even harsh measures—as fully justified "when for the good of the people." It is particularly telling that they saw themselves as continuing the ultimate mission of the Continental Army: fighting for a republic of liberty. They expressed this symbolically by carrying green twigs in their hats, patterned on the Continental Army's Fourth of July parade custom.[8] The Revolution had legitimized certain concepts that were so broadly framed that they were now useful as missiles in a very different struggle.

But the rulers built on the very same legacy to advance their stance. Government troops wore shreds of white paper in their hats to symbolize the Constitution. Massachusetts officials maintained that they represented nothing more than the people and so there was no ground for questioning their authority. Surely, they felt, the rebels misunderstood the very term, and consequently were confused as to who held legitimate title to power and who had the duty to obedience. Henry Knox complained that the principle of people as the sovereign had been perverted by many of the people themselves. In what must today seem a brilliantly accurate, if hostile, observation, Fisher Ames, writing about the arguments of the Shaysites, noted, "The people have turned against their teachers the doctrines, which were inculcated in order to effect the late revolution." Theodore Sedgwick saw the demands of the Shaysites as not only "absurd and ridiculous" but also ironic, because the government they attacked consisted of "servants of the public." In the eyes of the rulers, the rebels were not only incapable of understanding the new system but, worse, they *usurped* it by inserting unauthorized content into its vocabulary of freedom. Clearly, this was a battle over who controlled the meanings of the Revolutionary lexicon. At a deeper level, however, the issue was class. A similar case from contemporary England, described by Eliga H. Gould, can serve as an example. In 1761 the miners in the town of Hexham clashed with the government over the interpretation of the Militia Act, and in their argument the miners employed the concept of public good, taken directly from elite—and therefore conveniently legitimate—political rhetoric. The tactic, however, triggered a number of outraged publications condemning the miners and pointing out that the "lower" orders of society had no authority to take positions on "what is, or is not, expedient for the Good and Well-being of the whole Community." One indignant minister asked, "How can he get Wisdom that holdeth the Plough . . . and whose talk is of bullocks?" In the eighteenth-century British world, universalist political concepts did not in themselves imply that all social classes could interpret them. Even references to "self-evident" truths, which included liberty, were usually meant in the narrow sense of being evident only for those who had the ability to discern them as such.[9]

Inevitably, the anti-Shaysite missives turned to the meaning of liberty itself. The rebels were reminded that civil liberty by definition required a respect for official order, and that assemblies, as legal representations of the people, once elected, had power that was "supreme." If collective civil liberty was to be preserved, individuals were obliged to obey their representatives. Shays's Rebellion was thus an "attempt of a part of this community to unorganize government, preferring ferocious independence to civil liberty." The authoritative definition was still that "There is no other liberty than civil liberty," just as "All lawful government is derived from the people." But "when the people had consented to a form of government, the social compact was compleat. The state of nature was at an end; free to give or withhold, their consent, they became bound when they gave it." In civil society, "individuals are silent. . . . The minority are bound by the social compact to submit, but if they refuse obedience, force may be lawfully used to extort it." Mercy Otis Warren thought the demands of the Shaysites were "absurd in the extreme" because the rebels were "too ignorant to distinguish between an opposition to regal despotism and a resistance to a government recently established by themselves." The only fitting course for the rulers was to force them into "proper submission." On the other hand, she noted that Governor John Hancock's genteel qualities enabled him to quickly overcome this "factious and seditious spirit" and restore tranquility with his "disinterested conduct and masterly address." Samuel Adams believed that the new polity was a self-repairing one because it was based on representation; even if problems did emerge at some point, the nearest election would provide a remedy.

It was a measure of the still thriving, pre-Revolutionary, elite-centered world view that he did not even consider that the representatives could have been representing their constituents poorly.[10] Once elected, they were autonomous. The way the Shaysites formulated their demands undercut this traditional understanding; they wanted their representatives to be an extension of the current desires of their constituents. What matters is that their argument was made up of concepts supplied to them on a silver tray by their current antagonists. It was one of those moments when history smiles at its own sweet ironies.

Behind the veil of theoretical arguments, the political class also had a much more down-to-earth interpretation of events that called up a traditional cultural distinction between the gentry and the commonality: the rebels were an uncivil mob and, unlike the reason-driven gentry, they were primarily motivated by primitive emotions. Henry Knox argued that theirs was a "formidable rebellion against reason, the principles of all government, and the very name of liberty." The heart of the problem lay, according to him, in that free government was designed for civil citizens, not for the mob: "The source of evil is in the nature of the government, which is not constituted for the purposes of man possessing boisterous passions, and improper views." For Fisher Ames, "the bold startling creed of rebellion" was primarily "addressed to the passions and feelings of mankind." If the insurgents, this "rabble of offenders," were not suppressed, the government would come to depend on the "prejudice, caprice, and ignorant enthusiasm of a multitude of tavern-hunting politicians." A letter to the *Worcester Magazine* called them simply the "unthinking part of the community," while another, in the *Massachusetts Gazette,* saw the protesters as full of "vices and depravity." What annoyed the authors most was the rebels' supposed antipathy for property rights, which was interpreted as contempt for social rank. Two dangerous historical precedents were summoned: the egalitarian ideology of the Levellers, radical groups which surfaced during the English Revolution in the 1640s, and the tribal communalism of "savage" peoples. David Humphreys advised George Washington that the Shaysites were wedded to "a levelling principle" and wished "to annihilate all debts public and private." Henry Knox assailed them for wanting to abolish private property in favor of communalism, claiming the Shaysite creed was that "the property of the United States has been protected from the confiscations of Britain by the joint exertions of all, and therefore ought to be the common property of all." Springfield minister Bezaleel Howard noted that the government side "propegated that their [Shaysites] ultimate design was to Level al[l] Distinctions of person and property." Others warned that the rebels "contended for an equal distribution of property," which would bring American society back to a licentious state of nature, comparable to that of the Indians.[11]

Along similar lines, a group of conservative poets from Hartford known as the "Connecticut Wits" demonized the Shaysites as the epitome of "chaos" and the antithesis of civil society. As their "mobs in myriads" advanced, "anarch old, asserts its sway" over Massachusetts. Shays's was a "parricidous hand" with a sword pointed "against the bosom of their native land." There were no sacrosanct public values for the mutineers, not even the "sacred flame" of just-won American independence. They were negatively contrasted with idealized American leaders, such as Joseph Warren or Hugh Mercer, whose sacrifice for liberty would "live, immortal, in the patriot page." The authors hoped that these giants would inspire new, virtuous heroes to fight the rebels, who were ruled by vulgar passions. It mattered little that many of them had, in fact, valiantly fought for that noble cause themselves. Shays was especially targeted as a social upstart. Because he had obtained—despite his humble origins—the rank of a captain, elite writers made much of his selling, in a moment of need, of a sword that he had received from Lafayette, pointing out that only a virtueless man of low social station would thus put money before honor. Mercy Otis Warren, referring to his war record, wrote that veterans like him "had been very serviceable in the field during the late revolutionary war." Serviceable—not brave, patriotic, or committed to the cause of freedom—was the most acknowledgment she could come up with for this "former subaltern officer."[12]

A closer look at the language of the Shaysites also reveals that rather than opposing social hierarchy on principle, they primarily wanted to be admitted to the league of those who "owned" the various rights and liberties more fully. While the rulers feared that the rebels were carrying the meaning of equal freedom to "levelling" lengths, the Shaysites themselves still invoked their rights as deriving from "privileges" of liberty as freemen, not from equality. In this, they were closely following the pattern present in the complaints and demands placed before the king over a decade earlier by the American Revolutionaries: that they had been "degraded into a State of Servitude from the preeminent Rank of English Freemen," and that various acts of Parliament "have violated the dearest rights & most essential privileges which belong to us as freemen." In the 1786 Shaysite petition to the Massachusetts Assembly to ease the debt burden, fifty-seven farmers from Greenwich underscored that their primary desire was "to defend secure and promote the wrights and liberties of the people." They were "willing to pay our shares" toward the state's war debts as good citizens, but at the same time, they asked to be recognized as legitimate carriers of certain liberties, demanding the right to "injoy our shares in independency and constatutional privileges in the Commonwealth." Elsewhere the rebels stressed, "It is our hearts desire, that good government may be kept up in a constitutional way." The main privilege they claimed was to have elected representatives respond to their grievances. Rather than calling for an elimination of rank, they pointed to imprudent policies. Despite the economic difficulties, the governor was well paid out of people's taxes, and the government offered high "sallerys and grants to other gentlemen, as your honours very well know." The attorneys, who filed lawsuits against the farmers, were especially seen as "very extravigent and oppressive." For the petitioners, this contradiction not so much violated equality, but debased traditional New England anti-luxury values: "piaty, justice, moderation, temperance, etc."[13]

Consequently, suggestions that the use of the Revolution-sanctioned language of liberty by the Shaysites and other non-elite groups in 1780s and 1790s reflected a growing "class consciousness," as well as an increased awareness of a "ruling class," must be met with caution. For several reasons, the traditional categories of class do not easily fit the early modern agrarian society of Massachusetts, nor do they explain how the concept of liberty functioned at the time. An awareness of a ruling class is not the same as a rising class consciousness, which involves a perception of the ruling group as essentially antagonistic (a concept that would have to override the still entrenched organic assumptions of society). Nor could debtors and creditors be neatly polarized into opposing classes; they were present on both sides of the struggle, and so a simple opposition of the two groups is not very accurate. In any case, social order was rapidly shifting, with mobility, competing religious interests, and economic upheavals creating complex patterns of change, which might explain why this and other eighteenth-century protests were, as Pauline Maier has shown, relatively restrained (Shaysites melted away once they attained their specific purpose of closing down courthouses) and usually occurred only when legal avenues of obtaining redress failed to do so. This corresponds well with the rebels' language that indicated they were driven by a desire to be recognized as *privileged* in possessing certain liberties, rather than by a wish to overturn the privileges of the elites. The Shaysites, like the Whiskey Rebels or John Fries's tax protesters in Pennsylvania, wanted specific improvements of their lives, and the elimination of concrete burdens, rather than to bring down the established class. Finally, the farmers were not disenfranchised as a group; they had elected delegates in the General Court in Boston who represented them in their demands for paper money and tax relief, but were outvoted by the coastal, commercial, propertied majority.[14] They were well aware that they already exercised certain rights and liberties, and wanted to affirm them to increase their practical influence. They also wanted a share in the social respectability attached to the "ownership" of rights, something expressly indicated by their references to disinterested political virtue. In other words, the Shaysites demanded that the meaning of liberty be socially expanded so as to better include them among those owning certain rights. It was this process of broadening the cultural and social space of liberty, rather than an essentialized opposition to elite class interests, that was to bear progressive fruit in the two decades that followed.

It is intriguing that one of the most dramatic contemporary voices for such an expansion came not from the rebels but from a member of the local gentry. Massachusetts Justice William Whiting took the inclusiveness of the Revolutionary language of liberty literally, and, despite substantial political risk, acted upon that understanding, publicly taking the side of the Shaysites. He announced that the "future of Liberty" was in less danger from "the present Insurrections of the people" than from the government attempting to suppress their demands. He pointed out that it was unacceptable that "the Lower orders of the people Should be Reduced to absolute poverty and Slavery and thereby sap the foundation of our Republikin Government." But his key argument was that for the inhabitants of the state the language enshrined "in the fifth article of their bill of Rights that all Power is originally Vested in the people and is Derived from them" was not symbolic, but actually meant that all governments were "no other than their Substitutes and agents, and are at all times accountable to them." The magistrates were thus merely their "Creatures and servants." He reminded the public that "when Americans Took up Arms against Great Britain, it was . . . to obtain from them the free Exercise of those Liberties and previlages Which they had a natural Right to Enjoy." If this tradition were not respected, then "the boasted liberties of the inhabitants of every state are totally Insecure." As to the rebels, he admonished them not so much for protesting, but for their "Inattention to public affairs for Several years past, . . . the principle Door through Which those Evils in Government you now Complain of have crept in upon you; for had you Vigilantly and Carefully from time to time, Exercised those Governmental powers Which the Constitution has placed in your hands . . . you might probably have prevented any occasion for adopting the present Violent measures." In other words, Whiting fully expected a deeper politicization of the lower and middling orders of society *to reflect* the Revolutionary language of freedom. He also saw it as their genuine, not merely nominal, right, just as he saw the "indispensible duty" of their representatives to rule according to the "instructions" of the people. It was obviously not a majority view among the ruling class, but it unmistakably signaled the possibilities contained in the participatory rhetoric of the Revolution. Whiting firmly persisted in his view, even though it brought upon him the wrath of critics. Rufus King wrote that "all the virtuous men must feel the utmost indignation towards that unworthy magistrate the first Justice of Berkshire." Theodore Sedgwick, in turn, accused Whiting of seeking "momentary popularity" by "courting the voices or passions and prejudices of a miserably misguided and misinform'd people," a stand unbecoming a gentleman and "a man of abilities and education."[15]

Some scholars believe that Shays's Rebellion was primarily a conflict between commercial and agrarian ways of life, a precapitalist communal formation against a capitalist, individualistic one, focused mainly on the accumulation of money. But this macro-scale model does not capture well the slow and complex process of cultural change that enabled the enlargement of the sphere of liberty (it would not, for instance, help much in explaining a very similar struggle for the meaning of freedom and representation a decade earlier, between the Carolina Regulators from the farming backcountry and the Tidewater landed class). Furthermore, it glosses over the fact that the Shaysites wanted to be freed from very specific financial burdens that were not inherently capitalist in nature. A more fertile approach would be to realize that the rulers of Massachusetts saw themselves as gentry rather than entrepreneurs. They viewed their policy of maintaining public debt as a prime example of applying disinterested virtue to the larger public good—in this case, the need for the new republic to pay its debts in order to retain respectability. More importantly, the Shaysites, too, saw the elite as gentry, something that often escapes us when attention is placed on the antagonism between the two. They still viewed society in terms of hierarchies, an outlook especially strong in rebel areas populated by Scotch-Irish Presbyterians. They wanted to be recognized as owners of certain liberties, but they acknowledged that their liberties were not as extensive as those of the upper class, a view reflecting what Alan Taylor has aptly called a "protection covenant"—that is, a deeply traditionalist relationship by which the elites protected the farmers' property and liberties in return for deference. Petitioners from the town of Colerain, asking in January 1787 for a hearing of their grievances before the Massachusetts General Court, and for an amnesty for the rebels, employed a studied style of humility and appealed to the traditional upper-class virtues of the addressees: "We beg leave to lay this our request before your excellency and Council . . . relying on your Wisdom, patriotism and steady regard for the public Good as also on the wisdom and Integrity of the honourable legislative body of both houses."[16]

The Shaysite model of utilizing the Revolutionary vocabulary of freedom to demand certain rights was replicated in the last two decades of the century in various other episodes of rebellion, protest, and assertions of civil rights. For instance, in the lengthy struggle of squatters against land speculators in Maine, the rebels were demanding changes in law to reflect their interests. They, too, failed to question the existence of a social order of ranks, and in their protests appealed to such genteel values as virtue and public duty. In rejecting the rebels' demands, the elite also styled themselves as defenders of the larger public interest against licentiousness and put emphasis on the low social status of their opponents, labeling them a "mob" of "dirty, ragged fellows," mostly "ignorant." Equally characteristically, a group of Jews from a Philadelphia synagogue petitioned their state for broader civil rights by claiming that they were "fond of liberty" and that "the conduct and be-haviour of the Jews, in this and neighboring states, has always tallied with the great design of the Revolution." Similarly, the Newport, Rhode Island, Hebrew Congregation expressed hope and joy that "a government created by the majesty of the people . . . to bigotry gives no sanction, to persecution no assistance, but generously affording to all liberty of conscience and immunities of citizenship."[17]

Shays's rebels did not reject the political rhetoric produced and imposed on the culture by the rulers; instead they took it up and transformed it into a metaphor that became an instrument of their own ambitions and demands, undermining its meaning from within. It was a device of the weak, but it contained strengths derived from a prior legitimacy created by the powerful. The view from Mount Vernon met with the view from the farming towns of Massachusetts—but it was not a meeting of two alien worlds. It should be told as one story. The cultural capital of liberty created and legitimated by and for the elites became a vehicle for the non-elites to advance their collective interests. To say merely that such use was a case of "unintended consequences" of elite-made rhetoric, or of "appropriation" of the rulers' terminology by the oppressed, is to compress the complex process of cultural osmosis and collaboration between classes and groups into far too simple a framework. The non-elite could not have appropriated the elite vocabulary of rights before it was consecrated by the culture and inculcated into the collective consciousness. Universal and equal liberty as a proposition first had to be disseminated by the speaking class until it reached a critical mass when such idiom triggered what some scholars have called an "availability cascade," a process by which a growing number of people accept perceptions popularized by those with certain authority. Such beliefs thus become increasingly available, setting off a chain reaction as more and more people found them plausible and acceptable. It was essentially a communicative process—people domesticated new beliefs that they borrowed from others mainly because they took such beliefs to be already reputable.[18] In this case, the task of making them reputable was carried out by the political elite, forced by the Revolution out of closed rooms where such a conceptual repertory would otherwise have been mostly contained. Their domestication among ordinary people occurred when dramatic conflicts, such as Shays's Rebellion, called for an effective language to express the clashing positions.

Throughout this process, the rhetoric of liberty itself by no means remained static. Despite the suppression of the Shaysites, the rulers continued to democratize their political idiom—forced not only by the insurrection, but also by the need to live up to their new role as the voice of the people. One symbolic device that they increasingly employed to this end was to carefully replace the rebels' arguments with a rhetoric of freedom that nominally acquiesced to their demands. This counterdiscourse had the effect of neutralizing the challenges that the protesters posed to the rulers. For instance, the 1787 Massachusetts "Proclamation of Rebellion," which called for defeating the insurgents, also contained a magnanimous assertion that "every complaint of grievance was attended to, with disposition to grant all that relief which could be afforded consistent with equal justice and the dignity of government." A year later, after the fall of the Shaysites, George Minot summed up the treatment of the rebels as a case of a great "lenity of government" that "must attach every man to a Constitution . . . which governs its subjects without oppression and reclaims them without severity."[19]

The question, posed earlier, whether the rulers contradicted their own ideology is out of place in this story. Once Revolutionary rebels became the ruling elite, their roles were switched; while they held on to the founding language of liberty to frame political issues, they returned to the role of the establishment, albeit an altered one, and defending the status quo became their primary goal. This is one of the classical patterns in history: any order, once established, can be expected to take on those who oppose it. The seeming paradox of the Revolutionary radical Samuel Adams calling for the execution of the post-Revolutionary radical Daniel Shays was no paradox at all. What was truly novel was the tangible expansion of the meaning and usages of the Revolutionary language of liberty.

II. Party Struggles and the Expansion of Liberty

> The very idea of the power and the right of the People to establish Government presupposes the duty of every individual to obey the established Government. All obstructions to the execution of the Laws, all combinations and Associations, under whatever plausible character, with the real design to direct, controul, counteract, or awe the regular deliberation and action of the Constituted authorities are destructive to this fundamental principle and of fatal tendency. They serve . . . to put in place of the delegated will of the Nation, the will of a party.
>
> —George Washington, Farewell Address, 1796

IF SHAYS'S REBELLION demonstrated how the Revolutionary liberty talk was being picked up by non-elites in the pursuit of their own goals, the years that followed it witnessed further changes in political culture that pushed the now popular language of freedom even further away from its former, restrictive connotations. These changes took place as a result of factionalism—a seemingly odd development considering that the Founders reviled and denounced it as the main threat to liberty in America. "Party" was a dirty word; Madison was willing to acknowledge only one type of party division, that between friends and enemies of the United States, between those who supported "republican policy" and those who stood for the "spirit of usurpation and monarchy." But intense debates over constitutions, representation, rights, and foreign policy—all enhanced by the flourishing of newspapers—not only amplified divisions between emerging political factions, but also expanded the social composition of their memberships to include increasing numbers of middling and ordinary people. Another source of growing political participation by non-elites was the mobilization of military forces to fight in the Revolutionary War, a process that turned out to be a significant medium of politicizing the population. The Philadelphia militiamen, for instance, on returning from war, organized a pro-independence Committee of Correspondence, while many also became involved in public rallies and street demonstrations demanding economic relief. The perceived radicalism of their demands ultimately produced a conservative backlash, but their vocal presence on the public stage signified a major change that could not be ignored by the political class.[20]

The emerging factional allegiances served as powerful magnets; they crossed state and regional borders, with perhaps the most radical polarization occurring in the urbanized areas of New England. Public debate was still conducted mostly by members of the elite, but the divisions among them soon percolated into popular culture, as people came to support newspapers, taverns, and even churches, depending on their political loyalties. By the 1790s, most of those who paid attention were able to characterize themselves as "us" versus "them." These new engagements ran deep, cutting across cities and villages, even families, as in the well-known case of two figures in Dedham, Massachusetts—the lawyer Fisher Ames, a personification of High Federalism, and his Anti-Federalist brother, the physician Nathaniel Ames—both endowed with sharp pens. What until the mid-1780s used to be a fairly robust and stable gentry identity began to fracture. During Washington's second term, both Federalists and Anti-Federalists, seeking a broader base of support, were forced to allow—and even actively seek—a much greater politicization of ordinary people than was ever conceivable earlier. Much of this shift was caused by the fact that factionalism changed the function of newspapers; no longer a means of conducting ideological disputes and sagely reflecting on politics, they became a tool of intense, often harsh and inelegant, political struggle. This, in turn, further democratized, and often coarsened, the already open-ended, universalist language of politics inherited from the Revolution. The long-term effect was a de-gentrification of liberty.[21]

What were the sources of popular interest in factional rivalries? It appears that the main attraction was that ordinary people were invited to the table. Another was the still urgent need among the population to make sense of the new, post-Revolutionary America, and to develop a usable world view to interpret the new realities. Combined with an already increased engagement of American society in political life, the new, party-driven polarization was a major wellspring of heated public exchanges about proper relations between power and liberty. For most, the intensity of this discourse was not primarily driven by the seductive power of the intellectual and political theories that were being debated. Ordinary people who would not otherwise have knowledge of Locke or Hobbes, but who were now, for the first time, admitted to the debate, found in it an opportunity both to fill a cultural vacuum caused by the disruption of their earlier identity as Britons, and to develop a new, American selfhood, anchored to a vision of freedom and good government. This post-Independence cultural vacuum was not just a minor detail in what has so often been viewed as the triumphant march of progress. New, trustworthy concepts of order were still acutely needed to make up for the demolition of the familiar and long-established ones linked to British monarchic tradition. The genteel themes borrowed from that tradition had thus far served the American elite well, but once this elite invited the former outsiders into their exclusive circle of politics, they found the new guest brought different customs, experiences, expectations, and language to express them. The accommodation of lowbrow aspirations and energy by highbrow guardians of virtue became unavoidable, and the adjustment was far from painless.

The exploding struggle between Federalists and Anti-Federalists provided a vehicle for such democratizing revisions. The leaders of both factions built their arguments around claims that theirs was the only one capable of preserving freedom and representing the interests of the entire population. In other words, the principal strategy of both was to delegitimize the other side in order to gain better control of the public meaning of liberty, and emerge as its only true spokesmen. It was not originally intended to be a battle for a modern, egalitarian sense of freedom. Full freedom was to remain attached to the elite, even as the elite was becoming less homogeneous and increasingly spoke with more than one voice. The Anti-Federalist leaders were far from fully identifying with the mass of the people; they assumed the need to preserve an upper class, but in order to rally support for their faction chose to use a more inclusive language than the Federalists. The Federalists were much more cautious, but they too developed a new rhetoric to appeal to the common man. As a result of this competition, both parties found themselves— sometimes with grave qualms and reservations—marketing new spaces for political participation. The controversy launched a public debate that would become a staple of American politics for the next two centuries: where to draw the line between the state and the people.

The original battle is better understood if we realize that it was often literally a struggle for the right to name, to publicly label, certain political behaviors. A conflict over liberty poles that erupted in 1798 may serve as an illustration. The liberty pole by that time was already a popularly recognized political symbol, and renaming it to suit current ideological purposes could have the effect of promoting or diminishing the authority of a faction. When Anti-Federalists began erecting liberty poles across the country in opposition to the policies of the Adams administration, Federalist newspapers without delay renamed them "sedition poles" and "emblems of sedition." Because sedition was the antithesis of new patriotism, such relabeling invalidated the existing legitimacy of liberty poles as positive, and thus politically useful, symbols. Federalists could now claim that those who erected them were not capable of understanding the meaning of freedom, and were instead "ignorant and misguided followers, disorganizers and revilers of our virtuous administration."[22]

The struggle over meanings, and the cultural realignments that ensued from it, were especially visible in orations commemorating various events of the Founding. The motif of liberty was the most frequently recurring theme—whichever party was the organizer—and usually functioned as the axis of most arguments. Because such public events (often taking place in churches) had the capability to communicate to large numbers of people a unified vision of new, patriotic identity, this theme relatively quickly entered popular culture, and became a pillar of early national identity. The language of these speeches can be viewed as a barometer of such change. It was an unusual blend of genteel and popular styles, a motley mix of elevated vocabulary—with de rigueur references to public virtue—and picturesque, emotional rhetoric intended to exert a pull on ordinary people. This eclecticism revealed an ongoing process of fusion where elite and non-elite elements—previously jealously guarded as separate—came together in a bond of convenience. Elite speakers, even when they invoked gentry-made values, took meticulous care to present themselves as no more than spokesmen for the liberty of all Americans, and adjusted their style accordingly. It was a meeting of high and low culture, unthinkable only two or three decades earlier, when seeking the support of ordinary people would have been seen as inappropriate. Indeed, for many speakers this shift was still problematic, and not all were willing to surrender the lofty style associated with the upper ranks. For them, James Otis was one of the first to offer advice: use humility, stress the collective good, and avoid any appearance of elitism in rhetoric. No speaker will command respect until he "has some reverence for his hearers," he warned. He also recommended: "Study, the most early, natural ways of expressing yourself, both in the tone of your voice, and in the gesture of your body." The goal was to find a golden mean between "the rusticity of the boor, and the affectation of the courtier." This, of course, did not for a moment prevent him from seeing himself as a member of the upper echelons of colonial society, or from speaking with contempt of the "menial servants" of the deputies empowered by the Writs of Assistance, who "are allowed to lord over us," a state akin to suffering "the curse of Canaan" and being "the servant of servants, the most despicable of God's creatures." But he and others had to bow to the new reality, already signaled by the popular reception of Thomas Paine's *Common Sense,* which, as soon as it came off the press, was "greedily bought up and read by all ranks of people." One notably cheerful side effect of the newly colorful language used as political medicine was the growth of humor, parody, and caricature. The staunch Federalist David Humphreys discovered in 1786 that "in some instances, the force of ridicule has been found of more efficacy than the force of argument against the Anti Federalists and Advocates of Mobs and Conventions." As he noted, "It was pleasant enough to observe how some leading men, of erroneous Politics, were stung to the soul by shafts of satire."[23]

Despite their political differences, both Federalist and Anti-Federalist authors endeavored to fashion their language to meet the new populist criteria. The Anti-Federalists were especially careful to shun overtly genteel style because such avoidance aided their political line of accusing the Federalists of aristocratic leanings. A 1794 Anti-Federalist manifesto in the *Newark Gazette* stressed that "it must be the mechanics and farmers or the poorer class of people (as they are generally called) that must support the freedom of America; the freedom which they and their fathers purchased with their blood—the nobility will never do it—they will be always striving to get the reins of government into their own hands, and then they can ride the people at pleasure." The Federalists also developed more accessible poetics aimed at a wider audience. They were already to some extent doing so through the momentum created by the inclusiveness of the Revolutionary rhetoric; now the need to respond to the rival faction added another powerful stimulus. In his May 5, 1779, oration, the traditionalist lawyer William Tudor used emotional and picturesque language to paint a portrait of British soldiers during the Boston Massacre as an anti-image of Americans. The redcoats "contemptuously looked down on our peaceful orders of citizens" and "assumed a superiority," treating Bostonians as "slaves," and displaying "arrogance of carriage" as well as "licentiousness and brutality." He referred to metropolitan laws as receiving their force "from the mouths of cannon." Two years later, Judge Thomas Dawes in his speech on the same subject conjured equally colorful language: "Do we not see the darkened spring of 1770, like the moon in a thick atmosphere, rising in blood, and ushered in by the figure of Britain plunging her poignard in the young bosom of America?" Of the martyrs who died "at the foot of Liberty," he waxed sentimental: "Their melancholy ghosts will forever wander in the night of this noted anniversary."[24] Fisher Ames may have strongly believed that common people were not fit to fully participate in public life, but his political language was emotive and at times even passionate, attributes which would have been considered unseemly a few decades earlier.

This populist language was not merely a tool of communication. Both parties shared the same goal: acquiring more influence over the public. Both party elites saw themselves as necessary intermediaries between the republican system and the yet unenlightened masses. In other words, the new style was not only about better ways of reaching the masses, it was also about better ways for the party leaders and spokesmen to symbolically derive their authority from the people. It was a significant cultural change for the elites, a change about which many felt uneasy, warning about the spread of demagoguery—a code word for gaining power by means of appealing to common people.

Benjamin Rush was well known for his Revolutionary condemnations of the old British concept of the gentleman as a social parasite who did no useful work. Yet, years later, as he witnessed the growth of political participation, he lamented that government was no longer controlled by men of quality. Outbursts against demagoguery and partisan spirit abounded on both party sides. These attacks, often portrayed in historiography as mere propaganda against the other faction, had a much deeper underlying strain: a lamentation that "public virtue," formerly a gentry monopoly, was being sacrificed at the altar of vulgar populism, and replaced by "interest" that readily stooped to rabble-rousing. Madison feared this might even infect the upper levels of government. "How frequently too," he asked, "will the honest but unenlightened representative be the dupe of a favorite leader, veiling his selfish views under the professions of public good and varnishing his sophistical arguments with the glowing colours of popular eloquence?" Others were more blunt, noting that "the giddy multitude have enjoyed the bustle of parties, and have found amusement in destruction."[25]

Why would the gentry class undermine their own position as the dominant political power? The answer is that they did not feel they were undermining it, because members of both factions continued to take the social homogeneity of such an upper class for granted and believed that the *other* group behaved as a mere party, betraying the genteel ethos. They were both caught off guard by the rapidity of changes in the political arena that brought about the new divisions—the need to court support for independence from a wider public, and the fear, mostly local, of the excessive power of a centralized federal government. The strife between the two parties in the 1780s and 1790s was neither a form of class struggle nor, as some scholars portray it, a conflict between advocates of a society without rank on the one hand and disciples of a hierarchical order on the other. The tradition of pigeonholing the Anti-Federalist leaders as automatically progressive and the Federalist ones as retrograde is too simple and derives from taking the political language of the times too much at face value, while neglecting the fact that both groups continued to define themselves against the uneducated and the unenlightened. It is just as imprecise as taking the stress placed by republicanism on the collective good of society as signifying a thrust toward egalitarianism, or as taking the Lockean emphasis on property rights as pointing toward egoistic individualism.[26] In reality, the engagement between the two factions was primarily about authority. Both ideologies were devised by the elites, and the struggle took place mostly within one and the same social class. Both sides of the contest styled themselves as defenders of public good and custodians of people's liberty.

The language of polemical exchanges between the two parties reveals that, despite a rhetorical inclusion of ordinary people, both sides construed their arguments around elementary gentry values until the early nineteenth century. Perhaps the most frequent theme was that of betrayal—by the other side, naturally—of that most distinctive, defining attribute of the ruling class: loyal and impersonal service to the public. Anti-Federalist leaders—traditionally thought to have a more egalitarian outlook—consistently considered themselves legitimate gentry, and took for granted the distance between them and the non-elites. They were deeply affronted when the Federalists insinuated their low social rank. Elbridge Gerry, who himself had attacked the Federalists for their aristocratic leanings, was immensely distressed at being himself associated by them with the vulgar classes. "It is beginning to be fashionable," he observed wryly, "to consider the opponents of the Constitution as embodying themselves with the lower classes of the people." Such accusations, even when collectively aimed, were painful, because he knew they were meant to puncture his social identity. His disgust at attempts to declass him was palpable. Anti-Federalists, he wrote, were collectively treated "with the humiliation which attaches to an inferior and degraded caste." This was much more than nostalgia for the lost political solidarity of the Patriot elite; the rise of factions was a startling development because it turned their world upside down, destroying its reassuring security and constancy. Writing to General James Warren, Gerry noted that as a result of party struggles over the Constitution, the Federalists "have deprived you, Mr. S. Adams and myself in a great measure of that public confidence to which a faithful attachment to the public interest entitles us." Public office, increasingly taken over by the ungenteel, had lost the old luster of elite dignity, and now "the road to political honours lies through the mazes of intrigue, servility and corruption." What just over a decade earlier had been proud service as a member of a legislative body had now become "neither pleasant, lucrative, nor honourable."[27]

The Anti-Federalists were especially fond of exploiting another vintage genteel attribute—fidelity to the larger public good. They gleefully portrayed their rivals as having ties of loyalty to Britain rather than to America. Successfully conjuring up Revolution-inspired images of monarchic hostility to liberty, they pictured their opponents as haughty aristocrats as detached from the people as the old hereditary nobility of England. Nathaniel Ames saw the Federalist paper in his hometown of Dedham, the *Minerva,* as having "a base, British, aristocratical complexion," and its goal a dedication to "make public servants Lords." He was fond of referring to Theophilus Parsons and his Essex Junto as the "British Junto," unblushingly suggesting disloyalty, if not treason. Pierre Du Ponceau, the Anti-Federalist lawyer and organizer of the Law Academy of Philadelphia, saw America as permeated by a "spirit of freedom and equality," a proud new national identity which was being subverted by monarchically inclined Federalists representing "the pride of wealth and the arrogance of power." Elbridge Gerry felt that the Federalists wanted to "establish a nobility of opinion under whose control in a short time, will be placed the Government of the Union and of the States, and whose insufferable arrogance marks out for degradation all who will not submit to their authority."[28]

The Federalists returned the compliment by linking their opponents to another gentry-made category—the vulgar mob—as a means of invalidating their rivals' title to gentility. Associating the Anti-Federalists with the unlettered multitude—in their world view, a class no less inimical to liberty than the pedigreed aristocracy—packed a considerable punch. One pamphlet called Anti-Federalist sympathizers a "strange, unlettered, multifarious band" and "simple dupes of Anti-Federal arts," driven by passions rather than reason, a crowd whom "sense ne'er guided, virtue never knew." Only members of such a mobocracy and American "Sanscoulottes" would celebrate the September 21 anniversary of the founding of the French Republic by marching in the streets like "cattle or swine in a drove." And no wonder, because "the persons who composed this opposition, and who thence took the name of Antifederalists, were not equal to the Federalists, either in point of riches or respectability. They were in general, men of bad moral characters, embarrassed in their private affairs, or the tools of such as were. Men of this caste naturally feared the operation of a Government embued with sufficient strength to make itself respected, and with sufficient wisdom to exclude the ignorant and wicked from a share in its administration." Naturally, this meant they possessed no virtue; they made up for its lack by "a hypocritical anxiety for the preservation of the liberties of the people." Their wealth was questionable: "Few of them were men of property, and such as were, owed their possessions to some casual circumstance, rather than to family, industry, or talents." In the 1790s, remarks that Anti-Federalists were "unprincipled, insolent and abandoned miscreants" and "wretched patricides" were regular in the Federalist *Columbian Centinel.* It was also a staple of the *Centinel*'s editorial pages to label Anti-Federalists as "Jacobins" who "justified the hostile measures of France," and who were "'pretended' friends to Republican Government," possibly disloyal and "under the influence of France." Those Americans who idolized Revolutionary Paris were gently reminded that "the plague had once a beginning from a *dunghill,* but its Infection depopulated *cities.* The stream of French influence should be checked in its beginning." William Cobbett called the Anti-Federalists "Frenchified citizens of the United States."[29]

This duping of the lower classes, Federalists warned, posed grave consequences for liberty, because it disrupted social order, vital for freedom to flourish, and because it encouraged unqualified people to take up political activity. Anti-Federalist political texts were "published for the purpose of deceiving and irritating the simple, unsuspecting tillers of the earth who are remotely situated from the focus of intelligence." Others claimed that the Anti-Federalists were "seekers of popularity," "corrupters of the multitude," as well as "deceivers of the people," and that "the malady is endemical and incurable." They spread the disease of demagoguery through their newspapers, such as the *Boston Chronicle,* because these were read by "plain" people, whose "reasoning is from what they know, and they take facts from that paper." In other words, the Anti-Federalists compounded the threat to freedom by feeding the ignorance of the lower classes with subversive ideas. The result was that "false notions of liberty are pretty general among those who read, so that over and above the error into which the multitude is prone to fall from passion and prejudice, is that which is imposed upon them by authority." The Federalists, by contrast, were careful to point out that when they themselves developed a following by common folk, the latter were of the more reputable sort. It was noted, for instance, that at the Federalists' 1798 Fourth of July celebration in Dedham, Massachusetts, participants included "magistrates, men of influence in their several circles, enlightened farmers and mechanics," which made the occasion "respectable."[30]

But political rhetoric grew out of immediacy, and cultural beliefs out of a long historical process. The Anti-Federalists, with all their populist and egalitarian language, did not suddenly abandon the old, elite axiom that ordinary people were not ready for full political freedom because they lacked rational judgment. Nathaniel Ames saw the successes of the despised Federalists as being precisely due to the fact that politicians with golden tongues could easily mold common people's views. When one of them addressed a parish group in town, he so effectively "harangued them" that he "beat the people out of their senses, made them defeat their own wishes, and drum good citizens out of the meeting." For him, ordinary people were mostly passive recipients of elite arguments. From this premise, it was easy for him to rhetorically extend his contempt for the passion-driven and ignorant lower ranks to all followers of Federalism, who were "selfish wretches under foreign influence, that never had a conception of searching out the truth, and will neither read, see, nor hear anything contrary to their own narrow prejudices, wholly actuated by the impulse of the moment." This approach was common among other Anti-Federalist authors, who routinely attempted to paint the Federalists in the public eye as unrefined and vulgar. For instance, the Philadelphia bookseller and writer Matthew Carey called the Federalist William Cobbett "a wretch so far sunk in infamy" that he is "abhorred by all those whose good opinion can reflect honour," and represents "the insolence of a low-bred, cowardly alien." John Williams wrote of another Federalist editor that his writings were "only congenial with the mind and temperament of a low ruffian—who is ignorant of the responsibility of a gentleman to his honour."[31] Clearly, segments of the elite were going through a divorce, but this separation was mainly political, while the much older and more durable shared cultural assumptions continued to frame their thinking for at least a generation after the Revolution.

As they sought supporters for their agendas, both parties found themselves in a dilemma they did not anticipate. If new categories of persons were to be allowed an increased public voice and greater political participation—in other words, more freedom—they could not simply be added to the existing collection of the already more free. Those already more free would have to give up some of their hitherto privileged freedoms to accommodate the newcomers (gender historians were among the first to fully appreciate this pattern, noting that the culturally defined identity of men depended on the subordination of women, and consequently any change which increased the

FIGURE 5. A satirical portrayal of a dispute on the floor of the Congress on February 15, 1798, between Federalist Roger Griswold of Connecticut and Republican Matthew Lyon from Vermont. (Courtesy Library of Congress, Washington, D.C.)

freedoms of women would have to involve constraining the freedom enjoyed by the hitherto privileged men).[32] Any growth of the space of liberty in the two post-Revolutionary decades would have to have come at the cost of restricting the scope of liberty thus far owned by the elite. Since this would not ordinarily have been in their interest, it could only have taken place when circumstances of intense internal rivalry and factionalism forced both parties to encourage more political participation by ordinary people.

Whether it was symbolic or factual, this participation expanded the political sphere, changing the meaning of liberty in the process. Madison acknowledged as much when he wrote in Federalist No. 37 that political language available to him had become a "cloudy medium" and contained "inevitable inaccuracy." Apparently, what he meant was that this imprecision stemmed from a growing use of such language as a highly malleable tool, used inconsistently in incessantly shifting political struggles. He was right. For instance, "imperial power" was a bogeyman during the Revolution but became a positive concept by the 1790s, when a "republican empire" was to be the guarantor of liberty. That such shifts were happening was plainly evident in the campaign, begun in the late 1780s, to reveal the names of authors of political publications hiding behind pseudonyms. The Federalists were apprehensive about publications by "usurpers" who did not represent a genuine voice of the gentry. Anti-Federalists were more concerned about the vagueness of meanings in the constitutional documents, which governments could use to gain excessive power. In truth, both were concerned that anonymous authorship produced political statements detached from an overt source of authority. They had good reason to worry; the very same steps undertaken by the political class to channel the growing participation of ordinary people—rallies, anniversary celebrations, parades—often politicized people beyond the elite's ability to manage such developments. But the new idiom was fast becoming a fact of life. In 1774, Gouverneur Morris could still warn the American "gentry" and "people of property" that the rising political awareness of the common folk might soon create a situation when the "mob" would take over the country. By the late 1780s, such blunt language coming from a public figure would appear increasingly unfashionable, and politically impractical.[33]

The post-Revolutionary party debates and rivalries created an informational spill; knowledge of liberty moved from upper-class rooms through elite newspapers, public rituals, popular press, political and election rallies, party propaganda, and tavern talk, to the collective mind. The effect was not only to raise the consciousness of various rights and liberties across social ranks. It was, more importantly, to raise the awareness of the *existence of different options* of defining a free political system and individual freedom. When public discourse offered people the possibility of making a choice between two contrasting interpretations of liberty, conditions for cultural change were created.[34] Such choices supplied ordinary people with a more participatory sense of liberty, and engaged them in peacetime political action to an extent not practiced before. It is essential to appreciate that this process of altering shared perceptions took about three decades—a generation—and did not happen instantaneously in 1776, or even in 1787. Such change is always incremental; culture abhors sudden disruptions of order. The newly populist meaning of liberty only gradually undermined the one deriving primarily from social distinctions. That this progression was slow was indicated by the continued coexistence of the new concepts with much older values.

While the Revolution was still in process, only the most creative and imaginative non-elite individuals, able to look beyond the currently accepted reality, utilized the emerging concepts of liberty and applied them to new objectives. The writing of Lemuel Haynes may serve as an example. Haynes was a black militiaman and veteran who had seen Lexington and Concord and fought in the Battle of Bunker Hill in Boston. In his never published essay "Liberty Further Extended: Or Free Thoughts on the Illegality of Slave-Keeping," he asserted that an African had an "undeniable right to his liberty," and that because such privileges were given by God, "no one has the least right to take them from us without our consent." But after the culture-changing period of party debates, those voicing similar arguments showed much greater confidence and a sense of agency in navigating the rhetoric of liberty to promote their goals. One of the more noteworthy examples of a considered use of the Revolutionary idiom for new political ends can be found in James Forten's anti-slavery pamphlet, *Letters from a Man of Colour*. Forten, a veteran of the Revolutionary War, was a free black and a prominent Philadelphia businessman. He was reacting to a proposed bill in the state senate to restrict African American immigration. His argument was almost entirely based on the premise that the bill contradicted all the principles of the Founding. He opened his *Letters* with, "We hold this truth to be self-evident, that God created all men equal," and invoked "our noble Constitution" to make the point that "This idea embraces the Indian and the European, the Savage and the Saint, the Peruvian and the Laplander, the white Man and the African." He asked rhetorically if the delegates had read the Pennsylvania constitution, and suggested its writers originally understood this principle to mean that they had "no more authority to enslave us, than England had to tyrannize over them. They were convinced that if amenable to the same laws in our actions, we should be protected by the same laws in our rights and privileges." He universalized the meaning of freedom, pointing out that it was incredible that "the advocates of liberty, should conceive the idea of selling a fellow creature to slavery." As a prosperous citizen, he could, and did, bring up the link between property and freedom—but reversed its common, pro-slavery meaning: "Many of us are men of property, for the security of which, we have hitherto looked to the laws of our blessed state, but should this become a law, our property is jeopardized, since the same power which can expose to sale an unfortunate fellow creature, can wrest him from those estates, which years of honest industry have accumulated." He linked the issue of the bill with the virtue and patriotism of the Revolutionary struggle, writing: "Many of our fathers, many of ourselves, have fought and bled for the Independence of our country. Do not then expose us to sale." Finally, employing the same transcendent justifications of God and Reason used by the Revolutionaries, he asked whether "God who made the white man and the black, left any record declaring us a different species." Of his own remarks, he noted: "They are the simple dictates of nature and need no apology."[35] In a speech to the Ladies' Antislavery Society of Philadelphia, Forten directly invoked the Declaration of Independence, pointing out that freeing the slaves was equivalent to securing "a greater respect and obedience to Him who wills the happiness of all mankind, and who endowed them with life, and liberty, as conducive to that happiness." The party wars of the 1780s and 1790s were now bearing cultural and intellectual fruit—a democratized political discourse that included non-elite participants publicly applying the broadened notion of liberty to their own interests and aspirations.

III. The Ruling Class: A Crisis of Identity

> The excess of the passion for liberty, inflamed by the successful issue of the war, produced, in many people, opinions and conditions which could not be removed by reason nor restrained by government.
> —Benjamin Rush, *Medical Inquiries and Observations,* 1794

THE PERIOD BETWEEN 1786 and 1800 witnessed a growing counter-offensive against "usurpers" to liberty. There were two principal causes of this reaction. One was that the late colonial gentry had always taken for granted that they would remain in power in the post-Revolutionary world, but now were beginning to realize that it was no longer a certainty. The other was an increasing anxiety that the set of values which made up their distinctiveness and coherence as a class was eroding. They had built this distinctiveness around a certain ideal of liberty, in part inherited from Britain and in part a product of the Revolution. It presented them as progressive, enlightened, and benevolent rulers, destined to govern the new republic for the foreseeable future. What they did not anticipate was that the constitutional debates of the 1780s and the subsequent escalation of political rivalries would raise public awareness of various liberty-related issues to a point where the elite's ability to control their meanings would come into question.

The first and instinctive counterattack was directed at political populism. It was instinctive because there existed among the colonial upper class a long tradition of antipathy to such conduct. Laments were common against steps "many of the Members of Assemblies take to make themselves popular," a dangerous conduct which "can activate a mighty and many headed Multitude."[36] The Revolution did not eliminate this aversion, but swept it under the carpet in order to promote a soaring, universalistic ideology, which initially was not seen as a threat to elite authority. But by the late 1780s many among the political class became alerted to the fact that the popular usage of liberty language had begun to blur the traces of conventional social distinctions originally contained in it.

Nathan Dane, a delegate to Congress from Massachusetts, anxiously expressed the hope that this state of things would turn around soon, but his diagnosis was grim: "The revolution, popular harrangues made to effect it, and various circumstances have thrown us into extremes of disorder on the popular side. We have experienced the evils of a Government popular in its principles and too popular, on many occasions at least, in its administration." The original idealism and enthusiasm for the idea of a new nation of upright citizens was now being dampened by a growing disillusionment. It has been suggested that this disillusionment came from the discovery that the "high hopes" of the revolutionaries did not find sufficient reflection in the virtuous behavior of the people. But a closer look shows that the disappointment was not so much about too little virtue as about too much equality. "I myself have been an Advocate for a Government free as air; my Opinions have been established upon the belief, that my country men were virtuous, enlightened, and governed by a sense of Right and Wrong," noted Rufus King in 1786. He had assumed that "if our Republican Governments were subverted, it would be by the influence of commer[c]e and the progress of Luxury." "But," he went on, "if in opposition to these Sentiments, the great Body of the people are, without Virtue . . . there is but too much reason to fear, that the Framers of our constitutions, & laws, have proceeded on principles that do not exist, and that America, which the Friends of Freedom, have looked to as an

Asylum when persecuted, will not Afford that Refuge, which their hopes & wishes have suggested." The period was fast approaching when Americans might be faced with "the horrors of anarchy and licentiousness," wrote Henry Lee, blaming the "tardiness of the virtuous and worthy part of society" and the "concert and zeal of the vicious." "It is the anarchy," declared Charles Pinckney, "or rather worse than anarchy, of a pure democracy which *I fear— where the laws lose their respect, and the magistrates their authority; where no permanent security is given to the property and privileges of the citizens; and no measures pursued, but such as suit the temporary interest and convenience of the prevailing parties.*" "The public Checks upon the reserved licentiousness of the People are too weak to suppress their Clamors," warned James M. Varnum. "Seasons of general Heat, Tumult and Fermentation" create many problems, wrote John Jay, and one of the biggest among them was "a wide Field open for the Operations of Ambition-Men raised from low Degrees to high Stations, and rendered giddy by Elevation." As early as 1783, Virginia delegates to the Continental Congress concluded that "the prospect must be very disagreeable, when it is considered that congress may possibly be in danger of being mobbed, if they do not flatter the prejudices of the majority of the lower class of citizens." "We have thought," wrote one author, "that virtue, with so many bright rewards, had some solid power; and that, with ten thousand charms, she could always command ten thousand votes. Alas! These illusions are as thin as the gloss on other bubbles." William Cobbett had few doubts as to where the radicals came from: "The bulk of the political reformers is always composed of needy, discontented men, too indolent or impatient to advance themselves by fair and honest means." Benjamin Rush, otherwise well known for his Revolutionary egalitarianism, joined the chorus of malcontents. As he witnessed non-elite participation in politics swell, he felt it was time to compose an epitaph for American liberties:

> Here lie interred the liberties of the United States. They were purchased with much treasure and blood, and by uncommon exertions of talent and virtues. Their dissolution was brought on by the cheapness of suffrage in some of the states, by a funding system which begat banks and lotteries and land speculations, and by the removal of Congress to the city of Washington, a place so unfriendly to health, society, and instructing intercourse, and so calculated to foster party and malignant passions, that wise and good men considered a seat in it as a

kind of banishment, in consequence of which the government fell into the hands of the young and ignorant and needy part of the community, and hence the loss of the respect and obedience due to laws, and hence one of the causes of the downfall of the last and only free country in the world.[37]

What is surprising is how little attention has been paid to the nature of this defensive reaction from the elite, a reaction that in itself confirmed that tectonic shifts in culture were taking place. These shifts would in due time push the liberties nominally established on paper in 1787 into new territory of real-life practice. The gentry identified the problem quite clearly: the growing involvement of ordinary people in the political process, and their claims to new slices of the liberty cake. Both threatened to distort the original republican recipe. Contributing to this erosion of control were other historical forces, such as western expansion, that brought a decline in property qualifications for the franchise; widespread land ownership; and denominational diversity accelerated by the Great Awakening. According to Nathan Hatch, the last development—with its anticlericalism—combined with the Revolutionary changes to contribute to the decline of deference-based distinctions between elites and commoners. But ultimately it was the democratization of public conversation about politics that presented the greatest menace to the rulers, because it threatened to turn the stock of concepts related to freedom, which they had created, into a sword of Damocles pointed at them. It is important to note that this democratization was first taking place predominantly in the symbolic sphere, where meaning, condensed in signs and words, was easily accessible and immediately usable. The liberty cap may again serve as an example. Originally deriving from the *pileus,* a cap received by a slave at a manumission ceremony in ancient Rome, it had long been popular in England as a symbol of its freedoms. It was introduced as an icon of the American cause by Paul Revere in 1768. Almost immediately, it was appropriated by the colonists (with some help from English political cartoonists). The logic was dense: the symbol crossed the Atlantic because Americans were the new possessors of British liberty. The cap became omnipresent as a popular sign synthesizing the Revolutionary ideology, and, most importantly, it was accessible to all, including "the lower class of citizens," who could read their own meanings into it.[38]

This popular enthusiasm was exceedingly vexing for the gentry because it undermined their hitherto anointed position as interpreters of the true meaning of freedom. "It is really very curious to observe how the people of this world are made the dupes of a word," noted Edward Rutledge with consternation, " 'Liberty' is the motto; every attempt to restrain licentiousness or give efficacy to Government is charged audaciously upon the real advocates of Freedom as an attack upon Liberty." He found several of his friends "so highly disgusted with the artifices of some unworthy characters, that they had determined to withdraw from the theatre of public action." Theophilus Parsons despaired that the "idea of liberty has been held up in so dazzling colours, that some of us may not be willing to submit to that subordination necessary in the freest States." Noah Webster was distraught at how people had come to use popular symbols to express their yearning for freedom. "How is this?" he asked. "Why the answer is easy—the Egyptians venerated a cat and cow and our modern idolaters venerate a liberty cap.... Our people are perpetually exclaiming 'Liberty is the goddess we adore,' and the cap is the emblem of this goddess." But, he noted, it was no less an "act of superstition to dance around a cap or a pole in honor of liberty, than it was in Egypt to sacrifice a bullock to Isis." Timothy Ford warned those who demanded more equality to "beware, lest in arraying liberty with the omnipotence of a deity, or the captiousness of an arbitrary monarch, they convert it to a tyrant; and on the placid brow which naturall, beams peace and all the charming virtues, they stamp the scowl of malevolence and the terrific bodings of civil discord." Although Nature did make all equal in their rights, he noted, "the unavoidable conclusions is that inequality of conditions is one of nature's laws ... and it would be rather presumptuous to attempt to establish civil society upon principles repugnant to her laws." The *Anarchiad* caricatured demagogues who practiced such populism on common people: Mr. Wronghead was "busied, daily, planning pop'lar schemes, and nightly rapt in democratic dreams," aiming to please the "vulgar ears" with "*cant pretense of Liberty.*" The result of such activities could only be an alarming decline in proper respect for great leaders; politicians would from now on mainly aim to "awe the mob."[39] Demagogues of this kind represented not only a betrayal of impartiality, but also—by filling people's heads with excessive ambitions—a threat to social harmony.

The usual explanation offered for such developments was that "liberty is as apt to degenerate into licentiousness, as power is to become arbitrary.

Restraints therefore are as necessary in the former as the latter case." This was why it was becoming commonplace to bemoan the disparity between the virtuous, Revolutionary generation and what Mercy Otis Warren called the "degenerate, servile race of beings" that could take over America if "intoxicated ambition" and "licentiousness" prevailed. Jeremiah Atwater warned in his sermon before the legislature of Vermont that due to the weakness of human nature, "the people will easily suffer themselves to be duped and blinded by the crafty and designing," while "heat, passion, and prejudice, will drown the still voice of reason, and public offices be the purchase of venality, or the sport of faction." Others, eyeing these "causes of our disappointment," concluded in resignation that "the real truth is, our revolutionary schemes were too visionary . . . and our hopes too sanguine."[40]

Such apprehensions began in earnest during the administrations of Washington and Adams. They were in evidence in the Federalists' portrayal of Anti-Federalists as American "Jacobins" whose main sin was that they were inciting people to become politically active *beyond their stations*. Federalist Brahmins held venal contempt for those who subverted social hierarchy, calling them the "refuse, the sweepings of the most depraved part of mankind." Such reactions were usually occasioned by an "improper"—that is, unauthorized—usage of liberty language by ordinary people. George Cabot described this rhetorical epidemic spreading across the population as "the consummation of vice and tyranny," and warned, "It is justly to be feared, because it is propagated by eloquence and sophistry, and is exhibited in the garb of virtue and of liberty, whose sacred name it profanely usurps." Many were distressed that men of "abilities and integrity" had now "retired from the busy scene," while "Demagogues of desperate fortunes, mere adventurers in fraud, were left to act unopposed," preying on the "ductility of the Multitude." Timothy Dwight complained that individuals lacking virtue had taken over the government and displaced the genteel, as "sycophancy, servility, bribery, perjury, and numberless other spectres of vice, haunt all seats of power and trust, and force the friends of public integrity to retire with alarm and discouragement."[41] All of these reactions, which may be described as declension anxiety, can be attributed to the gentry's fear of disappearing in the Bermuda Triangle of an expanding "market" for liberty talk, the social unrest inspired by it, and the collapse of their unity as a class.

As to the first threat, we do not always appreciate that in the eighteenth-century British world language was not as homogenized in its usages as it is in today's age of mass communications and nationwide institutions. To a British colonist before 1764 it would have been immediately obvious that elite usage was different from non-elite usage. When in 1766 a group of South Carolina slaves rioted, using the conflict with England to demand freedom, the Charleston elite dismissed them as simply ridiculous, noting that "Some Negroes had mimick'd their betters in crying out '*Liberty.*'" Clearly, there were two different *markets* for the use of political language, and their corresponding publics were not interchangeable. Certain subjects (like certain styles) were assigned to specific publics, and issues of liberty were the province of the elite. Toward the end of the century, these markets began, for the first time, to overlap. Newcomers, both invited and uninvited, were trespassing on what used to be reserved territory. As James Warren of Massachusetts wrote to John Adams in 1779, "Fellows who would have cleaned my shoes five years ago, have amassed fortunes, and are riding in chariots." For him, such disruptions of the customary order were a most serious threat, resulting in no less than a "world turned topsy-turvy." Satires on parvenus were in high demand; literature tried to restore in fiction what in reality was a fading line of cultural separation between the elite and the commoners. Royall Tyler's heavily didactic play *The Contrast* (1787), the first professionally staged American drama, featured the contrasting figures of Dimple and Colonel Henry Manly. Dimple is snobbish (claiming to have read "Chesterfield and received the polish of Europe"), greedy, ignorant of the public good and virtue, and possessed of a talent for stealing into people's confidence by demagoguery, while Colonel Manly possesses all the old, genteel qualities of patriotism, honor, selflessness, and a rejection of luxury ("I have humbly imitated our illustrious WASHINGTON, in having exposed my health and life in the service of my country"). Dimple represented what was by then a fairly common stereotype of those who were raised to new wealth but lacked true gentility, and thus had no scruples in courting the mob (tellingly, the cast of characters also included a model of a "proper" commoner—Jonathan, a simple country fellow, who was nevertheless deferential to gentlemen like Manly). Other authors complained that some of the gentry, seduced by interest, betrayed their own class in the same manner, an ignoble act, because "to flatter the ignorant and inexperienced requires no skill, it scarcely requires any thing more than a disposition to flatter; for with that class of people the very disposition is accepted as an evidence of kindness." "I pray God," wrote Samuel Adams, "we may never see Men, filling the sacred Seats of Government, who are wanting in adequate Abilities, or influenced by any Motives or Feelings separate from the publick Welfare."[42] The very need for such prayers indicated that social barriers were already being crossed.

To many among the political class, such crossings took on a more sinister aura in the context of the social unrest that erupted during and immediately after the Revolution. Well before Shays's Rebellion gripped the country's attention, there were tensions in Virginia triggered by disputes over the creation of minutemen units, their pay, and ways of choosing their commanders; tumults following Patrick Henry not being reappointed commander of the army in 1775; riots in 1774 in Hanover over shortages of salt; and challenges to the Patriot elite by Loudoun County farmers. It was bad enough that common people were beginning to use the elite language of rights as if they had the virtue and knowledge to do so, but now some acted upon those concepts, at times even violently. Fear of lost authority was now compounded by the fear of actual anarchy. All this was, of course, gentry language for the gentry market. When a major Virginia figure like Carter Braxton, invoking the interests of "the people," warned that such "anarchy" would ultimately threaten "the enjoyment of our liberties and future quiet," he was not speaking to ordinary, working people, but to his social peers.[43]

The third source of apprehension was the growing sense that, in the context of factional schism, the necessity to accommodate ordinary people in the political process was hazardous to the integrity of the ruling class. The greater the schisms, the more each faction had to reach out to supporters beyond its own circles and fashion new public images for its leaders and for itself. This presented them with a formidable dilemma that cannot be explained by looking at political and legal history only. Patrick Henry tried to solve it by styling himself publicly as a simple, spontaneous representative of all people and adopting a popular style, often with dramatic gestures, including waving a dagger. But Jefferson thought such manner lacked refinement and was indicative of someone seeking cheap fame rather than virtue. To him, Madison's language was "pure, classical, and copious, soothing always the feelings of his adversaries by civilities and softness of expression," a stark contrast to "the fervid declamation of Mr. Henry." He praised Edmund Pendleton's "cool, smooth, and persuasive" style, adding sarcastically that he

certainly did not have "the poetical fancy of Mr. Henry, his sublime imagination, his lofty and overwhelming diction." Similarly, Edward Carrington
thought that it was "unfortunate that in the elections the passions instead of
the reasons of the people, were brought into operation too generally," and he
sarcastically referred to "the popular talents of Mr. H[enry]," while William
Bingham condemned the current fashion of working "on the passions of the
people" and referred to Henry's "most eloquent harangue" in the Virginia
Assembly.[44] All three were trying to preserve the world of the gentry as they
knew it.

The power of this identity was evident in the fact that even the most
politically antagonistic factions shared it. During the War of Independence,
American leaders could perfectly well attack their metropolitan counterparts
while *sharing* with them beliefs in an unequal social order, notions of virtue,
manners, taste, and styles of conduct. We saw how in the post-Revolutionary
decade, Federalists' and Anti-Federalists' sharing of certain deeply rooted
values belied political disagreements. Gentry identity—defined by property,
virtue, and the title to a full inventory of freedoms—was still strong enough
to transcend such divisions. But by the last decade of the century, this sense of
unity was dissipating, and the alarms were going off.

As far as the gentry could reach into their collective memory, this cultural
unity had been stable. Throughout the colonial period, both the provincials
and British officials used the same, elite-bound, virtue-premised subtexts of
liberty to argue for their otherwise opposing causes. A 1701 essay, probably
authored by the Virginia planter Robert Beverley and aimed against the
excessive and arbitrary power of governors, emphasized that its author was
speaking from a position of public virtue shared by all British subjects when
he censured royal officials, who "oftentimes of mean education and base
spirits, cannot bear their good Fortunes, but thinking absolute Command
only is their Province, either for private Interest, or to gratifie their Ambition,
Revenge, or some other Passion." Royal officials, for their part, used the
very same ethos to criticize the colonists. William Black, Governor William
Gooch's secretary to the Virginia Treaty Commission to the Six Nations,
used it to reproach members of the colonial Assembly for lacking sufficient virtue to make good policy. "Decorum," he noted in his diary in 1744,
"which justly regulated, is always a great addition to the Augustness as well as
Honour and Credit of any Public Body, was not to be observed . . . nothing but a confus'd multitude and Greater part of the meaner sort, speak as

make Patriotism their plea but Preferment their design, and that not for Honour but for Profit . . . most of them preferring Private Advantage to public Good."[45]

Metropolitan authors prominently attacked provincial leaders during the Revolution for violating this unified ethos, a conduct they blamed on factionalism springing from low social origins. In 1776 a British pamphlet directed against the colonial leaders declared that the voice of reasonable men in America "is drowned in the clamours of Faction and tumult of Party" and "terrified into silence by the tyranny of a misled rabble." This theme was echoed by American Loyalists, who saw the Revolutionary leaders as betraying the social obligations of their class by trying to "incite the ignorant and the vulgar to arms." Joseph Galloway observed caustically that Samuel Adams was "a man, who though by no means remarkable for brilliant abilities, yet is equal to most men in popular intrigue, and the management of faction."[46]

On the American side, shared values of the gentry manifested themselves across the front lines throughout the Revolutionary War. Loyalist Cadwallader Colden, irate at the American rebels who imprisoned him, questioned the cultural legitimacy of the new authorities when he sarcastically noted in his journal the "threatenings and insults I have received from our tarring and feathering gentry." He also cast doubt on their very understanding of rights when he complained that they had violated his birthright "English liberty" by putting him in jail, not for what he did, but for what he "may do." Yet, when he applied to American authorities for parole, he still very much counted on certain genteel assumptions presumably shared between himself and his tormentors. He fully expected the Revolutionary authorities to recognize that he would honor the noblesse oblige principle: "I do hereby promise and Engage upon my Honour as a Gentleman," he wrote, "to repair to Fish Kill . . . and there to apply to the Commissioners."[47]

A Loyalist, responding to Washington's 1777 proclamation requiring oaths of loyalty, accused the General of betraying public virtue for private gain: "That Mr. Washington, who once was esteemed a gentleman, should forget that character by becoming a tool of an impracticable ambition, is a matter of commiseration." But it was not unusual for a contemporary Patriot gentleman to invoke identical values when expressing the hope that eventual military victory over the British would bring a time "when America will establish her freedom and independence upon the permanent foundation of public virtue." This ethos was so closely shared that it sometimes made for inadvertently humorous situations. When Loyalist William Henry Drayton of Charleston was ostracized in a Patriot pamphlet, his published retort referred to the authors as "profanum vulgus"—pretending to be gentlemen but, being unread, capable of understanding only "rules [of] how to cut up a beast in the market to the best advantage, to cobble an old shoe in the neatest manner, or to build a necessary house." "Nature," he pointed out, "never intended that such men be profound politicians, or able statesmen." Within days, his Patriot addressees responded—using the same criteria to discredit him as ungenteel—by writing that he drew an "unmanly satisfaction of hacking and hewing" respectable men and gave "an ostentatious shew of learning, by spouting scraps of Latin at every turn and making a most illiberal application of such vulgar and low words, as would better become the high-bred dames of Billingsgate or Drury."[48]

It was a testimony to the durable power of this identity that its perceived fragmentation was fought strictly within the framework of the old ethos, through mutual accusations of factionalism as a deviation from the genteel norm. These typically took the form of denunciations of "the selfish and contracted spirit" in public officials as "odious and unpardonable," threatening to "destroy all harmony of sentiment," and causing "public resolutions" to show "more the complexion of party-attachment, than the public good." Commentators noted bitterly that "it is on points of private local utility, or on those of doubtful tendency, that men split into parties," and that when they do, "victory is the object and not public good." Such ethical decline would inevitably be followed by the loss of the political elite's ability to represent the true will of the population: "When tumultuous meetings of people, unknown to the law, and unrestrained by legal modes of procedure, undertake to direct the public will, faction succeeds; and faction begets disorder, force, rancorous passions, anarchy, tyranny, blood and slaughter." "I see much of that Jealousy & party Spirit by which some Gentlemen will perpetuate their detestable characters," wrote a disgusted delegate of the disagreements in the Continental Congress in 1779. A year later, when agreement among delegates was emerging, Connecticut member Roger Sherman observed with relief that "the people of the States should have the fullest confidence in Congress" because it showed signs of "Universal attention to the public good, & no appearance of party sprit." The advice on organizing a state constitutional convention offered by Caesar Rodney, a major general of the Delaware state militia, was to pursue "true patriotism" with "cool argument & reasoning," a tactic which would unite "all such as are not Governed with party spirit." It was not just a matter of arriving at decisions on finances or foreign policy. In all these comments, the key question was that of their authors' self-image, at the heart of which lay the claim that they constituted one unified, nonpartisan upper class. Sharpened political divisions shattered these defining attributes and, by extension, the social boundaries embedded in them. By the turn of the century, this loss of identity loomed as an impediment to all political progress. Griped John Adams, "I say Parties and Factions will not suffer, or permit Improvements to be made. As soon as one man hints at an improvement his Rival opposes it. No sooner has one Party discovered or invented an Amelioration of the Condition of Man or the order of Society, then the opposite Party, belies it, misconstrues it, misrepresents it, ridicules it, insults it, and persecutes it."[49]

The conviction among the American political elite that they were one upper class was still clearly discernible in the conduct of the Constitutional Convention. Its decorum, language, and style were all taken from the gentry playbook. It is important to understand that frequent condemnations of party in the 1770s and 1780s were fundamentally elitist, not egalitarian, in nature. When rivalries over policy surfaced, blaming factionalism became common, but behind these condemnations was a thinly veiled nostalgia for old unity. When Gouverneur Morris warned the Congress against party spirit in 1779, he still conjured up an idealized picture: "There is indeed in this House a chosen Band—of Patriots, who have a proper Respect for each others Opinions, A proper Sense of each other's Feelings and whose Bosoms glow with equal Ardor in the common Cause. But no party." Benjamin Rush compared the spread of factionalisms to "epidemic diseases," and bemoaned the fact that "Our country is divided into two great parties called Federalists and Democrats" that "hold different speculative opinions in government and different views of the proper mode of conducting public affairs." This was alien to the original republican ideals. "Suppose," he asked, "a ship be manned by sailors of six different nations, and suppose no one of them to understand the language of the other. Suppose the ship to be overtaken by a storm, and the captain and mates to be able to speak the language of but one class. What do you suppose would be the fate of that ship?" Impartiality, noted James Madison, is needed in all governments, but "in a *federal* Republic founded on local distinctions involving local jealousies, it ought to be attended to with a still more scrupulous exactness." When "party spirit" reigns, government can scarcely be expected to produce "harmony or the public good." When Thomas Burke of North Carolina attacked Thomas Paine in a satirical poem, he pointed to the threat to the unity of the old elite posed by overdemocratic parvenus grasping at political roles:

> On envy's altars hecatombs expire,
> And Faction fondly lights her Pupil's fire.
> That pupil most devoted to her will,
> Who for the worthless wags his quibbling quill;
> And with true democracy of spirit
> Bravely attacks the most exalted merit.[50]

Whether Loyalist or Revolutionary, Federalist or Anti-Federalist, the gentry typically shared the assumption that they were a single upper class unified by property, education, entitlement to office, and immunity to interest—and as such uniquely qualified as guarantors of liberty. This identity was older, deeper, and stronger than even the most dramatic political differences of the day. It was a distressing sight for its members to watch rising divisions drive wedges into what they had confidently considered to be an enduring fixture in American society.

IV. The Useful Mob

> Liberty consists in a power of acting under the guidance and controul of reason: Licentiousness in acting under the influence of sensual passions, contrary to the dictates of reason.
>
> —Moses Mather, *America's Appeal to the Impartial World,* 1775

LOOKING BACK ON THE Boston Massacre nearly five decades after the event, John Adams still saw a clear distinction between the two categories of actors involved: the helpful but unreliable street crowd, also known as the mob; and the "virtuous, substantial, independent, disinterested, and intelligent citizens" who, led by Whig leaders, congregated to debate the event at the Old South Church. There was little doubt in his mind that the latter were predestined to lead the republic, and the former were expected to follow. Despite the invention of the idea of the "people," the concept of the "mob" retained its utility in the Revolutionary era as a symbolic antithesis of republican virtue. As David Ramsay observed in one of his orations, "Genuine republicanism is friendly to order and a proper subordination in society," but "it is hostile to mobs and licentiousness of every kind." No amount of public identifying with the "people at large" could erase the elite's deeply seated fear and loathing of the "common herd." Corruption, the reverse of virtue, was increasingly identified with rudeness and simpletonness—in elite eyes, qualities of the common folk. Without erecting proper barriers to protect themselves, the American elite believed they too could easily degenerate into vulgarity. This thinking was bolstered by a new awareness of history that told them civilized people could slide back into "Indian savagery." Ramsay, who in principle believed "all mankind to be originally the same and only diversified by accidental circumstances," and who criticized Jefferson's portrayal of Africans in his *Notes on the State of Virginia* for having "depressed the negroes too low," was nevertheless convinced that "Our back country people are as much savage as the Cherokees." Fear of the mob was widely shared among diverse eighteenth-century British elites—whether colonial or metropolitan, newly wealthy or old money, landed or commercial. For instance, the Loyalist Ann Hulton, sister of Henry Hulton, commissioner of customs in Boston in 1769, had an all-embracing explanation for the rebelliousness of the colonists: the excessive power of the mob. "Tyranny of the Multitude," she noted, "is the most Arbitrary & oppressive; there is no justice to be obtain in any case, & many Persons awed by the people, are obliged to court Popularity for their own Security, this is only to be done by opposing Government at home."[51]

One response to these fears was a new emphasis on an old cultural device used to depict the relationship between the elite and non-elite: refinement. Although in colonial British America social distinctions were much less complex than in England, by the end of the eighteenth century both countries increasingly witnessed a flattening of old hierarchies into a simpler opposition of the polite and the vulgar. It was a measure designed for an age of upward mobility, and its greatest success was soon to be witnessed among the fast-growing middle class in the nineteenth century. Social climbing and new money were taking the gloss off the long-established distinctions of affluence, pedigree, and public virtue. Refinement, by contrast, retained its usefulness to set both new and old elites apart from ordinary folk. Those lacking it could serve as an educational anti-model for the socially aspiring. "The vulgar are always slaves to prejudice," a state of mind that "betrays a narrow, contracted soul, and ignorance of the world," cautioned a Philadelphian author in his "advice to a young gentleman."[52]

The meaning of refinement was not limited to the style of conduct; it had direct and serious connotations for the politics of liberty. The concept of politeness as an organizing principle of social order, as well as an engine for the advancement of freedom, found its most elaborate intellectual articulation in the works of Anthony Ashley Cooper, Earl of Shaftesbury (although we should bear in mind that he only supplied a theoretical expression for what the upper classes had already practiced). His view epitomized the shift in culture that replaced older models of authority, based on court and church, with one founded on good manners. Its essence was that politeness—elegant behavior, speech, wit, subtle distance from one's topic of conversation, and a generously tolerant attitude to others—supplied a broad ideal capable of regulating social interactions. Lawrence E. Klein has shown how this ideal of cultural politics was a response to the decline of the older, courtly model of societal domination, and reflected the expansion of the public arena beyond the gentry and aristocracy. More than just a set of desirable traits for those in authority, it was a larger project for a well-ordered society organized around polite sociability, one offering a cultural, rather than political, model of liberty. In its hope that all could someday become cultivated and moral, and therefore part of a politically active public, it was nominally an inclusive vision of a free society. In the future, reason would neutralize irrational emotions, currently dominant among ordinary folk. It would, of course, have to be a disinterested reason, calm and witty, not one promoted by "zealots" with "grim Aspect" and "ill Grace." "All politeness is owing to liberty," noted Shaftesbury. "We polish one another, and rub off our Corners and rough Sides by a sort of *amicable Collision*. To restrain this, is inevitably to bring a Rust upon Mens Understandings. 'Tis a destroying of Civility, Good Breeding, and even Charity itself, under pretence of maintaining it." It was a view in many ways resembling the one held by the American Revolutionary leaders—that when the future educates and civilizes the masses, all will become free to participate in political life. They would then become citizens in the image of members of Congress, so admired by John Dickinson for their "perfect Affection to the Liberty of America" and their "Enlightened understandings," and by Gouverneur Morris for their amicable generosity and tolerance ("Nothing is truer than this, that little minds are more resentful than great ones").[53]

The "mob" was indispensable to this vision of the world. Defined negatively by a *lack* of reasonableness and refinement, it effectively played the role of an anti-model of the enlightened and the civil, an ever-present hazard to the stability of social order and to the security of property. It was a broad cultural construct, a collective category homogenized out of an otherwise amorphous mass of people. It included the uncultured, the illiterate, the dependent, the poor, the servile, the laboring, and the propertyless. An examination of its usage tells us that it was employed to symbolize not just the lower orders, but also all those who were presumed to be *irrational* and *uncultivated*. It was this meaning that the English novelist Henry Fielding had in mind when he explained, "Whenever this word occurs in our writings, it intends persons without virtue, or sense, in all stations." It was, in practice, a device to define the elites themselves, and to draw borders between them and "others." The tension of such contrasts was seen as beneficial to maintaining a free society. This was what one Carolina author must have had in mind when he noted that "domestic slavery, far from being inconsistent, has, in fact, a tendency to stimulate and perpetuate the spirit of liberty."[54]

The concept of the mob was another example of how the speaking elite were able to create cultural reality by establishing certain norms and then producing representations of those who "violated" these norms. "It is not by contracted and narrow motives that a public Official should act," observed Arthur Middleton, "but on large and disinterested conduct only can a free Government be established and [largely?] supported. A Legislature should proceed with caution and coolness not with the heat of a distempered mob." Commenting on the unrest in Massachusetts, Henry Lee referred to "the Madness of the Malcontents," and worried that if not suppressed, the consequence for America would be "a mob government for a time, which will terminate in despotism among ourselves or from abroad." The unruly mob was unqualified to understand the risks posed to liberty by its actions, because "the objects of the malcontents are alluring to the vulgar and the impotency of government is rather an encouragement to, than a restraint on, the licentious." William Hooper, a signer of the Declaration of Independence, saw the radically democratic 1776 Constitution of Pennsylvania as the fulfillment of this kind of a threat: "The Mob made a second branch of Legislation-Laws subjected to their revisal in order to refine them, a Washing in ordure by way of purification. Taverns and dram shops are the councils to which the laws of this State are to be referred to for approbation before they possess a binding Influence." He called the new polity "a Beast without a head," a creation of instincts unmoderated by reason. Two years earlier, when he still supported reconciliation with Britain, he thought the Boston Tea Party an "intemperate folly of a rabble," and assured his mother that he was not willing to be "a licentious demagogue, but think cooly & dispassionately upon the conduct of government." Madison, in turn, worried about revivalist beliefs as a potential threat to good government, because when "religion is kindled into enthusiasm, its force, like that of other passions, is increased by the sympathy of the multitude."[55]

It was not surprising, therefore, that there was already considerable unease among the American political class during the earliest patriotic demonstrations involving the Stamp Act, which in some cases turned riotous; they needed them to support the cause but at the same time feared losing control over the protests. The historian William Gordon echoed these worries: "It is not to be supposed, that the disorderly proceedings above related, were chargeable solely to the dregs of the colonies. . . . The mobs consisted not of mere rabble; but were composed much of independent freemen and freeholders, so that some of the first people in the provinces were intimidated. . . . Merchants, assemblymen, magistrates, &c. united directly or indirectly in the riots, and without their influence and instigation the lower class of inhabitants would have been quiet; but great pains were taken to rouse them into action."[56]

The cultural depth of derision for the mob derived from a very long tradition, going back to medieval attitudes to the serfs and peasants, often portrayed as wicked and bestial, and therefore naturally fit for labor. In parts of early modern Europe where unfree labor was dominant, the ruling classes saw themselves as radically different from the peasants, a disparity that was sometimes racial and always deeply divisive. In Russia, the peasants were portrayed as inherently inferior, passive, and incapable of enjoying freedom;

FIGURE 6. An agitated street mob preparing to burn an unpopular government minister in effigy. British cartoon, 1756. (Courtesy Library of Congress, Washington, D.C.)

and in Poland, the landed class tenaciously held on to the myth that it historically derived from an altogether different stock than the peasants. The eighteenth-century gentry in Britain continued to assign the lower classes two distinctive characteristics: irrationality and moral depravity. As the Scottish author James Reid observed, "The rabble, that many-headed monster, is not capable of listening to the voice of sound reason."[57] This belief in depravity required that even relief programs directed at this group incorporate punishment in the Houses of Correction.

The most distinctive trait at the heart of the concept of the mob, both in European and American early modern history, was that it divided people into those who were driven by "reason" and those who were motivated by "passions." "The mobile, that many headed beast," explained the refined Maryland doctor, Alexander Hamilton, "cannot be reasoned into religious and pious duties. Men are not all philosophers. The tools by which we must work upon the gross senses and rough cast minds of the vulgar are such as form and lay before their eyes, rewards and punishments whereby the passions of hope and fear are excited." It was widely assumed among the ruling classes that this category of people were incapable of grasping the concept of political order, much less the notion of freedom. This was why it was a standard belief in European courts that a certain degree of ostentation and pomp was not only proper, but indispensable, so that the lower classes could understand power. Only through the language of decorum, ceremony, and equipage—all appealing to *the senses*—could the vulgar appreciate authority. "The common man," observed the Enlightenment philosopher Christian Wolff, "solely dependent on his senses, and unable to make much use of his reason, cannot comprehend the majesty of a king; but through things that fall in his eye and stir his senses, he receives . . . an idea of power and might." The Federalist patriarch Rufus King observed wryly that pomp and splendor in public celebrations, "of course draw the Huzzas and admiration of the Multitude." Passions led to dependence; reason, on the contrary, made cultivation and public spirit possible. "The people at large," noted Thomas Johnson, "are not a Body fit for Deliberation, they are gen[era]lly carried away with a warmth of Zeal that overleaps sedate & wise policy." "How ungenerous is the human Heart when under the Controul of tumultuous Passions," complained James M. Varnum, noting that in such situations the hard-earned merit of leaders is forgotten in an hour.[58] Passions, it was believed, lay at the root of chaotic, primitive peoples, where absence of order made liberty impossible. Against the Enlightenment backdrop of a civilized and harmonious society, the irrational "rabble" stood as the barbarians in the garden. They needed to be monitored and contained.

In Revolutionary America, the mob and its accompanying passion/reason dichotomy played a significant role in the debates over the new political system. The creation of the new nation and its polity were believed to have been an act of reason. "This single circumstance," wrote Joel Barlow, "will stamp a peculiar glory on the American revolution, and mark it as a distinguished aera in the history of mankind; that sober reason and reflection have done the work of enthusiasm and performed miracles of gods." Carter Braxton, who was skeptical of placing excessive expectations on the people at large and on "popular governments," warned that reasoned, altruistic actions could not be expected from the masses. The more politically radical Samuel Adams shared the very same premise. After a 1774 incident in which the poor of Marblehead, Massachusetts, fearful of an epidemic and angry at preferential treatment for some, set fire to a hospital, Adams observed: "The tumult of the people is very properly compared to the raging of the sea. When the passions of the multitude become headstrong, they generally will have their course: a direct opposition only tends to increase them; and as to reasoning, one may as well expect that the foaming billows will hearken to a lecture of morality and be quiet." The episode was not a rightful "rising" but "a lawless attack upon property," and therefore the Patriot elite ("the friends of liberty themselves") was fully justified in taking military action to protect citizens from the "fury of an ungoverned mob." This outlook did not essentially differ from that of Royalist Governor Thomas Hutchinson of Massachusetts, for whom the most obvious explanation of the rebellious nature of Boston's defiant legislative elections of 1769 was that the town meetings involved in the protests were "constituted of the lowest class of the people under the influence of a few of the higher class but of intemperate and furious dispositions." As he explained, "Men of property and of the best characters have deserted these meetings where they are sure of being affronted." Loyalist Joseph Galloway expressed indignation that during the 1774 session of the Continental Congress, "the republican faction in Congress had provided a mob, ready to execute their secret orders."[59]

What is important is that the opposing categories of reason and passion were so deeply ingrained in eighteenth-century culture that they became a part of the reigning definition of liberty. As William Byrd II noted in his *Commonplace Book:* "No man is so qualified to undergo the tyranny of an arbitrary Prince, as he who has been accustomed to be slave to his passions. This is the true reason, that private vertue is the safest Guard of publick Liberty." John Adams believed that common people, with their "vulgar, rustic imaginations," were too easily driven by emotions to sustain liberty. Moses Mather, a Connecticut Patriot and a minister, expressed much the same thought, noting, "Liberty consists in a power of acting under the guidance and controul of reason: Licentiousness in acting under the influence of sensual passions, contrary to the dictates of reason." Henry Cummings, preaching in Massachusetts on the sixth anniversary of the outbreak of the Revolution, stressed the ever present need for Patriots of a "calm and dispassionate temper," because "The generality are influenced by their passion only." Samuel Wales, addressing the General Assembly of Connecticut, condemned selfishness as unpatriotic, but distinguished between its effects on the elite and the common folk. In the former, it produced at worst "a mad pursuit of low popularity," but in the case of "the common people," there was a danger they would elect as their civil rulers only those "to whom they happen to be particularly attached by any private and sinister motives," or those "by whom they are most humoured in their prejudices and follies." Gouverneur Morris was far from being an isolated voice when he worried on the eve of Independence about a threat to social order from "the lower orders of mankind." He was only more blunt than others when he noted that "the heads of the mobility grow dangerous to the gentry; and how to keep them down is the question." The policies of London loomed as no more evil a prospect than the emergence of the mob on the political stage: "I see it with fear and trembling, that if the disputes with Great Britain continue, we shall be under the worst of all possible dominations; we shall be under the domination of a riotous mob."[60]

Putting aside for the moment the legal and constitutional considerations, from a cultural standpoint the Founders' wariness about the "tyranny of the majority" may be seen as a permutation of their fear of the irrational mob. Although today we tend to view Madison's worries about this issue as primarily a problem of protecting minority rights and of reconciling the parochial interests of the localities with those of the whole Union, he was also clearly concerned about the self-perpetuation of the elite in a situation of expanding voting rights. This concern was quite consistent with the widely held elite belief that the majority of people lacked the necessary virtue to make impartial decisions in the name of larger public good. He feared putting too much trust in the people themselves, and worried that their representatives' independence would be lost if the "courtiers of popularity" succumbed to the narrow, often passion-driven goals of the masses, putting in doubt majority rule as "the safest guardian of both the public Good and of private rights." Like other members of the gentry, he fully expected that the time-honored social order would continue, in that elections would "extract from the mass of the Society the purest and noblest characters which it contains," which, in turn, would alleviate the dangers posed by the interested and the vulgar.[61]

By the end of the century, the opposition between those guided by reason and those driven by emotions became one of the main criteria defining the eligibility for liberty. It was used to distinguish between those who were qualified for its full privileges, including office holding, from those who were not. When Elbridge Gerry was appointed envoy to France in 1797, Jefferson, concerned about a potential conflict with Paris, invoked impassionate virtue and appealed to him to accept the position, suggesting that if Gerry declined, "a substitute may be named, who has enlisted passions in the present contest, and by the preponderance of his vote in the mission, may entail on us calamities." This powerful ideal of conduct was well illustrated by the fact that one of the most common points of praise directed at George Washington during his lifetime was that he could, "at the dictate of reason, control his will and command himself to act." One author argued that Washington was "the best man living" because, conscious that the "principles on which he acts are indeed founded on virtue, he steadily and coolly pursues these principles, with a mind neither depressed by disappointments, nor elated by success." Joel Barlow thought Washington and other officers who fought in the War of Independence "an example of the noblest effort of human nature, *the conquest of self*, in obeying the voice of their country."[62]

Perhaps the most common pair of metaphors used during the Revolution to express the contrast between irrational and rational aspirants to liberty was the gendered duo of manliness and effeminacy. When in 1774 South Carolina statesman Thomas Lynch praised New Englanders for their restraint, he stressed that they behaved "without rashness, or any tumultuous proceedings that belong to mobs" and instead offered "a steady, manly, cool and regular conduct." Others invoked the need for the colonies to show "firm, manly and persevering opposition" to British tyranny. They advocated "showing independent Virility instead of colonial effeminacy" as the best foreign policy; warned that the success of the Revolution depended on the colonists curing themselves of "their vicious and luxurious and effeminate Appetites, Passions and Habits, a more dangerous Army to American Liberty than Mr. Howes"; and counseled that when English kings asked, "How shall we turn the Minds of the People from an Attention to their Liberties?" the answer was, "By making them extravagant, luxurious, effeminate." "Manly" was associated with "not subservient." When Samuel Ward praised the petition of Georgia to the king, it was for showing a proper "spirit of Freedom that Vein of Piety that good sense that manly Firmness & Decency void of all that low submissive creeping Address usually contained in Performances of that Sort."[63]

The prominence of the distrust of the irrational and unruly "mob" in political discourse did not indicate that the Revolutionary project of creating an enlightened and free state based on the sovereignty of the people was internally incoherent. Far from an incongruity, the simultaneous lionization and fear of common people were part and parcel of the Founders' grand vision, which needed both in order to maintain its overall coherence. An enlightened justification of the new state required a symbolic inclusion of the masses. On the other hand, perceptions of the common people as often uncivil and dangerous were indispensable to elite claims to authority and privileged liberty—both needed to keep the *mobile vulgus* in check. Short of descending to ahistoricism, it is not possible to explain the coexistence of these two views as a case of irony, because early modern elites never embraced a world view where ordinary people were equal to them in the first place. Their commitment to inequality was in easy agreement with their understanding of liberty as an entitlement for some, rather than a right of all. In fact, their fervent dedication to liberty cannot be fully understood without realizing that it was simultaneously a commitment to their own distinction and preeminence. Although by the mid-1780s the rulers were still referring to the common crowd, or mob, as if it occupied an entirely separate cultural space, in real life they were now beginning to talk to them, adjust the language to their needs, make more frequent appeals to them, sound out their sentiments, and at times seek their direct support. As an upper-class Bostonian, resigned to this reality, put it, "We must consult the rooted prejudices [of ordinary people] if we expect their concurrence in our propositions." The key word was "must." It is not likely that the word would have been used this context before the Revolution.[64]

V. A People's Aristocracy

Merit is the criterion of eminence.
—Simeon Baldwin, *An Oration*, 1788

ONE OF THE RESPONSES of the American political elite to the post-Revolutionary crisis of their identity was an attempt at a conceptual substitution of "natural aristocracy," or "aristocracy of merit," for the earlier "gentry," "aristocracy," "better sort," and other collective terms signifying the upper class. The new situation called for a usable notion that would accommodate both the primacy of the newly sovereign people and the existence of an elite. The notion of an aristocracy of merit satisfied this requirement more than well, which helps explain why it was promoted enthusiastically across political party lines, and soon became part and parcel of the new government's self-portrayal. It was firmly rooted in the tradition of the elite's "natural" preeminence, and yet it rejected inherited advantage. It carried a basically egalitarian suggestion that anyone could rise in social rank through individual effort. It emphasized the continued indispensability of an educated elite. It also revalidated the gentry as a class, and did it with good grace by implying that they were essentially of the people, and that their elevated rank was entirely due to personal achievement, and not privilege. At the same time, it upheld social distinctions and set off the elite from ordinary people.

Why would the ruling class make the effort to reinvent themselves as a new kind of elite? After the war, many still held economic wealth (which supplied the means to act on the public stage) and continued to occupy positions of power. With the monarchy—the main barrier to their local authority—removed, they dominated the political scene. Some scholars have suggested that natural aristocracy was fashioned because of the weakness of the American upper class. But a class that organized and led the Revolution, took the reins of government after its success, and wrote the Declaration of Independence, the Constitution, and the Bill of Rights was not weak. What they lacked at this point in time was legitimacy in a political order turned upside down. The ownership of acres of tobacco-producing land could not in itself categorize one as a member of the elite, nor justify one's high position in society. Only perceptions which translated such objective realities into valid signs of authority in the collective mind could achieve that. Self-fashioning was the means to perform such a conversion.[65] The fashioners already had a huge advantage in their ability to create and popularize such representations, and yet they could at no time afford to cease doing so, because as the social, economic, and political environment around them changed, the need to signal and confirm authority—to ordinary people, to competitors, and to members of their own class—only increased. With our hindsight, we know that the soon-to-follow western expansion, immigration, market economy, religious pluralism, growth of the electorate, and emergence of parties were to doom the project for a neo-aristocracy as conceived by Jefferson and Adams. But they did not know that. What mattered to them most was that the concept accommodated the new polity centered around "the people" by paying homage to equal opportunity. It promised that all could rise in society through personal effort and merit, while it simultaneously made sense of the continued usefulness of their own class.

It is important that we do not make this concept into an entirely novel, Revolutionary product, born out of a radically modern concept of freedom. Merit had long been asserted, alongside pedigree, as a key component of the identity of British ruling classes; American "natural" aristocracy designed itself in contrast to that model, but in reality it had at its core the same cluster of virtue, knowledge, and reason as the hereditary one. When in 1777 John Hancock appealed to the Massachusetts Assembly in defense of Joseph Hewes, whose ship had been seized, he used arguments out of the arsenal of the Revolution as well as out of the old culture of English nobility. "Mr. Hewes," he wrote, "was a Member of Congress for a considerable length of time in the Representation from the State of North Carolina. From the enclosed Memorial you will perceive, the Sense his Constituents entertain of his Merit—to which I shall only add, that his Conduct as an inflexible Patriot, and his liberality as a Gentleman, justly entitle him . . . to their Protection." Heredity was happily absent from definitions of a new American aristocracy, not so much because equality was made supreme, but because heredity had previously been an insurmountable handicap. "I dislike and detest hereditary honours, Offices, and Emoluments established by law," noted John Adams, one of the main promoters of natural aristocracy. Moreover, individually attained merit had already been held in greater respect in America than in Europe. Contemporary English nobility still had trouble freeing itself from the distaste for the nouveau riches, and French aristocrats defending their privileges during the 1790 debates on the abolition of primogeniture and titles had to make considerable efforts to overcome their detestation of the parvenu "nobility of wealth," and to learn to emphasize their own merit and professionalism rather than hereditary titles.[66] Americans had no indigenous traditions of considering recently achieved prominence as unvirtuous.

The concept of an aristocracy of merit was not, as some authors have suggested, a vision of a "classless meritocracy" that would help overcome the existing social divisions, but a rather traditional cultural argument, though fine-tuned for new circumstances and imbued with Enlightenment ideals, to safeguard the prominence of the elite. It was still self-evident to the creators of the concept that a civil society would by definition consist of different and unequal ranks, and that those who would assume the political responsibility for such a society would not come from the ranks of ordinary people, from whom a "subordination" to superiors was expected. In "equal and free governments," where "the PEOPLE are the fountain of power and authority," these elite men were to be "the guardians of the public liberty," because the superiority of their rank "entitle them . . . to the obedience and submission of the lower." Making people the source of all authority did not cancel out the desirability of "natural" inequalities in society. John Adams believed that natural inequalities among people were inescapable, given the differences in behavior and "understanding," but ardently condemned the elevation of some to high positions by means of aristocratic criteria of birth and title. He saw such fictitious inequalities as the prime cause of all despotism in world history. Instead, objective merit should be the source of distinction. In the same vein, the New Hampshire revolutionary Nathaniel Peabody railed against "the Tyrannic Strides of Certain Aristocrated Gentry now in and using their Hostile influence to subjugate the E. (States)," and New Jersey politician and professor William Churchill Huston was apprehensive about being "oppressed by a set of Landjobbers and Aristocratical Gentry."[67]

From the 1780s, justifications of the gentry's title to rule based on their collective "quality" became noticeably more frequent. They were still accompanied by expectations that ordinary people would "naturally" acknowledge this characteristic. Madison had "no doubt that there are subjects to which the capacities of the bulk of mankind are unequal and on which they must and will be governed by those with whom they happen to have acquaintance and confidence. . . . I infer from these considerations that if a Government ever be adopted in America, it must result from a fortunate coincidence of leading opinions, and a general confidence of the people in those who may recommend it." Pennsylvania's John Armstrong was more direct, writing that "the philosophy that teaches the equality of mankind & the dignity of human nature is founded on vanity & addressed to it alone—and in my opinion tho' there be less consolation there is infinitely more truth in the opposite doctrine, that the many were made for the few." Jefferson continued to refer to virtue or quality when identifying various subsets of American society. In 1776, reflecting on proper taxation, he noted that "all charges of war & all other expenses . . . shall be defrayed out of a common treasury, which shall be supplied by the several colonies in proportion to the number of inhabitants of every age, sex, & quality." New York merchant Melancton Smith assumed that in the new republic the elite would logically continue to be elected to offices, writing, "This Government is so constituted that the representatives will generally be composed of the first class in the community, which I shall distinguish by the name of natural aristocracy." He noted that although America had no "legal or hereditary distinctions . . . every society naturally divides itself into classes," and that "birth, education, talents and wealth, create distinctions among men as visible and of as much influence as titles, stars and garters." The only threat to this order was that "the populace" could create such pressures that "the considerate and good, who adorn private life, and such only can be safely trusted in public station, will never commit themselves to a situation where a conscientious discharge of duty may embitter the evening of life." Most authors agreed that liberty would be threatened by any major shift in the social status quo, for "there can be no fixed and permanent government that does not rest on the fixed and permanent orders and objects of mankind." The continuing connection between the characteristics exclusive to their class and the socially asymmetrical distribution of liberty linked the new aristocracy of merit to their predecessors. John Milton, who in calling for a republican government in 1660 England defined liberty as consisting of "civil rights and advancements of every person according to his merit," would not find the above arguments surprising.[68]

"Happy are the free and virtuous people," wrote the New England scholar and minister Elizur Goodrich, "who pay strict attention to the natural aristocracy, which is the institution of heaven; it appears in every assembly of mankind. . . . Happy the people who have the wisdom to discern the true patriot of superiour abilities, in all his counsels ever manifesting a sincere regard to the public good, and never with a selfish view." Others argued that the American elite's "personal influence" was qualitatively different from that of the old aristocracy because it was an "influence which men derive from offices, the merit of their services, age, talents, wealth, education, virtue." That "natural or customary aristocracy" existed "universally among men" was becoming an axiom. Reflecting on the appointment of American ambassadors, James Monroe drew much pride from the fact that the "motive or cause which originally gave birth to the office in Europe does not apply here." As he explained: "There a nobleman held the office in quality of his rank in the court . . . but with us this is not the case. We shall appoint the man, the minister, in consideration of his talents only."[69]

In the ideal plan, neither wealth nor lack of it was to be a sole criterion for office. "I hope our Country will never see the Time," wrote Samuel Adams, "when either Riches or the Want of them will be the leading considerations in the choice of publick officers." Reflecting upon the nature of government, John Adams observed dejectedly that a true nobility of "virtue and Talents" was essential to a free republic, but, unfortunately, the vulgar masses could not quite tell who was who. They would view even the "the meanest" characters—if only possessed of wealth—as noble: "The Many, will acknowledge no other aristoi." Elsewhere he noted that the "numerous multitude, not only become their Dupes, but even love to be Taken by their Tricks: I feel a stronger disposition to weep at their destiny, than to laugh at their Folly." Jefferson was less pessimistic about the easily deceived multitude, but agreed that "there is a natural aristocracy among men," based on "virtue and talents," and that it should be the very heart of a civil state. "The natural aristocracy," he noted, "I consider as the most precious gift of nature for the instruction, the trusts, and government of society." Indeed, it must have been part of a divine plan, for "it would have been inconsistent in creation to have formed man for the social state, and not to have provided virtue and wisdom enough to manage the concerns of the society." Must it not therefore follow that "that form of government is the best which provides most effectually for a pure selection of these aristoi into the offices of government?" Jefferson did share Adams's concern that an elite based on wealth only could someday replace those with virtue. To prevent the rise of such an "artificial aristocracy" he was prepared to call for laws to suppress it. Conservative Gouverneur Morris was not far behind with his position; he too was concerned that true public virtue simply could not be comprehended by ordinary people: "A Man of Sentiment has not so much Honor as the Vulgar suppose in risquing Life & Fortune for the Service of his Country. He does not Value them as highly as the Vulgar do." Liberty, furthermore, required a certain generosity and tolerance, and "great Liberality in vulgar Minds is not common even in America."[70]

The concept of natural aristocracy showed once again how claims of merit, wisdom, and virtue attached the elite to the liberty of the whole nation. "Public Virtue," observed John Adams, "cannot exist in a Nation without private, and public Virtue is the only Foundation of Republics." "Man is impatient of restraint," noted Virginian Edward Carrington, "nor will he conform to what is necessary to the good order of society, unless, he is perfect in discernment and Virtue, or, the Government under which he lives is effective. The Fathers of the American Fabric seem to have supposed the first of these principles, peculiarly, our lot, and have chosen it for a foundation: in the progress of experiment, the fallacy is discovered, and the whole pile must fall, if the latter cannot be supplied." When in 1771 Acting Governor William Nelson of Virginia spoke in honor of the recently deceased Lord Botetourt, he invoked the late governor's "constant and uniform exertion of every public and private Virtue." Distinguishing the two categories of virtue as separate domains of achievement was not a mere figure of speech. It was important because many could possess private virtue but public virtue continued to be seen as an exclusive province of the gentry, a distinction that translated into a cultural entitlement to rule.[71]

It should be plain by now that making "the people" the symbolic sovereign did not interfere with, or seriously diminish, the elite's belief that real people generally did not possess the necessary predispositions to rule, and that their needs and interests could be properly articulated only by the elite. James Madison explained that the idea was "to refine and enlarge public views, by passing them through the medium of a chosen body of citizens, whose wisdom may best discern the true interest of their country, and whose patriotism and love of justice will be least likely to sacrifice it to temporary or partial considerations." This, he argued, was not a matter of choice, because the people at large, unlike "established characters," did not possess the necessary qualities. Madison was disappointed that Massachusetts voted for the Constitution by a majority of only nineteen delegates, but noted with approval that the "prevailing party comprized however all the men of abilities, of property, and of influence," while in "the opposite multitude there was not a single character capable of uniting their wills or directing their measures."[72] Unlike the old elites, the new meritocracy would not simply decide what was good for society, but would mediate disinterestedly between the will of the people and the demands of government. Attributing to them any longings for a classless society would be historically more than premature.

If no one but members of the meritorious elite were capable of effectively protecting equal liberty for all, it followed that only they could properly hold political offices in the new republic. "It is our duty," wrote one of them, "to get the publick Departments, especially the most important of them, filled with Men of understanding & inflexible Virtue. It would indeed be alarming, if the United States should ever entrust the Ship in which our all is at Stake, with inexperienc'd or unprincipled Pilots. Our cause is surely too interesting to Mankind, to be put under the Direction of Men, vain, avaricious or concealed under the Hypocritical Guise of Patriotism, without a spark of publick or private Virtue." New merit was becoming interchangeable with old virtue; both were to ensure that the voters did not elect *unauthorized* social elements to office. It was to be a barrier in the form of a "mental qualification" that would serve as a "sufficient guard against the choice of men on account of pecuniary recommendation." The ideal was to "find a man independent in his fortune, of good sense and patriotism filling a public office: but when the last is wanting, the possession of the first is evil." If such ungenteel politicians were permitted to rise, they would artfully promote personal agendas instead of public good: "Some who are void of the least regard to the public, will put on the appearance and even speak boldly the language of patriots, with the sole purpose of gaining the confidence of the public, and securing the loaves and fishes for themselves, or their sons or other connexions." Edmund Pendleton insisted on a "firm" administration, "to preserve that virtue which they [political philosophers] all declare to be pillar on which the government, and liberty, its object, must stand." Simple realism dictated that there was not a sufficient "aggregate fund of virtue" in society at large to base a government capable of suppressing "licentiousness" solely on "the American spirit."[73]

It is striking how much this supposedly new mediating role promoted for the post-Revolutionary elite resembled the mythical role of the genteel in old England, "first in the World for virtuous Liberty . . . where Wisdom and sound Policy dropping from the Lips of venerable Sages have ever sustained their due Authority, kept the licentious in Awe, & even rendered them Subservient to their own & Publick Welfare." We have seen how the Founders closely identified themselves with this transatlantic ethos. After all, it was this ethos that enabled them to readily argue that they were the only true defenders of British freedom. This continuing connection with the Old World sometimes escapes us because of the habit of emphasizing what was new in the Revolution, but the long-term inertia of culture was much more powerful than we tend to think. Referring to England, Edmund Randolph noted that the "spirit of liberty will not be less prominent in America, I hope, than there." The presence of the old ethos was unmistakable in his pride in being a gentleman endowed with "conscious independence and rectitude of conduct," two virtues crucial to the British catalog of upper-class values. Carter Braxton made equally clear that the "same principles which led the English to greatness animate us," and that "however necessary it may be to shake off the authority of arbitrary British dictators, we ought, nevertheless, to adopt and perfect that system, which England has suffered to be grossly abused, and the experience of ages has taught us to venerate." Others warned about the perils of excessive democracy, and placed the only hope in the "spirit of the English Constitution" which "has yet a little influence left."[74] Although the public persona of the provincial gentry had evolved with the Revolution, the view of their role in society remained much more traditional.

The historical significance of the aristocracy of merit did not end with the post-Revolutionary decades. Like many intellectual fictions that express the deeper needs of societies, it persisted—with only slightly changed meaning—well beyond the historical circumstances that gave birth to it. Over the two centuries that followed, it has thrived as one of the most emblematic beliefs of modern American culture—that of meritocracy. It may have been created by and for the elite, but it was a concept that carried democratic promise and expressed the aspirations of countless people seeking opportunity and social advancement. Because it had served the Founding elite so well, it could ride on their authority and in time grow into the modern and progressive belief that anyone can rise in the ranks of society, a belief that was destined to become one of the pillars of national identity. Few Americans could resist the enthusiasm and the promise contained in the words of David Ramsay: "It is the happiness of our present constitution, that all offices lie open to men of merit, of whatever rank or condition: and that even the reins of state may be held by the son of the poorest man, if possessed of abilities equal to the important station. We are no more to look up for the blessings of government to hungry courtiers, or the needy dependents of British nobility; but must educate our own children for these exalted purposes."[75] Once again, a cultural device instilled into the collective consciousness by one interest group, with one rationale, took on a life of its own when picked up by others who used it to express new, egalitarian aspirations quite incongruous with the meaning given to it by its authors. Once again, a symbolic representation preceded real changes in society.

Conclusion

Liberty and the Web of Culture

The power to impose recognition depends on the capacity to mobilize around a name.

—Pierre Bourdieu, *Distinction*

THERE IS A DISTINCT strain of wishful thinking that haunts the historiography on Revolutionary liberty. Its presence is noticeable in studies of all methodological and ideological orientations. We, as the investigating culture, largely select the questions we ask of the past from our own lists of what is "natural," "just," and "up to standard." For many, it is already intellectually discomforting to realize that the eighteenth-century men and women involved in the struggle for liberty had lists of priorities dramatically different from ours. But it is almost painful to discover that inequality was often desirable and carried a positive value, even for those who rose, or aspired to rise, from the ranks of the underprivileged.[1] It has the ring of an anomaly. We are ill at ease accepting that the restricted, metropolitan meaning of freedom transmitted to the British colonies persisted throughout the eighteenth century and, consequently, that much of modern American liberty had its source in exclusion and hierarchy.

Only when we recognize that in the Revolutionary era the meaning of freedom was synonymous with privilege, and therefore made full sense only within the context of an unequal social order, can we appreciate the fact that a response to oppression was not the only driving force behind the term's evolution toward its modern meaning. The pursuit of advantage over others and the aspiration to move up the social rungs were equally weighty catalysts. They were particularly important in a fluid and mobile society that associated such goals with improvement and advancement and not with inherited entitlements "owned" by select groups. Furthermore, to understand the process of admitting new residents into the realm of liberty, we need to acknowledge that such progress involved an inversely proportional relationship between those who were already the most free and those who were at a given point able to raise claims to certain freedoms. Every successful new claim implied the loss of a certain fraction in the spectrum of liberties thus far exclusively controlled by those making the concession. This is important because today we often view rights and liberties as inexhaustible commodities that can be offered to all, without cost to any. This cost did exist and was the reason why there was so much resistance in history to the expansion of liberties. One of the best-known examples of such a reaction in American history was the case of poor whites in the South who, after the abolition of slavery, lost their privileges—their race-exclusive voting rights and their place on the social ladder above the African Americans. Their defense of segregation was a defense of the former scope of *their* exclusively held liberties, a scope that would shrink once these liberties were extended to new groups of people.

We should also be more sensitive to the fact that the emergence of any specific liberty was grounded in circumstances unique to a particular history of a particular people at a particular time, and therefore deeply rooted in the culture produced by those experiences. This liberty could neither be easily reproduced in another society, with another history behind it, nor could it be plausibly viewed as some deep structure of universal nature. Societies and their organizations (such as the United Nations today) may, and should, attempt to make some of these liberties universally honored, but success in this endeavor will depend on our awareness that such liberties would still contain traces of the unique, time- and place-specific historical experiences of those who created them in the first place. This awareness should at least give pause to those who presume that one people's norms of liberty (usually those of the presumers) can be mechanically inserted into other cultures that are the products of other historical experiences.

Only when all of this is taken into account can we fully appreciate the striking uniqueness of the American Revolution. One does not have to subscribe to the now outdated theories of American exceptionalism to do so. Unlike many other revolutions, it did not develop out of internal tensions in society, but in opposition to outside pressure that threatened the relative independence of local political and economic elites. Its success did not produce a dramatic replacement of the established ruling class, in part because the whole struggle was undertaken to preserve this class. Its distinctive feature was that it was a political revolution rather than a systemic one. It removed the imperial superstructure over a base that was able to sustain itself. It had to change the polity, but it did not have to undertake major social engineering in order to endure.[2] This helped conserve the old socioeconomic order and its network of values. The Revolution sanctioned some new freedoms but did not introduce others (and, most dramatically, left slavery intact), but the continuity of the old culture should not be interpreted solely as a roadblock on a trajectory toward the progress of liberty. There already existed in this culture many seeds of such progress: a denominational system, long traditions of respect for the rule of law, deeply rooted local government structures, and beliefs venerating British liberty. They too were preserved thanks to the nonsystemic nature of the Revolution.

The Revolution produced a rich narrative of liberty, but its language was designed to justify opposition to the power of the metropolis and not to fuel the struggle of one social class against another for local authority. It was not a case of the bourgeoisie overthrowing the power of hereditary aristocracy, or of laborers overthrowing capitalists, or peasants rising against feudal lords— where those who won would have to develop and introduce dramatically new values in order to rule. In consequence, there was both less radicalism among the ruled and more ideological flexibility on the part of the rulers toward the ruled. Because the ruled never became a real threat to the rulers, it was possible to transform them into a symbolic sovereign, a key step toward the broadening of the meaning of liberty.

The century-old debate over whether the Revolution was about "home rule" or about "who should rule at home" thus needs revision. The success of the original struggle for independence led to an unanticipated internal split *within* the American political class about who should rule at home. Both of the factions that emerged adopted Revolutionary constitutional concepts as the foundations of their agendas. But both soon found themselves framing these agendas—often reluctantly, for fear of upsetting the social order—in terms that included ordinary people. Unlike the French revolutionaries, they downplayed class divisions as they attempted to gain broad support. The laboring and middling classes eagerly picked up this language to express their own interests. As a result, a new space for liberty was created that by the early nineteenth century became too big to sustain the social claims of its genteel promoters. Although Jefferson's disappointment with the new and younger Lady Liberty entering the stage was palpable, she was reading from his script.

The Revolutionary narrative rested on the premise of happiness for all. However, as the various revolutions of the past two centuries tell us, there is a world of difference between enforcing a state of happiness and declaring the right to pursue happiness. Because the leaders focused on the political system rather than on social change, they kept governing relatively *separate* from issues of social order. This was one of the reasons why post-Revolutionary America did not become radicalized. Its transformation of government, however dramatic, did not require—as the French Revolution did—having to reconcile the existing, historically encoded cultural norms and values with an entirely new, experimental social order. Such a clash would have inevitably involved restrictions on the already existing rights, and the need for a more authoritarian rule to implement any drastic restructuring of traditional world views. America did not witness anything resembling the introduction of the French Revolutionary calendar, or the abolishment of religion in the name of Reason. The lack of a rigid, prescriptive formula of progress to be immediately imposed on the people reduced the degree of potential coercion and intolerance, inherent in any revolutionary effort. Perfect models of happiness are deeply contradictory in themselves: they presuppose a despotic governmental power required to impose them, and that, in turn, spells further unfreedoms as the enforcers enforce their version of perfection. Because the Founders were political figures, not *bien-pensants* primarily dreaming of a universal utopia, they were pragmatic and did not seek to immediately achieve perfect equality, as did the French and, much later, the Bolsheviks. The avoidance of this trajectory thus brought not only negative consequences, such as preserving many existing unfreedoms, but also tangible benefits for the evolution of democracy.

Theoreticians of the French Revolution like Abbé Sieyès prided themselves on the fact that rights were no longer granted as a deal or a bargain between two groups with sufficient power, but were derived from the authority of the people. Earlier, American revolutionaries, too, professed to rule solely in the name of the people. But because they were already the ruling class, the pressure to use this potent new legitimacy to amass more power was less significant than in France, where it ended up undermining representation, deemphasizing the rule of law, and putting the rights of all people above the rights of individuals. This was why it was not a paradox that the otherwise preservationist American upheaval became ultimately hospitable to the expansion of liberty. Liberty as such can only be individual (even as it is realized only as a relation between groups of people), because only the individual's body or property can be protected. Collective protection puts the individual person in a position secondary to the collective "interest," which is invariably defined by the powers that be. The anti-despotic and individualistic understanding of freedom, expressed in documents such as the Declaration of Independence and the various bills of rights, was so strong in America because it historically grew out of attempts to secure common-law liberties against the excessive power of the monarchy, and because of a deep mistrust (dating back to the Stuarts) of "tyranny" in the form of a centralized government.[3] This sentiment, enhanced by the primarily local, not imperial, interests of the provincial representative assemblies, did not allow the new state to dominate society and to diminish the locally rooted, decentralized authority of the political class. The social meaning of the Revolutionary language of liberty was not yet egalitarian—it still referred only to those qualified for freedom—but even with this limitation, it contained presumptions of individualism strong enough to begin reshaping the political culture even before the new polity was codified in the Constitution.

Taking all this into consideration would help advance studies that move beyond the canonical frameworks of interpretation and the growing aroma of mold around them. The mastery of culture over people's actions, including political ones, remains underestimated in the historiography of the Revolutionary era, despite the prevailing emphasis on themes of race, class, and gender. While these approaches have been tremendously productive in revealing previously disregarded aspects of the past, they have by nature tended to be framed primarily in terms of fairly straightforward oppositions (the oppressed vs. the oppressors, the privileged vs. the unprivileged, male vs. female, poor vs. rich, etc.). When the dense network of cultural values did make an appearance, it was usually only to the degree that some of these values selectively fitted into such oppositional frameworks. While issues of power will always remain crucial to studying the past, cultural history does not lend itself well to clean-cut conceptual oppositions, does not deal with subjects governed by rules of internal consistency, and does not naturally follow any linear route toward the realization of this or that ideal goal (such as, for instance, equal liberty for all). If inequality in a modern, moral sense were made our chief analytical category, we would assuredly find endless evidence of its presence in history, but this would not necessarily explain why a certain liberty surfaced in the first place. To reconstruct the story of early modern liberty primarily in terms of inequality is to presuppose inclusive equality as a norm and a point of reference. However, no such norm existed in the culture at the time. If, as has been argued, the provincial gentry assumed and expected their dominance to continue in the new republic, then our view of the relation between their rights talk and their commitment to inequality must move beyond conventional historiographical wisdom and recognize such inequality as intrinsic, not contradictory, to the genesis of modern American liberty. Taking off the glasses of purely oppositional analysis will allow us to see the true drama of history that we have been largely missing: that elite culture as well as popular culture can be both progressive and reactionary, intolerant and charitable, and consequently can propel or hinder the positive evolution of liberty. It may seem counterintuitive, but it is exceedingly common in history that good causes produce bad consequences, and bad causes produce good outcomes (for instance, the wealth derived from exploitation financed great art, and the leisure time of the privileged, made possible by the labor of others, was used to write fine literature). Likewise, historical advances of liberty should not be understood as automatically entailing the universalism of such progress. In fact, the American Revolution's stress on provincial liberties and property rights not only did not expand equality to all, but in some aspects it substantially strengthened the legal and ideological premises on which slavery rested.[4]

It would therefore be helpful to put behind us another frequent, though often invisible, assumption: the use of highly perfectionist criteria for viewing the past. Such criteria focus our attention on the things which *do not* meet the ideal (past or present)—that is, on shortcomings, inequalities, ironies, and contradictions. To tell the story of freedom in terms of inconsistencies presupposes some perfect, orderly framework against which to measure these inconsistencies. But looking for perfection is like looking for absolute certitude; the former symbolically erases injustices, the latter neutralizes the randomness of life. Both are pleasant illusions. Cultural history flows, however, driven by constant tensions between chaos and order, between perfect ideals and the imperfect reality of existence. Our real goal should be to discover how and why liberties—however partial and inadequate, or merely nominal—emerged. The story of American liberty after 1764 was one of persistent friction between the language of equal rights and the reality of various unfreedoms, between the possession of exclusive freedoms by some and the exclusion of others from such freedoms. A perfectionist perspective simply cannot capture this dynamic. It may instead lead us to an assumption that admitting all social groups equally to full liberty would have been a culturally viable proposal in the 1770s and 1780s had it not been resisted by a conservative ruling class. In this view, the story of Revolutionary liberty becomes the story of a contradiction. The leaders' rhetoric of freedom merely "masked the political exclusion of certain groups," and only much later, "when the rules and the reality come together does the Rule of Law become more than an apology or a masquerade."[5] We ought to take another look at the venerable concept of this "central paradox of American history" *as a framework* for explaining the coexistence of a "dedication to liberty and dignity among the leaders of the American Revolution" with a socioeconomic system that "denied human liberty and dignity." The coexistence was true, but the concept of paradox is incapable of explaining it. Instead, it inevitably leads to the question of whether "the vision of a nation of equals [was] flawed at the source." The anachronism of such a flawed-versus-perfect schema surfaces fully when we realize that the leaders' dedication was largely nonparadoxical, because it was a dedication to a pre-egalitarian, elite-made, inequality-premised liberty. They no more deserve to be dismissed because their point of departure was not a more modern meaning of freedom than they should be caricatured because they "aped the style of the English country gentleman." In both cases, they drew on self-evident legitimacies. British colonial culture, as Alan Tully and Robert Olwell have aptly observed, was a product of a tension between two interacting but contrary forces: "New World experience or possibilities and Old World inheritance or imitation."[6]

Oppositional and perfectionist models have by no means been marginal or exceptional; they show up in the most respected and sophisticated studies. They are typically used when the scope of historical inquiry is largely confined to political ideas, with little connection to the larger cultural matrix. For instance, in her book on elitism and egalitarian democracy in the 1790s, Joyce Appleby juxtaposes two presumably antagonistic concepts of liberty circulating in America at the time. One, a "classical" concept held by the Federalists, assumed a society divided between the virtuous and the rest, and stressed such notions as the right of a corporate body to self-determination and local government, the idea of free and independent men participating in politics, and the right of "secure possession" of property. Its opposite, a "liberal concept of liberty," was based on assumptions that were "individualistic, egalitarian, abstract, and rational," and rejected classical beliefs in social rank and disinterestedness as foundations of civic virtue. That these contradictory "meanings of liberty" co-occurred after the Revolution was a wonder, considering their "fundamental incompatibility." "So at odds were these two liberties," writes the author, "that it is hard to understand how they could have coexisted together in the same political discourse. This is a puzzle yet to be solved."[7]

A fuller acknowledgment of the symbolic nature of public conversation could go a long way toward resolving this puzzle. It would reveal that the classical and the liberal notions of liberty were not as different, or opposing, as they might seem, because they both derived from the same core meaning, historically shaped by the ethos and privileges of the ruling classes, and because behind these notions stood one and the same social elite, albeit with differing views on government. They all shared a highly individualistic cult of personal independence based on property, an assumption that such independence was a source of disinterestedness (the foundation of public virtue), and a veneration for equality (but within the elite only). To counterpose the Federalists' and the Jeffersonians' sense of liberty is to make a case similar to that of the much overstated difference between the "Country" and "Court" factions in early modern England (although there was a resemblance, in that the former defended local—in America, state—interests and the latter, centralized authority). The Country party represented itself as a defender of order, tradition, and common law against the Court, accused of assuming historically unwarranted powers.[8] In reality, there was no substantial social or prestige distinction between the two sides as subsets of the same ruling class, and their struggle was mostly political. The Federalists and the Jeffersonians were just as far from being fundamentally divided on the question of authority. One can certainly point to significant differences among their followers in terms of distinction and dignity, as seen in the disgust of ambitious men such as Patrick Henry and Thomas Jefferson with the social hermeticism of the old planter oligarchy. But these were rivalries for influence *within* the gentry class, and while Henry may have publicly criticized old-style patronage, he was by no means reluctant to seek it to advance himself. What in contemporary language may appear to be an idea of a "classless society" was mostly an abstraction, a device directed against hereditary privilege but not against ranks and privilege as such. The difference between the two groups identified by Appleby was that one openly stressed the need for ranks, while the other promoted an idealized vision for an egalitarian *future*. Both took for granted that in their time they should continue as the dominant class. Finally, it is not likely that Jefferson, with his "liberal liberty," rejected selflessness as the basis of civic virtue. His passionate promotion of land ownership as the ideal foundation of future, yeoman-based, republican citizenship was deeply rooted in the old, landed gentry ethos of disinterestedness and independence, achievable exclusively through landholding.

Many such controversies rooted in the question of how much the Revolution can be credited with creating modern liberty would be moot if we fully acknowledged that the entire episode unfolded at two different but closely overlapping levels, the factual and the symbolic. The latter one, where all communication took place, determined how people knew things. If we pay no heed to the powerful role of this duality, or worse, if we reconstruct the history of liberty by organizing it around singular categories only (such as, for instance, class confrontation), we miss this vital makeup of the past. It also makes it impossible for us to properly appreciate that symbolic representations, so often dismissed as fictional, nominal, or incongruent with "reality," were in fact prerequisites of real, enforceable liberties. Such appreciation would effectively end the debate about whether Revolutionary liberty was already modern or merely a radical façade born out of contingency. It would reveal that it was neither.

It would also help to put an end to another quandary. The unfounded but frequent intellectual fear of appreciating more fully the symbolic capacity of words in the history of liberty—as opposed to a strict focus on legislation and purportedly "literal" descriptions of reality—creates a needless obstacle to a full and balanced, neither prosecutorial nor hagiographic, acknowledgment of American accomplishments in this sphere. To say that the Founders' contribution to American liberty was immense and that many of them were extraordinary characters is not to propose an overly heroic or filopietistic narrative. It is to recognize that, in the final analysis, not only the legal documents but also the symbolic realm they fashioned created new room for liberty. Their words of equal rights turned out to be Hamlet's daggers that ultimately pierced not only the privileges of their authors, but also the constrained meanings of liberty imported from British culture to colonial America.[9] In its time, this rhetoric may have been in good part nominal, but it just so happened that it corresponded perfectly to the peculiar needs of a territorially expanding, upwardly mobile, economically growing, and denominationally pluralistic America. Liberty grew by new meanings and interpretations superimposed on this original script by subsequent generations. The Founders' contribution, therefore, should be considered in toto, and must include both their role in establishing freedoms guaranteed by law, as well as their input—in the form of grand fictions and representations of liberty—into the cultural capital of American society. It was the combination of the two that constituted a true quantum leap in the progress of modern freedom, unlocking the gates of the political arena for the people. To be appreciated for their part in this process, the Founders did not have to singlehandedly and intantaneously create literal, modern, egalitarian liberty. Their best justification lay in the fact that to this day the Revolutionary narrative lives on and remains a vibrant resource for new liberties. The numerous attempts of other countries since the eighteenth century to model their constitutional law and language of rights on American blueprints are but one indication of the scale of its success.[10]

This is not to say that liberty's post-Revolutionary expansion was simply an "unintended consequence" of the Founders' actions. That would erroneously disconnect such consequences from their actions. Although the full edifice of American liberty that arose with time was not foreseen by the original architects, its construction was organically and causally tied to their designs. For that to happen, intentionality was not needed on the part of the originators of change, nor did they need to achieve perfection. Indeed, they had already achieved very much for their moment in time—they created a liberal polity codified in law and produced a hugely popular narrative of equal rights and liberties that in its cultural impact went far beyond the codifications. To fully reconstruct the genesis of modern liberty, we ought to consider the results that differed from original intentions but were caused by the actions of those who held those intentions. This would restore the Founders to the place where they truly belong—as neither intentional creators of full modernity nor its betrayers, but as remarkably resourceful originators of progressive change. It would also enable Americans to uphold their deep emotional attachment to them—but for the right reasons. We will simply understand them better in their historical context when we realize that their commitment to social distinctions was not only not contradictory to their enthusiasm for liberty, but was one of the circumstances that magnified their zeal. Liberty as such was created not only when people reacted to "adverse conditions," but also when those who exclusively possessed it idealized and popularized it, thereby attaching *value* to it for the entire American culture.[11] It is true that they did not glorify it in order to immediately extend it universally, and that they were much preoccupied with safeguarding their own rank, identity, and authority. But it is also true that their new and inclusive depictions of liberty soon began to *compete* in a very real way with the older ones based on social difference.

Their accomplishment was that a new cultural space was created for liberty long before full liberty for new classes of people became legalized. This space emerged because of, not in spite of, the fact that the late colonial political class was able to formulate and present their own interests in terms of a national discourse of freedom. Only they could have done it—not simply because they had a huge stake as a class in doing so, but also because they alone possessed the ability to frame on such a scale the meaning of events and situations, and to furnish the language and metaphors by which they were described. This discourse contained new conceptual standards (all are born equal and have natural rights) which—whether we label them fictions or not—became components of a shared tradition. They became cultural givens, a part of commonsensical reality. Only then was it possible to frame issues of rights and liberties for new segments of society in terms of this new reality. As people became conscious that alternative views of who could possess liberty were available, these new conceptual standards were applied to new classes not originally included in them by the authors of these standards.[12] This new area, within which certain practices would be seen as natural and acceptable, had to be created in the culture first, in order for political, legal, and constitutional liberty to move there.

No such space materialized without a struggle. American revolutionaries invoked the existing British space when they brought up taxation without representation, and accused London of violating it. In turn, when they became the rulers of the newly established republican space, they were surprised that rebels, opponents, and critics challenged them by invoking the new republican standards. In a sense, the progress of liberty resembled a domino effect. The cultural approval of one liberty was followed in time by its codification, which, in turn, opened the way for other liberties. Social relationships change constantly, and new needs to act freely in one sphere or another accompany such changes. People at a given time do not know what new liberties the existing ones will give birth to in the future. In that sense, there will never be a completion of liberties.

If these suggestions for a new interpretation of the Revolution are to bear fruit, we need to become much more aware of just how deeply all interpretations blend historical facts with our own presuppositions. A bit of respect for our subjectivity should not conjure up undue fears of relativism. As Leszek Kolakowski has pointed out in his study of Husserl, the debate between relativism and certainty has been going on for centuries, but it is the tension between the two that should be of greatest interest to a historian, because it has driven so much of intellectual and cultural life. (One might add that it is tension, not finality, that lays at the heart of modern democracy, which tolerates different, often fiercely opposing, views).[13]

This would help bring the meanings of people's experiences into a sharper focus and allow us, without needless self-reproach, to see the Revolution in its true light—not as an implausibly sudden break with the past in favor of wholly modern liberty, but as a marvelously dramatic moment in time when the historical contingencies, the traditional world views, the newly democratic political language, the visions of enlightened progress, the entrenched class identities, the sophisticated leadership, the issues of governmental legitimacy, the hard truth of slavery, and the aspirations of ordinary people converged in an intricate and tense competition. Setting our sights on culture— the space where shared meanings were formed, identities were negotiated, beliefs were expressed, values were reproduced, and symbolic representations of reality and order were fashioned—would bring Revolutionary liberty down to earth, where it actually resided.

We know that when the Revolution's leaders wrote and spoke about liberties, practically the whole relevant vocabulary used was supplied to them by the preceding century of British history. Assertions of personal freedom, equality, happiness, habeas corpus, trial by jury, protection of property, rights anchored in nature, parliamentary representation, and religious toleration were not only not new, but they had widely functioned under the rubric of liberty in public discourse at least since 1688. It is not realistic to assume that during the Revolutionary years the *meanings* of this vocabulary suddenly ceased to contain inherent traces of the old social relationships and order. The durability of such meanings is lost to us if we use a looking glass that filters out their cultural context and shows only the sign, but not its significance. Then, indeed, the revolutionaries may appear before us as leading "the greatest utopian movement in American history"—trying to create a society based on abstract, ideal principles.[14]

The Founders were not utopian dreamers. They were driven by a combination of their interests as a class and their strong identification with the Enlightenment vision of progress. They were not primarily articulators of ideas. They owned land, exported commodities, employed people, loaned money, speculated, ran stores, governed, passed and executed laws, occupied offices, and created powerful political and kinship networks. They required legitimacy for all of this, just as they required it for their Revolutionary project, and legitimacy could not be invented—it had to build on what was already culturally valid, on what had status conferred on it by some earlier authority. The more they wanted to press for change in the old system, the more they needed the stepping-stone of existing legitimacies. This is why the song of liberty they wrote for the new republic was based on what they viewed as the best compositions of the preceding century. Future actors would read the lyrics in new ways and translate them into action, just as British history had earlier provided the Founders themselves with a usable vocabulary of liberty that they employed in their struggle against Britain. There is no reason why this liberty could not have been both conservative in its elitism and progressive in the way it embedded a set of inclusive standards in the culture.[15] Future newcomers to politics who would follow the old elite also needed a foothold on an existing legitimacy—and the Founder-made standards provided it.

One of the most important conclusions we can draw from all of this is that liberties—that is, specific rights, protections, and enfranchisements—first had to be invented and legitimized by some (as a rule, by those who were able to assert them as privileges, and who could define them in ways that contributed to preserving this privilege) before they could be claimed by others. We know that the poor in eighteenth-century Britain did not fully enjoy the right of habeas corpus, even if it was widely referred to as a basic British liberty; they could still be imprisoned, enlisted, or transported to the colonies without their consent. But the right of habeas corpus first had to be invented (in this case negotiated and established in the public sphere as an exclusive right of a certain class) in order to be subsequently available as a distinct, legitimate standard to all those who had never before commanded such a right but who would, at an opportune moment, demand it. Each such invention, however constrained in its application, added to the existing batch of liberties recognized by the culture. In this sense, privilege contributed significantly to the long-term progress of liberty, but we would not know it if we viewed privilege exclusively as an obstacle to such progress. The emergence of freedom was not just a response to unfreedom; it was also an outcome of the practices of the ruling class, because they were already the most free, they held cultural authority, and they were able not only to circumscribe particular liberties but also bestow worth and reputation on them. To appreciate this, we need to look less at political theories and more at the activities of the consumers of liberty.

Modern American liberty grew less from a simple rejection of earlier, exclusivist liberty than from the social expansion of the old privileges (indeed, the Revolution itself is a prominent example of this principle: it used rights invented earlier in Britain to justify a separation from Britain). The old liberty should not be looked upon as a mere anti-model of modernity, waiting to be replaced with a new, "liberal" model. Rather, it should be studied as a shell within which the various future components of modern liberty were born, and from which they were over time extracted, in a piecemeal fashion, to occupy a broader social space. Despite the fact that the Founders still believed that a well-ordered society should be based on rank, the *symbolic* model of American liberty that emerged from the Revolution contained strongly individualistic traits because its authors were themselves fiercely attached to personal liberty. This model—when stripped of its exclusionism —also happened to be eminently suited to the needs of a society of ambitious immigrants, enterprising pioneers, and highly motivated social climbers striving to improve their condition. By the early nineteenth century, it had become the cultural property of ordinary Americans, and served well as an expression of their fundamental aspirations. In feeding the republican government its own words of rights and liberties, Shays's Rebellion was a forerunner of the many other voices that would call for an expansion of liberty, including those of African Americans like James Forten and Frederick Douglass in their cases against slavery.

Revolutionary-era changes in the meaning of liberty did not involve replacing its existing sense with one antithetical to it. It expanded in its own time, and its periodization depended not so much on events (the Revolutionary War) or documents and laws (the Declaration of Independence, the Constitution) as on the slow and protracted transformation of culture. The process of broadening its social boundaries had begun in the 1770s, but it was not—nor could it have been—an abrupt, qualitative shift, nor was it the willful act of a single, progressive group. Instead, it was the beginning of a long, chaotic, and halting transformation, only much later to be marked with such highlights of modernity as the abolition of slavery, the granting of the franchise to women, and civil rights legislation. The core characteristic of this process was that broader freedom was very gradually extracted from socially specific and exclusive liberties; it did not emerge from some axiomatic, timeless design. When a particular unfreedom was rejected and condemned, it was usually with the help of a previously existing cultural standard of freedom, internal to an already advantaged group rather than some abstract, "universal" one. Accustomed by the Founders' language and the long tradition it engendered of thinking about the post-1764 events as a "revolution in favor of universal liberty . . . which opens a new prospect in human affairs, and begins a new aera in the history of mankind," we do not always properly acknowledge this jagged progression. But each step in this process was a singular concession, made in large part because cultural changes that altered the meaning of liberty made them conceivable. It is therefore not very realistic to imagine that the Revolutionary leaders threw the class-linked sense of liberty, together with monarchy, into the dustbin of history, and replaced it with its diametrical opposite, in an episode where "overnight modern conceptions of public power replaced older archaic ideas."[16]

It took several decades to de-gentrify the meaning of liberty—a process of intertwined political and cultural change driven by strained relations between the provincial ruling class and their metropolitan counterparts who denied them legitimacy; between the elite-bound concept of liberty and the need to propagate it more widely to gain internal support and external validation of Revolutionary political claims; and between the public's gradual absorption of the new discourse of freedom and the desire of the elites to preserve the existing relations of power. No simple dichotomy can explain the unexpected results of these frictions, for instance, as in the case of back-country North Carolina, where oaths of loyalty came to be required in 1778 and where some of the common folk opposed to taking them used the Patriot language of resistance to "arbitrary power" against the very Patriot elite that demanded the oaths.[17]

The historical ontology of liberty is too entangled in the complex web of culture to be reduced solely to power relations, legal formulations, or symbolic means of expression. Nor can the early modern episodes during which its social realm expanded be explained as having been driven mainly by a shared, broad idea of freedom. Instead, the idea of liberty unfolded in a pattern somewhat resembling the Archimedes principle, where the weight of the water displaced by an object immersed in it is equal to the weight of the object. In most cases, one privileged group reluctantly relinquished a certain area of liberty that it had possessed, so that another group could occupy it and exercise that portion of liberty. Specific, definable rights for new categories of people, who thus far had never owned them, were usually recovered and reconstituted from those secured earlier as exclusive assets by other groups. Ultimately, the full beauty and richness of liberty that emerges from the Revolutionary era lay not in the discovery of some timeless, cosmic rule of universally equal rights, but in the perennially human tension between the privileged and the nonprivileged, between those who had the power to be more free than others and those who were constrained but came to see the various freedoms of the former as templates for their own hopes and aspirations. The history of early modern American freedom was not a story of attacks on the exclusive club of owners of liberty in order to destroy it or replace it with an entirely new one. Rather, it was a lengthy chronicle of diverse groups pounding at the gates and demanding membership.[18]

Notes

Abbreviations

AHR   *American Historical Review*

APW   Charles S. Hyneman and Donald S. Lutz, eds. *American Political Writing during the Founding Era, 1760–1805.* Indianapolis: Liberty Fund, 1983.

HL   Huntington Library manuscripts, San Marino, Calif.

JJ   Charles Warren. *Jacobin and Junto: Early American Politics as Viewed in the Diary of Dr. Nathaniel Ames, 1758–1822.* Cambridge, Mass.: Harvard University Press, 1931.

LDC   Paul H. Smith, ed. *Letters of Delegates to Congress.* Washington, D.C.: Library of Congress, 1976.

LEG   James T. Austin. *Life of Elbridge Gerry.* Boston: Wells and Lilly, 1828.

VHS   Virginia Historical Society manuscripts, Richmond, Va.

WMQ   *William and Mary Quarterly*

Introduction

1. Nash, *Unknown American Revolution;* Holton, *Forced Founders;* A. Young, *Beyond the American Revolution.* For a recent sample of the controversy between elite-centered and people-centered history, see Guyatt's review of Gordon Wood's *Revolutionary Characters* (Guyatt, "Father Knows Best"). On the presumed radical rejection of rank, see Wood, *Radicalism of the American Revolution,* 179. On witches, see Norton, *In the Devil's Snare,* 295. On recovering the nature of eighteenth-century culture from superimposed frameworks of modern scholarship, see Barzun, *The Culture We Deserve,* 3–22.

2. On representations, see Lefort, *Democracy and Political Theory,* 92.

3. Ibid., 93.

4. On the risks and advantages of poststructuralist approaches to colonial America, see Cornell, "Early American History in a Postmodern Age."

5. Other cultures, with different histories and dominated by different values, either developed concepts of freedom different from the Western one or developed none at all (Patterson, *Freedom,* 1:x; Wolf, *Anthropology,* 96).

6. On such pursuits, see Kolakowski, *Freedom, Fame, Lying, and Betrayal,* 84.

7. See Femia, "Gramsci's Patrimony," 347–48.

8. Legal history, as Bruce H. Mann put it, must in an important sense be autonomous and hegemonic; it must move through time "forcing all who live near it to fashion individual and collective accommodations with its presence," because that is what makes law law (Mann, "Death and Transfiguration," 446).

9. Braudel, *The Mediterranean;* Goff, *Time, Work, and Culture.*

10. Certeau, *Practice of Everyday Life,* 32–33.

11. Bloch, *Strange Defeat,* 154.

12. On the ontological aspect of freedom, see Kolakowski, *Freedom, Fame, Lying, and Betrayal,* 95–103; and Bauman and Tester, *Conversations with Zygmunt Bauman,* 113. On the sociogenesis of freedom, I am deeply indebted to Zygmunt Bauman's brilliant insights in his *Freedom.* On balancing limitations within a larger system, see Rawls, *Theory of Justice,* 203.

13. Mather, "America's Appeal," in Sandoz, *Political Sermons,* 1:450 (habeas corpus); Patrick Henry's Draft of Address to the King, Oct. 21? 1774, in *LDC,* 1:223 (trial by jury); James Duane's Speech to the Committee on Rights (Sept. 1774), ibid., 1:54 (representative government); John Zubly to Lord Dartmouth, Sept. 3, 1775, ibid., 2:2 (taxes); "Thomas Burke's Notes on the Articles of Confederation" (ca. Dec. 18, 1777), ibid., 8:433 (franchise). For specifically legal definitions of liberty, see Primus, *American Language of Rights,* 43, 238; and Hohfeld, *Fundamental Legal Conceptions.*

14. Bauman, *Freedom,* 9; Fisher, *Liberty and Freedom,* 113 (terms).

15. Silverman, *Cultural History of the American Revolution;* Eagleton, *Idea of Culture,* 34.

16. Rosen, "Integrity of Cultures," 612 (coherence); Bauman, *Postmodernity and Its Discontents,* 133 (categories), 130 (meaning), 6 (dirt).

17. On prereflexive givens, see Gadamer, *Truth and Method,* 245; Bailyn, *Ideological Origins of the American Revolution;* and Pocock, *Machiavellian Moment.*

18. Isaac, *Transformation of Virginia,* 43.

19. Bourdieu, *Language and Symbolic Power,* 39. Historians have been increasingly aware of this fact since Lucien Lefebvre's pathbreaking study of Rabelais, *Problem of Unbelief in the Sixteenth Century.*

20. Finkelman, *Slavery and the Founders,* 105. On directional paths, see Bauman, *Postmodernity and Its Discontents,* 133; and Huizinga, *Waning of the Middle Ages,* 5.

21. Eco, *Theory of Semiotics,* 54–57.

1. A Critique of Self-Evident Liberty

1. See Kolakowski, *Freedom, Fame, Lying, and Betrayal,* 18, 98.

2. Taylor, *American Colonies,* x–xvii.

3. T. West, *Vindicating the Founders,* 179, xi; Wood, *American Revolution: A History,* 102; Countryman, *American Revolution,* 224.

4. Bailyn, *Ideological Origins of the American Revolution,* 319; Wood, *Creation of the American Republic,* 615; Wood, *Radicalism of the American Revolution,* 368.

5. Zinn, *People's History,* 74–75.

6. The economic argument was first made forcefully by Charles Beard in 1913 (*Economic Interpretation of the Constitution,* 73–151); for consensus views, see Bailyn, *Ideological Origins of the American Revolution;* and Boorstin, *Americans: The Colonial Experience.* It is a view in certain aspects continued by Wood.

7. Zinn, *People's History;* Rediker and Linebaugh, *Many-Headed Hydra;* Holton, *Forced Founders;* Raphael, *Founding Myths;* A. Young, *Beyond the American Revolution.*

8. T. West, *Vindicating the Founders,* 113, 179. See also Glendon, *Rights Talk,* 47–48.

9. Authors both on the left and on the right tend to represent liberty in terms of political theory as universal, rather than as attached to particular groups (see, for instance, Dworkin, *Taking Rights Seriously,* 92; and Rawls, *Theory of Justice,* 3–4).

10. Greene, "All Men are Created Equal," 238.

11. R. W. Davis, series foreword in Konig, *Devising Liberty,* vi.

12. Ingersoll, "Riches and Honour," 61–62. For a similar approach, see O'Brien, "Thomas Jefferson: Radical and Racist," 53–74.

13. John Phillip Reid, *Concept of Liberty,* 45 (amaurosis); Harris, *Plain Folk and Gentry,* 10 (hypocrisy); Jennings, *Creation of America,* 99 (Carolinians); Temperley, "Jefferson and Slavery," 85 (hypocrite); Griswold, "Rights and Wrongs," 210–11 (tranquility); Frey, "Liberty, Equality, and Slavery," 243, 245 (incompatibility); Frey, *Water from the Rock,* 45 (absurdity); Hoffer, *Law and People,* 115 (promises unfulfilled).

14. Royster, "Nature of Treason," 178 (betrayal); Zuckerman, "Rhetoric, Reality, and the Revolution," 698 (aristocratic ambitions); Appleby, *Capitalism and a New Social Order,* 102 (contradiction); Wood, *Creation of the American Republic,* 615 (partisan purposes); Levy, *Jefferson and Civil Liberties,* 171 (generalities); Levy, *Origins of the Bill of Rights,* 5 (error).

15. Finkelman, *Slavery and the Founders,* 137, 135. The rare author who has pointed out that there is no evidence that such a criterion of coherence was present in the Revolutionary era is Primus in his *American Language of Rights,* 93.

16. Hartz, "Theory of the Development of New Societies," 73.

17. Kolakowski, *Freedom,* 96.

18. Primus, *American Language of Rights,* 73.

19. Rediker and Linebaugh, *Many-Headed Hydra,* 352–53 (solidarity); Holton, *Forced Founders,* 212 (common traits).

20. Bauman, *Conversations,* 113. We have long abandoned attempts like those of James George Frazer (*Golden Bough*) to show a deep commonality of rituals, customs, and beliefs among vastly differing cultures and societies in different epochs.

21. See Colley, *Forging the Nation.*

22. Pocock, *Machiavellian Moment* (Florence); Foucault, *Archeology of Knowledge,* 149 (coherence); Brooke, *Heart of the Commonwealth,* xiii; Koschnik, *"Let a Common Interest Bind Us Together";* Neem, *Creating a Nation of Joiners,* 172; Onuf, *Jefferson's Empire,* 75. Earlier groundbreaking work on culture and politics had been done by Isaac in his *Transformation of Virginia.* For cultural rather than economic and political perspectives on revolutionary developments in Britain and France at the threshold of modernity, see Jones and Wahrman, *Age of Cultural Revolutions.*

23. Waldstreicher, *In the Midst of Perpetual Fetes;* Warner, *Letters of the Republic.*

24. Kolakowski, *Main Currents of Marxism,* 237.

25. "An entire population took part in that robust dialogue [over the Declaration of Independence]. . . . The dialogue itself deserves celebration, not just its practical conclusion" (Raphael, *Founding Myths,* 123).

26. Gilje, *Liberty on the Waterfront,* 105, 127.

27. On such differences, see Bauman, *Freedom,* 97.

28. Bridenbaugh, *Gentleman's Progress,* 55. On goal attainment, see Rawls, *Theory of Justice,* 204.

29. Rediker, *Between the Devil and the Deep Blue Sea,* 5, 298.

30. On comparative servitude, see Drescher and Engerman, *Historical Guide to World Slavery.*

31. For a philosophical comment on this, see Kolakowski, *Freedom,* 99.

32. Hill, *World Turned Upside Down.*

33. On the socialization of cultural norms, see Wrzosek, "The Problem of Cultural Imputation," 135.

34. Frey, "Inequality," in Pestana and Salinger, *Inequality,* 87.

35. P. Morgan, *Slave Counterpoint,* xv, xxiii–xxiv.

36. Moses Finley aptly called this recurring problem the "free-will error" (Finley, *Slavery in Classical Antiquity,* 70).

2. British Legacies

1. Eric Foner, in his fine survey of freedom in American history, recognizes that "echoes of this old restricted idea of liberty survived in early America," but he treats it as a mere relic of the past (Foner, *Story of American Freedom,* 6).

2. Patterson, *Freedom,* 365 (spectrum), 220 (Rome); Bauman, *Freedom,* 30 (freedmen).

3. R. Johnson, *Commons Debates,* 3, 487. I am obliged to Daniel Hulsebosch for drawing my attention to this quote. For an analysis of how colonial legal norms were differently adhered to by different social groups, see Offut, "Limits of Authority."

4. Mączak, *Rządzący i rządzeni,* 27–29.

5. Maitland, *Constitutional History of England,* 15 (anti-Stuarts); Penn, "Letter from a Gentleman in the Country" (birthright); Stubbs, *Constitutional History,* 1:595 (collective act); Candidus III, "American Independency Defended," in *Large Additions to Common Sense,* 82 (limited dependence).

6. Pym, "Speech or Declaration of John Pym," 21.

7. Primus, *American Language of Rights,* 46 (preexisting privileges); Rakove, "Parchment Barriers and the Politics of Rights," 105 (traditionalism). The Declaration of 1689 reflected the various autocratic violations by James II but did not demand toleration, nor did it negate the established church (see Ryan, "The British, the Americans, and Rights," 384 [Declaration of Rights]).

8. Hutson, "Bill of Rights," 93 (de Witt), 94 (Randolph). Burlamaqui, well known to Jefferson, thought a right was best defined as a "power" (Hutson, "Bill of Rights," 92).

9. Trenchard and Gordon, *Cato's Letters,* 1:429 (natural liberty), 429 (lust), 429 (pillaging).

10. Bush, *Noble Privilege,* 18, 120.

11. Mączak, *Rządzący i rządzeni,* 22–24; Patterson, *Freedom,* 221 (Cicero), 222 (achievement); Finley, *Politics in the Ancient World,* 85.

12. Bauman, *Freedom,* 35.

13. "From the Craftsman," by Aequus, *Massachusetts Gazette and Boston Newsletter* (1776), in *APW,* 1:63 (privilege); Henry Parker, *An Answer to a Paper* (1651), quoted in Tuck, *Natural Rights Theories,* 151, 5–6 (passive rights).

14. Abraham Williams, *Election Sermon* (Boston, 1762), in *APW,* 2:5, 9; Americanus, *Constitutionalist* (Charleston, 1794), 35; J. Allen, *An Oration* (Boston, 1773), 1–2.

15. Eltis, "Europeans and the Rise and Fall of African Slavery," 1408.

16. Fletcher, *Second Discourse,* 55 (vagabonds), 47, 56–58; Slack, "Vagrants and Vagrancy," 360–79 (employment); Fletcher, *Second Discourse,* 46–47. See also Leonard, *Early History,* vii. Enslavement projects are discussed in greater detail in Rozbicki, "To Save Them from Themselves," 29–50.

17. Fletcher, *Second Discourse,* 47–49 (the idle); 49, 52 (master).

18. Ibid., 50–51, 56, 50; Journal of Cadwallader Colden, 97 (benefit of clergy), HL. See also Joseph Jones to Unknown, Philadelphia, Sept. 18, 1781, in *LDC,* 18:55, in which he approves "the benefit of clergy" for an accused.

19. Berkeley, *The Querist,* 6:136–37.

20. Ibid. (act of charity); Berkeley, "A Word to the Wise or an Exhortation to the Roman Catholic Clergy of Ireland" (1749), in *Works of George Berkeley,* 240, 244 (lusty vagabonds); Berkeley, *The Querist,* 137 (terror); Fletcher, *Second Discourse,* 56 (galleys).

21. Berkeley, *The Querist,* 136–37 (hard labor); T. Young, *Completing Berkeley's Project,* 22–23 (religious equality).

22. Berkeley, *Proposal for the Better Supplying of Churches* (1725), in *Works of George Berkeley,* 7:347; Gaustad, *George Berkeley in America,* 25 (Berkeley's slaves); Berkeley, *Proposal,* 346 (gospel-liberty). On Berkeley in America, see Rand, *Berkeley's American Sojourn;* Berman, "Irish Philosophy," 28–39; Skemp, "Berkeley's Newport Experience"; and McGowan, "George Berkeley's American Declaration."

23. McDonald, *Novus ordo seclorum,* 54–55, 188 (influence on Jefferson); Hutcheson, *System of Moral Philosophy,* vol. 2, bk. 2, 105.

24. Hutcheson, *System of Moral Philosophy,* vol. 2, bk. 3, 199, 211–12, 201.

25. Ibid., vol. 2, bk. 3, 201.

26. Ibid., vol. 2, bk. 3, 202 (seven years), 201 (natural rights and right to defense), 202 (contracts), 205 (captivity in war), 202–3 (voiding of rights), 202 (just foundation).

27. Davis, *Problem of Slavery,* 378.

28. Hutcheson, *Inaugural Lecture on the Social Nature of Man* (Glasgow, 1730), in Hutcheson, *On Human Nature,* 145 (genteel elites); Hutcheson, *System of Moral Philosophy,* vol. 2, bk. 1, 123 (sensuality), 120 (inferior orders), bk. 3, 209–11 (perpetual slavery), bk. 2, 84–85 (captives).

29. Robbins, "When Is It That Colonies May Turn Independent?" 214, 217 (American colonies); Davis, *Problem of Slavery,* 119–20.

30. This gamut stretched from the monarch down to the slaves, but even among the latter one found a subcategory of runaway slaves considered "outlawed," as in the Virginia code of 1705, indicating that regular slaves retained some rights (T. Morris, *Southern Slavery and the Law*, 286–88).

31. Kussmaul, *Servants in Husbandry*, 33–34, 166 (statutes); Dean, *Constitution of Poverty*, 36–37, 59; Thompson, *Customs in Common*, 37 (masterless men); Richard Brome's poem quoted in Hill, *World Turned Upside Down*, 48 (beggars); [Donaldson], *Undoubted Art of Thriving*, 57; *Gentleman's Magazine* 5 (1735): 93 (appeal to slaves).

32. Fletcher, *Second Discourse*, 50; John Phillip Reid, *Concept of Liberty*, 119; Roy Porter, "Enlightenment in England," 7–8 (distinctions); Tuck, *Natural Rights Theories*, 3–5, 8 (ius and dominium).

33. Jennings, *Creation of America*, 281–82, 284 (imperialism); "Exhibit Number Eight, Referred to in Judge Chase's Answer" (May 2, 1803), in Banning, *Liberty and Order*, 298 (state of nature).

34. Leonard, *Early History of English Poor Relief*, 229–30 (court books); Donne quoted in Howard Mumford Jones, "The Colonial Impulse," 147 (Bridewell); Hugh Jones, *Present State of Virginia*, 118 (legal compulsion); Oldmixon, *British Empire in America*, 1:xv (value to nation); Tuck, *Natural Rights*, 19 (theorists). On British bond servants in America, see A. Smith, *Colonists in Bondage;* and Galenson, *White Servitude*.

35. Pole, *Pursuit of Equality*, 49n79 (literal commitment). The increasing cultural acceptance of the enslavement of Africans was not necessarily inversely proportional to the growing rejection of slavery for Europeans (see Drescher, *Capitalism and Antislavery*, 27).

3. The Transmission of Restricted Liberty to Colonial America

1. Maier, *American Scripture*, 191.

2. Grasso, *Speaking Aristocracy*, 14 (aristocracy); Day quoted in Greene, "Social Structure and Political Behavior, 122; Grasso, *Speaking Aristocracy*, 14 (shoemaker). On Southern elites, see Rozbicki, *Complete Colonial Gentleman*, chap. 2.

3. Beard, *Economic Interpretation of the Constitution*, 17; Hartz, "Development of New Societies" (consensus); Wood, *Radicalism of the American Revolution* (dominant class); Kolp, *Gentlemen and Freeholders;* Rozbicki, *Complete Colonial Gentleman*, 28–75 (traditionalism).

4. On such criteria, see Mączak, *Rządzący i rządzeni*, 277.

5. Bourdieu, *Distinction*, 68.

6. Ibid., 472, 479 (condescension strategies); Bauman, *Freedom*, 23 (equilibrium). I am describing here a general pattern only; there were, of course, compromises—for instance, the sale in eighteenth-century England of titles to wealthy commoners.

7. Samuel Adams to James Warren, Nov. 4, 1775, in *LDC*, 2:299; Kirkpatrick and Wood quoted in Longmore, *Invention of George Washington*, 58; [Richard Henry Lee], The Federal Farmer, letter from Oct. 10, 1787, in McDonald, *Empire and Nation*, 103 (the virtuous); Adams quoted in Keane, *Tom Paine*, 126.

8. Rozbicki, *Complete Colonial Gentleman*, 43–52 (Defoe); Langford, *Public Life*, iv

(nouveaux riches), chaps. 3–4 (parliament); Defoe, *Compleat English Gentleman,* 18 (plaebeii).

9. Marambaud, *William Byrd of Westover,* 59; Greene, *Diary of Landon Carter,* 910; Richard Henry Lee to George Mason, New York, Oct. 1, 1787, in *LDC,* 24:458; James Duane to George Washington, Philadelphia, Dec. 9, 1780, ibid., 16:422.

10. John Adams to Horatio Gates, April 27, 1776, Philadelphia, in *LDC,* 3:588; John Adams to Mercy Otis Warren, April 16, 1776, ibid., 3:538 (spirit of commerce); John Keane, *Tom Paine,* 171 (business ethos); The Federal Farmer, in Pole, *American Constitution,* 30, 28, 30 (Anti-Federalists); Maddox, *Sermon Preached before the Incorporated Society,* 27; [Ward], *Trip to New England,* 16 (peddlers).

11. Jonathan Blanchard to Josiah Bartlett, Annapolis, April 20, 1784, in *LDC,* 21:532; John Adams to John Hawley, Nov. 25, 1775, ibid., 2:385, 3:519; Ephraim Paine to Robert R. Livingston, May 24, 1784, ibid., 21:640; Charles Thomson to Hannah Thomson, July 25, 1783, ibid., 20:454; officer cited in Raphael, *People's History,* 203.

12. Ingersoll, "Riches and Honour," 48–58 (levelling); Instructions to Charles Calvert, *Archives of Maryland,* 15:16. On upward mobility, see Bushman, *Refinement of America,* 409–13.

13. Mączak, *Rządzący i rządzeni,* 22.

14. Richard Henry Lee's draft Address to the People of Great Britain and Ireland, Oct. 11–18, 1774, in *LDC,* 1:174; and his "Draft Address to the King," ibid., 226 (English constitution); Zagorin, *History of Political Thought,* 37 (Levellers); "General Laws and Liberties of the Province of New Hampshire," 18–19; Jefferson to Edmund Pendleton, Philadelphia, Aug. 26, 1776, in *LDC,* 5:66; Lutz, *Colonial Origins,* 377 (Confederation).

15. The Preceptor, "Social Duties of the Political Kind," *Boston Massachusetts Spy* (May 21, 1772), in *APW,* 1:178 (subordination), 180 (common interests); John Adams to James Sullivan, Philadelphia, May 26, 1776, in *LDC,* 4:75; Thomas Jefferson to George Rogers Clark, Jan. 1, 1779, in Boyd, *Papers of Thomas Jefferson,* 3:259.

16. On such divisions, see Schultz, "Class Society?" 203, 212.

17. Skinner, "Blackstone's Support for the Militia," 13 (Tories); Isaac, *Transformation of Virginia,* 105.

18. Chartier, *Cultural Origins of the French Revolution,* 185–86 (French monarchy); Higonnet, *Class, Ideology, and the Rights of Nobles,* 258 (French bourgeoisie), 16 (duty to state).

19. Rozbicki, *Colonial Gentleman,* 77–79.

20. John Phillip Reid, *Concept of Liberty,* 25 (property in liberty); *Encyclopédie méthodique* (1784–87), quoted in Bien, "Offices, Corps, and a System of State Credit," 1:92 (exclusive liberties), 94 (trading liberty).

21. Mayhew, "Election Sermon," 293; "Account of the Vices Peculiar to the Savages of N. America," *Columbian Magazine* 1, no. 1 (Sept. 1786); Son of Liberty [Silas Downer], "A Discourse at the Dedication of the Tree of Liberty" (Providence, 1768), in *APW,* 1:101; Richard Henry Lee's draft Address to the People of Great Britain and Ireland, in *LDC,* 1:177; John Adams to James Sullivan, Philadelphia, May 26, 1776, ibid., 4:74; James Madison to Thomas Jefferson, Oct. 24, 1787, ibid., 24:506.

22. On socially constituted schemes of perception, see Bourdieu, *Distinction,* 482

(representations); and Bridenbaugh, *Gentleman's Progress,* 13–14 (Holland shirts). Economic relations may underlie many of such relationships, but signs of class are immediately communicable (see Thompson, *Making of the English Working Class,* 9). On class and language, see G. Jones, *Languages of Class.*

23. Silas Deane to Samuel B. Webb, Philadelphia, Nov. 22, 1775, in *LDC* 2:371. See also Bourdieu, *Language and Symbolic Power,* 230–31.

24. Bourdieu, *Distinction,* 24, 69 (essentialism); Morris quoted in Keane, *Tom Paine,* 178–79.

25. Grace Galloway to Elizabeth Nickleson, Nov. 6, 1758, Galloway MS, HL.

26. George Mason to George Mercer, Oct. 2, 1778, *Virginia Historical Register* 1 (1848): 30; Benjamin Franklin to Richard Howe, July 20, 1776, Cooper MS. On cartoons, see Olson, *Emblems of American Community,* 247, 72–123.

27. William Byrd II to Peter Beckford, Dec. 6, 1735, in Tinling, *Correspondence of the Three William Byrds,* 2:464. On identity, see Greene, "Empire and Identity," 208–30.

28. Bailyn, *Ideological Origins of the American Revolution,* 378; John Phillip Reid, *Concept of Liberty,* 68–73 (abstraction); Arthur Lee to Dr. Theodorick Bland, Aug. 21, 1770, Bland Family MS (Rousseau); [Braxton], "An Address to the Convention of the Colony," 1:334; "The Tribune," *South Carolina Gazette* (Oct. 6, 1776), ibid., 1:95. On preferment, see Samuel West, "On the Right to Rebel against Governors" (Boston, 1776), ibid., 1:443. On autonomy as the premise underlying the meaning of freedom in the Declaration of Independence, see Furstenberg, "Beyond Freedom and Slavery," 1295–1330.

29. Pole, *American Constitution,* 86, 93 (the "Farmer" is thought to be the framer and non-signer of the Constitution, John Francis Mercer); William Hooper to Joseph Hewes, Nov. 19? 1776, in *LDC,* 5:520; Edward Hand to Jasper Yeates, Annapolis, Aug. 6, 1784, ibid., 21:757.

4. The Revolution

1. Wood, *Radicalism of the American Revolution,* 124 (superficiality); 124–25 (fragility); 230 (reconstitution).

2. Samuel Adams to James Warren, Philadelphia, Dec. 26 1775, in *LDC,* 2:521.

3. Ong, *Interfaces of the Word,* 103, 3.

4. The term "conceptual package" is used here after d'Anjou, *Social Movements and Cultural Change,* 231.

5. Hill, *God's Englishman,* 262–65; Cochin, "Theory of Jacobinism"; Raphael, *People's History,* 145–85 (loyalists); Paine, *Rights of Man,* 54, xvii.

6. Virginia Delegates to George Washington, Philadelphia, July 26, 1775, in *LDC,* 1:669; William Franklin to Earl of Bute, London, July 3, 1762, and July 29, 1762, in "Colonial Patronage," 132–33.

7. Maier, *American Scripture,* 237–38.

8. Bourdieu, *Language and Symbolic Power,* 230.

9. Jack Rakove has shown how this language was assembled from metropolitan histori-

cal traditions, common law, and the Enlightenment discourse of freedom (Rakove, *Original Meanings,* 290–97).

10. On such need in culture, see Kolakowski, *Presence of Myth,* chap. 1.

11. Lockridge, *The Diary and Life of William Byrd II,* 49, 65, 157.

12. John Selden, *De jure naturali* (1640), quoted in Tuck, *Natural Rights Theories,* 91; "Note during the Convention for amending the Constitution of Virginia," in Meyers, *Mind of the Founder,* 407.

13. May 1754, *Letters of Horace Walpole,* 2:5 (Beckford); Edmund Pendleton to Joseph Jones, Feb. 10, 1781, in Mays, *Letters and Papers of Edmund Pendleton,* 2:335; Lafayette to Mme. Lafayette, June 7, 1777, quoted in Gottschalk, *Lafayette Comes to America,* 135.

14. Hancock to Charles Lee, Philadelphia, Feb. 19, 1776, in *LDC,* 3:282; George Washington to Robert Mackenzie, Philadelphia, Oct 9, 1774, ibid., 1:166; Virginia delegates to unknown, Oct. 16, 1775, ibid., 2:194 (common cause); Thomas Lynch to Ralph Izard, Philadelphia, July 7, 1775, ibid., 1:608; Joseph Reed, draft of a letter to George Johnstone, Valley Forge, July 13, 1778, ibid., 10:99; Furet, *Interpreting the French Revolution,* 54 (general will); Thayer, *Discourse Delivered at the Roman Catholic Church in Boston* (1797), in Sandoz, *Political Sermons,* 2:1344 (insurrection); Otis, *Rights of the British Colonies,* in Kurland and Lerner, *Founders' Constitution,* 1:52; Silas Deane to Thomas Mumford, Philadelphia, Oct. 16, 1774, ibid., 1:201; William Pierce to St. George Tucker, [Sept. 28, 1787], ibid., 24:447; Samuel Adams to James Warren, Philadelphia, Dec. 12, 1776, ibid., 5:601.

15. Hutson, "Bill of Rights," 66 (rights), 76 (Magna Charta), 69 (precedents). On serviceable concepts, see Bauman, *Freedom* 29.

16. Otis, *Rights of the British Colonies,* 71; John Adams, "Dissertation on the Canon and Feudal Law," 1:111–12; [Silas Downer], "A Discourse at the Dedication of the Tree of Liberty," in *APW,* 1:101; Sir Edward Coke, "Prohibitions del roy" (1607) in Malcolm, *Struggle for Sovereignty,* 1:18. On the use of natural law by the Enlightenment ruling classes, see Rommen, *Natural Law,* 67–96.

17. "Address on Liberty," *Providence Gazette,* Jan. 21, 1769 (poem); Jefferson, *Notes on the State of Virginia,* 163; Noll, *America's God,* 91 (churches); Allison, *Spiritual Liberty,* 17; John Witherspoon, "Sermon Delivered at a Public Thanksgiving after Peace," in Witherspoon, *Works of the Rev. John Witherspoon,* 3:79.

18. Quoted in Greene, *Nature of Colony Constitutions,* 19 (Laurens), 186 (Lee); "Tous les pouvoirs publics, sans distinctions, sont une émanation de la volonté generale; tous viennent du peuple" (quoted in Higonnet, *Class, Ideology, and the Rights of Nobles,* 255).

19. Henry, Speech to the Virginia Ratifying Convention, June 5, 1788, in Pole, *American Constitution,* 123; Pendleton, "Address to the Virginia Ratification Convention," in Mays, *Letters and Papers of Edmund Pendleton,* 2:523, 524.

20. Richard Brown, *Knowledge Is Power,* 102 (legal speech); Thomas Hutchinson to Lord Dartmouth, Dec. 3, 1773, quoted in A. Young, "George Robert Twelves Hewes," 590. On the written word, see Rozbicki, "Cultural Development of the Colonies," 75–76.

21. Henry Cumings, A Sermon Preached at Lexington, in Sandoz, *Political Sermons,*

1:674; Butterfield, *Earliest Diary of John Adams,* 74. On the topic of rhetoric, I rely heavily on Sandra M. Gustafson's unsurpassed analysis of contemporary changes in political rhetoric in her *Eloquence Is Power.*

22. John Adams to Benjamin Rush, June 21, 1811, in Schutz and Adair, *Spur of Fame,* 197; *The Patriots,* in Munford, *Collection of Plays,* 122; "Liberty," *Connecticut Gazette* (New London) July 7, 1775 (poem). On the politics of the play, see McDonnell, "A World Turned 'Topsy-Turvy,'" 235–70.

23. Bland, *An Inquiry into the Rights of the British Colonies,* 10; Benjamin Franklin to Jonathan Shipley, Philadelphia, July 7, 1775, in *LDC,* 1:606; James Duane, "Notes for a Speech in Congress," ibid., 1:394; Jennings, *Creation of America,* 280 (Northwest Ordinance); Warren quoted in foreword by Lester H. Cohen in M. O. Warren, *History,* 1:xvii.

24. On the coherence-generating role of language, see Bauman, *Culture as Praxis,* xiii– xiv. On defining the meaning of reality, see d'Anjou, *Social Movements,* 231. On the fictionality of language, see Bourdieu, *Language and Symbolic Power,* 41–42.

25. Paine, *Common Sense,* 8 (tyranny); Theodorick Bland Jr. to Farrel and Jones (merchants in Bristol), Dec. 1, 1774, in Campbell, *Bland Papers,* 1:33 (aristocracy); Carter Braxton Diary; [Macpherson], *Rights of Great Britain Asserted,* 45 (smuggler); Querno, *American Times,* 1–2 (rats); Samuel Ward "Notes for a Speech in Congress," Oct. 12, 1774, in *LDC,* 1:184 (elite of quality).

26. Rozbicki, *Complete Colonial Gentleman,* 45–46.

27. Jefferson to Madison, Paris, Sept. 6, 1789, in Koch and Peden, *Life and Selected Writings of Thomas Jefferson,* 492.

28. Johnson, "Taxation No Tyranny," 416, 431; Macpherson, *Rights of Great Britain Asserted,* 11; Edmund Jenings to Robert Beverley, April 9, 1766 (cobbler), Edmund Jenings MS.

29. Edward Rutledge to John Jay, Philadelphia, June 29, 1776, in *LDC,* 4:338; Alexander McDougall to George Clinton, Philadelphia, March 12, 1781, ibid., 17:54; John Adams to John Lowell, Philadelphia, June 12, 1776, ibid., 4:197; Jonathan Dickinson Sergeant to John Adams, Princeton, April 11, 1776, ibid., 3:507.

30. John Adams to Elbridge Gerry, April 25, 1785, in *LEG,* 1:427, 430; Massachusetts delegates to James Bowdoin, New York, Sept. 3, 1785, in *LDC,* 22:613; M. O. Warren, *History,* 2:617, 619; Burke quoted ibid., 2:620 (grandeur); William Ellery to Francis Dana, Philadelphia, Dec. 3, 1783, in *LDC,* 21:178, 179 (usurped nobility); Rufus King to Elbridge Gerry, July 4, 1786, ibid., 23:386; Jefferson to Washington, Annapolis, April 16, 1784, ibid., 21:522.

31. M. O. Warren, *History,* 622 (upper class); Cassius, *Considerations on the Society or Order of Cincinnati,* 3; David Osgood, "The Wonderful Works of God Are to Be Remembered" (1794), in Sandoz, *Political Sermons,* 2:1233; Darnton, "High Enlightenment and the Low-Life of Literature," 90–91 (le monde).

32. Lefort, *Democracy and Political Theory,* 92.

33. *Boston Evening Post,* Aug. 22, 1768.

34. Baradziej, *Rozważania,* 8; Kroeber, *Anthropology,* 102.

35. Samuel Whitwell, Oration on July 4, 1789, Boston, in Loring, *Hundred Boston*

Orators, 228 (darling rights); Waldstreicher, *In the Midst of Perpetual Fetes,* 38 (fusion); Adams to Warren, July 3, 1776, Philadelphia, in *LDC,* 4:376; Ellis, *Founding Brothers,* 216; Howe, *Language and Political Meaning,* 96 (oaths).

36. Ramsay, *History of the American Revolution,* 1:10, 30.

37. Quoted in Newman, *Parades and Politics,* 100–101, 113 (sovereignty), 111 (original intent), 102 (women).

38. *JJ,* 47 (procession), 81, 83–84 (cockades); Abigail Adams to her sister, April 26, 1798, in Banning, *Liberty and Order,* 225 (theater).

39. Waldstreicher, *In the Midst of Perpetual Fetes,* 26. See also Shaw, *American Patriots.*

40. Letter to the editor by Locke, *Daily Universal Register,* Jan. 26, 1785, 1 (bondage); "The Progress of Liberty in England," *Times,* June 10, 1788, 3 (laws); "The Progress of Liberty," *Times,* Jan. 6, 1790, 3 (no wrongs); *Times,* Dec. 22, 1791, 3 (Albion); Mazareen in *Times,* Jan. 12, 1790, 4 (France).

41. Samuel Adams to Samuel Freeman, Philadelphia, Aug. 15, 1777, in *LDC,* 7:413; Edward Carrington to Thomas Jefferson, New York, June 9, 1787, ibid., 24:311; John Francis Mercer to the Public, ibid., 21:33; William Emerson, Oration (Boston, 1802), in Sandoz, *Political Sermons,* 2:1563 (degeneracy).

42. Charles Thomsen to David Ramsay, New York, Nov. 2, 1786, in *LDC,* 23:627; Waldstreicher, *In the Midst of Perpetual Fetes,* 25 (funerals), 41 (song); Hobsbawm, "Introduction: Inventing Traditions," 1. See also Gustafson, *Eloquence Is Power,* 147.

43. Washington's Farewell Address, Sept. 19, 1796, in Banning, *Liberty and Order,* 218.

44. Zamoyski, *Holy Madness,* 34. On Leiden and the language of inalienable rights of "the people," see Shama, *Patriots and Liberators,* 64–135. On Sarmatians, see Symmons-Symonolewicz, *National Consciousness in Poland,* 23–40.

45. For instance, Waldstreicher, *In the Midst of Perpetual Fetes,* 111; and Warner, *Letters of the Republic,* 173.

46. On contests over the symbolic foundations of power as a dimension of Revolutionary radicalism, see Darnton, "High Enlightenment and the Low-Life of Literature," 81–115.

47. Samuel Adams to James Warren, Dec. 26, 1775, in *LDC,* 2:52.

48. Furet, *Interpreting the French Revolution,* 49.

49. [Ramsay], *Address to the Citizens of South-Carolina,* 11 (one rank); Ramsay, "Oration," 192, 194 (medium).

50. Morgan, *Inventing the People,* 13.

51. Blackstone, *Commentaries,* 29.

52. Gadamer, *Truth and Method,* 267 (hermeneutics); Hewes quoted in A. Young, "George Robert Twelves Hewes," 588.

53. The Virginia Bill of Rights, June 12, 1776, in Pole, *Revolution in America,* 519, 521 (uniform government); Washington to John Jay, Aug. 1, 1786, in Fitzpatrick, *Writings of George Washington,* 28:502–3; Jefferson to William Smith, Nov. 13, 1787, in Ford, *Writings of Thomas Jefferson,* 4:466; John Adams, "Thoughts on Government," March 19, 1776, in *LDC,* 3:402; Paine, *Common Sense,* 1776, 2.

54. Marxists are wary of accepting this because they often still assume—despite the

arguments of postmodern epistemology—that such collective subjects exist objectively, resting firmly on people's relation to the means of production (Bourdieu, *Language and Symbolic Power,* 250–51).

55. "The Presentment of the Grand Jury," in Gibbes, *Documentary History,* 1:290.

56. Gross, *In Debt to Shays,* 310 (personas); Howe, *Language and Political Meaning,* 154, 151, 169 (pseudonyms); Samuel Adams to Elbridge Gerry, Philadelphia, Sept. 26, 1775, in *LDC,* 2:64; Elias Boudinot to Hannah Boudinot, Philadelphia, Aug. 13, 1778, ibid., 10:439; Benjamin Rush to Julia Rush, Philadelphia, July 22, 1776, ibid., 25:583; Timothy Dwight, "Greenfield Hill: A Poem in Seven Parts" (New York, 1794), in McTaggart and Bottorff, *Major Poems of Timothy Dwight,* 402.

57. Thomas Jefferson to Edmund Pendleton, Philadelphia, Aug. 26, 1776, in *LDC,* 5:65; Pole, *Revolution in America,* 521 (Virginia); "Farmer Refuted," quoted in Wood, *Creation of the American Republic,* 271 (compact); "Federalist No. 84" (1787), in Kurland and Lerner, *Founders' Constitution,* 5:10 (power of people).

58. W. P. Adams, *First American Constitutions,* 84–85 (New York); Pittsfield Town Petition, May 29, 1776, in Pole, *Revolution in America,* 419–20; W. P. Adams, *First American Constitutions,* 147 (polarization); Onuf, "Federalism, Democracy and Liberty," 132–59, 78–79. I am very grateful to Peter Onuf for letting me read his manuscript before it was published.

59. Raphael, *People's History,* 393.

60. John Adams to John Penn, March 19 1776, in *LDC,* 3:405; David Ramsay to Thomas Jefferson, New York, May 3, 1786, ibid., 23:262.

61. Theophrastus, "A Short History of the Trial by Jury," in *APW,* 1:700–701.

62. David Griffith, *Passive Obedience Considered,* 12; "The Farmer," March 2, 1788, in Pole, *American Constitution,* 93, 95; Ramsay, "Oration," 185; Theophilus Parsons, "The Essex Result" (Newbury, 1778), in *APW,* 1:490–501; Israel Evans, "A Sermon Delivered at Concord" (1791), in Sandoz, *Political Sermons,* 2:1071; Worcester Speculator, *Worcester Magazine* (Oct. 1787), in *APW,* 1:700; John Adams, "Thoughts on Government," ibid., 1:408; Samuel Adams to James Warren, Dec. 27, [1775], in *LDC,* 2:525 (youth).

63. Theodorick Bland to Theodorick Bland, Sr., n.d., in Campbell, *Bland Papers,* 1:17.

64. Thomas Jefferson to James Madison, Paris, Dec. 20, 1787, in Onuf, *Thomas Jefferson,* 129; John Adams to John Sullivan, May 26, 1776, in *LDC,* 4:74; Farrand, *Records of the Federal Convention,* 1:402; Keane, *Tom Paine,* 171; Hume, "Of Refinement in the Arts," in Hume, *Essays and Treatises,* 1:289.

5. The Sway of Symbolic Power

1. James Duane's Speech to the Committee on Rights, Sept. 8, 1774, in *LDC,* 1:51 (impartial part); Samuel Adams to the Public, March 13, 1781, ibid., 17:55; [Green], *Observations,* 8 (hope for ages); [Tucker], *Conciliatory Hints,* 10 (usurpation).

2. James Madison to Edmund Randolph, Philadelphia, April 1, 1783, in *LDC,* 20:129; Samuel Adams to Thomas Jefferson, Nov. 18, 1801, in Cushing, *Writings of Samuel Adams,* 4:411.

3. John Adams to John Penn, [March 19–27], 1776, in *LDC*, 3:400; John Adams to Archibald Bulloch, Philadelphia, July 1, 1776, ibid., 4:346 (Jerusalem); John Adams to Josiah Quincy, Philadelphia, July 29, 1775, ibid., 1:676 (providence); Benjamin Rush, "Notes for a Speech in Congress," Aug. 1, 1776, ibid., 4:602; Elias Boudinot to James Searle, Philadelphia, April 1, 1783, ibid., 20:125–26; George Washington, Circular to the States, June 14, 1783, in W. B. Allen, *George Washington*, 240–41; Madison, *Discourse*, 9; Onuf, *Jefferson's Empire*, 15.

4. Massachusetts Delegates to James Bowdoin, New York, Sept. 3, 1785, in *LDC*, 22:613 (happiness); Roy Porter, "Enlightenment in England," 11.

5. Tench Coxe to Benjamin Rush, New York, Feb. 12, 1789, in *LDC*, 25:497; Samuel Adams to Elbridge Gerry, Philadelphia, Nov. 27, 1789, ibid., 16:387.

6. John Adams to John Penn, [March 19–27?], 1776, in *LDC*, 3:400.

7. Edward Carrington to Thomas Jefferson, New York, June 9, 1778, *LDC*, 24:311 (will of the people); David Howell to William Greene, Annapolis, Feb. 5, 1784, ibid., 21:340 (tyranny); James Madison to George Washington, New York, Feb. 8, 1788, ibid., 24:641.

8. Edward Carrington to Thomas Jefferson, New York, June 9, 1787, in *LDC*, 24:311 (sacred rights); Samuel Holten to Aaron Ward, Philadelphia, April 8, 1780, ibid., 15:21; George Partridge to Samuel Adams, New York, Feb. 25, 1785, ibid., 22:220; Philip Freneau, "On Mr. Paine's Rights of Man" (1795), in H. Clark, *Poems of Freneau*, 125.

9. Robespierre, *Report upon the Principles of Political Morality*, 2–4, 7, 10–11.

10. John Quincy Adams, *An Oration*, 7; Loring, *Hundred Boston Orators*, 158 (Warren); Jacob Duché's first prayer in Congress, in *LDC*, 25:551; John Francis Mercer to the Public, in *LDC*, 21:32. On stylistic privilege, see Bourdieu, *Language and Symbolic Power*, 72, 152, 156.

11. Bowdoin, *Proclamation*.

12. *Virginia Gazette*, May 19, 1774, quoted in Davidson, *Propaganda and the American Revolution*, 135.

13. Peter D. G. Thomas, "The Grenville Program, 1763–1765," in Greene, *Companion to the American Revolution*, 121.

14. Saillant, review of *Epistles and Elexicons*.

15. Isaac Kramnick suggests, to the contrary, that Anti-Federalists wanted representatives to be "directly responsible to their constituents" (Kramnick, "Great National Discussion," 15). Edward Carrington to Thomas Jefferson, New York, June 9, 1787, in *LDC*, 24:312; William Pierce to St. George Tucker, [Sept. 28, 1787], ibid., 24:445; Konig, introduction to *Devising Liberty*, 3; J. Clark, *Language of Liberty*, 8 (constitutional proceedings); Blackstone, *Commentaries*, 160–61.

16. [William Ball], *The Peoples Right Briefly Asserted* (London, 1649), in Malcolm, *Struggle for Sovereignty*, 1:364, 368; Giles Hickory [Noah Webster], *American Magazine*, Dec. 1787, 13–14, 75–76.

17. James Madison, "Federalist No. 10," in Pole, *American Constitution*, 154; Noah Webster, "An Oration on the Anniversary of the Declaration of Independence" (1802), in *APW*, 2:1233 (dependence); The Federal Farmer (1787), in Pole, *American Constitution*,

32, 35–36 (common people); Meriwether Smith to the Public, Philadelphia, March 9, 1779, in *LDC*, 12:182. On the contemporary sense of "the public," see Chartier, *Cultural Origins of the French Revolution*, 33–37.

18. Thomas Jefferson to Edmund Pendleton, Philadelphia, Aug. 26, 1776, in *LDC*, 5:65; Noah Webster, "An Oration on the Anniversary of the Declaration of Independence" (New Haven, 1802), in *APW*, 2:1230–34; Theodore Sedgwick to Pamela Sedgwick, New York, July 18, 1786, in *LDC*, 23:408; Hobbes, *Leviathan*, 87.

19. Ramsay, "Oration," 187, 189; John Adams to Jonathan Dickinson Sergeant, Philadelphia, July 21, 1776, in *LDC*, 4:505; Sydnor, *American Revolutionaries in the Making*, 44–59 (elections).

20. Committee on Secret Correspondence to Silas Deane, Philadelphia, July 8, 1776, in *LDC*, 4:405 (universal demand); Georgia Delegates to Nathanael Greene, Philadelphia, July 27, 1781, ibid., 17:450; Henry Marchant to William Greene, Philadelphia, Oct. 26, 1779, ibid., 14:123.

21. On this mechanism, see Bourdieu, *Language and Symbolic Power*, 208; and Gustafson, *Eloquence Is Power*, 184–99.

22. Primus, *American Language of Rights*, 85–87; The Federal Farmer, letter no. 2, in McDonald, *Empire and Nation*, 98; Primus, *American Language of Rights*, 85, 87 (right to participate); Webster, "An Oration," 1230.

23. Baron de Montesquieu, *Spirit of the Laws*, 150; S. Johnson, "Taxation no Tyranny," 427.

24. Ladurie, "Rangs et hiérarchie dans la vie de coeur"; letter by Atticus, Dec. 27, 1787, in Sheehan and McDowell, *Friends of the Constitution*, 340 (three classes); The Federal Farmer, letter from Oct. 12, 1787, in Pole, *American Constitution*, 32 (share of influence); Pendleton to Carter Braxton, May 12, 1776, in Mays, *Letters and Papers of Pendleton*, 1:177; *New York Daily Advertiser*, Oct. 17, 178, in Sheehan, *Friends of the Constitution*, 323; Jonathan Edwards, "The Necessity of the Belief of Christianity" (Hartford, 1794), in Sandoz, *Political Sermons*, 2:1215–216. On organic society, see Wood, *Creation of the American Republic*, 59, 179.

25. John Dickinson's draft Letter to Quebec, Oct. 24, 1774, in *LDC*, 1:239 (equitable energy); The Federal Farmer, letter no. 7, Dec. 31, 1787, in Banning, *Liberty and Order*, 4 (proper station). These letters were formerly attributed to Richard Henry Lee; more recently Melancton Smith emerged as a possible author (ibid., 3).

26. Knud Haakonssen, "From Natural Law to the Rights of Man: A European Perspective on American Debates," in Lacey and Haakonssen, *Culture of Rights*, 10, 53–56. On the understandings of natural law in the Revolutionary era, see Hutson, "Bill of Rights," 62–97.

27. Bailyn, *Ideological Origins of the American Revolution*, 307 (Bland); Greene, "All Men Are Created Equal," 245. On the function of the concept of equality as a colonial argument against the metropolitans, see W. P. Adams, *First American Constitutions*, 164–71.

28. Rakove, "Parchment Barriers and the Politics of Rights," 109; Greene, *Quest for Power*.

29. Jennings, *Creation of America*, 197; Paine, *American Crisis* (1783), in Paine, *Rights*

of Man, 77. On attributes appropriating their owners, see Bourdieu, *Language and Symbolic Power,* 122.

30. Soame Jenyns, "Valour, Patriotism, and Friendship," 169 (Gooch); Rhode Island General Ezekiel Cornell to Governor William Greene, Philadelphia, Aug. 15, 1780, in *LDC,* 15:580 (Rochambeau); Stoddard, *Way for a People to Live,* 4, 6, 5; Stoddard, *God's Frown in the Death of Useful Men,* 6 (honor).

31. Adams to Gerry, Philadelphia, Sept. 1775, in *LEG,* 1:113–14; John Adams to Elbridge Gerry, Philadelphia, June 18, 1775, ibid., 1: 90 (Washington); Pencak, "Samuel Adams and Shays's Rebellion," 141–43 (leniency); Henry Laurens to Marquis de Lafayette, March 4, 1778, in *LDC,* 9:213; "American Patriot's Prayer," in *Large Additions to Common Sense,* 1; George Mason quoted in Maier, *From Resistance to Revolution,* 137–38 (model citizen); Gerry letter to James Warren, (probably 1789), in *LEG,* 2:97; Oct. 18, 1789, ibid., 43. On identity and honor, see Bourdieu, *Language and Symbolic Power,* 122.

32. Benjamin Rush, "An Address to the Inhabitants of the British Settlements in America upon Slave-Keeping" (Philadelphia 1773), in *APW,* 1:228–29; Crito [Stephen Hopkins], Essay on the African Slave Trade (1787), in Sheehan and McDowell, *Friends of the Constitution,* 446; David Rice, "Slavery Inconsistent with Justice and Good policy" (Augusta, 1792), in *APW,* 2:886; David Cooper, "A Serious Address to the Rulers of America" (Trenton, 1783), in Nash, *Race and Revolution,* 124–25; St. George Tucker, *A Dissertation on Slavery* (Philadelphia, 1796), ibid., 152; A Letter from Benjamin Banneker to the Secretary of State (Philadelphia 1792), ibid., 179; Kruman, *Between Authority and Liberty,* 105 (widows).

33. Quoted in *LEG,* 2:59–60; Howe, *Language and Political Meaning,* 220 (Madison); Jefferson to Elbridge Gerry, Philadelphia, May 13, 1797, ibid., 2:138 (duties).

34. Michael Keane to Samuel Lynch, St. Vincent, Oct. 3, 1788, Michael Keane Letterbook MS, VHS, 134; Robert Munford to Theodorick Bland Sr., Aug. 4, 1758, in Campbell, *Bland Papers,* 13–14; Henry Laurens to Joseph Brown, Charleston, Oct. 28, 1765, in Rogers et al., *Papers of Laurens,* 5:29, 31.

35. Patrick Henry to Theodorick Bland, May 10, 1779, quoted in Campbell, *Bland Papers,* 1:125; Henry Laurens to John Wereat, Aug. 30, 1777, in *LDC,* 7:577, 576; Samuel Adams to Elizabeth Adams, Philadelphia, Feb. 1, 1781, ibid., 16:651; Robert Morris to Joseph Reed, Hills of Shuykill, July 21, 1776, ibid., 4:510; Edward Langworthy to William Palfrey, York Town, March 19, 1778, ibid., 9:311.

36. Camillus I, in *Boston Independent Chronicle,* Feb. 15, 1787, in W. B. Allen, *Works of Fisher Ames,* 1:57.

37. Ousterhout, "Controlling the Opposition in Pennsylvania," 14–15; M. O. Warren, *History,* 1:14 (superiority); Weir, *Colonial South Carolina,* 342.

38. Raphael, *People's History,* 9 (violence).

6. Usurpers and Dupes

1. Fisher Ames, Republican VIII, *Boston Gazette,* Aug. 23, 1804, in W. B. Allen, *Works of Fisher Ames,* 1:330; Phocion IV, "The Palladium," May 1, 1801, ibid., 1:283; James

Madison to Edmund Randolph, New York, March 19, 1787, in *LDC*, 24:156 (usurpers); Minot, *History of the Insurrections*, 170.

2. Richards, *Shays's Rebellion*, 9.

3. Samuel Adams to Richard Henry Lee, Philadelphia, Jan. 15, 1781, in *LDC*, 16:599.

4. In this and the following paragraphs, I rely heavily on the documentary material in David Szatmary's *Shays' Rebellion*. Minot, *History of the Insurrections*, 120 (values); Petition of Shaysites, in Morison, 208–9 (virtue); Attleborough to *Independent Chronicle*, Aug. 31, 1786 (yeomanry); A Freeman to *Worcester Magazine*, Oct. 1786 (aristocracy), quoted in Lienesch, "Reinterpreting Rebellion," 164; Richards, *Shays's Rebellion*, 21 (tyrants, tyranny), 25 (slavery); Lienesch, "Reinterpreting Rebellion," 166 (aristocratical principle), 163 (Tories); Szatmary, *Shays' Rebellion*, 68 (justice), 41 (luxury), 41 (interests).

5. Handlin and Handlin, *Popular Sources of Political Authority*, 550, 483.

6. George Washington to David Humphreys, Mount Vernon, Dec. 26, 1786, in Abbot and Twohig, *Papers of Washington*, 4:478; Lucius Junius Brutus III [Ames], Oct. 26, 1786, in W. B. Allen, *Works of Fisher Ames*, 1:50–51; Miller, *Sam Adams*, 374. On Adams, see Pencak, "Samuel Adams and Shays's Rebellion."

7. Samuel Adams to Noah Webster, April 30, 1784, quoted in Maier, "Popular Uprisings and Civil Authority," 29 (enemies), 35 (role of people); Szatmary, *Shays' Rebellion*, 74–75 (monarchy); Pencak, "Samuel Adams and Shays's Rebellion," 70 (luxury); Lienesch, "Reinterpreting Rebellion," 166 (despots); Camillus I [Fisher Ames], *Boston Independent Chronicle*, Feb. 15, 1787, in W. B. Allen, *Works of Fisher Ames*, 1:57 (danger); Lucius Junius Brutus I [Fisher Ames], *Boston Independent Chronicle*, Oct. 12, 1786, in W. B. Allen, *Works of Fisher Ames*, 1:40 (treason); Minot, *History of the Insurrections*, 96 (despotism).

8. Minot, *History of the Insurrections*, 121 (officers of the people); Szatmary, *Shays' Rebellion*, 97 (body of the people); Attleborough letter to *Boston Independent Chronicle*, Aug. 31, 1786, quoted in Lienesch, *Reinterpreting Rebellion*, 167 (militia); "Member of the convention" to *Worcester Magazine*, Oct. 1786, ibid., 165 (good of the people); Pencak, "Fine Theoretic Government," 128 (green twigs).

9. Szatmary, *Shays' Rebellion*, 98; [Fisher Ames] Camillus III, *Boston Independent Chronicle*, March 1, 1787, in W. B. Allen, *Works of Fisher Ames*, 1:72; Riley, "Dr. William Whiting," 66, 138; Hexham controversy discussed in Gould, *Persistence of Empire*, 93; Pole, *Pursuit of Equality*, 52 (self-evident truths).

10. Lucius Junius Brutus I, Oct. 12, 1786, in W. B. Allen, *Works of Fisher Ames*, 1:41–42 (supreme power of assemblies); Lucius Junius Brutus II, Oct. 19, 1786, ibid., 1:47 (unorganizing government); Camillus II, *Boston Independent Chronicle*, Feb. 22, 1787, ibid., 1:64 (civil liberty); ibid., 65 (state of nature); Camillus I, ibid., 66 (obedience); M. O. Warren, *History*, 2:651–52, 654 (submission); 665 (Hancock); Pencak, "Samuel Adams and Shays's Rebellion," 67 (self-repair).

11. Henry Knox to George Washington, New York, Oct. 23, 1786, in Abbot and Twohig, *Papers of George Washington*, 4:300, 460; [Fisher Ames] Camillus I, in W. B. Allen, *Works of Fisher Ames*, 1:59 (passions); Lucius Junius Brutus III, Oct. 26, 1786,

1:50 (rabble); Lucius Junius Brutus I, Oct. 12, 1786, ibid., 1:40–41 (tavern-hunters); Cassius, to *Worcester Magazine,* Jan. 1787 (unthinking part); letter by a "A Citizen," quoted in Lienesch, *Reinterpreting Rebellion,* 163 (depravity); David Humphreys to George Washington, New Haven, Nov. 9, 1786, in Abbot and Twohig, *Papers of Washington,* 4:351 (levelling); Henry Knox to George Washington, New York, Oct. 23, 1786, ibid., 4:300 (common property); Brown, "Shays's Rebellion and Its Aftermath," 603; Camillus, *Boston Independent Chronicle,* March 8, 1787, in W. B. Allen, *Works of Fisher Ames,* 1:85 (Indians).

12. Riggs, *Anarchiad,* 6 (chaos, mobs), 20 (anarchy), 23 (sword, sacred flame), 56, 58 (heroes); Rachel Porter, "Shays' Rebellion," 105 (gang); Gross, *In Debt to Shays,* 309 (sword); M. O. Warren, *History,* 652 (subaltern).

13. John Dickinson, "Draft Address to the King," Oct. 22, 1776, in *LDC,* 1:230 (servitude); Patrick Henry's Draft Address to the King, Oct. 21? 1774, ibid., 2:222 (rights); Morison, *Sources and Documents,* 208 (petition), 208 (independency); Minot, *History of the Insurrections,* 127 (good government); Morison, *Sources and Documents,* 209 (high salaries), 209 (moderation).

14. A. Young, afterword to *Beyond the American Revolution,* 328 (class consciousness); Maier, "Popular Uprisings," 13–17 (restraint); Slaughter, *Whiskey Rebellion,* 181; Jennings, *Creation of America,* 131 (Fries); Stephen E. Patterson, "The Federalist Reaction to Shays's Rebellion," in Gross, *In Debt to Shays,* 103 (General Court).

15. William Whiting, "Some Remarks on the Conduct of the Inhabitants of the Commonwealth of Massachusetts," in Riley, "Dr. William Whiting," 140–41 (future of liberty), 145 (slavery), 146 (substitutes), 148 (servants), 148 (natural right), 148 (insecurity), 152 (violence), 154 (instructions); Rufus King to Theodore Sedgwick, New York, Oct. 22, 1786, in *LDC,* 23:612; Theodore Sedgwick to William Whiting, Stockbridge, Sept. 14, 1786, in Riley, "Dr. William Whiting," 136.

16. Szatmary, *Shays' Rebellion,* xiv, 11 (agrarian way of life); Richard Buell Jr., "The Public Creditor Interest in Massachusetts Politics, 1780–86," in Gross, *In Debt to Shays,* 55 (respectability); Alan Taylor, "Regulators and White Indians: The Agrarian Resistance in Post-Revolutionary New England," in Gross, *In Debt to Shays,* 150; Petition from Coleraine to the Governor and Council, "Documents Relating to the Shays Rebellion, 1787," *AHR* 2, no. 4 (July 1897): 696–97.

17. Taylor, "Regulators," 146 (Maine), 147, 150 (licentiousness); Petition for Equality by the Philadelphia Synagogue, 1783, in Sarna and Dalin, *Religion and State in the American Jewish Experience,* 72–73; Letter from the Hebrew Congregation of Newport to George Washington, 1790, ibid., 79.

18. Chartier, *Cultural Origins of the French Revolution,* 18 (vocabulary of rights); Kuran and Sunstein, "Availability Cascades," 683–768.

19. Pencak, "Samuel Adams," 72 (proclamation); Minot, *History of the Insurrections,* 192.

20. Madison quoted in Elkins, *Age of Federalism,* 267; Rosswurm, *Arms, Country, and Class.*

21. Waldstreicher suggests that in the emerging first party system "partisanship re-

mained mostly an accusation, not a widely legitimized (much less theorized) practice" (Waldstreicher, *In the Midst of Perpetual Fetes,* 201). On the profound consequences of this political polarization for the character of the election of 1800, see Lewis, "What Is to Become of Our Government?"

22. *Columbian Sentinel,* Aug. 19, 1798, and *Alexandria Advertiser,* Dec. 21, 1798, quoted in *JJ,* 104.

23. James Otis, "A Dissertation on Letters," in *Rudiments of Latin Prosody,* 51, 50; see also Gustafson, *Eloquence Is Power,* 155; Wroth and Zobel, *Legal Papers of John Adams,* 2:142 (servants); Josiah Bartlett to John Langdon, Philadelphia, Jan. 13, 1776, in *LDC,* 3:88 (Common Sense); David Humphreys to George Washington, New Haven, Nov. 16, 1786, in Abbot and Twohig, *Papers of Washington,* 4:373.

24. *Newark Gazette,* March 19, 1794, in Banning, *Liberty and Order,* 171; Loring, *Hundred Boston Orators,* 137 (Tudor), 142 (Dawes).

25. Benjamin Rush to John Adams, Oct. 2, 1810, in Schutz and Adair, *Spur of Fame,* 184; James Madison's notes, April, 1787, in *LDC,* 24:269; Fisher Ames, "History Is Philosophy Teaching by Example," *Palladium,* Feb. 2, 1802, in W. B. Allen, *Works of Fisher Ames,* 1:85 (multitude).

26. Appleby, *Capitalism,* 21 (society without ranks); Lacey and Haakonssen, *Culture of Rights,* 9 (Locke).

27. Elbridge Gerry to James Warren, (1788?) in *LEG,* 2:86 (inferior caste), 86 (public interest); Elbridge Gerry to James Warren, Cambridge, Feb. 15, 1789, ibid., 96 (corruption).

28. *JJ,* 10 (Lords), 8 (Essex Junto), 53 (Du Ponceau); Elbridge Gerry to James Warren (1788?), in *LEG,* 2:86 (nobility).

29. *JJ,* 54 (dupes), 62 (swine); Porcupine [Cobbett], *History of American Jacobins,* 8 (respectability, hypocrisy), 22 (wealth); letter to the editor by "Decius," *Columbian Centinel,* April 24, 1799 (Jacobins); letter to the editor by "Epaminondas," *Columbian Centinel,* May 8, 1999 (dunghill); Cobbett, *Works of Peter Porcupine,* 122.

30. *Massachusetts Mercury,* Nov. 1, 1798, quoted in *JJ,* 101 (tillers); Fisher Ames to Oliver Wolcott, Nov. 14, 1796, in W. B. Allen, *Works of Fisher Ames,* 2:1202–2; *Columbian Centinel,* July 11, 1798, quoted in *JJ,* 78 (plain people); Fisher Ames to Oliver Wolcott, Jan. 12, 1800, in W. B. Allen, *Works of Fisher Ames,* 2:1347 (multitude); Fisher Ames to Timothy Pickering, July [6], 1798, ibid., 2:1284 (mechanics).

31. Diary of Nathaniel Ames, quoted in *JJ,* 11 (parish group); 134 (selfish wretches); *Plumb Pudding,* 6 (cowardly alien); John Williams quoted in *JJ,* 95.

32. Joan Scott, "Women's History," in Burke, *New Perspectives on Historical Writing,* 58.

33. *The Federalist* (New York, 1788) 2:7; Howe, *Language and Political Meaning,* 203 (empire), 10 (pseudonyms), 11 (vagueness); Waldstreicher, *In the Midst of Perpetual Fetes,* 12 (politicization); Gouverneur Morris to John Penn, May 20, 1774, in Force, *American Archives,* 1:342–43.

34. On this process, see Giovanni Levi, "On Microhistory," in Burke, *New Perspectives on Historical Writing,* 107.

35. Haynes quoted in Nash, *Unknown American Revolution,* 224; [Forten] *Letters from a Man of Colour,* 1 (Constitution), 4 (authority to enslave, advocates of liberty), 2 (honest industry, independence), 3 (different species), 5 (nature); Forten, *Address Delivered before the Ladies' Anti-slavery Society,* 4. I am very grateful to Julie Winch for providing me with materials on Forten. On Forten, see Winch, *A Gentleman of Color.*

36. Diary of William Black MS (1744), VHS.

37. Nathan Dane to Moses Brown, New York, June 7, 1788, in *LDC,* 25:149; Wood, *Radicalism of the American Revolution,* 366 (high hopes); Rufus King to Theodore Sedgwick, New York, Oct. 22, 1786, in *LDC,* 23:612; Henry Lee to George Washington, New York, Sept. 8, 1786, ibid., 23:53; Charles Pinckney's Speech to the New Jersey Assembly, March 13, 1786, ibid., 23:192; James M. Varnum to Horatio Gates, Philadelphia, Feb. 15, 1781, ibid., 16:716; John Jay to George Washington, Philadelphia, April 21, 1779, ibid., 12:363; Virginia Delegates to Benjamin Harrison, Philadelphia, April 19, 1783, ibid., 20:162; Fisher Ames, "No Revolutionist" (1801), in W. B. Allen, *Works of Fisher Ames,* 1:8; Porcupine [Cobbett], *History of American Jacobins,* 22; Benjamin Rush to John Adams, Oct. 2, 1810, in Schutz and Adair, *Spur of Fame,* 184.

38. Hatch, *Democratization of American Christianity,* 44; Korshak, "Liberty Cap as a Revolutionary Symbol," 55 (pileus); Rauser, "British Political Prints," 153 (liberty cap).

39. Edward Rutledge to John Jay, Charleston, Nov. 12, 1786, in Johnston, *Correspondence and Public Papers of Jay,* 3:217; Theophilus Parsons, *Essex Result* (Newburyport, 1778), in *APW,* 1:486; Edward Rutledge to John Jay, Charleston, Nov. 12, 1786, in Johnston, *Correspondence and Public Papers of John Jay,* 3:217; Parsons, *Essex Result,* 1:486; Noah Webster, *The Revolution in France* (New York, 1794), in Sandoz, *Political Sermons,* 2:1256; Americanus [Timothy Ford], *Constitutionalist* (Charleston, 1794), 31, 33; Riggs, *Anarchiad,* 29–31.

40. Benjamin Rush to Anthony Wayne, Philadelphia, Sept. 24, 1776, in *LDC,* 5:235 (restraints); M. O. Warren, *History,* 2:646; Jeremiah Atwater, *A Sermon* (Middlebury, 1801), in *APW,* 2:1174; Noah Webster, *An Oration on the Anniversary of the Declaration of Independence* (1802), in *APW,* 2:1235 (sanguine hopes).

41. Noah Webster to John Pickering, July 7, 1797, quoted in *JJ,* 87 (refuse); George Cabot to Alexander Hamilton, Oct. 11, 1800, ibid., 87 (improper usage); Edward Carrington to Thomas Jefferson, New York, June 9, 1787, in LDC, 24:311 (ductility); Dwight, *True Means of Establishing Public Happiness,* 7 (sycophancy).

42. Henry Laurens to John Lewis Gervais, Charleston, Jan. 29, 1766, in Rogers et al., *Papers of Henry Laurens,* 5:53 (Negroes); James Warren to John Adams, Boston, June 23, 1779, in *Warren-Adams Letters,* 1:105; Tyler, *Contrast,* 104, 49, 27; Fisher Ames, "The Mire of Democracy" (1805), in W. B. Allen, *Works of Fisher Ames,* 1:4 (the ignorant); Samuel Adams to James Warren, Oct. 24, 1789, in *LDC,* 16:245 (welfare).

43. Holton, *Forced Founders,* 168 (minutemen), 170 (Henry), 176–77 (salt), 179–80 (farmers); Braxton, "Address to the Convention of the Colony," 1.

44. Thomas Jefferson, *Autobiography,* in Peterson, *Thomas Jefferson,* 37, 33; Edward Carrington to William Short, New York, April 25 1788, in *LDC,* 25:78; William Bingham to Benjamin Rush, New York, Aug. 19, 1788, ibid., 25:309.

45. Wright, *Essay upon Government,* 36; William Black Diary MS (May 18, 1744), 8, VHS.

46. [Macpherson] *Rights of Great Britain Asserted,* 70 (rabble); Galloway, "Historical and Political Reflections," 9:801.

47. Cadwallader Colden Journal MS, 1, 93, 57, HL.

48. Moore, *Diary of the American Revolution,* 1:384–86, 503 (Washington); William Henry Drayton, Charleston, Sept. 16, 1769, in Weir, *Letters of Freeman,* 31 (nature), 113 (Billingsgate).

49. Elizur Goodrich, *The Principles of Civil Union and Happiness Considered and Recommended* (Hartford, 1787), in Sandoz, *Political Sermons,* 1:927 (public good); Webster, *Revolution in France,* ibid., 2:1274 (parties), 1284 (tumultuous meetings); Nathaniel Peabody to Josiah Bartlett, Philadelphia, July 3, 1779, in *LDC,* 13:141 (jealousy); Roger Sherman to Oliver Ellsworth, Philadelphia, Sept. 5, 1789, ibid., 16:24; Caesar Rodney to Thomas Rodney, Philadelphia, Aug. 3, 1776, ibid., 4:618; Adams to Jefferson, Quincy, July 9, 1813, in Cappon, *Adams-Jefferson Letters,* 351. On change in social boundaries, see Bourdieu, *Language and Symbolic Power,* 238; and Wood, *Creation of the American Republic,* 471–518.

50. Gouverneur Morris's speech in Congress, Jan. 7, 1779, in *LDC,* 11:426; Benjamin Rush to John Adams, Aug. 21, 1812, in Schutz and Adair, *Spur of Fame,* 265; James Madison to Edmund Pendleton, New York, Oct. 20, 1788, in *LDC,* 25:436; Thomas Burke, "Epistle," ibid., 13:226.

51. John Adams to William Tudor, April 15, 1817, in C. F. Adams, *Works of John Adams,* 10:249; Ramsay, "Oration," 196; David Ramsay to Thomas Jefferson, New York, May 3, 1786, ibid., 23:261; Hulton, *Letters,* 18.

52. Letter to the editor by YZ, *Columbian Magazine* 1, no. 1 (Sept. 1786): 12, 11 (the vulgar).

53. Klein, *Shaftesbury and the Culture of Politeness,* 4–5, 14, 212, 196; Cooper, *Sensus Communis,* 8–9; John Dickinson's notes for a speech in Congress, May 23–25, 1775, in *LDC,* 1:378; Gouverneur Morris to *Pennsylvania Packet,* Feb. 27, 1779, ibid., 12:116.

54. Fielding, *History of Tom Jones,* 1:28; [Ford], *The Constitutionalist,* 40 (slavery).

55. Arthur Middleton to Aedanus Burke, June 10, 1782, in *LDC,* 18:568; Henry Lee to Richard Bland Lee, New York, Nov. 11, 1786, ibid., 24:25; Henry Lee to James Madison, New York, Oct. 25, 1786, ibid., 23:615 (the licentious); William Hooper to Samuel Johnston, Philadelphia, Sept. 26, 1776, ibid., 5:245; William Hooper to Mary Hooper, New York, Nov. 7, 1774, ibid., 1:225; James Madison's notes, April 1787, ibid., 24:270.

56. Gordon, *History of the Rise, Progress, and Establishment,* 1:149.

57. Davis, "Constructing Race," 13 (peasants); Kolchin, *Unfree Labor,* 170–71 (Russia); Symmons-Symonolewicz, *National Consciousness in Poland,* 23–38 (Poland); James Reid, "Religion of the Bible," 54.

58. Bridenbaugh, *Gentleman's Progress,* 33; Christian Wolff, *Vernünfftige Gedancken von dem gesellschaftlichen Leben der Menschen* [Rational Thoughts on the Social Life of Man] (Frankfurt, 1740), 505, quoted in Mączak, *Rządzący i rządzeni,* 256, trans. author;

Rufus King to Elbridge Gerry, July 4, [17]86, in *LDC,* 23:386; Thomas Johnson to Samuel Purviance, Jr., Annapolis, Jan. 23, 1775, ibid., 1:300; James M. Varnum to Horatio Gates, Philadelphia, Feb. 15, 1781, ibid., 16:716.

59. Barlow, *Oration,* 6; Braxton, "Address to the Convention of the Colony," 15; Samuel Adams to Elbridge Gerry, Boston, March 25, 1775, in *LEG,* 1:37; Hutchinson quoted in Robert E. Brown, "Democracy in Colonial Massachusetts," 313; Galloway, "Historical and Political Reflections," 802.

60. William Byrd II Commonplace Book MS, 49, VHS; Adams quoted in Wood, *Radicalism of the American Revolution,* 27; [Moses Mather], "America's Appeal to the Impartial World" (Hartford, 1775), in Sandoz, *Political Sermons,* 1:486; Henry Cummings, "A Sermon Preached at Lexington" (Boston, 1781), ibid., 1:674–75; Samuel Wales, "A Sermon Preached before the General Assembly of the State of Connecticut" (Hartford, 1785), ibid., 1:851; Gouverneur Morris to John Penn, May 20, 1774, in Force, *American Archives,* 1:342–43.

61. James Madison, Memorandum of April 1787, quoted in Rakove, *Original Meanings,* 48, 49, 50 (elections), 51.

62. Jefferson to Gerry, Philadelphia, June 1797, in *LEG,* 2:155–56; Gouverneur Morris to John Marshall, June 26, 1775, in A. Morris, *Diary and Letters of Gouverneur Morris,* 2:492; Moore, *Diary of the American Revolution,* 1:356–57; Barlow, *Oration,* 14.

63. Thomas Lynch to Ralph Izard, Philadelphia, Oct. 26, 1774, in *LDC,* 1:247; Samuel Adams to the Boston Committee of Correspondence, Philadelphia, Sept. 14, 1774, ibid., 1:71 (opposition); James Lovell to John Adams, Nov. 1, [1779], ibid., 14:138 (effeminacy); John Adams to Abigail Adams, Philadelphia, Sept. 8, 1777, ibid., 7:627 (passions); Samuel Adams to John Scolloy, Philadelphia, Dec. 30, 1780, ibid., 16:514 (kings); Samuel Ward to Henry Ward, Philadelphia, Sept. 21. 1775, ibid., 2:43 (petition).

64. Nathaniel Gorham quoted in A. Young, *Beyond the American Revolution,* 336.

65. Waldstreicher, *In the Midst of Perpetual Fetes,* 68 (weakness of elites); Bourdieu, *Distinction,* 482 (signs of authority).

66. John Hancock to the Massachusetts Assembly, Philadelphia July 10, 1777, in *LDC,* 7:332; Adams to Jefferson, Quincy, Nov. 15, 1813, in Cappon, *Adams-Jefferson Letters,* 401; Higgonet, *Class, Ideology, and the Rights of Nobles,* 61.

67. Waldstreicher, *In the Midst of Perpetual Fetes,* 72 (meritocracy); The Preceptor, "Social Duties of the Political Kind," *Boston Massachusetts Spy,* May 21, 1772, in *APW,* 1:179, 181 (subordination); John Adams to Elbridge Gerry, April 25, 1785, in *LEG,* 1:430; Nathaniel Peabody to Josiah Bartlett Aug. 17, 1779, in *LDC,* 13:384; William Churchill Huston to Robert Morris, Philadelphia, March 6, 1780, ibid., 14:469.

68. James Madison to Edmund Randolph, New York, Jan. 10, 1788, in *LDC,* 24:609; John Armstrong to Horatio Gates, New York, May 30, 1788, ibid., 25:128; Thomas Jefferson's Notes of the Proceedings in Congress, July 12-Aug. 1, 1776, ibid., 4:438; Melancton Smith, Speech at the New York Ratifying Convention (1788), in Pole, *American Constitution,* 102, 84–85; [John Milton] "The Readie and Easie Way to Establish a Free Commonwealth" (1660), in Malcolm, *Struggle for Sovereignty,* 1:522.

69. Elizur Goodrich, "A Sermon Preached before His Excellency Samuel Huntington"

(Hartford, 1778), in Sandoz, *Political Sermons,* 1:920; Webster, *Revolution in France,* ibid., 2:1289; James Monroe to William Short, New York, Jan. 23, 1786, in *LDC,* 23:112.

70. Samuel Adams to Elbridge Gerry, Philadelphia, Jan. 2, 1776, in *LDC,* 3:15; Adams to Jefferson, Quincy, July 9, 1813, in Cappon, *Adams-Jefferson Letters,* 352; Adams to Jefferson, Quincy, Nov. 15, 1813, ibid., 398 (dupes); Jefferson to Adams, Monticello, Oct. 28, 1813, ibid., 388; Gouverneur Morris to George Washington, Philadelphia, Aug. 2, 1778, ibid., 10:383 (man of sentiment); Gouverneur Morris to Henry Laurens, Camp, Jan. 26, 1777, ibid., 8:658 (liberality).

71. John Adams to Mercy Otis Warren, April 16, 1776, in *LDC,* 3:538; Edward Carrington to Edmund Randolph, New York, Dec. 8, 1786, ibid., 24:42; Van Horne, *Correspondence of William Nelson,* 154.

72. Federalist No. 10, in Pole, *American Constitution,* 154; James Madison to Thomas Jefferson, New York, Feb. 19, 1788, in *LDC,* 24:652 (multitude).

73. Samuel Adams to Richard Henry Lee, Philadelphia, Jan. 15, 1781, in *LDC,* 16:598 (publick departments); Elbridge Gerry to Samuel Adams, Watertown, Dec. 13, 1775, in *LEG,* 1:124, 123 (pecuniary recommendation); Samuel Adams to Elbridge Gerry, Philadelphia, Oct. 29, 1775, ibid., 121 (loaves and fishes); Edmund Pendleton, "Address to the Virginia Ratification Convention," in Mays, *Letters and Papers of Edmund Pendleton,* 520–21. See also John Phillip Reid, *Concept of Liberty,* 116–17.

74. Joseph Galloway to Samuel Verplanck, Trevois, Dec. 30, 1774, in *LDC,* 1:282 (venerable sages); Greene, *Diary of Colonel Landon Carter,* 55, 86–87 (British freedom); Edmund Randolph, in Elliot, *Debates in the Several State Conventions,* 3:65 (rectitude); Braxton, "Address to the Convention of the Colony," 1:333; Gouverneur Morris to John Penn, May 20, 1774, in Force, *Archives,* 1:342–43 (perils).

75. David Ramsay, "Oration," 183.

Conclusion

1. See Burnard, *Creole Gentlemen,* 237–58.

2. On systemic and nonsystemic revolutions, see Bauman, *Intimations of Postmodernity,* 156–72.

3. Baker, "Idea of a Declaration of Rights," 96, 98.

4. Eagleton, *Idea of Culture,* 129. Peter Onuf develops this point superbly in his "Federalism, Democracy, and Liberty."

5. Hoffer, *Law and People in Colonial America,* 123.

6. E. Morgan, *American Slavery, American Freedom,* 4, 387, 368; Olwell and Tully, *Cultures and Identities,* 11.

7. Appleby, *Capitalism,* 21, 17–19, 22, 21.

8. Zagorin, *Court and the Country,* 55–56.

9. Shakespeare, *Hamlet,* 965.

10. Blaustein, "Influence of the United States Constitution Abroad."

11. Primus, *American Language of Rights,* 124 (adverse conditions).

12. Bourdieu, *Distinction,* 417, 468 (discourse), 467 (reality). Thomas Kuhn observed

that Johannes Kepler would not have written his laws of planetary motion had he not had the Copernican paradigm at his disposal (Kuhn, *Structure of Scientific Revolutions,* 154–56). See also Gellner, *Legitimation of Belief,* chap. 8.

13. Gadamer, *Truth and Method,* 267 (presuppositions); Kolakowski, *Husserl and the Search for Certitude,* 81–85. On problems of knowledge and the creation of modernity, see Kelley, *History and the Disciplines.*

14. Roy Porter, "Enlightenment in England," 8–9 (public discourse); Wood, *Radicalism of the American Revolution,* 230 (utopia). A brave but limited attempt to break out of the "paradigm shift" model and to show that monarchic ways of thinking and writing were not swept away by the Revolution is made by Paul Downes in his *Democracy, Revolution, and Monarchism.*

15. On the debate over whether late eighteenth-century America was liberal or republican, see Kruman, *Between Authority and Liberty,* xi, 156. On relations between idealized egalitarianism and market economy, an illuminating study is Shankman's *Crucible of American Democracy.*

16. Price, *Observations,* 2 (new aera); Wood, *Radicalism of the American Revolution,* 187 (archaic ideas).

17. Escott and Crow, "Social Order and Violent Disorder," 385.

18. The rise of the middle class in the nineteenth century was analogous to this process; many of those among the working class who were able to do so wanted to become *like* the bourgeoisie because it was the only shared cultural model of success and upward mobility available for adoption.

Bibliography

Manuscript Sources

Black, William. Diary, 1744. VHS.

Bland Family Papers, 1713–1825. MS. VHS.

Braxton, Carter. Diary. MS. VHS.

Byrd, William, II. Commonplace Book. MS. VHS.

Colden, Cadwallader. Journal. MS. HL.

Cooper, Samuel. Papers, 1718–1798. MS. HL.

Galloway, Joseph. Papers. MS. HL.

Jenings, Edmund. Letterbook, 1753–1769. MS. VHS.

Keaner, Michael. Letterbook. MS. VHS.

Published Sources

Abbot, W. W., and Dorothy Twohig, eds. *Papers of George Washington. Confederation Series.* Charlottesville: University Press of Virginia, 1992.

"An Account of the Vices peculiar to the Savages of N. America." *Columbian Magazine,* no. 1 (1786).

Adams, Charles Francis, ed. *The Works of John Adams.* 10 vols. Boston: Little, Brown, 1850–56.

Adams, John. "A Dissertation on the Canon and Feudal Law." 1765. In *Papers of John Adams,* edited by Robert J. Taylor. Cambridge, Mass.: Belknap Press of Harvard University Press, 1977.

Adams, John Quincy. "An Oration, Pronounced July 4 1793." In *The Hundred Boston Orators,* edited by James Spear Loring. Boston: John P. Jewett, 1853.

Adams, Willi Paul. *The First American Constitutions: Republican Ideology and the Making of the State Constitutions in the Revolutionary Era.* Translated by Rita and Robert Kimber. Chapel Hill: University of North Carolina Press, 1980.

Allen, John. *An Oration, upon the beauties of liberty.* Boston, 1773.

Allen, W. B., ed. *George Washington: A Collection.* Indianapolis: Liberty Fund, 1988.

——, ed. *Works of Fisher Ames.* Indianapolis: Liberty Fund, 1983.

Allison, Hugh. *Spiritual Liberty: A Sermon.* Charleston, 1769.

"American Patriot's Prayer." In *Large Additions to Common Sense.* Philadelphia, 1776.

Americanus [Timothy Ford]. *The Constitutionalist.* Charleston, 1794.

Appleby, Joyce. *Capitalism and a New Social Order: The Republican Vision of the 1790s.* New York: New York University Press, 1984.

Austin, James T. *Life of Elbridge Gerry.* Boston: Wells and Lilly, 1828.

Bailyn, Bernard. *The Ideological Origins of the American Revolution.* 1967. Cambridge, Mass.: Belknap Press of Harvard University Press, 1992.

Baker, Keith Michael, ed. *The French Revolution and the Creation of Modern Political Culture.* Vol. 1, *The Political Culture of the Old Regime,* edited by Baker. Oxford and New York: Pergamon Press, 1987.

——. "The Idea of a Declaration of Rights." In *The French Revolution: Recent Debates and New Controversies,* edited by Gary Kates. London: Routledge, 1998.

Banning, Lance, ed. *Liberty and Order: The First American Party Struggle.* Indianapolis: Liberty Fund, 2004.

Baradziej, Jerzy, and Janusz Gockowski, eds. *Rozważania o tradycji i ethosie* [Reflections on Tradition and Ethos]. Kraków: Baran i Suszyński, 1998.

Barlow, Joel. *An Oration, Delivered at the North Church in Hartford.* Hartford, 1787.

Barzun, Jacques. *The Culture We Deserve.* Hanover: Wesleyan University Press, 1989.

Bauman, Zygmunt. *Culture as Praxis.* London: Sage, 1999.

——. *Freedom.* Minneapolis: University of Minnesota Press, 1989.

——. *Intimations of Postmodernity.* London: Routledge, 1992.

——. *Postmodernity and Its Discontents.* New York: New York University Press, 1977.

Bauman, Zygmunt, and Keith Tester. *Conversations with Zygmunt Bauman.* Cambridge: Polity Press, 2001.

Beard, Charles. *An Economic Interpretation of the Constitution of the United States.* New York: Free Press, 1986.

Berkeley, George. *The Querist.* In *The Works of George Berkeley, Bishop of Cloyne,* edited by A. A. Luce and T. E. Jessup. London: Thomas Nelson, 1953.

Berman, David. "Irish Philosophy and the American Enlightenment during the Eighteenth Century." *Eire-Ireland. A Journal of Irish Studies* 24, no. 1 (1989): 28–39.

Bien, David D. "Offices, Corps, and a System of State Credit: The Uses of Privilege under the Ancien Régime." In *The French Revolution and the Creation of Modern Political Culture,* edited by Keith Michael Baker. Oxford: Pergamon Press, 1987.

Blackstone, William. *Blackstone's Commentaries on the Laws and Constitution of England.* London, 1820.

Bland, Richard. *An Inquiry into the Rights of the British Colonies.* Williamsburg, 1766.

Blaustein, Albert P. "The Influence of the United States Constitution Abroad." In *European and American Constitutionalism in the Eighteenth Century,* edited by Michal Rozbicki. Warsaw: American Studies Center, 1990.

Bloch, Marc. *Strange Defeat: A Statement of Evidence Written in 1940.* New York: Octagon Books, 1968.

Boorstin, Daniel. *The Americans: The Colonial Experience.* New York: Random House, 1958.

Bourdieu, Pierre. *Distinction: A Social Critique of the Judgment of Taste.* Translated by Edward Nice. Cambridge, Mass.: Harvard University Press, 1984.

——. *Language and Symbolic Power.* Edited by John B. Thompson; translated by

Gino Raymond and Matthew Adamson. Cambridge, Mass.: Harvard University Press, 1991.

Bowdoin, James. *A Proclamation for a Day.* Boston, 1786.

Boyd, Julian P., ed. *Papers of Thomas Jefferson.* Princeton: Princeton University Press, 1950–.

Braudel, Fernand. *The Mediterranean and the Mediterranean World in the Age of Philip II.* Berkeley and Los Angeles: University of California Press, 1995.

[Braxton, Carter]. "An Address to the Convention of the Colony and Ancient Dominion of Virginia." In *American Political Writing during the Founding Era, 1760–1805,* edited by Charles S. Hyneman and Donald S. Lutz. Indianapolis: Liberty Fund, 1983.

Bridenbaugh, Carl, ed. *Gentleman's Progress: Itinerarium of Dr. Alexander Hamilton, 1744.* Chapel Hill: University of North Carolina Press, 1948.

Brooke, John. *The Heart of the Commonwealth: Society and Political Culture in Worcester County, Massachusetts, 1713–1861.* New York: Cambridge University Press, 1989.

Brown, Richard. *Knowledge Is Power: The Diffusion of Information in Early America 1700–1865.* New York: Oxford University Press, 1989.

——. "Shays's Rebellion and Its Aftermath: A View from Springfield, Massachusetts, 1787." *William and Mary Quarterly* 40, no. 2 (1983): 598–615.

Brown, Robert E. "Democracy in Colonial Massachusetts." *New England Quarterly* 25, no. 3 (1952): 291–313.

Browne, William Hand, ed. *The Archives of Maryland.* 72 vols. Baltimore: Maryland Historical Society, 1883–1972.

Burke, Peter, ed. *New Perspectives on Historical Writing.* University Park: Pennsylvania State University Press, 2001.

Burnard, Trevor. *Creole Gentlemen: The Maryland Elite 1691–1776.* Routledge: New York: 2002.

Bush, Michael L. *Noble Privilege.* Manchester: Manchester University Press, 1983.

Bushman, Richard L. *Refinement of America: Persons, Houses, Cities.* New York: Knopf, 1992.

Butterfield, L. H., ed. *The Earliest Diary of John Adams.* Cambridge, Mass.: Belknap Press of Harvard University Press, 1966.

Campbell, Charles. *Bland Papers, Being a Selection from the Manuscripts of Colonel Theodorick Bland, Jr.* Petersburg, Va., 1840–42.

Cappon, Lester J., ed. *The Adams-Jefferson Letters: The Complete Correspondence between Thomas Jefferson and Abigail and John Adams.* Chapel Hill: University of North Carolina Press, 1987.

Cassius [Aedanus Burke]. *Considerations on the Society or Order of Cincinnati.* Philadelphia, 1783.

Certeau, Michel de. *The Practice of Everyday Life.* Translated by Steven F. Rendall. Berkeley and Los Angeles: University of California Press, 1984.

Chartier, Roger. *The Cultural Origins of the French Revolution.* Translated by Lydia G. Cochrane. Durham: Duke University Press, 1991.

Clark, Harry Hayden. *Poems of Freneau.* New York: Harcourt, Brace, 1929.

Clark, J. C. D. *The Language of Liberty: Political Discourse and Social Dynamics in the Anglo-American World*. Cambridge: Cambridge University Press, 1994.

Cobbett, William. *The Works of Peter Porcupine*. Philadelphia, 1795.

Cochin, Augustin. "The Theory of Jacobinism." In *Interpreting the French Revolution,* edited by Francois Furet. Cambridge: Cambridge University Press, 1981.

Coke, Sir Edward. "Prohibitions del roy." 1607. In *The Struggle for Sovereignty: Seventeenth-Century English Political Tracts,* edited by Joyce L. Malcolm. Indianapolis: Liberty Fund, 1999.

Colley, Linda. *Forging the Nation, 1707–1837*. New Haven: Yale University Press, 1992.

"Colonial Patronage: Two Letters from William Franklin to the Earl of Bute, 1762." *William and Mary Quarterly* 59, no. 1 (2002): 123–34.

Cooper, Anthony Ashley, Earl of Shaftesbury. *Sensus Communis: An Essay on the Freedom of Wit and Humour*. London, 1709.

Cornell, Saul. "Early American History in a Postmodern Age." *William and Mary Quarterly* 50, no. 2 (1993): 329–41.

Countryman, Edward. *The American Revolution*. New York: Hill and Wang, 1985.

Cushing, H. A., ed. *The Writings of Samuel Adams*. New York: G. P. Putnam's Sons, 1904–8.

d'Anjou, Leo. *Social Movements and Cultural Change: The First Abolition Campaign Revisited*. New York: De Gruyter, 1996.

Darnton, Robert. "The High Enlightenment and the Low-Life of Literature in Pre-Revolutionary France." *Past and Present* 51 (1971): 81–115.

Davidson, Philip Grant. *Propaganda and the American Revolution 1763–1783*. Chapel Hill: University of North Carolina Press, 1941.

Davis, David Brion. "Constructing Race: A Reflection." *William and Mary Quarterly* 54, no. 1 (1997): 7–18.

———. *The Problem of Slavery in Western Culture*. Ithaca: Cornell University Press, 1966.

Dean, Mitchell. *The Constitution of Poverty: Toward a Genealogy of Liberal Governance*. London: Routledge, 1991.

Defoe, Daniel. *The Compleat English Gentleman*. Edited by Karl D. Bülbring. London, 1891.

"Documents Relating to the Shays Rebellion, 1787." *American Historical Review* 2, no. 4 (1897): 693–99.

[Donaldson, James]. *The Undoubted Art of Thriving*. 1700. Reprint, *Promoting Prosperity: Two Eighteenth Century Tracts*. New York: Arno Press, 1972.

Downes, Paul. *Democracy, Revolution, and Monarchism in Early American Literature*. New York: Cambridge University Press, 2002.

Drescher, Seymour. *Capitalism and Antislavery: British Mobilization in Comparative Perspective*. New York: Macmillan, 1987.

Drescher, Seymour, and Stanley Engerman. *A Historical Guide to World Slavery*. New York: Oxford University Press, 1998.

Dwight, Timothy. "Greenfield Hill: A Poem in Seven Parts." 1794. In *The Major Poems of Timothy Dwight (1752–1817),* edited by William J. McTaggart and William K. Bottorff. Gainesville: Scholars' Facsimiles and Reprints, 1969.

———. *The True Means of Establishing Public Happiness.* New Haven, [1795].

Dworkin, Ronald. *Taking Rights Seriously.* Cambridge, Mass.: Harvard University Press, 1977.

Eagleton, Terry. *The Idea of Culture.* Oxford: Blackwell, 2009

Eco, Umberto. *A Theory of Semiotics.* Bloomington: Indiana University Press, 1978.

Elkins, Stanley, and Eric McKitrick. *The Age of Federalism: The Early American Republic, 1788–1800.* New York: Oxford University Press, 1993.

Elliot, Jonathan, ed. *The Debates in the Several State Conventions on the Adoption of the Federal Constitution.* Philadelphia: Lippincott, 1901.

Ellis, Joseph. *Founding Brothers: The Revolutionary Generation.* New York: Knopf, 2001.

Eltis, David. "Europeans and the Rise and Fall of African Slavery in the Americas: An Interpretation." *American Historical Review* 98, no. 5 (1993): 1399–423.

Escott, Paul D., and Jeffrey J. Crow. "The Social Order and Violent Disorder: An Analysis of North Carolina in the Revolution and the Civil War." *Journal of Southern History* 52, no. 3 (1986): 373–402.

Farrand, Max, ed. *Records of the Federal Convention of 1787.* New Haven: Yale University Press, 1911.

Femia, Joseph V. "Gramsci's Patrimony." *British Journal of Political Science* 13, no. 3 (1983): 327–64.

Fielding, Henry. *The History of Tom Jones, a Foundling.* London, 1775.

Finkelman, Paul. *Slavery and the Founders: Race and Liberty in the Age of Jefferson.* Armonk, N.Y.: M. E. Sharpe, 1996.

Finley, Moses. *Politics in the Ancient World.* Cambridge: Cambridge University Press, 1983.

———, ed. *Slavery in Classical Antiquity.* Cambridge: W. Heffer, 1960.

Fisher, David Hackett. *Liberty and Freedom: A Visual History of American Founding Ideas.* New York: Oxford University Press, 2005.

Fitzpatrick, John C., ed. *The Writings of George Washington.* Washington: Government Printing Office, 1938.

Fletcher, Andrew. *The Second Discourse Concerning the Affairs of Scotland.* In *Andrew Fletcher of Saltoun: Selected Political Writings and Speeches,* edited by David Daiches. Edinburgh: Scottish Academic Press, 1979.

Foner, Eric. *The Story of American Freedom.* New York: Norton, 1998.

Force, Peter, ed. *American Archives.* Washington, 1837–53.

Ford, Paul L., ed. *The Writings of Thomas Jefferson.* New York: G. P. Putnam's Sons, 1894.

Forten, James. *An Address Delivered before the Ladies' Anti-slavery Society of Philadelphia.* Philadelphia: Merrihew and Gunn, 1836.

[———]. *Letters from a Man of Colour.* Philadelphia, 1813.

Foucault, Michel. *The Archeology of Knowledge.* Translated by A. M. Sheridan Smith. New York: Pantheon Books, 1972.

Frazer, James George. *The Golden Bough: A Study in Magic and Religion.* New York: Macmillan, 1935.

Freneau, Philip. "On Mr. Paine's Rights of Man." 1795. In *Poems of Freneau,* edited by Harry Hayden Clark. New York: Harcourt, Brace, 1929.

Frey, Sylvia F. "Liberty, Equality, and Slavery: The Paradox of the American Revolution." In *The American Revolution: Its Character and Limits,* edited by Jack P. Greene. New York: New York University Press, 1987.

——. *Water from the Rock: Black Resistance in a Revolutionary Age.* Princeton: Princeton University Press, 1991.

Furet, Francois, ed. *Interpreting the French Revolution.* Cambridge: Cambridge University Press, 1981.

Furstenberg, François. "Beyond Freedom and Slavery: Autonomy, Virtue, and Resistance in Early American Political Discourse." *Journal of American History* 89, no. 4 (2003): 1295–330.

Gadamer, Hans-Georg. *Truth and Method.* Translated by William Glen-Doepel. London: Sheed and Ward, 1979.

Galenson, David W. *White Servitude in Colonial America: An Economic Analysis.* Cambridge: Cambridge University Press, 1981.

Galloway, Joseph. "Historical and Political Reflections on the Rise and Progress of the American Rebellion." 1780. In *English Historical Documents,* edited by Merrill Jensen. New York: Oxford University Press, 1955.

Gaustad, Edwin S. *George Berkeley in America.* New Haven: Yale University Press, 1979.

Gellner, Ernest. *Legitimation of Belief.* New York: Cambridge University Press, 1974.

"General Laws and Liberties of the Province of New Hampshire." 1680. In *Colonial Origins of the American Constitution: A Documentary History,* edited by Donald S. Lutz. Indianapolis: Liberty Fund, 1998.

Gibbes, Robert W., ed. *Documentary History of the American Revolution.* New York: Appleton, 1855.

Gilje, Paul A. *Liberty on the Waterfront: American Maritime Culture in the Age of the Revolution.* Philadelphia: University of Pennsylvania Press, 2004.

Glendon, Mary Ann. *Rights Talk: The Impoverishment of Political Discourse.* New York: Free Press, 1991.

Goff, Jacques Le. *Time, Work, and Culture in the Middle Ages.* Translated by Arthur Goldhammer. Chicago: University of Chicago Press, 1980.

Gordon, William. *The History of the Rise, Progress, and Establishment, of the Independence of the United States of America.* New York, 1789.

Gottschalk, Louis. *Lafayette Comes to America.* Chicago: University of Chicago Press, 1935.

Gould, Eliga H. *The Persistence of Empire: British Political Culture in the Age of the American Revolution.* Chapel Hill: University of North Carolina Press, 2000.

Grasso, Christopher. *A Speaking Aristocracy: Transforming Public Discourse in Eighteenth-Century Connecticut.* Chapel Hill: University of North Carolina Press, 1999.

[Green, Jacob]. *Observations on the Reconciliation of Great Britain, and the Colonies.* Philadelphia, 1776.

Greene, Jack P. "All Men Are Created Equal: Some Reflections on the Character of the American Revolution." In *Imperatives, Behaviors, and Identities: Essays in Early American Cultural History,* by Greene. Charlottesville: University Press of Virginia, 1992.

——, ed. *The Diary of Colonel Landon Carter of Sabine Hall, 1752–1778.* Charlottesville: University Press of Virginia, 1965

——. "Empire and Identity from the Glorious Revolution to the American Revolution." In *The Eighteenth Century,* edited by J. Marshall. Oxford: Oxford University Press, 1998.

——, ed. *The Nature of Colony Constitutions: Two Pamphlets on the Wilkes Fund Controversy.* Columbia: University of South Carolina Press, 1970.

——. *The Quest for Power: The Lower Houses of Assembly in the Southern Royal Colonies, 1689–1776.* Chapel Hill: University of North Carolina Press, 1963.

——. "Social Structure and Political Behavior in Revolutionary America: An Analysis of John Day's 'Remarks on American Affairs.'" In *Understanding the American Revolution: Issues and Actors,* by Greene. Charlottesville: University Press of Virginia, 1995.

Greene, Jack P., and J. R. Pole, eds. *A Companion to the American Revolution.* Malden: Blackwell, 2000.

Griswold, Charles L. "Rights and Wrongs: Jefferson, Slavery, and Philosophical Quandaries." In *A Culture of Rights: The Bill of Rights in Philosophy, Politics, and Law 1791 and 1991,* edited by Michael J. Lacey and Knud Haakonssen. Cambridge: Cambridge University Press, 1991.

Griffith, David. *Passive Obedience Considered.* 1775. In *Revolutionary War Sermons,* edited by David R. Williams. Delmar: Scholars' Facsimiles and Reprints, 1984.

Gross, Robert, ed. *In Debt to Shays: The Bicentennial of an Agrarian Rebellion.* Charlottesville: University Press of Virginia, 1993.

Gustafson, Sandra M. *Eloquence Is Power: Oratory and Performance in Early America.* Chapel Hill: University of North Carolina Press, 2000.

Guyatt, Nicholas. "Father Knows Best." Review of *Revolutionary Characters,* by Gordon Wood. *Nation* 283, no. 11 (November 9, 2006): 29–33.

Handlin, Oscar, and Mary Handlin, eds. *The Popular Sources of Political Authority: Documents on the Massachusetts Constitution of 1780.* Cambridge, Mass.: Belknap Press of Harvard University Press, 1966.

Hanson, Robert Brand, ed. *The Diary of Dr. Nathaniel Ames of Dedham, Massachusetts, 1758–1822.* Camden, Me.: Picton Press, 1998.

Harris, J. William. *Plain Folk and Gentry in a Slave Society.* Middletown: Wesleyan University Press, 1985.

Hartz, Louis. "A Theory of the Development of New Societies." In *The Founding of New Societies,* edited by Hartz. New York: Harcourt, Brace and World, 1964.

Hatch, Nathan O. *The Democratization of American Christianity.* New Haven: Yale University Press, 1991.

Higonnet, Patrice. *Class, Ideology, and the Rights of Nobles during the French Revolution.* Oxford: Clarendon Press, 1981.

Hill, Christopher. *God's Englishman: Oliver Cromwell and the English Revolution.* New York: Harper and Row, 1970.

———. *The World Turned Upside Down: Radical Ideas during the English Revolution.* New York: Viking, 1972.

Hobbes, Thomas. *Leviathan, or, The Matter, Forme, and Power of Commonwealth Ecclesiastical & Civill.* London, 1651.

Hobsbawm, Eric. "Introduction: Inventing Traditions." In *The Invention of Tradition,* edited by Hobsbawm and Terence Ranger. Cambridge: Cambridge University Press, 1983.

Hoffer, Peter C. *Law and People in Colonial America.* Baltimore: Johns Hopkins University Press, 1992.

Hohfeld, Wesley. *Fundamental Legal Conceptions as Applied in Judicial Reasoning.* Westport, Ct.: Greenwood Press, 1978.

Holton, Woody. *Forced Founders: Indians, Debtors, Slaves, and the Making of the American Revolution in Virginia.* Chapel Hill: University of North Carolina Press, 1999.

Horn, James, Jan Ellen Lewis, and Peter Onuf, eds. *The Revolution of 1800: Democracy, Race, and the New Republic.* Charlottesville: University of Virginia Press, 2002.

Howe, John. *Language and Political Meaning in Revolutionary America.* Amherst and Boston: University of Massachusetts Press, 2004.

Huizinga, Johan. *The Waning of the Middle Ages.* New York: Doubleday Anchor, 1956.

Hulton, Ann. *Letters of a Loyalist Lady.* Cambridge, Mass.: Harvard University Press, 1971.

Hume, David. *Essays and Treatises on Several Subjects.* London, 1784.

Hutcheson, Francis. *On Human Nature.* Edited by Thomas Mautner. Cambridge: Cambridge University Press, 1994.

———. *A System of Moral Philosophy.* 1755. Reprint, New York: Augustus M. Kelley, 1968.

Hutson, James H. "The Bill of Rights and the American Revolutionary Experience." In *A Culture of Rights: The Bill of Rights in Philosophy, Politics, and Law 1791 and 1991,* edited by Michael J. Lacey and Knud Haakonssen. Cambridge: Cambridge University Press, 1991.

Hyneman, Charles S., and Donald S. Lutz, eds. *American Political Writing during the Founding Era, 1760–1805.* Indianapolis: Liberty Fund, 1983.

Ingersoll, Thomas N. " 'Riches and Honour Were Rejected by Them as Loathsome Vomit': The Fear of Levelling in New England." In *Inequality in Early America,* edited by Carla G. Pestana and Sharon V. Salinger. Hanover: University Press of New England, 1999.

Isaac, Rhys. *The Transformation of Virginia, 1740–1790.* Chapel Hill: University of North Carolina Press, 1982.

Jefferson, Thomas. "Autobiography." 1821. In *Thomas Jefferson, Writings,* edited by Merrill D. Peterson. New York: Viking, 1984.

———. *Notes on the State of Virginia.* 1781. Edited by William Peden. New York: Norton, 1982.

Jennings, Francis. *The Creation of America through Revolution to Empire*. Cambridge: Cambridge University Press, 2000.

Jenyns, Soame. "Valour, Patriotism, and Friendship Weighed in the Ballance of Christianity." In *Annual Register, or a View of the History, Politics, and Literature, for the Year 1776*. London: Dodsley, 1782.

Johnson, Robert C. *Commons Debates, 1628*. New Haven: Yale University Press, 1977.

Johnson, Samuel. "Taxation no Tyranny." 1775. In Samuel Johnson, *Political Writings*, edited by Donald J. Greene. Indianapolis: Liberty Fund, 2000.

Johnston, Henry P., ed. *The Correspondence and Public Papers of John Jay*. New York and London: G. P. Putnam's Sons, 1890–93.

Jones, Colin, and Dror Wahrman, eds. *The Age of Cultural Revolutions: Britain and France, 1750–1820*. Berkeley and Los Angeles: University of California Press, 2002.

Jones, Gareth Stedman. *Languages of Class: Studies in English Working Class History, 1830–1982*. Cambridge: Cambridge University Press, 1984.

Jones, Howard Mumford. "The Colonial Impulse: An Analysis of the 'Promotion' Literature of Colonization." *Proceedings of the American Philosophical Society*, 90, no. 2 (1926).

Jones, Hugh. *The Present State of Virginia*. London: J. Clarke, 1724.

Kates, Gary, ed. *The French Revolution: Recent Debates and New Controversies*. London: Routledge, 1998.

Keane, John. *Tom Paine: A Political Life*. Boston: Little, Brown, 1995.

Kelley, Donald R., ed. *History and the Disciplines: The Reclassification of Knowledge in Early Modern Europe*. Rochester: University of Rochester Press, 1997.

Klein, Lawrence E., ed. *Shaftesbury and the Culture of Politeness: Moral Discourse and Cultural Politics in Early Eighteenth-Century England*. Cambridge: Cambridge University Press, 1994.

Koch, Adrienne, and William Peden, eds. *The Life and Selected Writings of Thomas Jefferson*. New York: Modern Library, 1944.

Kolakowski, Leszek. *Freedom, Fame, Lying, and Betrayal: Essays on Everyday Life*. Boulder, Colo.: Westview Press, 1999.

——. *Husserl and the Search for Certitude*. Chicago: University of Chicago Press, 1987.

——. *Main Currents of Marxism: Its Origin, Growth, and Dissolution*. Oxford: Clarendon Press, 1978.

——. *The Presence of Myth*. Translated by Adam Czerniawski. Chicago: University of Chicago Press, 2001.

Kolchin, Peter. *Unfree Labor: American Slavery and Russian Serfdom*. Cambridge, Mass.: Harvard University Press, 1987.

Kolp, John Gilman. *Gentlemen and Freeholders: Electoral Politics in Colonial Virginia*. Baltimore: Johns Hopkins University Press, 1998.

Konig, David T., ed. *Devising Liberty: Preserving and Creating Freedom in the New American Republic*. Stanford: Stanford University Press, 1995.

Korshak, Yvonne. "The Liberty Cap as a Revolutionary Symbol in America and France." *Smithsonian Studies in American Art* 1, no. 2 (1987): 53–69.

Koschnik, Albrecht. *"Let a Common Interest Bind Us Together": Associations, Partisanship, and Culture in Philadelphia, 1775–1840.* Charlottesville: University of Virginia Press, 2007.

Kramnick, Isaac. "The 'Great National Discussion': The Discourse of Politics in 1787." *William and Mary Quarterly* 45, no. 1 (1988): 3–32.

Kroeber, Alfred L. *Anthropology: Culture Patterns and Processes.* New York: Harcourt, 1963.

Kruman, Marc W. *Between Authority and Liberty: State Constitution Making in Revolutionary America.* Chapel Hill: University of North Carolina Press, 1997.

Kuhn, Thomas. *The Structure of Scientific Revolutions.* Chicago: University of Chicago Press, 1996.

Kuran, Timur, and Cass R. Sunstein. "Availability Cascades and Risk Regulation." *Stanford Law Review* 51 no. 4 (1999): 683–768.

Kurland, Philip B. and Ralph Lerner, eds. *The Founders' Constitution.* Chicago: University of Chicago Press, 1987.

Kussmaul, Ann. *Servants in Husbandry in Early Modern England.* Cambridge: Cambridge University Press, 1981.

Lacey, Michael J., and Knud Haakonssen, eds. *A Culture of Rights: The Bill of Rights in Philosophy, Politics, and Law 1791 and 1991.* Cambridge: Cambridge University Press, 1991.

Ladurie, Emmanuel Le Roy. "Rangs et hiérarchie dans la vie de coeur." In *The French Revolution and the Creation of Modern Political Culture.* Vol. 1, *The Political Culture of the Old Regime,* edited by Keith Michael Baker. Oxford and New York, Pergamon Press, 1987.

Langford, Paul. *Public Life and the Propertied Englishmen, 1689–1798.* Oxford: Clarendon Press, 1991.

Large Additions to Common Sense. Philadelphia, 1776.

[Lee, Richard Henry]. "Letters from the Federal Farmer." 1787. In *Empire and Nation,* edited by Forrest McDonald. Indianapolis: Liberty Fund, 1999.

Lefebvre, Lucien. *The Problem of Unbelief in the Sixteenth Century: The Religion of Rabelais.* Cambridge, Mass.: Harvard University Press, 1983.

Lefort, Claude. *Democracy and Political Theory.* Minneapolis: University of Minnesota Press, 1988.

Leonard, E. M. *The Early History of English Poor Relief.* London: Barnes and Noble, 1965.

The Letters of Horace Walpole, Earl of Orford. London: R. Bentley, 1840.

Levy, Leonard. *Jefferson and Civil Liberties: The Darker Side.* Chicago: Ivan R. Dee, 1989.

———. *Origins of the Bill of Rights.* New Haven: Yale University Press, 1999.

Lewis, James E. " 'What Is to Become of Our Government?': The Revolutionary Potential of the Election of 1800." In *The Revolution of 1800: Democracy, Race, and the New Republic,* edited by James Horn, Jan Ellen Lewis, and Peter Onuf. Charlottesville: University of Virginia Press, 2002.

Lienesch, Michael. "Reinterpreting Rebellion: The Influence of Shays's Rebellion on American Political Thought." In *In Debt to Shays: The Bicentennial of an Agrarian Rebellion,* edited by Robert Gross. Charlottesville: University Press of Virginia, 1993.

Lockridge, Kenneth. *The Diary and Life of William Byrd II of Virginia, 1674, 1744.* Chapel Hill: University of North Carolina Press, 1987.

Longmore, Paul K. *The Invention of George Washington.* Charlottesville: University Press of Virginia, 1999.

Loring, James Spear. *The Hundred Boston Orators.* Boston: John P. Jewett, 1853.

Lutz, Donald S., ed. *Colonial Origins of the American Constitution: A Documentary History.* Indianapolis: Liberty Fund, 1998.

[Macpherson, James]. *The Rights of Great Britain Asserted against the Claims of America.* London, 1776.

Mączak, Antoni. *Rządzący i rządzeni: Władza i społeczeństwo w Europie wczesnonowożytnej* [The Rulers and the Ruled in Early Modern Europe]. Warsaw: PIW, 1986.

Maddox, Isaac. *A Sermon Preached before the Incorporated Society for the Propagation of the Gospel.* London, 1734.

Madison, James. *A Discourse on the Death of General Washington.* London, 1800.

Maier, Pauline. *American Scripture: Making the Declaration of Independence.* New York: Knopf, 1997.

——. *From Resistance to Revolution: Colonial Radicals and the Development of American Opposition to Britain, 1765–1776.* New York: Knopf, 1972.

——. "Popular Uprisings and Civil Authority in Eighteenth-Century America." *William and Mary Quarterly* 27, no. 1 (1970): 4–35.

Maitland, A. F. W. *The Constitutional History of England.* Cambridge: Cambridge University Press, 1961.

Malcolm, Joyce L., ed. *The Struggle for Sovereignty: Seventeenth-Century English Political Tracts.* Indianapolis: Liberty Fund, 1999.

Mann, Bruce H. "The Death and Transfiguration of American Legal History." In *The Many Legalities of Early America,* edited by Christopher L. Tomlins and Bruce H. Mann. Chapel Hill: University of North Carolina Press, 2001.

Marambaud, Pierre. *William Byrd of Westover, 1674–1744.* Charlottesville: University Press of Virginia, 1971.

Mayhew, Jonathan. "An Election Sermon." In *The Wall and the Garden: Selected Massachusetts Election Sermons, 1670–1775,* edited by A. W. Plumstead. Minneapolis: University of Minnesota Press, 1968.

Mays, David John, ed. *The Letters and Papers of Edmund Pendleton, 1734–1803.* University Press of Virginia: Charlottesville 1967.

McDonald, Forrest. *Novus ordo seclorum: The Intellectual Origins of the Constitution.* Lawrence: University Press of Kansas, 1985.

——, ed. *Empire and Nation.* Indianapolis: Liberty Fund, 1999.

McDonnell, Michael A. "A World Turned 'Topsy-Turvy': Robert Munford, *The*

Patriots, and the Crisis of the Revolution in Virginia." *William and Mary Quarterly* 61, no. 2 (2004): 235–70.

McGowan, William. "George Berkeley's American Declaration of Independence." *Studies in Eighteenth-Century Culture* 12 (1983): 105–13.

McTaggart William J., and William K. Bottorff, eds. *Major Poems of Timothy Dwight (1752–1817).* Gainesville: Scholars' Facsimiles and Reprints, 1969.

Meyers, Marvin, ed. *The Mind of the Founder: Sources of Political Thought of James Madison.* Hanover: University Press of New England, 1981.

Miller, John C. *Sam Adams: Pioneer in Propaganda.* 1936. Reprint, Stanford: Stanford University Press, 1964.

Minot, George. *The History of the Insurrections, in Massachusetts, in the Year 1786.* Worcester, Mass., 1788.

Montesquieu, Baron de. *The Spirit of the Laws.* Translated by Thomas Nugent. New York: Hafner Press, 1949.

Moore, Frank., ed. *Diary of the American Revolution: From Newspapers and Original Documents.* New York: Charles T. Evans, 1863.

Morgan, Edmund. *American Slavery, American Freedom: The Ordeal of Colonial Virginia.* New York: Norton, 1975.

——. *Inventing the People: The Rise of Popular Sovereignty in England and America.* New York: Norton, 1988.

Morgan, Philip. *Slave Counterpoint: Black Culture in the Eighteenth-Century Chesapeake and Lowcountry.* Chapel Hill: University of North Carolina Press 1998.

Morison, Samuel Eliot, ed. *Sources and Documents Illustrating the American Revolution, 1764–1788.* New York and London: Oxford University Press, 1965.

Morris, Ann Cary., ed. *The Diary and Letters of Gouverneur Morris.* New York: Da Capo Press, 1970.

Morris, Thomas D. *Southern Slavery and the Law, 1619–1860.* Chapel Hill: University of North Carolina Press.

Mumford, Jones Howard. "The Colonial Impulse: An Analysis of the 'Promotion' Literature of Colonization." In *Proceedings of the American Philosophical Society* 90, no. 2 (1926): 147.

Munford, Robert. *The Patriots.* In *A Collection of Plays and Poems by the Late Robert Munford.* Petersburg: William Prentis, 1798.

Nash, Gary B. *Race and Revolution.* Lanham, Md.: Rowman and Littlefield, 2001.

——. *The Unknown American Revolution: The Unruly Birth of Democracy and the Struggle to Create America.* New York: Viking, 2005.

Neem, Johann N. *Creating a Nation of Joiners: Democracy and Civil Society in Early National Massachusetts.* Cambridge, Mass.: Harvard University Press, 2008.

Newman, Simon. *Parades and Politics of the Street: Festive Culture in the Early American Republic.* Philadelphia: University of Pennsylvania Press, 1997.

Noll, Mark A. *America's God: From Jonathan Edwards to Abraham Lincoln.* New York: Oxford University Press, 2002.

Norton, Mary Beth. *In the Devil's Snare: The Salem Witchcraft Crisis of 1692.* New York: Vintage, 2002.

O'Brien, Connor Cruise. "Thomas Jefferson: Radical and Racist." *Atlantic Monthly* 278, no. 4 (1996): 53–74.

Offut, William M., Jr. "The Limits of Authority: Courts, Ethnicity, and Gender in the Middle Colonies, 1670–1710." In *The Many Legalities of Early America,* edited by Christopher L. Tomlins and Bruce H. Mann. Chapel Hill: University of North Carolina Press, 2001.

Oldmixon, John. *The British Empire in America.* 1741. Reprint, New York: Augustus M. Kelley, 1969.

Olson, Lester C. *Emblems of American Community in the Revolutionary Era.* Washington: Smithsonian Institution Press, 1991.

Olwell, Robert, and Alan Tully, eds. *Cultures and Identities in Colonial British America.* Baltimore: Johns Hopkins University Press, 2006.

Ong, Walter. *Interfaces of the Word.* Ithaca: Cornell University Press, 1977.

Onuf, Peter. "Federalism, Democracy and Liberty in the New American Nation." In *Exclusionary Empire: English Liberty Overseas, 1600–1900,* edited by Jack P. Greene. New York: Cambridge University Press, 2009.

——. *Jefferson's Empire: The Language of American Nationhood.* Charlottesville: University Press of Virginia, 2000.

——, ed. *Thomas Jefferson: An Anthology.* New York: Brandywine Press, 1999.

Otis, James. *The Rights of the British Colonies Asserted and Proved.* 1764. In *The Founders' Constitution,* edited by Philip B. Kurland and Ralph Lerner. Chicago: University of Chicago Press, 1987.

Ousterhout, Ann M. "Controlling the Opposition in Pennsylvania During the American Revolution." *Pennsylvania Magazine of History and Biography* 105, no. 1 (1981): 3–34.

Paine, Thomas. *Common Sense.* Philadelphia, 1776.

——. *Rights of Man, Common Sense and other Political Writings.* Edited by Mark Philp. New York: Oxford University Press, 1995.

Patterson, Orlando. *Freedom.* New York: Basic Books, 1991.

Pencak, William. " 'The Fine Theoretic Government of Massachusetts Is Prostrated to the Earth': The Response to Shays's Rebellion." In *In Debt to Shays: The Bicentennial of an Agrarian Rebellion,* edited by Robert Gross. Charlottesville: University Press of Virginia, 1993.

——. "Samuel Adams and Shays's Rebellion." *New England Quarterly* 62, no. 1 (1989): 63–74.

Penn, William. "A Letter from a Gentleman in the Country." In *The Political Writings of William Penn,* edited by Andrew R. Murphy. Indianapolis: Liberty Fund, 2002.

Pestana Carla G., and Sharon V. Salinger, eds. *Inequality in Early America.* Hanover: University Press of New England, 1999.

Peterson, Merrill D., ed. *Thomas Jefferson: Writings.* New York: Viking, 1984.

A Plumb Pudding for the humane, chaste, valiant, enlightened Peter Porcupine. Philadelphia, 1799.

Pocock, J. G. A. *The Machiavellian Moment: Florentine Political Thought and The Atlantic Republican Tradition.* Princeton: Princeton University Press, 1975.

Pole, J. R. *The Pursuit of Equality in American History.* Berkeley: University of California Press, 1978.

——, ed. *The American Constitution: For and Against.* New York, 1987.

——. *The Revolution in America, 1754–1788.* London: Macmillan, 1970.

Porcupine, Peter [William Cobbett]. *History of American Jacobins.* Philadelphia, 1796.

Porter, Rachel R. "Shays' Rebellion: An Episode in American State-Making." *Sociological Perspectives* 34, no. 1 (1991): 95–113.

Porter, Roy. "The Enlightenment in England." In *The Enlightenment in National Context,* edited by Roy Porter and Mikulas Teich. New York: Cambridge University Press, 1981.

Price, Richard. *Observations on the Importance of the American Revolution.* London, 1784.

Primus, Richard A. *The American Language of Rights.* Cambridge: Cambridge University Press, 1999.

Pym, John. "The Speech or Declaration of John Pym." In *The Struggle for Sovereignty: Seventeenth-Century English Political Tracts,* edited by Joyce L. Malcolm. Indianapolis: Liberty Fund, 1999.

Querno, Camillo. *The American Times: A Satire.* London, 1780.

Rakove, Jack N. *Original Meanings: Politics and Ideas in the Making of the Constitution.* New York: Vintage Books, 1997.

——. "Parchment Barriers and the Politics of Rights." In *A Culture of Rights: The Bill of Rights in Philosophy, Politics, and Law 1791 and 1991,* edited by Michael J. Lacey and Knud Haakonssen. Cambridge: Cambridge University Press, 1991.

[Ramsay, David]. *An Address to the Citizens of South-Carolina.* Charleston, 1778.

——. *The History of the American Revolution.* 1789. Indianapolis: Liberty Fund, 1990.

——. "An Oration on the Advantages of American Independence." 1794. Edited by Robert L. Brunhouse. *Transactions of the American Philosophical Society* 55, no. 4 (1965).

Rand, Benjamin. *Berkeley's American Sojourn.* Cambridge, Mass.: Harvard University Press, 1932.

Raphael, Ray. *Founding Myths: Stories That Hide Our Patriotic Past.* New York: New Press, 2004.

——. *A People's History of the American Revolution: How Common People Shaped the Fight for Independence.* New York: Perennial, 2002.

Rauser, Amelia. "British Political Prints and the Struggle for Symbols in the American Revolution. *Oxford Art Journal* 21, no. 2 (1998): 153–71.

Rawls, John. *A Theory of Justice.* Cambridge, Mass.: Harvard University Press, 1971.

Rediker, Marcus. *Between the Devil and the Deep Blue Sea: Merchant Seamen, Pirates, and the Anglo-American Maritime World, 1700–1750.* New York: Cambridge University Press, 1993.

Rediker, Marcus, and Peter Linebaugh. *The Many-Headed Hydra: Sailors, Slaves, Commoners, and the Hidden History of the Revolutionary Atlantic.* Boston: Beacon Press, 2000.

Reid, James. "The Religion of the Bible And Religion of K.[ing] W.[illiam] County Compared." In *The Colonial Virginia Satirist. Mid Eighteenth-Century Commentaries on Politics, Religion and Society,* edited by Richard Beale Davis. *Transactions of the American Philosophical Society* 57, no. 1 (1967).

Reid, John Phillip. *The Concept of Liberty in the Age of the American Revolution.* Chicago: University of Chicago Press, 1988.

Richards, Leonard L. *Shays's Rebellion: The American Revolution's Final Battle.* Philadelphia: University of Pennsylvania Press, 2002.

Riggs, Luther G., ed. *The Anarchiad: A New England Poem.* Gainesville: Scholars' Facsimiles and Reprints, 1967.

Riley, Stephen. "Dr. William Whiting and Shays' Rebellion." *Proceedings of the American Antiquarian Society* 66 (1956): 119–66.

Robbins, Caroline. " 'When Is It That Colonies May Turn Independent?': An Analysis of the Environment and Politics of Francis Hutcheson, 1694–1746." *William and Mary Quarterly* 11, no. 2 (1954): 214–51.

Robespierre, Maximilien. *Report upon the Principles of Political Morality.* Philadelphia: Benjamin Franklin Bache, 1794.

Rogers, George C., et al., eds. *The Papers of Henry Laurens.* Columbia: University of South Carolina Press, 1976.

Rommen, Heinrich A. *The Natural Law: A Study in Legal and Social History and Philosophy.* Translated by Thomas L. Hanley. Indianapolis: Liberty Fund, 1998.

Rosen, Lawrence. "The Integrity of Cultures." *American Behavioral Scientist* 34, no. 5 (May 1991): 612.

Rosswurm, Steven. *Arms, Country, and Class: The Philadelphia Militia and the "Lower Sort" during the Revolutionary War.* New Brunswick, N.J.: Rutgers University Press, 1988.

Royster, Charles. "The Nature of Treason: Revolutionary Virtue and American Reactions to Benedict Arnold." *William and Mary Quarterly* 36, no. 2 (1979): 164–93.

Rozbicki, Michal. *The Complete Colonial Gentleman: Cultural Legitimacy in Plantation America.* Charlottesville: University Press of Virginia, 1998.

——. "The Cultural Development of the Colonies." In *A Companion to the American Revolution,* edited by Jack P. Greene and J. R. Pole. Malden, Mass.: Blackwell, 2000.

——, ed. *European and American Constitutionalism in the Eighteenth Century.* Warsaw: American Studies Center, 1990.

——. "To Save Them from Themselves: Proposals to Enslave the British Poor, 1698–1755." *Slavery and Abolition* 22 (2001): 29–50.

The Rudiments of Latin Prosody. Boston: B. Mecom, 1760.

Ryan, Alan. "The British, the Americans, and Rights." In *A Culture of Rights: The Bill of Rights in Philosophy, Politics, and Law 1791 and 1991,* edited by Michael J. Lacey and Knud Haakonssen. Cambridge: Cambridge University Press, 1991.

Saillant, John. Review of *Epistles and Elexicons: Reading the Letters of Delegates to Congress, 1774–1789,* vols. 1–25. *H-Review,* April 1999. www.h-net.msu.edu/reviews/showrev.cgi?path=115.

Sandoz, Ellis, ed. *Political Sermons of the Founding Era, 1730–1805.* Indianapolis: Liberty Fund, 1998.

Sarna, Jonathan D., and David G. Dalin, eds. *Religion and State in the American Jewish Experience.* Notre Dame: University of Notre Dame Press, 1997.

Schultz, Ronald. "A Class Society?: The Nature of Inequality in Early America." In *Inequality in Early America,* edited by Carla G. Pestana and Sharon V. Salinger. Hanover: University Press of New England, 1999.

Schutz, John A., and Douglass Adair, eds. *The Spur of Fame: Dialogues of John Adams and Benjamin Rush, 1805–1813.* Indianapolis: Liberty Fund, 2001.

Scott, Joan. "Women's History." In *New Perspectives on Historical Writing,* edited by Peter Burke. University Park: Pennsylvania State University Press, 2001.

Shakespeare, William. *The Complete Works of William Shakespeare.* London: Spring Books, 1958.

Shama, Simon. *Patriots and Liberators: Revolution in the Netherlands 1780–1813.* New York: Vintage, 1992.

Shankman, Andrew. *Crucible of American Democracy: The Struggle to Fuse Egalitarianism and Capitalism in Jeffersonian Pennsylvania.* Lawrence: University Press of Kansas, 2004.

Shaw, Peter. *American Patriots and the Rituals of the Revolution.* Cambridge, Mass.: Harvard University Press, 1981.

Sheehan, Colleen A., and Gary L. McDowell, eds. *Friends of the Constitution: Writings of the "Other" Federalists, 1787–1788.* Indianapolis: Liberty Fund, 1998.

Silverman, Kenneth. *A Cultural History of the American Revolution: Painting, Music, Literature and the Theatre in the Colonies and the United States from the Treaty of Paris to the Inauguration of George Washington.* New York: Random House, 1986.

Skemp, Sheila. "George Berkeley's Newport Experience." *Rhode Island History* 37, no. 2 (1978): 53–63.

Skinner, Stephen. "Blackstone's Support for the Militia" *American Journal of Legal History* 44, no. 1 (2000).

Slack, Paul. "Vagrants and Vagrancy in England, 1598–1644." *English Historical Review* 27 (1974): 360–79.

Slaughter, Thomas P. *The Whiskey Rebellion.* New York: Oxford University Press, 1986.

Smith, Abbot E. *Colonists in Bondage: White Servitude and Convict Labor in America, 1607–1776.* New York: Norton, 1947.

Smith, Paul H., ed. *Letters of Delegates to Congress.* 26 vols. Washington, D.C.: Library of Congress, 1976.

Stoddard, Solomon. *God's Frown in the Death of Useful Men.* Boston: Green and Allen, 1703.

——. *The Way for a People to Live Long in the Land That God Hath Given Them.* Boston: Bartholomew Green and John Allen, 1703.

Stubbs, William. *The Constitutional History of England.* Oxford: Clarendon Press, 1880.

Sydnor, Charles. *American Revolutionaries in the Making: Political Practices in Washington's Virginia.* New York: Free Press, 1965.

Symmons-Symonolewicz, Konstantin. *National Consciousness in Poland: Origins and Evolution.* Meadville: Maplewood Press, 1983.

Szatmary, David. *Shays' Rebellion: The Making of an Agrarian Insurrection.* Amherst: University of Massachusetts Press, 1980.

Taylor, Alan. *American Colonies.* New York, Viking: 2001.

———. "Regulators and White Indians: The Agrarian Resistance in Post-Revolutionary New England." In *In Debt to Shays: The Bicentennial of an Agrarian Rebellion,* edited by Robert Gross. Charlottesville: University Press of Virginia, 1993.

Temperley, Howard R. "Jefferson and Slavery: A Study in Moral Perplexity." In *Reason and Republicanism: Thomas Jefferson's Legacy of Liberty,* edited by Gary L. McDowell and Sharon N. Noble. Lanham, Md.: Rowman and Littlefield, 1997.

Thompson, E. P. *Customs in Common. Studies in Traditional Popular Culture.* New York: New Press, 1993.

———. *The Making of the English Working Class.* New York: Pantheon, 1964.

Tinling, Marion, ed. *The Correspondence of the Three William Byrds of Westover, Virginia, 1684–1776.* Charlottesville: University Press of Virginia, 1977.

Tomlins, Christopher L., and Bruce H. Mann, eds. *The Many Legalities of Early America.* Chapel Hill: University of North Carolina Press, 2001.

Trenchard, John, and Thomas Gordon. *Cato's Letters.* Edited by Ronald Hamowy. Indianapolis: Liberty Fund, 1995.

Tuck, Richard. *Natural Rights Theories: Their Origin and Development.* New York: Cambridge University Press, 1979.

[Tucker, Thomas Tudor]. *Conciliatory Hints.* Charleston, 1784.

Tyler, Royall. *The Contrast: A Comedy.* New York: Bert Franklin, 1970.

Van Horne, John C., ed. *The Correspondence of William Nelson as Acting Governor of Virginia, 1770–1771.* Charlottesville: University Press of Virginia, 1975.

Waldstreicher, David. *In the Midst of Perpetual Fetes: The Making of American Nationalism: 1786–1820.* Chapel Hill: University of North Carolina Press, 1997.

[Ward, Edward]. *A Trip to New England.* London, 1699.

Warner, Michael. *The Letters of the Republic: Publication and the Public Sphere in Eighteenth-Century America.* Cambridge, Mass.: Harvard University Press, 1990.

Warren-Adams Letters, Being Chiefly a Correspondence among John Adams, Samuel Adams, and James Warren. Boston: Massachusetts Historical Society, 1917–25.

Warren, Charles. *Jacobin and Junto: Early American Politics as Viewed in the Diary of Dr. Nathaniel Ames, 1758–1822.* Cambridge, Mass.: Harvard University Press, 1931.

Warren, Mercy Otis. *History of the Rise, Progress and Termination of the American Revolution.* Edited by Lester H. Cohen. Indianapolis: Liberty Fund, 1989.

Weir, Robert M. *Colonial South Carolina: A History.* Millwood: KTO Press, 1983

———, ed. *The Letters of Freeman, etc.: Essays on the Nonimportation Movement in South Carolina, Collected by William Henry Drayton.* Columbia: University of South Carolina Press, 1977.

West, Samuel. *On the Right to Rebel against Governors.* Boston, 1776.

West, Thomas G. *Vindicating the Founders: Race, Sex, Class, and Justice in the Origins of America.* Lanham, Md.: Rowman and Littlefield, 1997.

Williams, David R., ed. *Revolutionary War Sermons*. Delmar: Scholars' Facsimiles and Reprints, 1984.

Winch, Julie. *A Gentleman of Color: The Life of James Forten*. New York: Oxford University Press, 2002.

Witherspoon, John. *Works of the Rev. John Witherspoon*. Philadelphia, 1802.

Wolf, Eric R. *Anthropology*. New York: Norton, 1974.

Wood, Gordon S. *The American Revolution: A History*. New York: Random House, 2002.

——. *The Creation of the American Republic, 1776–1787*. New York: Norton, 1969.

——. *The Radicalism of the American Revolution*. New York: Vintage, 1991.

——. *Revolutionary Characters: What Made the Founders Different*. New York: Penguin, 2006.

Wright, Louis B., ed. *An Essay upon Government of the English Plantations on the Continent of America*. 1701. Reprint, San Marino, Calif.: Huntington Library, 1945.

Wroth, Kinvin, and Hiller B. Zobel, eds. *Legal Papers of John Adams*. Cambridge, Mass.: Belknap Press of Harvard University Press, 1965.

Wrzosek, Wojciech. "The Problem of Cultural Imputation in History." In *Historiography between Modernism and Postmodernism,* edited by Jerzy Topolski. Amsterdam and Atlanta: Rodopi, 1994.

Young, Alfred. *Beyond the American Revolution: Explorations in the History of American Radicalism*. DeKalb: Northern Illinois University Press, 1993.

——. "George Robert Twelves Hewes (1742–1840): A Boston Shoemaker and the Memory of the American Revolution." *William and Mary Quarterly* 38 (1981): 562–623.

Young, Theodore A. *Completing Berkeley's Project: Classical vs. Modern Philosophy*. Lanham, Md.: University Press of America, 1985.

Zagorin, Perez. *The Court and the Country: The Beginning of the English Revolution*. New York: Athenaeum, 1971.

——. *A History of Political Thought in the English Revolution*. London: Routledge and Paul, 1954.

Zamoyski, Adam. *Holy Madness: Romantics, Patriots, and Revolutionaries, 1776–1871*. New York: Viking Books, 2000.

Zinn, Howard. *A People's History of the United States*. New York: Harper, 1980.

Zuckerman, Michael. "Rhetoric, Reality, and the Revolution: The Genteel Radicalism of Gordon Wood." *William and Mary Quarterly* 51, no. 4 (1994): 693–702.

Index

Adams, John: on aristocracy of talent, 219; on Boston Massacre, 204–5; on common people driven by emotions, 211; on democracy, 61; on emotive rhetoric, 95–96; on factionalism, 203; on good government, 136; on good laws' effects on society, 128; on hereditary privilege, 216; on inequality, 217; on landownership as condition of virtue, 130; on Mayflower Compact, 37; on mercantile pursuits, 62; on people's dignity in a republican system, 126; as Humphrey Ploughjogger, 121; on power and property, 71; on property qualifications for voting, 67; on public and private virtue, 219; on Revolution as a providential event, 133–34; on Society of the Cincinnati, 102; on Southern planters, 63; on treating common people well, 146; on George Washington's theatrical talents, 96; on George Washington's virtue, 155

Adams, John Quincy, 139

Adams, Samuel: on America as refuge of liberty, 111; on America's future, 133, 135; claims disinterestedness, 155; on corruption, 165–66; on merit as qualification for office, 219; on party spirit, 159; on political modesty, 121; representative government is self-repairing, 170; on Shays's Rebellion, 167; on street riots, 210–11; on unqualified men in government, 199

Allen, John, 42

Allison, Hugh, 92

American Revolution: abolitionist demands inspired by Revolutionary language of liberty, 18, 156, 157, 191–92, 237; certitude and the historiography of, 228; consensus interpretation of, 20, 21; creates new cultural space for liberty, 225–26, 233–24, 235–38; and distrust of centralized government, 227; dynamics of, 5; as an episode in the history of ideas, 27; federalism prevents centralization of power, 227; "from the bottom up" approach, 27; historiography of, 2, 19–21; as a history of constraints on liberty, 18; idealized interpretive frameworks for, 228; limited explanatory value of analysis in terms of paradoxes, 229; Marxist interpretation of, 20; and meaning of "the people," 115–16; its model of happiness, 226; and modern culture of equal rights, 32; narrative of, 8, 80–81, 225; political history of, 14; preservationist goals of, 81–84; radicalism of, 78–79, 86; representations of, 5, 85; republican government as an emanation of the people, 133; and slavery, 22–23; and the speed of historical

slavery (*continued*)
    tudes toward, 32; voices for the aboli-
    tion of, 191–92, 156, 157
Smith, Adam, 130
Smith, Melancton, 218
Smith, Meriwether, 145
society in colonial British America: at-
    tempts to reproduce social hierarchy,
    56–64; class divisions, 68–69, 71;
    emergence of a creole upper class, 57;
    gentry values, 59; link between prop-
    erty and freedom, 70–72; material
    symbols of rank, 72; organic concept
    of, 66–67; provincial elite, 58–59, 101;
    regional differences among the ruling
    class, 62–64
Society of the Cincinnati, 102–4
Sons of Liberty, 105
Statute of Artificers (1562–63), 52
Statute of Labourers (1350–51), 52
Steuben, Friedrich Wilhelm, baron von,
    100
Stoddard, Solomon, 154
Stubbs, William, 37

Taylor, Alan, 18, 176
Thompson, John, 164
Thomson, Charles, 64, 111
Tucker, St. George: on slavery being irrec-
    oncilable with American liberty, 157
Tudor, William, 183
Tully, Alan, 229
Tyler, Royall: *The Contrast,* 198

Varnum, James M., 194, 210
Virginia, 21, 36, 39, 54, 62, 75, 83, 89, 93,
    129, 154, 157, 193, 194; Bill of Rights,
    122; elections, 146; entrenched politi-
    cal elite, 161; militia, 68; planters, 12;
    social ranks in, 14; tumults, 199
virtual representation: 120, 142
virtue, 40, 41, 49, 51, 73, 75, 130, 133, 137,
    138, 143, 145, 146, 150, 152, 153, 154,

155, 158, 159, 160, 162, 164, 172, 175,
176, 180, 181, 185, 186, 193, 196, 197,
200, 204, 205, 207, 211, 212–13, 216,
217, 218, 219–20, 221–22; public, 165,
166, 201, 291
Voltaire (François-Marie Arouet), 104

Wales, Samuel, 211
Ward, Samuel, 213
Warren, James, 198
Warren, Joseph, 139, 172
Warren, Mercy Otis, 103, 170; on liberty
    degenerating into licentiousness, 197;
    political writing of as transgressing
    gender role expectations, 97; on
    Daniel Shays, 172
Washington, George, 21, 33, 60, 201; on
    British army, 89; desires coat of arms,
    73, 100; on duty of citizens to obey
    government, 112; as embodiment of
    British traditions of liberty, 111; la-
    ments Shays's Rebellion, 167; sensitive
    of his public image, 152; steady charac-
    ter of, 213; stylizes Mount Vernon, 73
Webster, Noah, 144–45; distraught that
    ordinary people idolize liberty too
    much, 196; on the sovereign power of
    the people, 148
Whiting, William, 174–75
Whiskey Rebellion, 139, 174
Wilkes, John, 93
Williams, Abraham, 42
Williams, John, 188
Witherspoon, John, 92
Witt, John de, 39
Wolff, Christian, 210
women, 2, 9, 18, 66, 67, 97, 116, 149, 157,
    188–89, 237; invisible on public stage,
    116; rights of, 108
Wood, Gordon, 78–79
Wood, James 60,

Young, Alfred F., 2

JEFFERSONIAN AMERICA